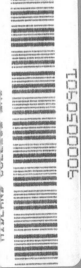

CHINESE DIARIES: 1941-1946

CHINESE DIARIES
1941-1946

ROBERT PAYNE

Originally published in two volumes as *Forever China* and *China Awakes*. Approximately one half of the original text appears in this new selection.

WEYBRIGHT AND TALLEY

NEW YORK

TO ALAN WITH LOVE

CONTENTS

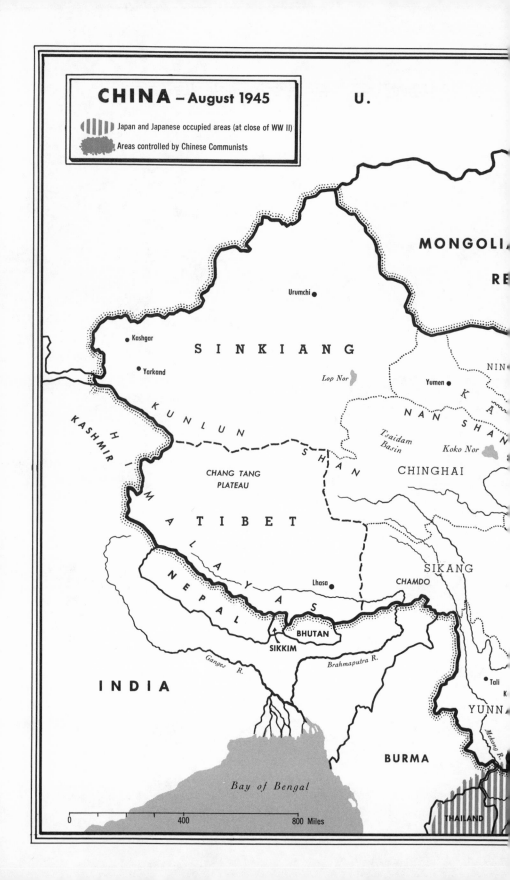

CHINA – August 1945

Japan and Japanese occupied areas (at close of WW II)

Areas controlled by Chinese Communists

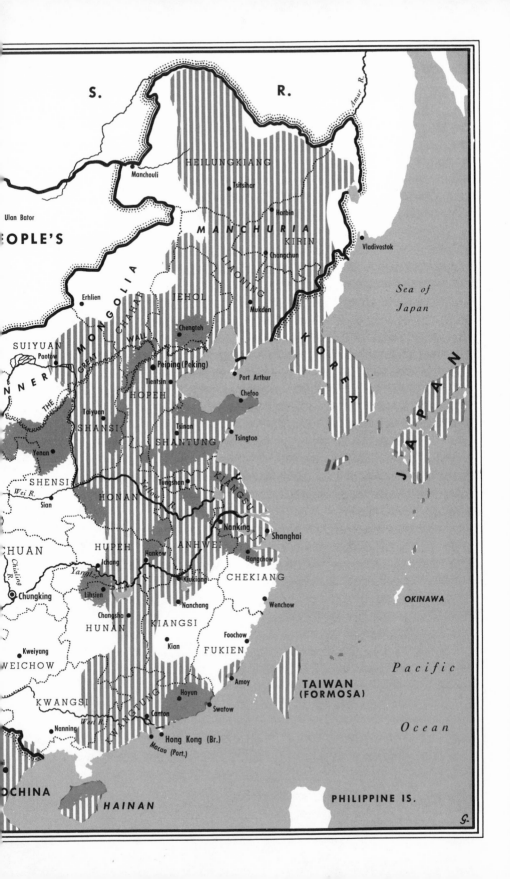

INTRODUCTION

I

When I was a child, China was a place where I traveled in my dreams.
I remember wallpaper patterned with pagodas and wheeled sailing
vessels which floated over immense stretches of desert, and I must
have been four or five when an old woman who looked like a witch,
swathed in long billowing purple garments, opened up for me her
collection of Chinese figurines. I can remember her bustling about a
small dark room in search of the key to unlock the cabinet, and the
precise moment when the glass door flew open and for the first time
I was allowed to touch the porcelain and ivory figures which were so
utterly unlike anything I had seen before. There were old men with
vast bulbous foreheads and rippling beards which reached to their
feet, warriors armed with strangely shaped swords, and maidens who
wore costumes in rainbow colors and whose round faces and black eyes
suggested ripe fruit. I examined the figures gravely one by one—there
must have been at least twenty of them altogether—and then they
were replaced in the china cabinet, never to be touched again. The
glass door was closed, the bright light which had shone on them was
moved away, and the figures vanished.

I no longer remember the name of the old witch, who was the
widow of a sea captain. She exists for me in an agreeable limbo, forever about to open the glass doors of a cabinet, forever swathed in
her voluminous purple robes. I do not remember her speaking about
China, and I suspect that she knew very little about the country. The
porcelain and ivory figures invaded my dreams, and I would find myself telling stories about them. At intervals in the stories there would
come the image of the Green Dragon, who derived, I think, from the

wallpaper in the witch's house. He was an amiable dragon, about ten thousand miles long, and he had the power to do anything he pleased.

When I was seven years old, I wrote a long epic called "The Adventures of Sylvia, Queen of China and Denmark." I had a firm belief that the work would establish my fame. Some twenty notebooks were filled with her adventures, and a few fragments have survived. Sylvia's adventures included a sleigh ride across Russia in the dead of winter; she had reached the borders of China when the sleigh was attacked by wolves. The most poignant incident in the epic described how one by one her servants and finally the Crown Prince of Denmark dropped off the sleigh in order to preserve the life of the Queen, who entered China alone and unrecognized. After many wars she established her right to the Chinese throne, and she continued to rule over China and Denmark to the end of her days.

When I came to China in 1941 I was at first puzzled by the sensation of déjà vu. In wartime Chungking, in the ruins of a bombed city, the figurines in the glass cabinet came to life, but they were scarcely more living than they had been in my dreams. These people had the vivid colors of dreams; their singsong voices and ample gestures were familiar to me, because I had imagined them; and throughout the years I spent in China there was never any feeling of strangeness, because I had been there so often. Night after night, year after year, I had been traveling in China, staying in the wayside inns, wandering up the steep slopes of the mountains, or stepping along the thin borders of rice fields. The Yangtse and the Chialing rivers roared at my feet, as years before I had seen them pouring through the glass cabinet.

I had always known I would live in China, marry a Chinese princess, and live in a palace in Peking. How these things would come about, and what dangers I would meet on the way, did not concern me: they were inevitable and worth no more than a passing thought. I would go to sleep one night and wake up in China. I had not the slightest doubt that it would happen very simply and quietly, without the least effort. Another witch would open another cabinet, only this time the cabinet would be as large as China.

In the thirties I wandered from one university to another, worked in a shipyard, traveled across Europe, and became briefly a war correspondent in Spain. It was a period of unremitting confusion, dominated by the raucous voices of dictators, and having seen the Spanish Republic go down to defeat, I sailed for the Far East. My father was the constructive manager at the Singapore naval base, with Malays,

Indians, and Chinese working for him. I could never have imagined that a naval base would be so like paradise, but it was. Flame of the forest trees grew in the base; the air was scented with frangipani blossoms; king cobras streaked through the high grass. Malay princes worked side by side with Chinese coolies in the machine shops. Under the rainbow colors of the Union Jack all the nations of the East seemed to be living in peace. I did not know that I was watching the last days of Britain's oriental empire. The sun was setting, and we thought it was the dawn.

I would look out from my house across the blue straits of Johore at the misty hills and the battleships gliding into harbor, and wonder whether there was any place in the world where peace was so impregnable, so tangible. I traveled to Java and Bali, where peace was woven into the fabric of men's lives. Then I returned to Singapore, the immense drydocks, the humming of machinery, the turbaned Sikhs standing guard, the big guns facing out to sea. One day in December 1941 the peace came to an end.

On the night of December 7 Japanese warplanes flew high over the naval base, lit by our searchlights. They had dropped a few bombs on the island to inspire us with a proper respect. The Prince of Wales and the Repulse opened fire, but the silver planes flew serenely overhead, out of range of the guns. I was duty officer that night, and one of my tasks, as soon as I heard of the presence of the Japanese planes, was to see that all the lights in the base went out. I gave the order over the telephone, and suddenly the whole base was plunged into darkness except for the floating dock moored in the straits, blazing with lights like a Christmas tree. I kept calling frantically to the floating dock, but there was no answer. At last I got the head of the night crew and cursed him. "I know all about that," he said, "but I can't find the bloody switch!" By this time the Japanese planes were out of sight, flying northward to their bases in Indochina.

The following day I watched the Prince of Wales and the Repulse steaming out of the straits, so vast and ponderous that they appeared indestructible. They bristled with guns and armor. In forty-eight hours they had been sunk, and the naval base was nearly defenseless.

I should have been among those who spent their last hours in Singapore blowing up every mortal thing we possessed. I was an armament officer, and with three others I was in charge of the vast quantities of high explosives, shells, and mines hidden away under the small hills in the naval base. It was our job to blow things up. But when Singapore was falling and the demolition experts were at work, I was thousands of miles away in China.

Three weeks before the Pacific war broke out, a certain Robert Scott summoned me to the Cathay Hotel in Singapore. He was a tall, ruggedly built Scotsman, mild-mannered, imperturbable, accustomed to command. He said he was thinking of sending me to Chungking, and I explained that I had other fish to fry. The armaments depot was understaffed, I was probably indispensable, and my superiors were not likely to let me go. What was I supposed to do in China? On this subject he was exceedingly vague. I was to be attached to his staff, and beyond that there was little he could tell me. Later in the day I learned that he was head of British intelligence in the Far East.

I did not know that the doors of the china cabinet were being flung open by a witch dressed in modern clothes and armed with imperial power. At his bidding airplanes were summoned out of the sky, secret treaties were signed, traitors were executed. He was probably the most powerful Briton in the Far East.

A few days later the war came to Singapore, and I forgot the interview at the Cathay Hotel. The war was on our doorstep, and Chungking was a thousand light years away. I had not reckoned with Robert Scott. Suddenly I was told that all the papers had come through, and I would be flown with a young lecturer from Bristol University to Chungking. We were the advance staff of Robert Scott, heirs to the secrets of British intelligence in China, bearing letters of appointment addressed to the British Ambassador, Sir Archibald Clark Kerr. It was heady wine, and we made the most of it. A special seaplane had been placed at our disposal to fly us to Rangoon; then we went by train to Lashio, and by air to Chungking.

The Ambassador was cordial. We dined with him, drank his wine, talked learnedly about the problems facing China, and waited for Robert Scott. I sharpened the Ambassador's goose-quill pens, wandered through the streets of Chungking, and went off to look at the Chinese universities, where the professors were pitiably poor, the students bright-faced and eager. From Singapore there came occasional telegrams: Robert Scott was coming; he was not coming. Then there was silence. Singapore fell, and nothing more was heard of him until the end of the war.

He was one of those men who stay to the end. Many years later I learned that the Japanese placed him high on their death list; they intended to cut off his head and parade it through the streets of Singapore. Arrested, he assumed another name, another identity, and it was some months before they discovered him in a prison camp; and by this time they were weary of cutting off heads. Instead they beat him very nearly to death and kept him in solitary confinement, so that at the end of the war he was little more than a malaria-ridden skeleton. When the British landed in Singapore, he had just enough strength to crawl out of his cell on his hands and knees, and some hours later a friendly Chinese found him lying motionless by the side of the road. There was still a little life in him, and the Chinese carried him in a wheelbarrow to the nearest hospital. When he recovered, he was knighted, and Sir Robert Scott became the new High Commissioner for Malaya.

We never discovered what he had intended to do with us. I suspect that the young lecturer from Bristol University was intended for high political affairs, while I would be sent out to blow up railroads. Meanwhile we did as we pleased, secure in the Ambassador's affections, and more privileged than we had ever guessed we would be, for we alone in the embassy had status without responsibility. When a battle broke out in Changsha, I decided to have a look at it and appointed myself the London Times correspondent. The young lecturer spent his days in the Chinese Foreign Office and was soon absorbed in the problems of the Chinese Red Cross.

One day, while I was sharpening his goose-quill pens, the Ambassador announced casually, "They are sending me to Moscow." I asked him whether he wanted to go, but he said nothing, looking out of the window at the desolate compound of the embassy. His wife had left him, he was beginning to drink heavily, age was creeping over him. He had the fine patrician features of a Scottish laird, with a great hooked nose and enormous eyes, which were dark brown and lit with gold lights. For a long time he gazed out of the window, and at last he said, "China is my home. What in hell am I going to do in Russia?"

He was not a good ambassador in Russia, but he was magnificent in China. He knew the pulse of the people, surrounded himself with young Chinese, and was adept at intrigues because he possessed a singular honesty and was therefore not bound by the laws of intrigue. He was on terms of intimacy with many Chinese, and preferred poor students to rich officials. During the bombing he refused to hide in the underground shelters, but would usually find some high spot to look out at the airplanes. He was furiously inquisitive, patient, generous, saturated in Chinese culture, brave to excess. When he left, we went into mourning.

On the night before his departure I was summoned to his small study in the embassy compound. He talked somberly about the journey to Russia, and even more somberly about his successor. "The poor fellow doesn't know a damned thing about China, and never will," he said. "The dark ages are coming. If you have any sense, you will leave the embassy and go into the Chinese universities." Then he gave me his collection of goose-quill pens.

In this way, in wartime, I went into the Chinese universities.

II

It sometimes happens that a diary by its very nature remains impersonal, remote from the author, like a mirror which he holds out at arm's length, turning it away from himself. I wanted to record the Chinese world, the cities, the fields, the farms, the soldiers, the students, the colors of an age, and what especially concerned me were the changing colors of the atmosphere, the shapes of the coming storm. It seemed to me that I was making a film, and if you held up the page to the light you would see the bottle-green misty colors of Chungking or the brilliant yellow colors of Kunming, and through these colors you would see the Chinese walking and going about their affairs in a time of war. Like film the diary was fluid. It would record what I saw from day to day, and out of the flow of events there would come a picture of China as it was, with little or nothing of myself. Even if I had wanted to, I could not impose a pattern on anything as vast and chaotic as China. I was the mirror, and I hoped the hand holding the mirror was steady.

Today, rereading the book nearly a quarter of a century later, it occurs to me that impersonality can be practiced too assiduously. I sometimes wrote about the people who were close to me, but it puzzles me that I wrote so little about those who were closest of all. So there is nothing about Rose Hsiung, whom I married because she was willful and beautiful, and there are only fleeting glimpses of her brilliant children. I wrote about General Feng Yu-hsiang as though he were an acquaintance, forgetting to say that I had been adopted by him, went in and out of his houses as I pleased, and was very well aware of the advantages and penalties of being the adopted son of the man who in those days bore the feudal title of Vice-Generalissimo, and would theoretically have come to power if anything had happened to the Generalissimo. When I wrote about the poet Wen Yi-tuo, I attempted always to see him in the middle distance, though we were blood brothers. I wrote nothing at all about Chang Tung, the handsome broad-shouldered student who looked as though he had stepped out of a medieval epic and laughed gaily the day after he had been tortured by the secret police, though he too was my blood brother. For a year and a half I lived in the abandoned theater of a Yunnanese warlord, my living quarters being a small portion of the gallery which I shared with Professor Ernest Hughes, a learned Oxford don, but he never appears in the pages of this diary.

I suspect there must have been some reasons for this silence. I did not leave them out because they had nothing to say. Indeed, they were all immensely talkative, capable of talking for many hours without interruption, and between them they taught me nearly all I knew about China. Hughes was a small gray-haired man with gentle manners and a biting tongue, happiest when translating obscure Chinese philosophers. The Chinese professors, who were living in the same abandoned theater, regarded it as perfectly natural that an Oxford don should travel halfway across the world to spend his days in a small corner of wartime China, translating texts of such intolerable difficulty that he sometimes spent a week puzzling out the meaning of a single page. We had one desk between us; he worked by day, and while he slept I would work into the night by the light of a rapeseed oil lamp. Though he adored China, he could never quite reconcile himself to the fact that I had a Chinese wife. Haunted by Victorian morality, he would sometimes hint that I had behaved improperly by marrying a native. Decent men, I was told, did not marry Chinese women, but kept them as concubines. Later, when he met her, he came to a different conclusion, and sometimes wondered aloud why she had married beneath her. He was pleased when she helped him with those tormentingly difficult passages in ancient Chinese philosophy.

Rose Hsiung was born in Peking and carried the air of Peking around with her. Her father was Hsiung Hsi-ling, who was Prime Minister of China during World War I. As a child, living in a vast palace on the Shih Fu Ma Tachieh, she was the playmate of the boy Emperor Pu Yi and the privileged spectator of the traditional ceremonies which continued in the Forbidden City long after the revolution had theoretically banished the Manchu dynasty. It was an age of brocaded costumes and shadowy courtyards, of gentle gestures and terrifying ruthlessness. Over the yellow roofs of Peking floated the gaily colored kites with little flutes inserted in them; and the song of the flutes poured over the city.

She grew up among brocades, and became weary of them. The Empress Dowager had sent her father on a mission to America and Europe; he returned with Western books which he never learned to read and clocks which he enjoyed winding up. Rose had no patience with the clocks, but she enjoyed the books. Soon she was announcing that she intended to be educated in America, and went off to Mount Holyoke, where she learned languages by day and attended dances every night. Her special preference was for Italian, which she spoke well, and for English, which she spoke with a New England accent. She returned to Peking with the determination to introduce American ways to an ancient and dying capital, and wore flapper costumes and danced all night. In winter, huddled in furs, she would drive out to the family estate in the Western Hills and compose Chinese poems while walking in the snow among the silver birches.

There was always something strange about her; and this she would put down to her complicated ancestry, for her father was not wholly Chinese. He was descended from Miao tribesmen who have inhabited the province of Hunan from time immemorial and were never completely assimilated by their Chinese conquerors. She had slanting eyes, full red lips, high cheekbones, a skin of ivory, but she did not look distinctively Chinese. There was the suggestion of a primitive tribal quality, a disturbing dissonance which made her beauty seem exaggerated. She had a "kill-kingdom smile," which came suddenly like a flash of lightning. They said of Yang Kuei-fei, the consort of the Emperor Ming Huang, that her smile was so ravishing that it led to the destruction of his kingdom. In the benediction of Rose's smile all thought ceased and one could only marvel.

She was perfectly aware of her beauty, and it pleased her that she had wealth, a high position in society, and innumerable admirers. She settled down, married an official in the Chinese foreign service, and had two children, Mary and Jon. Her husband died suddenly. The Japanese invaded Peking. They approached Hsiung Hsi-ling, ordered him to become the puppet Prime Minister of the conquered territory, and seem not to have been unduly surprised when he slipped away to Hong Kong. Rose remained in Peking with her two children and married a French diplomat. Mary was growing up to be a beauty. She was thirteen when she joined a group of patriotic school children who declared war on Chinese puppets serving the Japanese. The

Japanese-appointed salt commissioner at Tientsin was a powerful and brutal man who executed many Chinese slow to obey Japanese orders. The school children held a secret meeting in an ice-cream shop and solemnly sentenced him to death. They learned that he often went to the cinema, accompanied by two armed guards. One week Gunga Din was being shown. At the end of the film a violent battle breaks out, and they decided to shoot him at the height of the battle. Everything happened exactly as they had planned. Mary sat behind the salt commissioner, and when the cinema was filled with the din of machine-gun fire, she shot him in the back of the head. He died instantly. In the confusion all the school children escaped. Then they went to a corner store to eat ice cream, and an hour later they were on the train bound for Peking.

There were times when I thought Mary more beautiful than her mother. She had a dark Spanish beauty, and looked even less Chinese than Rose. She wrote once that she could never understand herself; she was a dark glass in a dark room, and she never knew what the glass contained. But in fact she knew herself reasonably well, and she had few illusions. From Peking she made her way to Chungking, where she was regarded as a heroine and banqueted by Kuomintang officials. She stayed in the house of Tai Li, the head of the secret police, a man long accustomed to assassinations. Then, as though nothing had happened, she went back to school.

Eventually she became a student in the great complex of universities in Kunming, where I was teaching. She stood out among the students by her reserve, her beauty, her legend. What interest she had in politics gradually vanished, and in her second year she married a young civil engineer. She said it was painful to be so happy when China was at war, but she persisted in her happiness until five years later when the Communists conquered Peking. She became an ardent Communist, and with many other students she was sent through the lines to prepare the way for the Communist army. One day, not long after the Communist victory over the whole of China, someone remembered that she was once the darling of the Kuomintang. There was a summary trial and she was sentenced to an indeterminate period of hard labor. Many years later she was released from jail, prematurely old and dying of tuberculosis. In this way the revolution rewarded its most dedicated followers.

Her younger brother Jon fared better. In appearance he resembled Pao Yu, the young hero of The Dream of the Red Chamber. He looked as though he had stepped straight out of the china cabinet, being made of ivory. When finally we all went to live in the palace in Peking, he alone seemed to be in full possession of it, moving about the courtyards like a prince of an earlier dynasty. There was violence in him, and during the civil war in Kunming, when the students were being killed, he was one of the leaders of the protest movement. I learned then that the boy who was so quiet at home could deliver rousing speeches when he stepped onto a platform, and I feared that he would become a politician. Instead he came to America and became a student of international politics.

In this improbable family, Jacqueline, the daughter of the French diplomat, was the most improbable of all. Distance had lent her enchantment; she had spent all the war years, and all the years of her life, in Peking. From time to time, at long intervals, there would come news from her. I would imagine her walking beside lotus pools in rainbow-colored garments, at ease among the painted palaces, even more beautiful than the other members of her family because she was far away, invisible, and therefore legendary. When we reached Peking at the end of the war, she was standing outside the ornamental gates of the palace, her hair flying in the gusty wind, her cheeks rosy, her eyes on fire because the long exile from her family had come to an end; and if her brother resembled a prince who prowled across the palace courts by right of immemorial descent, she resembled the princess in whose honor the palace was built. She was all gaiety and beauty, quietness and grace. She was twelve, and she was "Sylvia, Queen of China and Denmark" to the life. I might have known that I would discover her at the end of the journey.

I left Peking and never returned, but Rose remained. It was her city, and she refused to leave it. She gave her palace to the Communists, and as long as she could paint and write poems she was perfectly content. Poverty was no stranger to her; painting and poetry gave her detachment; it was enough to be able to wander through the enchanted city, observing the strange new forms of life around her. She wept a little when Jacqueline married a Scotsman and went to live in England, but she was too busy watching Peking and painting and caring for Mary's children to weep very often. When she was born, the Manchus ruled over China, and it seemed to her the most natural thing in the world to grow up in a palace and play with a boy Emperor. Now, as she grew old, it seemed equally natural to her to live in the world of the Red Guards. Peking was in her blood, and whatever storms raged, she would remain faithful to her city.

The people in the china cabinet came to life, but far more abundantly, more vividly, than I had ever expected. I had not known, and could not have guessed, how urgently the Chinese lived, and how much tragedy was involved in their dreams. I had thought of China as a place of heavenly peace, only to learn that it was a battlefield. It was a country where massacres were commonplace, floods drowned whole provinces, famine was more likely than food, and generals carved up empires for themselves without any care for the people they ruled or threw into their wars. To survive in China, one had to be unbelievably resilient. What made it worth while was the beauty of the land, the pride in an ancient civilization, the sense of an abiding perfection almost within reach, yet never to be grasped, because the Chinese character works always toward anarchy and the center never holds. Sun Yat-sen described China as "shifting sands," and he despaired of ever bringing the country under a stable government. The Kuomintang came to power, and for a few years there was an illusory peace. The Communists came to power, and for a few years there was a semblance of peace. So it has been throughout Chinese history: the country was always at war with itself. Even when there was peace, it was only on the surface, while the storms raged below.

1941

December 16th. It was dark when we crossed the airfield at Lashio, but suddenly the searchlights went on, and we saw a ring of machine guns trained on us, moving and following us as we moved across the silver field. In the darkness of the journey from the railway station to the airfield we had seen nothing except clumps of trees and houses, but in the sudden brilliant light of the searchlights we saw one another more clearly than we ever shall again, shining with a kind of metallic sheen which poured out of our dark overcoats. Blinded, we walked in the direction of the DC-3, and Bergery kept on whispering: "In Germany, when you are about to be shot, they have the kindness to blind you with searchlights." But the machine guns were as silent as the dark airplane on the edge of the field, and here and there were guards with fixed bayonets.

We are high above Burma, but one half of my mind is still on the landing ground at Lashio. I remember we crossed the field very slowly. The searchlights went off, there was a faint spluttering as of a fire being damped down with water, and then there was only the blue light of the airplane to guide us across the frozen ground. The moment of glory, when we saw each other as figures of heraldry, was extinguished so quickly that it seemed to have been a dream. Meanwhile the propellers were slowly revolving, shining with thin silver rings of light, and a comforting blue light from the cabin shone in the faint snow.

All over Europe, Africa, America, and Asia men are walking across dark fields to waiting airplanes. The rustle of grass, the frost melting on trees, the whistle of unseen leaves, and the sudden apparitions of silver moonlight—coming from the sky or from the earth or from a secret river—are taking possession of men's minds, and perhaps there is a new reverence for the silence of the night. . . .

As we climbed into the airplane, Bergery said something to this effect, but I was too drowsy and cold to understand what he was saying. He stood there, on the folded steps, his great cape billowing in the wind, looking out over the darkness of Asia with eyes which were dusted with snow. The blue light shone on one half of his face, and the silver light from the propellers shone on the other; and he smiled grimly, like a man stepping up to the scaffold. "A journey into the interminable darkness," he murmured, and was silent, for some birds flying low had disturbed the machine gunners, who thought they were enemy planes. In the shadow of the airplane the snow melted from our coats, but inside the cabin we could still hear the wind blowing. I am writing in the dark. They have turned out the lights. A few moments ago, while I was writing this, the engine began purring and two immensely powerful searchlights from the wings illuminated the propellers still more brilliantly, so that they resembled two immense stars revolving close to our eyes. A few moments later the searchlights were switched off again, the airplane left the earth, the bumpy field died away and we were moving suddenly into something smoother and softer than silk. It is a dark night, murderously cold, with a howling wind shaking the wings, and now that the propellers no longer shine like immense stars, the faint white towers of the clouds rush purposefully toward us and we seem to be imprisoned in their grasp. We flew low over the fields three times, catching glimpses of the customs shed and the trees bending in the wind, but the clouds are low and it is difficult to see clearly—a few stars, a ghostly mist, the earth rushing below, and a few dark trees. We are traveling on a dark ribbon of air, high above the uplands of northern Burma, and it is strange to think that only a few hours ago we were flying over the Irrawaddy delta, looking down at golden rice fields and the spires of gilt temples. The blinding light of the searchlight at Lashio has cut us off from the past.

I can hear the soft purring of the motors, and very faintly the whistle of the wind. The night is so thick that even the few stars disappearing in the haze of mist comfort us. Outside the blue windows snow is falling silently, and there is no comfort in the ice-cold world beneath. Snow everywhere, and on the wings are faint layers of ice.

Bergery has just turned the little bell-shaped ventilator, and the wind begins to ruffle his gray hairs. He looks old and worn in this light, which softens all outlines but changes the color of flesh until it resembles those curiously veined bluish rocks which are found in deserts.

"What is so extraordinary is that we haven't seen Lashio," he said. "It might have been anywhere—some European houses, taxis, a station courtyard, dark trees, a few faint lights burning behind shuttered doors. It's exactly like all the cities in Europe. From Berlin to Lashio—everywhere blackout!" A little while later he said: "In the future the historians will say that we were afraid of the light, and they will be wrong. What we are afraid of is the blinding light of an explosion, and the still more blinding light of truth." He was silent then, gazing out of the blue window. It was very warm in the airplane—too warm. He smiled, settled himself comfortably in the armchair with *The Statesman*, and went to sleep.

He is asleep now, but even in sleep he looks weary—the weariness which comes to all war correspondents in time, for traveling is the most rigorous occupation in the world and leaves its stigmata, as the years leave rings on trees. I met him first in Munich, in the summer of 1938. Nine months later we were together in Austria, taking part in some absurd scheme to kill Hitler. I met him again in Spain. I had not expected to meet him at the windswept airport in Lashio on his way to Kunming. He is sleeping lightly, his ears keened to the vibrations of the airplane, and I remember his saying in Austria that he had seen too much of war ever to sleep perfectly again. "When I am sleeping, I think I can always see what is happening all round me, and I am sure I can hear everything. I sleep deeply—with one eye open. It is not a question of nerves. It is a question of being eternally vigilant." Sometimes he smiles in his sleep, and sometimes he seems to be about to cry; and it is always curious to watch him as he sleeps, his head bent a little to one side—that immense head with the iron-gray hair—his silk scarf fluttering in the wind from the bell-shaped ventilator. Bergery was one of the greatest of the American war correspondents during the Great War. Retired, he lived in a small flat in Florence or in a gray stone building in Peking, entirely absorbed by the world but completely remote from it, until the Greater War caught him up in its folds, and once more he began to fly across continents in airplanes at night.

I am quite sure I have not slept. The starlight has come out, thick waves of clouds appear from the direction of China, and the small moon, curving and diving among the clouds, is so beautiful that I cannot take my eyes from the window. Gradually the moon grows brighter, and a thick white light falls on his sleeping head.

I must have fallen asleep. It is broad daylight. Green fields, red hills, small thatched houses with yellow roofs, and long purple shadows—and the blue sky, this above all. The blue of a thrush's egg, but deeper, an immensity of sky, falling or sweeping to the earth like a blue coat or curtain, and like a curtain rippling as it falls. I do not think that this is an inaccurate desctiption. Imagine an immense blue silk tent and the wind rippling the surface, its coolness and the faint ripples on the surface. It glitters with silver while in Malaya the sky glitters with bronze. Perhaps the color of the sky is due to the reflected color of the earth—a deep red, with here and there a few patches of green rice. We are already flying over Kunming. The walls of the city throw long purple shadows, and over the airfield there are small white objects glittering in the sun. Are they pebbles?

Bergery says quietly: "There is smoke over the city. She is burning." He looks pale, his face pressed against the window glass.

A moment later: "There are nearly a hundred airplanes on the airfield. Where have they come from?"

In the dazzling blue sunlight airplanes lie on the landing field to the northeast of the city. The city is blood-red and biscuit-yellow, the walls very high. And beside the city, stretching toward the bronze hills in the distance, lies an almost circular lake the color of emeralds dipped in milk. They have asked us to pull the curtains over the windows. Why? No one knows. Or perhaps the pebbles are really airplanes?

There are hundreds of airplanes on the field, painted dead white, the fuselages inscribed with the teeth of tigers. As we step out of the airplane someone says: "Haven't you heard? We were bombed yesterday. Four hundred were killed. There are no shelters. You have to run into the country, outside the walls. Twenty-seven airplanes—always twenty-seven in three groups of nine—came over in the morning. The 'Flying Tigers' came in the afternoon." He pointed to the airplanes lined up on the tarmac, the young Chinese mechanics in blue overalls, the armorers with their immense serpentine belts of silver-and-bronze machine-gun bullets. He said slowly: "Waal, I guess the tiger is growing wings."

The air is so pure that we can see the faintest incisions in the distant mountains. We are a mile above sea level. My heart is thumping. There is a lane of poplars leading from the airport to the city. In the mist-laden morning, the roads and the poplars and the small wooden carts driving down the shadowy road remind me of France. We have spent a few minutes in the *estaminet*, where there is a girl who is obviously French, though her features are Chinese and she wears a pair of dark blue slacks. Drinking hot coffee out of enamel mugs, we envy the American airmen in their heavy furs. They call themselves "Flying Tigers," as though they were acrobats taking part in an aerial tournament. Stamping the blood back into our legs and breathing the cold frosted air, we hardly dare go out into the frozen field. And when at last we return to the waiting airplane, we watch the milk-white mist rising about the long rows of planes. The mist is like silk; you can touch it and it flows in your hands. Suddenly, out of this mist, a silvery-white airplane begins gliding over the field. I have taken up a handful of Chinese earth. It is red like blood, the same color as the earth in Catalonia, Cornwall, and Malaya.

We are flying again. The blue lake mysteriously turns red. Small fishing vessels glide over the lake, their orange sails turning an even deeper red than the lake. Sunlight is coming over the hills, and behind us Kunming sparkles like orange juice. Everything red—bare foothills, faint tracks curving over the summits, small houses, gardens, peasants working in the misty fields; and then for some reason the earth's redness disappears and everything is blue. It is like looking through a stereoscope—the patterns in the bright liquid colors of China. Blue everywhere—the blue lake, the blue city, the long stretches of blue fields the color of the sea. We have been seeing the earth through the shadow of the airplane's wing, which cuts out the sun, but even now, with the sun ahead of us, the colors are so clear they appear to have been painted. On the horizon a great white cloud like a sea of milk is slowly moving towards us.

We are still in the cloud. According to Bergery we shall be in the cloud until we reach Chungking. It is pure white, and here and there faint rainbows springing from the wing tip and following us relentlessly color the cliffs of the cloud. For though the cloud is shapeless, there are occasional immense cliffs, vertical darknesses, and we look down through the cliffs at the misty green world beneath. In this whiteness we travel the road to Chungking.

When I was a child, I was always dreaming of China, but I never dreamt of anything so beautiful as Kunming. And yet the moment I saw it, I knew I had been perfectly familiar with it since the earliest days. The high biscuit-colored walls were the fortresses I played with; the temples and the lakes accompanied my dreams. Somewhere, perhaps in *Grimm's Fairy Tales*, I read of an old man who kept a princess of China in a bottle at the bottom of a deep well, and I would think of her late at night when my mother brought the night lamp into my room. The princess was small and perfectly formed, with waxen features and oiled black hair, dressed in a gown of some delicate silk material, and there were glass slippers on her feet and roses in her hair. Later I discovered that there were no longer any princesses in China, and the highest aim of the Chinese poet or scholar was to marry the daughter of a prime minister, and particularly his youngest daughter. Then, surrounded by courtiers in silk, with jade bracelets on their wrists and jade necklaces hanging over their shoulders, writing delicately with an ivory brush while one of the courtiers laid a chrysanthemum on the table in order that his handwriting should imitate the softness and strength of the petals, he would write a few lines of greeting to the bride he had never seen.

I have been thinking of this legendary China as we ride through the white cloud, wondering whether it still exists and whether I shall ever again see it in my lifetime. In the ancient dynasties of China there existed an ordered beauty of gesture and benevolence which has disappeared from the rest of the world, and may have disappeared still more completely in China herself. I remember an old man in Singapore, who would talk at length of the last days of the Ch'ing dynasty, for he had taken part in the political maneuvers of the time, financing Sun Yat-sen's revolutions, devoting himself to the care of the dispossessed and the exiled. A few days ago I saw him for the last time, and as we walked along the muddy beach at Tanglin, he asked me what I thought I would do in China. I told him I wanted to see everything there was to be seen, because I wanted to exorcise the demons and fairies who had tormented and delighted my youth.

"But China has changed—changed—changed——" He repeated the words perhaps twenty times. "There is no longer grace in my country. The reverence and love for things has gone from the earth. It has disappeared even from China. This war has made us all soldiers."

"Do you regret the change?"

He said nothing, though there was pain in his eyes. He asked me about the future of Singapore.

"I am quite sure it will hold out," I replied. "The best roads are in the south. We have the communications, and we have learned a lot from the loss of Penang. In a week or so we shall drive them out again."

"It is like the wars in China." He smiled, and nodded his head in agreement. "A village is captured, the people flee to the mountains, a week later it is recaptured, and then the village is forgotten. Perhaps it is mentioned in a military communiqué, but more likely it is wholly forgotten—it is always so! "

We walked back to the small white house on Amber road. The fishing smacks were still riding among the islands, and they shone for a moment like those jewels of the sea, for which an early Chinese emperor sacrificed his kingdom, since so much wealth was expended on their expeditions. In the Mongol dynasty Malaya paid tribute to the Emperor in Peking, and the Chinese who work in the rubber fields of Malaya are only returning to a country over which they once possessed sovereignty. Singapore was so peaceful that it was easy to understand the Chinese philosopher who said he could recapture the atmosphere of the T'ang dynasty more easily in Malaya than in Peking, for it was easier to contemplate under a living palm tree than in the decaying dust of the Chinese capital.

A few hours ago, in a cold blizzard, the airplane dropped out of the clouds flying low over the river, flashing past the white rocks on which Chungking is built. For the last two hours we were traveling by beam. The cloud thickened and seemed to turn black, and occasionally there were blue tongues of flame on the wings, and sometimes the cloud was so thick that it was impossible to see the wing tips. Sitting there, drowsy with the heat of the airplane, looking at our pale blue faces reflected in the blue window glass, at the swift-flowing river and the white cliffs and towers of Chungking, we felt like strangers about to enter an undiscovered country as visionary as any we had ever seen in our childhood dreams.

The airplane flew low over Chungking, and we caught a glimpse of white housetops, burned-out buildings, small, black paddle steamers riding the broad river, and far away in the west a yellow sandspit in midstream. We flew low over the sandspit and then roared up into the windy sky. A few minutes later we turned back, wings dipping, the silk on the wings rippling in the wind and rain, slowly circling over Chungking and gaining height. It was then that I noticed for the first time the immense height of the rocky cliffs upon which Chungking is built, for when we descended and skimmed over the river, Chungking towered above us, gleaming white in the faint sun. The gray towers of a cathedral, the blackened ruins near the water's edge, wattle and bamboo huts perched on cliffs, steps carved out of rock and leading down to the gray, smoky water. We were gliding lower and lower, until the wheels were touching the wave caps and a white spume was flung over the wings and over the windows. When the spume had been washed clean from the windows, we were following the chalk line on the sandspit to the end. Near some bamboo huts, the airplane came to a halt, and we were surprised by the engines' silence, for it seemed as though the airplane would go on forever, as elemental a thing as a bird, fuelless, perfectly proportioned to the air.

In the air everything was white and peaceful, but on the sandspit a storm was raging. White spray was flung on the sand, and the small ships on the river looked as though they would be dashed to pieces on the rocks. It began to rain in torrents. We shivered. We wished we were back in Malaya, where the rain is warm and does not wound with sharp points of frost. At the far end of the sandspit we found a small boat to take us over the river. The river was in spate, black and oily, the rain streaking whiteness on the black troughs of waves. The rain lashed everything within sight. Cowering in the small boat, the luggage piled in the bow, with the blinding rain cutting us like knives, we looked at Chungking through a mist of rain and gray descending clouds and saw only a gray smoky rock and a few lights burning. Bergery sat hunched up on the sternsheets. It was midday, the river a mile wide, and we were rowing against the current for fear of being swept downstream. It grew darker. In the sternsheets Bergery was repeating in bewilderment: "Is this Chungking?"

December 21st. We have been wandering in the city all morning. At seven o'clock we left the south bank, wandering down a muddy road carved out of rock and filled with horse droppings, slippery with ice and in places almost vertical. There was a white mist over the river, but the mist cleared when we were halfway across, and suddenly Chungking rose in splendor on the north bank, resembling once again a white ship, superb in her mourning bands of dead streets and blackened chimneys. At the top of the Wang Lung Men steps the enormous broken stumps of blackened chimneys pointing heavenward have a kind of prophetic menace, and we hurried past them in the direction of the center of the city, escaping by the skin of our teeth the green buses crowded with five times as many passengers as they were meant to hold and throwing up black, poisonous clouds of wood-oil smoke.

Sunk in his great overcoat, Bergery walked down the long road which runs along the river bank, complaining bitterly of the ugliness.

"Nearly all Chinese cities are beautiful, and only this one is ugly, but you must remember that nearly all Chinese cities are built for the night and for the full blaze of sunlight. There are towns where no one should go except in a winter darkness, and other towns where no one should go except at noonday. The Chinese countryside, of course, loves the mist, but the towns love only the extremes of darkness and light."

It was not light and it was not dark. There was no sun. The buildings were the color of old water, and the nightmare was made worse by the presence of Chinese characters written over the doorways in every imaginable form of degraded calligraphy. Again and again Bergery returned to the subject of these Chinese letters painted over the doorways or modeled in plaster.

"If you want to understand the greatness of a nation, look first at its lettering. Do you remember the tombstones of the Dutch conquerors in Malacca? And the Trajan column? There has never been a great period in a nation's history when there was not great lettering. The characters of the Chinese language are the most beautiful in the world; but modern industrialization has allowed the inefficient and the insane the privilege of writing the letters in the streets of Chungking."

He was angry as I have ever seen him, raging at the miserable letters as though he expected them to burst into powder under his vituperation. It became comic. He would look up at the gold characters written over a bank, shaking his fist. "Look at it! The fat swollen body of 'chung'—no character, a fat pig of a character. No Chinese will learn anything by looking at pigs. Pigs have no structure—no lines! If you make a character look like a horse or a fly or a tiger, that's something, there's grace in it. But the man who painted that character knows nothing except pigs."

"It looks all right to me."

"It looks all right to you! You're myopic, you're insensitive, you're beyond hope. Some of the greatest art in the world comes from Chinese characters—and look what they do to it. Calligraphy is the key to China. You can read a man's character from his Chinese handwriting, and you can read the progress of a civilization in China by the handwriting of the people. I thought the war would produce a calligraphy as firm and molded as the calligraphy of the Han dynasty. Look at that sign for 'chia.' It's a flea dipped in ink. And that sign for 'ying.' It's like a sickly girl, dying of an incurable disease. This is impossible. I beg you not to lift your head—the pavements at least have no characters written on them."

He had taken an immediate dislike to Chungking, but shortly afterward it became clear that he was like a lover who finds more faults in the beloved as his ardor increases. It was damp and misty, the gray sky almost within arm's reach. Buses groaned past, and inside the buses men, women, and children were crowded together in black confusion. The postmen in green, the policemen in black, the soldiers in every conceivable shade of blue and brown were lost in the immense crowds—colorless like water. Color was so rare that even the bleached white sackcloth of the mourners fell pleasantly on our eyes, but a single mourner with white headband, white apron, and white belt would have passed unnoticed, so colorless is the air and so dark are the skies. There are no red cheeks in these crowds. Many are diseased, and in one street which we passed through we saw a dead child lying in the mud of the roadside, the body of a man covered with a tarpaulin, and seven people suffering from deformities—a woman without a nose, a child with only one arm, a man who hobbled on crutches, waving in front of him a naked and paralyzed foot. But suddenly in this same street, at the moment when we thought we had entered a nightmare from which there was no return, we saw a bride in red silks coming from her home. Crackers were lit, and a flaming torch was waved backward and forward in front of her path and before her eyes. Her face was painted dead white, but her lips were pomegranate red and her eyebrows were thickly arched. She was pretending to struggle, but she was smiling, and when at last she was locked in her red and gilt bridal chair, the long carrying poles wound in green silk and green ribbons descending from the crown of the chair, it was as though our eyes were flooded with color. Her appearance in these gray streets produced an effect like that of a rippling stream that springs over sand, over pebble, through sunlight and shadow.

And so we wandered down the colorless damp lanes overlooking the river, remembering the sudden glory of red and green. We were hungry for color. The smallest spark of red, even a cigarette glowing in the distance, quickened our heartbeats. Occasionally there passes us a young student, in his blue Sun Yat-sen uniform, and on his cheeks there are the two red circles of a consumptive. A green automobile slid past. We paused for five minutes before a shop window filled with crumpled silver and gold paper, a Christmas tree, and three or four colored dolls. By midday it was raining, but the rain did not absorb the mist, for the mist remained. In this darkness and in this misery we wandered back to the swollen river.

Bergery disappeared in the afternoon. He came back in the evening covered with mud, saying that in the whole of Chungking he had found only one thing beautiful—a courtyard and a bridge on the south bank, and a dead plum tree standing against a high wall.

"You must come," he insisted.

It was nearly dark. The rain was still falling, and Chungking on the north bank is almost invisible in the mist, though the lights are shining down the Wang Lung Men steps. We scampered along muddy roads in the half-darkness, listening to the scurry of rats and the bark of the night dogs. The narrow streets on the south bank are covered with granite stones, but sometimes the stones are missing and you plunge into a morass of treacle. Here, in the darkness, yellow light coming from the paper windows of houses and a faint white illumination coming from the sky, you are conscious of a darkness greater than any imaginable blindness. Shapes of the night come from the dark walls. In the silence your footsteps are echoed by footsteps in a parallel road, and it is impossible to tell whether they are your own footsteps or another's. We climbed up a slag heap. It was black, and neither of us knew whether the slag heap was solid. Crouched against the walls, black beggars threw out pale white hands.

Bergery was more excited than at any moment since we left Kunming. He walked with quick steps, continually talking about China.

"You understand. . . . China at night. . . . This is something that is alive, terribly alive. Can you hear it?"

We stood still. From far away, or from the earth, we heard a dull roar like the roar of the blood in your ears when you have been running hard. I have heard the same kind of sound once in Spain when, walking over a deserted field at night, I heard through the earth the engines of an underground armament factory.

"What can you hear?"

"Nothing—a kind of dull roar."

"You'll hear it nowhere else—it is particularly Chinese, and no one has been able to explain it."

We were crossing a small bridge. At the bottom of an immense ditch there was a faint trickle of silvery water passing under the bridge. Bergery turned around, and there it was—the plum tree, the wall, the small bridge all white in the pale moonlight.

"Is this what you want me to see?"

"Yes, for God's sake, look at it! Look at the proportions! Look at the height of the wall and the shape of the dead plum tree and the curving arches of the bridge, and ask yourself whether they are not made for one another. A Chinese must have spent hours working out these proportions. Don't tell me it is an accident. The bridge was built first, then the wall, then the plum tree was planted. There can be no doubt about it. Look how splendidly the plum tree reflects the curve of the bridge and how the height of the wall——"

He stood there very silently, and it must have seemed to him that all the squalor of Chungking had disappeared. The black branches were gnarled and rimmed with silver, and this silver was reflected upward from the bottom of the foul-smelling ditch; and we heard the tinkle of water over rough stones. He stood there for perhaps five minutes, completely absorbed in the beauty of proportions and these reflections of silver in which he must have seen, as by a miracle of accomplishment performed by a Chinese scholar who once inhabited a garden in Chungking, the answers to innumerable questions long since forgotten by the Chinese who inhabit these desolate lanes.

"There was perhaps a garden," he said, as we made our way over slag heaps to the house where we were living. "I imagine a merchant from Szechuan who retired from business early. He devoted himself to art. He built this wall and this tree—and this is Chinese civilization."

When we returned, the moon had disappeared completely from behind the clouds. It was the dusk of night, when a faint illumination shines from the sky, but it is impossible to tell where it comes from. Muffled in our coats, we sat on the verandah, gazing at the lights of Chungking twinkling on the opposite bank. Some sampans, black against black water, passed in the direction of Ichang. It was very silent. Suddenly, on the opposite bank, a forked tongue of red flame leapt into the still sky, as though an immense match had been struck on the rough surface of the city. The flames were deep red, the color of blood. They grew violently and changed into other things

—the faces of golden cats, falling pillars, ceremonies of revolving cherubs. There were so many flames, each leaping from a different source, that we instinctively stepped back. The glow of the flames shone on the black waters.

We watched the flames for a long time. We heard the fire engine, and we saw, like faint silver ropes of rain, the jets of water scurrying sky-high above the flames. But the flames continued. Chungking is built on rock, but the houses are paper, matchwood, and plaster. There was something terrible and revengeful in the sudden reddening of the rock on the other side of the river. The flames continued all night. We heard the crash of dynamite, a long, silky, yellow flame came roaring and splashing out of the roof of a house which was burning, and slowly—very slowly—like the drooping wave of a waterfall, this house perished. Occasionally we heard screams, and once we saw a riverboat two hundred feet below the houses attempting to spray the cliff edge of the rock with its white jets. There was nothing that could be done. We went back to bed, but all night the red flames flickered on the bedroom wall.

December 23rd. At night columns of soldiers are marching through the streets. They are Kwangsi troops, wearing heavy greatcoats which reach to the feet, gray packs on their backs, straw sandals on their feet. They look healthy, and in the glow of the street lamps their faces are deep red like apples. I have seen them because I have been wandering at night with Bergery. We have seen nothing to compare with the dead plum tree against the gray wall; but there are moments, walking down the great canyons of streets near the river's edge, when the height of the buildings and the sudden apparition of a curving roof in the moonlight, in the vague whiteness which shines overhead; seems to presage a sudden awakening into beauty; but though we wait, nothing beautiful arrives.

But last night, hearing the distant tramp of feet at three o'clock in the morning, the city awakened into life.

I do not know why it is, but the sight of soldiers moving through dusk or darkness, even when they are moving silently, fills me with sudden excitement. The gleam of bayonets, the officer riding at the end of the procession with his sword swinging over the pony's rump, the fixed gaze of the soldiers, and the *relentlessness* of their marching steps fill me with amazed delight.

As we were crossing the river this morning, a Chinese officer came up to us and saluted smartly. He wore the usual yellow uniform and leather belt; on his collar were the three-barred gold triangles which denote a colonel. He looked very young, and later when we learned that he was twenty-three and had taken part in the battle for Chapei ten years ago, it was astounding to think that a man so young could be so experienced. We talked of many things, and as the paddleboat reached the opposite side, he asked us to dinner the next day.

At least once in every half-hour Bergery returns to the subject of the boy: "The youth of these people! In the old days, if you had a beard, you were on the way to becoming prime minister. None of the great soldiers were young. Think of Tseng Kuo-fan and Yuan Shih-k'ai, who were brought back into the army to win their greatest victories after their retirements." We passed some soldiers near Liang Lou K'o. They carried paper umbrellas, and many of them were walking barefoot, their feet bleeding. "They are so young—they are only children!" he exclaimed, like someone thunderstruck. "The most extraordinary thing is that they are all peasants—perhaps fourteen years old. In Szechuan, of course, a boy who looks fourteen may be eighteen—the people are small. But surely these boys——" Then he would look again, looking for the signs which reveal their character; and finding none, for it was dusk and the rain was coming out of low cotton-wool clouds, he stamped his feet in impatience. "How do they expect to fight the Japanese with boys?"

The rain came down, soaking them, but they laughed cheerily. We watched them as they marched down the road until they disappeared in the mist.

December 24th. Christmas Eve dinner with the young colonel. He lives in a small white brick house high up on the cliffs. You reach it through many archways, climbing innumerable stone steps. There is no sign of the sun, but the clouds are whiter than yesterday and the misery of the unbroken cloud is relieved by the presence of a faint glow in the sky.

The rooms are terribly bare. The leaves have fallen from the high trees outside, and only the spears of yellow bamboo remain. There is the soldier, his mother, and his wife, who will soon have a child. In all the three rooms the only splash of color comes from the heavily embroidered quilt on the large double bed. Through the house three black kittens wander like dissolute eighteenth-century emperors.

"It is an honor, it is an honor," the young colonel keeps on saying. Although he spoke English perfectly yesterday, the presence of his wife and his mother has made him tongue-tied.

Bergery is almost angry. We notice that a fortune has been spent on food. There is a whole chicken, a great cask of rice, seven or eight courses. We mumble apologies over our lack of finesse in eating with chopsticks. He is ashamed of his mother's hobbled feet and her lack of English, and when we laugh at frail jokes, we are conscious that his mother is laughing out of politeness. The colonel works at military headquarters.

"In Shanghai I was captured by the Japanese. I escaped. I decided I would make it my mission in life to kill Japanese. I have not killed very many yet, and so I am dissatisfied. I have been ordered to teach in the Staff College." He shrugs his shoulders. He is trying to convey that he can teach nothing, he is too ignorant. He asks Bergery endless questions about the war in Europe and in the Far East. He begins to talk about the Generalissimo who preaches to the staff college every Monday morning. He speaks of the Generalissimo in hushed voices—many voices. He is not one person, but three or four people. He is the young soldier who escaped miraculously from the dark lanes of Chapei; he is the young husband; he is the soldier who stands for three or four hours every morning while the Generalissimo makes a speech; he is the old man, ten thousand years old, who has seen invasion after invasion of conquerors in China.

He admired the Generalissimo above all men, living or dead, yet he could say that the speeches were too long, they were all the same, there were times when he was a little bored with them. When the Generalissimo makes a speech, he writes down the headings on a sheet of paper—perhaps three or four words, but the speech is endless. The same words are heard every morning. Loyalty, Death, the Japanese, the Spirit of the New Life Movement. The soldier said that the Generalissimo was probably quite conscious of the length of his speeches; he was repeating deliberately and endlessly in the hope that a few simple ideas would be understood by the officers and those who served under him. His voice dropped in reverence and regret. "But recently he has been getting old. He looks tired after his long speeches. Physically he is as active as ever, and mentally perhaps he is more understanding and compassionate, less like a priest. But we fear for him. The loneliness, and the terrible responsibilities. And what will happen when the Generalissimo dies?"

I have already heard this question many times in China. The kingpin is inviolate. Even Chou En-lai, the Communist member of the Supreme Military Defense Council, believes that he is completely necessary for the future of China. "And what will happen when the Generalissimo dies?" The words are spoken not in haste but in anguish. What will happen? In England, Russia, and America men know that the death of the elected leader will cause barely a ripple on the surface of the country. In China it is different. There is heartache in the question; for though not all the men around the Generalissimo are universally beloved, and he himself is revered rather than loved, there is no one else to take his place.

We spoke of many things in the bare rooms, where the wind came through the open windows. Here darkness came early, and we watched the small Tibetan ponies on the rocks beneath. They are a little larger than Kansu ponies, and they have a curious resemblance to the ponies shown on Han dynasty reliefs. They are sure-footed, sturdy, with heavy manes and long tails. As they fly across the rocks, the bells ring and they seem to be shaking their heads from side to side to produce a continuous ringing sound. In the morning I had said to Bergery, "I would like to see a boy riding one of these horses at night and carrying in his hand a bamboo flare." These bamboo flares are offered to passengers from the ferry on dark nights, when it is impossible to see the steps carved out of the rock. They shine with a blood-red, smoky light, which turns the rocks into crimson pools and the faces of passengers into ripe apples. And now, looking down from the house perched on the cliffs, we saw a small white pony ridden by a boy carrying a red, smoking light.

It was late. We had an appointment with a famous philosopher on the other side of the river. The soldier pressed something into our hands. We did not know what it was, and we did not look until we had reached the ferry, for the rocks were dark and the boy with the twisted bamboo flare had already disappeared. At the ferry we looked in our hands. Neatly folded lay a sheet of silk the size of a handkerchief. On the silk there was embroidered in large red letters the character for "good luck."

Climbing the steps. Climbing the steps. Climbing the steps. There are ten million steps in Chungking. There are steps from the ferry, there are steps in the main roads, there are steps in houses. One imagines there are invisible steps leading up through the clouds into the sunlight.

But tonight we did not cross the river by ferry. The ferry is out of action, and we crossed by sampan. The river was high, and we measured the current by the sampans which passed by so quickly that they seemed to be instantaneous photographs—appearing suddenly and disappearing still more suddenly.

The river was angry, and the passengers crouching in the bottom of the sampan were muttering prayers. I don't think anyone trusted the boatman. When we were alone in the middle of the river, looking up at the high black rocks, it was such a loneliness that one might almost go mad. The swirling current, the river's darkness, the depth of the river and the masts of three or four sampans standing above the water in midstream did not inspire confidence, and Bergery whispered pleasantly, "No one has ever come out of the Yangtse alive." Three boats were wrecked in the morning. More would be wrecked tomorrow, and many more in the days that followed. We lay in the bottom of the boat, wondering whether we were already sinking, lost in the dark river among the groans of the passengers, the curses of the boatmen, and the silvery gleams on the river like knives. The tide was so swift that we passed the landing-stage, a rickety affair of wooden planks laid out over the shallow water; but in the darkness we did not know that the water was shallow, and we were impatient to land. It was already eight o'clock. The philosopher had been waiting for us since seven. Climbing up the lanes of steps, we began to wonder whether the philosopher had already gone to bed.

In the center of the city, not far from the British embassy, the Street of the Seven Stars curves northward and at the same time climbs steeply. Between the high stucco frontals of the shops occasional small alleyways lead toward the river. We went down one of these small, dark alleyways, noisome with the smell of dead rats and refuse, and came to an unexpectedly well-lit courtyard where a few clumps of bamboo and small pines rustled in the evening wind. One side of the square courtyard was open to the Chialing river, which joins the Yangtse at Chungking; and looking down at the lights twinkling in the distance and the black serpentine flow of the river beneath we felt dizzy and at the same time surprised by the immense height we had climbed. The philosopher lived in a small room, hardly larger than a cupboard and occupied almost entirely by an enormous bed.

He wore a blue gown embroidered with flower patterns of a

darker blue. His long forked beard was gray, nearly white. On his wrists he carried ivory bracelets.

"You have come a long way," he said. "I should have sent a car for you, but unfortunately it was too late."

We wondered whether he possessed a car, for cars are rarities outside official circles.

We began to talk about India and Singapore. The Chinese are beginning to believe the rumors which have been spreading fast during the past few days. The Japanese have command of the air. Singapore was defended from the coast, but there were no defenses in the land. The Burmese are preparing to co-operate with the Japanese. The Chinese had offered to send expeditionary forces overseas, but these were refused. A note of bitterness crept into his voice until we turned the subject of conversation to China.

"You mustn't judge us by our failures, you must judge us by our victories. In economics our victories are greater than foreigners believe. The industries of China have been removed from the coast to the southwestern provinces, and if you think of our appalling lack of transport, then you will say that it is a miracle. We are like one of those old Chinese houses. The rafters are falling in, the walls are breaking open, and we have decided to live in the courtyard. The Chinese race is nomadic. We can live in the courtyard for many years, but the time will come when we want to return to the house. And then——" He paused for a while, handed us handleless bowls of sweet flowered tea, and then plucked three notes in quick succession on the Chinese lute, a beautiful instrument which once belonged to the Imperial Court. "I do not believe in revolution," he concluded, and it was some time before we realized that the last statement was indissolubly connected with the ominous phrase, "and then——"

Down below, the bowl of the night was indistinguishable from the bowl of the earth. Scattered lights glittered, and the earth and the sky seemed to be uniformly starred from top to bottom. Only the faint glimmering line of the Chialing river, cutting its way through the mountains, broke the scattering of these heavenly stars.

Bergery began to speak as though the revolution were already upon us. The philosopher smiled.

"It is said in the *Book of Changes:* 'The symbol of the earth and that of brightness entering into the midst of it give the idea of "wounded brightness." There will be advantage in crossing the great stream.' I do not know how you translate these old hexagrams into European languages. They were invented, they say, by the Duke of

Chou. It may be true. But the symbol of 'wounded brightness' is very much in my mind. The Revolution has not yet succeeded. Sun Yat-sen made his fatal journey to the north in the hope of discovering a method through which the popular will can be determined, and still we have not discovered the method. Perhaps it is because the country is so large, perhaps it is because we are not yet politically mature —though we are four thousand years old!—perhaps it is because we have lost contact with the heavenly principle. We are still young. What is four thousand years in the history of the world?"

He spoke of the decay of manners since his childhood. "The pure reverence and love for things have gone from the world. We are all materialists. There was a time when filial respect meant something deeper than you can imagine. It meant that the father was burdened with immense and terrible responsibilities. Now no one loves respon-sibility."

He possessed in this small bedroom in the hotel all those things that characterized the old philosophers. There was a fly whisk, an incense burner, paintings and scrolls on the wall, a small bamboo bookcase containing paperbacked Chinese books neatly arranged in rows. With the fly whisk he would occasionally flick entirely imagi-nary flies from Bergery's coat.

"Do not think that I am against the government. I welcome al-most everything they have done, and praise their courage. The New Life Movement has shocked me to the core, but——" He waved his hands in a gesture which sent the ivory bracelets revolving wildly on his thin wrists. "It will pass, like all the other curious importations we have brought from abroad. But the other things——" His face be-came grave. "The lack of reverence and understanding for the past, the breaking of the city walls, the lack of respect paid to scholars, the knowledge even of our past already forgotten, the Americanization and Britishization of all our old and most respected customs—that is what is terrible, and it is still more terrible when you remember that it has been brought about by the wars. I who am speaking to you have one foot in the grave. It is necessary that I should protest. If I could alter the course of Chinese history by hanging myself on a tree—in the old days one could commit suicide and thereby rebuke the emperor—I would do so. But whom shall I rebuke? Certainly not the Generalissimo. Certainly not the Chinese people. I rebuke his-tory, and history pays no attention to suicides."

As he spoke we grew accustomed to the small room and began to look at the beautiful carvings and oriental scrolls on the wall. The room was full of priceless objects, moonstones, jade inkstands, stone rubbings. There were paintings of valleys in the mist, not unlike the valleys of the Chialing river. On these paintings blue and green mountains were placed, not according to the conventions of perspective, one behind the other, but as though each were suspended in airy vapor, independent of one another and yet somehow touching one another by their proximity. The black jaw of the window was wide open. Occasionally the scrolls would move in the wind, and the sound of the wooden roller which hung at the bottom of the scroll, as it continually tapped the wall, had a nightmarish quality, reminding us that the words of the old man in the flowered blue gown were spoken from the grave of his cherished illusions.

"I believe that China has no future if she surrenders her soul to the West.

"The birthplace of the revolution was Honolulu, but we must not be expected to believe that the culture of Honolulu has anything to offer us.

"It is time the West learned from us the arts of calligraphy. The writing of Westerners is shocking beyond words.

"The image of China in the future is something I cannot discern; but that we must go back to our old virtues, and revive the nobility of scholars—of this I am convinced."

He said many other things, some bitter and trenchant, some lukewarm, as though he were already tired of the problems which a rejuvenated China imposed upon him. He wrote scrolls for us. He presented us with small jade rings, and refused to let us go. Bergery delighted him with his knowledge of international politics, and his sudden suavity of manner. In Bergery's understanding glance the old philosopher saw evidence of a pupil.

"Would you say that if China retains her reverence for things, she will still be able to compete with the West? Can you have reverence for battleships?"

The old philosopher thought for a while. "Yes, certainly," he said at last, "but what is more difficult to understand is whether we can have reverence for bureaucracy. Perhaps bureaucracy is as old as China, but my heart bleeds when I go into some of our government offices and see the young boys and girls doing nothing—nothing whatsoever. They look up at the clock with their arms folded over their desks. No task has been given to them. They are there because their fathers or mothers were related to the manager of the office. I would have all the youths in the banks and government offices in the war. If they were learning something, I could forgive them, but they are learning nothing at all."

He was bitterly disturbed by the fate of the young generation. The students in the universities, the soldiers and even the social workers possessed no traditions. They were too young to have learnt anything from the traditional authority of the dynasties. The New Life Movement, though admirable in many ways, failed as a substitute for the ancient traditions. They were purposeless. They lived in a world where there were no accepted customs and everything was being invented for the first time. And yet there was no freshness, they had not leaped into a new culture, they were hagridden by the old and incapable of seeing the new.

"I have been asked by the Generalissimo to write on the new culture. What can I do? Am I to invent a culture out of my head? We must wait patiently for the light, and I fear it will be a long time coming."

Just before we left, Bergery reminded him that the same problem was being faced in the West and no solution was in sight. The generation which returned from the last war was helpless in the face of historical necessity. In this small room overlooking the river, the wind knocking the scrolls against the wall, he recited the lines of *The Waste Land* which moved him above all others:

> What is that sound high in the air
> Murmur of maternal lamentation
> Who are those hooded hordes swarming
> Over endless plains, stumbling in cracked earth
> Ringed by the flat horizon only
> What is the city over the mountains
> Cracks and reforms and bursts in the violet air
> Falling towers
> Jerusalem Athens Alexandria
> Vienna London . . .

As we left, the Chinese philosopher said: "The plains do not go on forever, sometimes we find the city over the mountains. After this war you must come and help us to find these ancient cities."

We were sorry to leave the old philosopher, with his books, his small collection of scrolls, his delightful view over the river. In the dark night the tremendous city was humming still, though it was nearly midnight. A few green buses were still climbing the Street of the Seven Stars, throwing up immense black pillars of wood-oil vapor. The red banners over the streets were blowing gustily, and the silvered paper characters sewn on the banners still announced the coming of Christmas. Bergery repeated under his breath: "Falling towers—Paris, Singapore, Rangoon—Moscow, London. . . ."

December 25th. I have been up with Bergery in the hills. We had two small white ponies with bushy tails and straggling manes. There were no blinkers and only an apology of a saddle. From the south bank we climbed over the wet rocks toward Huang-k'o-ya, where a slender white pagoda commemorates an ancient empress of China who was born on the hill. The road winds through narrow villages, under the shadow of the old German embassy, until it comes out in a pine forest. The road is granite stone weaving up the mountain slope, and so well graded that the ponies can trot up the steps without growing tired. Under the coldish white of the pale sky, under the dark bulk of the gray mountains, the ponies scattered the sedan chairs and the peasants who came down from the heights. They rolled their necks from side to side, so that the sound of the bells could be heard in the farthest valleys, down in the green slopes and canyons full of broken and stripped pines, up among the yellow villas on the mountain tops, far away across the river. Already we could see the river above the green foothills. The river was like a silver spoon, the thin handle facing Chungking and the broad estuary glinting silver amid sandbanks in the west. We rode single file, Bergery on his sleek white pony the color of ivory, I on a mare who frisked and fretted and disliked her rider from the first.

As we climbed higher, the mist which had been hovering over Chungking all morning turned gray-blue. Ever since childhood I have had a passion for walled cities, and from the narrow stone road leading to Huang-k'o-ya it was possible to see traces of the ancient walls of Chungking on the north bank. A walled city has an unmistakable quality of pride. Impenetrable, throwing down gaunt brown shadows, the Chinese walled city in a plain stands isolated as an island, self-sufficient as a ship, unassailable in its own fortress. On the pure white rock, shining in the blue misty morning, Chungking resembled more than ever a ship inclining in a storm. The whiteness of the walls and towers under a white cloud, the faint grays and blues of the open roads, the mountains beyond and the wide-flowing river beneath added to the illusion, and there may be some significance in the fact that the ship points toward the east and the Japanese. In the west among shelving sandbanks and wide estuaries, the Yangtse flows

into the River of Golden Sands; but in the slanting light of morning,
the sun not yet risen high above the mountains, the western river
shone silver like floods, and we caught our breaths at the sweep of the
encircling river and the purple mountains rising in the distance.

The road narrowed and became rocky. Huang-k'o-ya stretches a
quarter of the way down the hillside, winding in blue shadow among
the silvery barks of pine trees. Already we could hear the "wave" of
the pines on the summit and the tramp of soldiers in the muddy
streets. The shops were crowding in on every side. We rode in single
file, while children ran for shelter and old women remained motionless on the stones, so that we brushed our shoulders against the
stucco houses and wondered whether any of the houses we had
touched had fallen into the valley below. Here, on the heights, enormous banyan trees and scrub oaks litter the narrow cobbled streets,
where the foundation walls of the houses are old tombstones. But the
village is dull, and nearly everyone is suffering from a disease of the
eyes which swells the eyeball and turns it violet. At a turning in the
road we paused and looked at the river away below, the horses struggling up the rock face, the foothills, and the silence of the bare trees.
The plum trees were black. There were no flowers. We rode down
the street like men who have hoped in these altitudes to find an answer to all their problems, and find only a more complete disillusion-
ment.

But once past the village, there is an extraordinary light on the
hills. Behind these hills are more valleys and more mountains, and
the light spreads out, no longer hemmed in as in Chungking. The
main road was blocked by a landslide. We took a smaller road, the
horses scrambled down slippery red mud hills, splashed across a
stream between rice fields, frightened the colored ducks in the yellow
ponds and the blue magpies, slithered on the edge of fields where
neither rice nor winter barley was growing, across gray-green lakes and
meres. They plunged onward in silence. They were accustomed to us
and no longer shook their heads from side to side, but moved with a
slow effortless tinkling of bells. We felt that we had come out of
prison. There was an immense area of sky above. High up, away in
heaven, larks were singing. The resinous sap of the pines filled our
nostrils.

"Do you see the bird——" An eagle swept out of the sky,
seized a field rat with its talons, and swept into the sky again, bearing the rat gently in its curved and sharpened cornelian claws, flying
against the yellow-green mountains and the white chalk road, flying

horizontally——away, away into the silence of the morning light. We watched the eagle as though there were some magic in its solitary flight. Like memory it disappeared into a small space of sky, pale turquoise-blue, the first pale stretch of blue sky we had seen in Chungking. We prayed that the sun would move swiftly from its place in the clouded east to this small square of pale blue in the west. But the clouds hung above us still, and sometimes we watched wisps of clouds above the rice fields rising to meet the white sheet above our heads.

We were fairly high at last, having crossed the chalk road which leads to Kweichow. There was little traffic on the road, though here as everywhere innumerable lorries lurk under pine branches. There is an automobile road leading from these high cliffs to a ferry across the Yangtse, and we have promised that we shall find the best car in Chungking and drive recklessly around thirteen hairpin bends. But there is quietness in the hills and misty mornings dropping dew.

In the evening, when it was quite dark in the streets except for candles—for the lights have gone out—we wandered through the streets. A few red and gold scrolls, with pictures of Father Christmas, hang across the roads, and there are small fir branches in the shop of my favorite pastry cook. But on the whole Christmas is dark and solemn, and the gray river flowing between the high rocks is still rising.

But just as we were about to descend the interminable steps to the ferry, we noticed an old coolie selling lanterns. They were not like ordinary lanterns. They were made of wood and green paper, and small porcelain bowls of rapeseed oil were suspended on wires inside them, and also suspended on wires were curious shapes cut out of cardboard which revolved and threw their shadows on the green paper frame. There were two shapes of cardboard—one representing an army on the march, bearing a flag on which the Chinese character for the Han dynasty had been inscribed, and another showing a peaceful scene in a country village—a goose girl followed by a long line of waddling geese, a marriage cart with ribbons hanging from the posts, an old farmer with his scythe and his buffalo. These two shapes re-volved in opposite directions and at different speeds. "This is so Chinese," Bergery exclaimed. "No one else would have thought of the world as two revolving rings of peace and war." We lit the oil lamp, and carried the lantern tenderly down the steps, afraid that the wind might blow out the light or break through the thin paper screen. And at the bottom of the steps there was no paddle steamer, and we were compelled to search among the broken rocks and the sand for a small boat which would take us across. The current was strong. We waited for more than half an hour, shielding the lantern with our bodies. And when at last we were rowed across the river, the shapes on the lantern continued to revolve and young children and old men craned forward and peered at it, their faces illuminated by the pale green light. Even the river shone with the faint reflected green light; and though we were often lost in midstream, and nothing of the shore was visible except the distant glow of candles, we watched the revolving shapes with extraordinary exhilaration, and the Chinese shouted out, "*Hao jee-la,*" delighted at the continual progress of the shapes.

I shall remember this Christmas for the faint green light of spring which shone on the waters, and the faces of the children as they craned forward, for they, too, were like the faces of idols painted green to announce the coming of spring.

December 27th. "We have come to the end of one civilization and we are beginning another. Perhaps today, or perhaps yesterday, a whole civilization was destroyed. But civilizations do not entirely disappear—they revive, as the dead mummy seeds in Egyptian tombs revive, and new splendors may come out of what has been destroyed."

He looked ill and dazed as he looked down on the river. Hongkong had fallen; he had a cold and a feverish temperature, but he insisted on gazing at the river. The lights shone, and in the distance we could hear the throbbing of invisible dynamos, dogs barking and the song of a singsong girl who lived in a house high up on the hills.

"I now have little hope for Malaya or the Philippines," he said a little later. "It is not that we have committed faults, or that you have committed faults; but we did not understand the people we ruled. We must learn to understand." And a little later he said, "In the *Analects* it is related that Confucius stood by a stream and wept because everything passes away."

"Yes, this civilization will perish, as perhaps it deserves to perish. We have had sympathy for the races we have ruled, we have learned their languages, we have sent ethnologists and anthropologists to take part in their rituals; but we have failed to love them, and therefore they did not trust us. But if we learn to love——"

He did not go on. Small black boats like beetles were creeping into moonlight. A faint red glare shone from a distant furnace; and as we stood there, on a piece of rock jutting out over the Yangtse, it seemed that we were standing on the bridge of an immense ocean liner, which at any moment would escape from its moorings. Bergery looked exactly like the captain of a ship, and we could almost hear the creaking of the wheel as it turned to and fro, and we could see the blue mast lamp and, the helmsman nodding over the charts. "Well, we're sailing now—there's nothing to stop us. But the charts won't be any use, and the reefs are dangerous, and we have more valuable cargo on board than we have ever had before." A mist came floating up the river. There was nothing to be seen, for even when the eyes had grown accustomed to the darkness, we saw only the candles, the dark, starless sky and a darker river, and two pale wakes where the prow of some river boat or other pried the water apart and sped it backward.

And then, after a long silence: "I hope *they* realize that it is a dangerous moment in the most complete sense. Europe is threatened by the attack on the East as she has never been threatened before. We preserved the spirit of Europe against the Huns, the Mohammedans, the Turks, and the Goths. We preserved it against the Northmen, and absorbed them, and in absorbing them we lost nothing except some of our graces. But this time we are faced with greater problems than ever simply because the Japanese are a more authentic foe than the Germans. The Germans can be fought and the issue of the battle can be decided without destroying the spirit of Europe, for the Germans are inevitably Europeans and cannot stay for long outside the fold. The Japanese can stay *forever* outside the fold. They are not built like us, they do not think like us, they possess nothing in common with us; and therefore we must destroy them or they must destroy us. Not a single value in their civilization is cherished by us, and not a single value of European civilization is cherished by them. We cannot agree; and yet we must learn to love them."

I asked him what he meant by love.

"Surely the love we have for beautiful people and for beautiful objects is the same as the love we have for beautiful civilizations. In the *Symposium* Socrates describes the nature of love. 'He is not delicate and lovely as most of us believe, but he is a hardy youth, barefoot and homeless, sleeping on the naked earth, in doorways or in the very streets beneath the stars of heaven, and always partaking of his mother's poverty.' So we must love nations as though we were beggars, holding out our alms bowls and hoping that out of the charity of their hearts they will sometimes offer us food and nourishment; sleeping naked on their earth and looking at their stars throughout the night; in tempest and storm; and fearing their animals and taking part in their sacrifices. We have not learned to love. The Americans and the British in China have lived in houses apart. They have not learned the language. They have not been equals. They have always ordered. Like the Japanese, we filled the estuary of the Yangtse with our warships, and like the wild tribes on the frontiers we plundered their goods. And this is our reward—that at a time when we are allies, they no longer trust us."

It was very late. Down below, great waves shot up from the rocks viciously, exhausting their energies in furious hissing sprays. But now there were almost no boats creeping beetle-like along the faint silvery river; and though a faint moon shone, and the slender black plum tree waved in the breeze, Chungking seemed to be a desert, black and remote, where a few candles like fireflies shone beneath a cold black wintry sky.

"It is not too late," Bergery kept saying. "But nations must know that it is not enough to send ambassadors—we must send the best spirits of our age. How many of the best spirits of England and America have come to China? We have sent tradesmen, not philosophers. We have sent pirates, not legislators. We have sent the dregs of our public schools, and we have never sent our sons to be educated in Chinese universities, though they have sent the best brains of China to Oxford and Harvard. We have only a few years left in which we can repair this wrong, and perhaps already it is too late."

December 29th. We have been invited to lunch with the British ambassador. In the gray morning we set out on a small black launch, waving the Union Jack—the only dash of color in this remote whiteness of fog. We hear bells and cries, but the sounds come from a long way away. The *remoteness* of morning in China—nearly all night Bergery has been attempting to conjure up his memories of mornings in China. "It is then that she is magnificent beyond every country on earth. The hot sun rising across the lake at Hangchow, the sudden illumination of a pagoda, which resembles a figure of white frost rather than something solid which you can see with your eyes, and then the sunlight slowly descending the whole length of the pagoda, and the green reeds, and the long level lines of pine trees planted by Su Tung-p'o nearly a thousand years ago. Remoteness, as of something ancient and permanent, and yet impermanent, for every moment it changes. . . . " But in this damp fog, the oily mist of fog trickling through our upturned coats, I saw no beauty and understood nothing of what he said. Besides, it was nearly twelve o'clock and the morning had turned stale and colorless, the wind had died down and still the thick vapor hung over the streets and the river.

Once, as the car which fetched us from the river traveled along the long winding muddy road to the Ambassador's house perched on a cliff, we saw the river below. There was a magic circle where no fog entered. And there, in that small circle, like a blue eye radiantly blue, we saw small ships like grasshoppers moving silently down river. There was a ghostliness about the scene which shocked us, for we had not expected it and there were moments as we gazed down at the blue eye of the river when we seemed to be gazing at a mirage. And slowly the eyelid of mist folded over the blue eye, and still more slowly the car wound up the muddy road, where even the stucco buildings exuded moisture and the trees resembled green fountains continually dripping.

But once inside the Ambassador's house we were in another world. In a small room, which was once the pavilion of a Chinese general, a great log fire was blazing. There were photographs, enormous bookcases, a collie dog, comfortable armchairs—a sense of security and good taste, of quiet contemplation and infinite common sense. In Singapore George Yeh told me, "Please be careful of him. He comes into your room, rolls up his shirtsleeves, takes out his pipe, and says quietly, 'Let's get down to the root of the matter'; and before you know where you are, you agree upon everything, there are no clouds in the sky, and you wonder what all the fuss was about." It was, I felt, a good description. The pipes on the mantelpiece, the collie dog sprawled out before the fire, the table in the anteroom set for dinner in Chinese style, with small blue bowls and ivory chopsticks, the books and the candles and the mahogany radio were carefully chosen and belonged to a man who rolled up his sleeves and got "down to the root of the matter."

Sir Archibald Clark Kerr came in five minutes later. He had been walking along the cliffs, and he brought with him the tang of winter on the Scottish moors. He wore a checked coat and gray flannel trousers; the long aquiline nose, the sunburn, and the bushy eyebrows were those of a Scottish laird, and his enormous hands were like the hands of an artist. But what was so extraordinary was that from a man so tall there should come a voice so quiet and gentle, and

even hesitant; and when he went into another room to order the dinner, Bergery whispered, "It is not the voice of a Scottish laird, or even
of an artist, but of a musician." We waited. A clock was ticking sonorously on the mantelpiece—an English clock, even to the little whirring sound before the chimes. And once more he returned, and the
room was flooded with the scent of heather and pines, and in our
imagination we were traveling through some distant landscape of
Scotland, where the mist was the same as the mist of Chungking and
even the sampans and the people in the crowded streets were the
same.

"And later on," the Ambassador was saying, "it becomes even
more like Scotland. In spring the mountains on the south bank remind me of the mountains of Scotland, very gray and green, and the
air has the same quality of mist and light as in Scotland."

He said he was happy there; he liked the Chinese and spoke of
their tolerance and magnificent staying power. The Chinese love informality with a kind of passion, and it was clear that he shared their
passion and would have been even more informal if circumstances
had allowed. He read omnivorously. Joyce's *Finnegans Wake* stood
proudly on his shelves in its blazing orange cover, and before long the
Ambassador and Bergery were deep in an argument about Joyce.
Bergery opened the book and began to read in his deep, heavy voice
the passage about Anna Livia Plurabelle, until it seemed that not
only the mountains of Scotland but also the rivers of Ireland were
wandering through Chungking, till at last, wearying of argument, the
Ambassador began to read a passage toward the end of the book on
night and death, a passage so heavily laden with the shadows of elms
and yews that it resembled the birth of the night and of all nights;
and reading it in that quiet voice, peering through horn-rimmed spectacles, his face colored by the yellow flames of the log fire, he had
surrendered so much to the charm of Joyce's prose that he forgot the
sound of the dinnerbell and the new guest who had just been announced, he forgot his secretary's quiet reminder of the passing of
time, and absent-mindedly taking a perfectly white feather pen from
the table, he began to wave it up and down in tune with the majestic
sonority of the prose. The sunlight was beginning to creep into the
room, a faint yellow sunrise which would disperse in a moment or
two. The collie dog uncurled at his feet and walked solemnly across
the room; and when at last he had finished the passage and placed
the book silently on the shelf, he smiled with a smile of such beauty
that Bergery was immediately conquered. And like someone in a

dream I watched them going into the dining room with their arms on each other's shoulders.

The sunlight flooded the green windows in the dining room; it flooded the blue porcelain bowls and spilled over the dead white tablecloth. White-robed servants entered silently with great bronze tureens. The conversation changed from the state of the defenses of Singapore to *Alice in Wonderland,* from the second battle of Changsha to Chinese novels. The Ambassador had cultivated Chinese novelists. He invited them to his house and discussed the technique of novel-writing with them. He was proud that a recent novel had been dedicated to him, and prouder still of his connections with the Sackville-Wests and Virginia Woolf. He had a deep love for Chinese paintings and porcelain, and spoke regretfully of the difficulty of transporting them from Peking. A black dispatch box came in. In white letters there was printed the inscription: "The British Embassy, Peking," but there was no British embassy left in the old capital of China, and he gazed at the letters tenderly, opened the box with his key, glanced for a moment at the papers inside, and then resumed his conversation with Bergery on the merits of Japanese painting. On the glass door separating the dining room from the circular drawing room the firelight flourished and gleamed, and sometimes the collie dog would nestle at his feet, and he would throw a bone in the air and watch the dog with an extraordinary affection.

1942

On January 2 the author was sent as Times' correspondent to the battle of Changsha, which had broken out on the night of December 23 when the Japanese crossed the Milo river. No heavy engagements took place until the last day of the year, when the Japanese attempted to rush the gates of the city. A short, critical battle took place, lasting three days, but on the fourth day the Japanese, harassed by guerrillas and the main forces of Lieutenant-General Hsueh Yueh's army, retreated in the direction of Yochow.

January 4th. The river has been covered with a faint mist ever since we left Hsiangtan early this morning, before daybreak. There was a wet cold in the air, and we shivered on the sweeping edge of land, so cold that our fingers were like icicles, and the dawn coming over the mountains was even colder than the night. The curlews cry on the great granite steps which lead down to the river. In the small town, everything was dark, and the beggars sleeping in doorways paid no attention as we passed. And then suddenly, just as we stepped onto the small launch, the bamboos began to quiver, the blue jays or magpies burst out cawing, and all the trees began to shake. It had rained during the night, and the trees on the foreshore seemed to be ornamented with small pieces of jade which touched one another and separated with the passing of the wind, leaving in the air the sound of distant bells and the sudden sparkle of water. And the river lay before us, dark green, the color of malachite, and the grayish-red hills took light from the ascending sun, till at last our fingers thawed and we climbed down into the small dark cabin, with the broken windows shuttered over with pine boards, and made ourselves comfortable around the small table, where an empty flowerpot and a samovar surprisingly accompanied us down the Hsiang river.

The thumping of the gasoline engine prevented us from sleeping; and gradually as we watched the low green hills giving place to copper-red mountains, we took heart and escaped from the overheated cabin into the cold wind of the deck. We swept between the white columns of an immense bridge which has never been completed, and watched with a sensation of awe the great white-sailed sampans sweeping downriver. They are bigger than the sampans in the Yangtse—bigger and cleaner—and they glide softly like sea birds, silent and leaving no wake, and with no sign of life except the small coke fires burning redly on the foredeck. A few fishermen with black cormorants were fishing near the high banks. It is the height of the banks which astounds us—the river flows deep below the surface of the land, and on this green pool with white wave-caps, nosing our way against a blustering north wind, our faces like ice, our hands frozen to our sides, we make our way to Changsha under a cloudless sky the color of the brightest steel.

The sampans came down river like immense swans, gliding gently and noiselessly, the wind creeping along the sails but never altering their shape. The ships were painted all colors, but the sails were white; and still there was no life on them. They were like ghost ships swiftly coming down the green river.

Afternoon came. The voices downstairs are becoming softer and drowsier. We are throwing up great mountains of spray, and sometimes the water fowl which hangs obstinately over our bows is blinded by the spray and slides toward the center of the river, screaming. We are gliding near the bank, perhaps because we want to avoid the attentions of Japanese airplanes, and all the ships are gliding near the bank, so that it seems as though the center of the river possessed some magical quality. We could see the plowman on the banks plowing through the frost, and as night came and we were still chugging slowly close to the banks, bridges began to pass more frequently, we passed small islands and sandbanks, and it was clear that we were drawing toward the capital. And all night we chugged still more slowly along the bank by the light of a faint circle of moon, and in the morning the air was colder. We went out on deck to see the landscape unchanged—the same green-and-red cliffs, the same small temples, and the same fishermen were throwing out their lines with wide-winged black cormorants into the blue river.

I have no idea how far we have traveled. Wet and dripping in the misty cabin, the oil lamp continually flickering out, the gray-blue discolored windows, and the boards seem to have been accomplices since the beginning of time The river is in spate, very blue and sweetly cold. The wind rushes up the river, billowing out the white sails which are beginning to drift upstream—strange transformation!—and we no longer ride close to the bank. And suddenly out of the mist and the white morning, low on the horizon, behind the red cliffs and the islands, Changsha shines in the sunlight, all white in the frosted air, flanked by the white sails of sampans, luminous and clear, a rock of white marble amid the red hills.

And so we come ashore. We have flown from Chungking to Kweilin; from there we have taken the Blue Express to Hengyang and Hsiangtan; and from there, since the railway has been cut by the Japanese, we have taken the motor launch to Changsha. It stands there gleaming, "the city of the sands." We climb ashore, make our way slowly through the knee-deep sand, while gusts of wind blow in our faces, and at the moment when the Japanese airplane appears we are already walking along a road, between the sunken fields white with broken ice, while the magpies crawk on the branches.

Later. We are living in a small country house painted green. There are plank beds which smell strongly of pine resin, very sweet in this frosty air.

Within half a mile from here lie the ruins of the University of Hunan, and all that is left of one of the greatest libraries of central China are two stone Doric columns. I have walked up among the small green hills, where Chinese officers have made small models of cities out of colored clay—cities which they will capture later—but more impressive even than the green pine-clad slopes of Yulosan or the distant spires of Changsha are these solitary columns on the plain. The Japanese came two years ago. They destroyed the whole university without warning; they burned and plundered. We sit along benches beside the great table downstairs. A Chinese military officer is recounting the story of the battle for Changsha, which ended two days ago; and his voice goes on, droning mysteriously in the candlelit darkness, and his fingers move across the map, a map which is still to us imaginary, for we have been in Hunan only a short time and cannot translate the names of cities into the walled fortresses we shall perhaps see later. And at night strange lights flicker in the gardens, soldiers stand guard at their posts, and in the distance we hear the explosions of bombs.

January 6th. In the darkness we were given breakfast. Wrapped in furs or padded cotton, we walked down the bare wooden steps and marched out into the morning. And then suddenly the sun rose over the red hills and threw down long spears on the broken squares of ice in the fields. Already the peasants were ploughing up the soil, and the blackbirds (which are really blue) were cawing in that harsh, ungainly tongue which mirrors perfectly the austerity of these fields in the early morning.

We climbed through the thick sand to the waiting launch, drove out into the middle of the river, and watched the yellowish-red hills slide past. Changsha suddenly appeared behind an island, whiter than ever, the foreshore littered with the stumps of broken buildings, but the factory chimneys still pointing to the sky. Better than yesterday, for as we come closer it shows its scars, and somehow those scars only add to the impression of beauty. When the current drove us close to the banks, we saw the body of a Chinese soldier in sky-blue uniform spread-eagled on the red earth close to the water line. He was the only soldier we saw there—killed perhaps by an unlucky shot from a low-flying airplane, or by the small group of Japanese who are known to have reached the river in an effort to encircle the town. The white city, the dead boy on the red cliff, and the gulls swooping low over the blue river—till at last we came to leeward of the wind, hiding in the island's shadow from the airplane overhead, and salt spray flew up over the bow and stern. We were already coming close to the white city in the miraculous morning air.

We saw the shell holes and the bomb craters gaping red in the moist earth; the broken ships at anchor with holes in their bows like sharks' mouths; the smoldering debris of a house blackened by bombs; the blue-clad soldiers following a coffin swung on yellow ropes across the shore. Details—a curving chimney stack, blown out of shape by an explosion, a red stain high up on the wall of a house, a body floating in the glacier-green river, and yet not moving, for the bare legs were caught in barbed wire; and then the city, whose name was inscribed on the front pages of newspapers all over the world, towering high above us, brooding in the morning silence among wraiths of smoke. Someone had inscribed, in yellow paint which glistened in the sunshine, the words, "Changsha will not fall." The Chinese characters were vigorous with action. "Chang" means "long" and "sha" means "sand," and there is a line like a descending spearhead in the character for "sand" which looks like a vigorous incitement to battle. But on the left bank of the river there are no sands at all, and as the motorboat bobbed in the swift transparent water, we could see high above us the slowly descending rubble of the city—a few trickles of stones, a few bricks, a few pillars, which tumbled in clouds of black dust toward the river's edge.

We marched ashore, picking our way carefully through rubble. Bergery was humming:

> *Sie werden lachen,*
> *Ich liebe*
> *Meine eigene Frau . . .*

"What makes you sing this kind of nonsense?" I asked.

He laughed gently and turned toward the city. "I am so used to bombed cities," he said sadly, "and now it is almost as though I am married to them. When I go into a city which isn't bombed, it seems that something is wrong. In Lisbon, I felt that nothing was so necessary as a bomb, I couldn't find my bearings, I felt completely lost. To be comfortable my legs must be searching for a foothold among debris. *Sie werden lachen. . . .* "

We didn't laugh. At that moment, making our way through broken walls, we saw the first white coffin. There were no flowers, and no cock was tied to the coffin lid. Swinging on the bamboo poles so heavily that you could hear the movement of the body inside, it passed along the ruined road in front of us in the direction of the burial mound at the East Gate.

And now from everywhere there appeared blue-helmeted soldiers in light blue padded-cotton uniforms. They were all young. They walked in the sunlight out of the shelter of bomb holes with an unexpected swagger, their bayonets gleaming. We photographed them. They smiled. They were very eager to talk about the battle, and they mentioned Colonel Li, who had defended the city from within, with extraordinary respect and affection. A general or an officer who obtains the respect of his soldiers in China can work miracles, someone

said, and it was easy to believe him, for these youths, fingering their
bayonets and gazing dreamily at the passing coffins, are soldiers of
whom any country could be proud. They were nearly all Hunanese,
fighting for their homes—farmers' lads, mostly, with faces like ripe
apples and a gay swing in their movements. All winter they had been
waiting. To while the time away, they had planted vegetables on
their blockhouses, and it was curious to turn into a side street and
see, through a curtain of bayonets, lettuces sprouting above corrugated iron houses.

We followed the soldiers along a broken street, where the
charred buildings were still smoking. Occasionally only a single
wooden post would remain standing. A tree stump or a lamp post
with bullet holes was like a wound still bleeding, but those bullet
marks on wooden posts were so fresh that they seemed to have been
made only a few moments before. Here the nakedness of war appeared in all its violence, for bodies still lay in the houses and the
sound of pickaxes echoed in the still, wintry morning. It was strangely
quiet. The magpies with their white collars sang on the branches, and
the footsteps of the soldiers echoed against stone walls. High above
the city airplanes flew and fought in the cold winter sun. Sentries
blew their whistles, and we were told to seek shelter near the river
edge; but no one took notice and shortly afterward the airplanes disappeared. When they had gone, the city was more silent than ever,
until suddenly we heard the sound of squealing pigs, and turning a
corner we watched three Hunanese peasants wheeling their barrows—with immense center wheels and curved flanks, which were so
delicately carved that they would grace a museum of modern industrial art. The barrows contained children in bright red leggings and
woolen mufflers, and their expressions were oddly at variance with
the expressions of the peasants, who looked grimed and sad with too
much wandering. Behind the peasants came the squealing pigs. The
peasants told us that they were going back to their homes on the west
bank of the river, and their faces under their black turbans lit with
relief when the soldiers gave them a right of way. And still we wandered through the burned-out debris, and we well understood the
number of bodies lying there. But the sun shone on the walls and in
the yellow puddles, and steam rose from the coffins lying beside the
road, and slowly the film of water disappeared from the smooth surface of pine, leaving the fresh, scented wood golden in the burst of
sunlight.

There may be some beauty in cities when they are bombed, but the outskirts of Changsha were bleak with an agony of black rubble, and at the East Gate the bleakness became intensified by the presence of Japanese dead. They lay in the mangled earth where they had been shot down with rifle fire and hand grenades, their faces swollen and broken, naked, the flesh turning green. They were not pleasant. They had, as the dead often have, supercilious expressions, and their bared teeth did not commend them to our souls. Their toes were turned outward—our first lesson in recognizing the Japanese—and some of them had beards. They lay there in a small enclosure behind an armament store, and the grass was already curling around their bodies. The photographers knelt down and took the inevitable close-ups, and occasionally it was necessary to change the position of an arm or a leg.

The hill was steep and overlooked the river; here and there the green turf was stained with blood. The day was warm and a cool breeze came up the Hsiang river. We walked up the hill toward the grey tombstones on the summit, conscious only of the clear beauty of the day and the white puffs of transparent cloud in the sky until suddenly, stumbling over the first of the naked bodies in the grass, seeing the prints of the machine gun legs in the mud—prints like black claws—and down below the red roof of the arms factory white with pigeons, we knew at once that the rest of the day would revolve about this dead soldier in the grass, as a universe revolves about its suns.

All the bodies were young, and many of them showed no signs of wounds. In the cold air, among the columns of the tombs, their flesh as white as paper, they embraced the grass and smiled in death like men who have found their home, though they were surprised at finding it so quickly. And this is what has always seemed to me so strange about war; the noise, the shouting, and the anger are followed inevitably by the silence. No birds called. In the white haze the white sands of Changsha were shining, and already peasants in blue smocks, old women mostly, were burying the bodies which were as yet untouched by Chinese earth.

We walked back through the charred black roads of the city and through wide thoroughfares where no bombs had fallen. The city was immense. Burned down in 1927 and again in 1938, it had been rebuilt in plaster. There were shops where the plaster was still fresh, with window decorations smiling under plate glass. Less than ten days ago, the governor of the province ordered the evacuation of the civilians; the houses were to be left exactly as they were and he

promised that everything would be returned intact. In the streets
there were notices calling upon the people to evacuate. There were
also small red squares of paper dropped by Japanese airplanes, calling
upon the people to surrender:

> The Great Pacific War has started—Abandon your fight and
> tell your soldiers to abandon this senseless war. Our imperial
> army is once again entering Hunan. We have killed no Hunanese
> people. We are opposed to killing. We fervently hope your war of
> resistance will cease. Lay down your arms if you wish to preserve
> the land and restore peace to the people. This is our advice.

The pamphlet was signed by the commander-in-chief of the Japanese armies in China.

In the center of the city, in a small building in a courtyard
flanked by stone lions, General Li, who had been in command of the
defense of the city, was waiting for us. In a small upstairs room, filled
with magazines, small handleless cups of grayish-brown tea, scrolls,
and comfortable sofas, we listened to his report of the progress of the
battle from the moment when, on the evening of the 31st, less than a
week ago, the Japanese attacked the suburbs from the south, east,
and northeast to the moment three days later when they were in full
flight to the north. He had received orders from General Hsueh
Yueh that the city must not be abandoned. He had fought well. He
had made three sorties from the West Gate, eight sorties from the
East Gate, he had cleaned up the small Japanese column which
penetrated into the city, and he had done all this without a single
reconnaissance airplane. There were guns on Yulosan manned by
Russian and Chinese artillerymen, but they alone could not have put
the Japanese to flight. There were many dead Chinese, and they were
still being buried. There were many buildings destroyed, but the
center of the town had been preserved. . . .

I cannot follow military discussions. I can understand battles
better without maps, for what is important is not the names of places
but "the tree," "the house," "the ridge between the rice fields" where
the defenders took cover, and "the river" which they cross at night
and defend till daybreak. These are things which the ordinary mind
appreciates, while the maps, even when they are faithfully inscribed
on great sheets of paper in thirteen colored inks, are nearly meaningless. It was better to look at the face of the young general, a face
tanned almost gray by the sun and full of mysterious spiders' webs of

wrinkles. He looked—his dumpy arms sprawled over the map—like someone who has been afraid and is no longer afraid; who has given orders—defend that tree, that wall, that house—and who has known the enjoyment which comes when orders are actually obeyed; and as he continued speaking, in a gaunt, clipped Hunanese voice, it was easy to imagine the concentration of power in the small ugly hand on the table. It was not well formed. It was a soldier's hand, scarred not by wounds but by continual knocking against solid objects, and the thick green jade ring seemed somehow out of place. He smiled. "So the defenders became the attackers—yes?" It was the only English he spoke, and it was like a sudden revelation of how victories are accomplished in China.

In a courtyard three miles away, blood-soaked Japanese flags, machine guns, rifles, diaries, poison gas bombs were littered in confusion against the wall. Only the bullets were carefully stacked in neat little piles. The sun shone on the thick, dried blood; it shone on the broken helmets and the fur-lined gloves, the green tent cloths and the photographs which had escaped from some pocketbook. A white horse, also captured from the Japanese, neighed, and sometimes it would start to run round the courtyard and then stop dead; a magnificent horse, no longer cared for but once belonging to a young officer who took a special pride in its appearance. Shell-shocked, whinnying, it continued to make these sudden furious little spurts round the bare sunlit courtyard until we had left.

And so we returned through the deserted streets of Changsha. A few guards stand at the crossroads. A few peasants make their way through the charred and burned out houses on the eastern corner of the streets. A pillbox covered with mud and green lettuces growing from the roof—and always the scent of gunpowder and danger. The city has been burned down to the ground so many times that no one cares to remember how many times it has had to be rebuilt; but very little has been destroyed, the shops are still standing, and the bullet marks leave curious little vertical traces, showing that they have come from airplanes. It was not always like this. Ten years ago there would have been no vertical traces, the shops would have been pillaged, and there would be no foreign correspondents riding through the walled city.

Toward evening we came to the ruins of Yale-in-China. The great roofless walls of the immense buildings are charred and blackened; the floorboards have fallen in; the radio-therapy installations and the X-ray equipment are black wires and molten metal. There is nothing left—nothing at all; even the beds are twisted strips of iron still hot to the touch.

Dr. Petit, who left for the south ten days ago and returned this morning, surveys the buildings without resentment, without bitterness, and without realizing exactly what has happened. "The damage is about two million dollars gold." He is still dazed, and those enormous black eyes as they survey the scene reflect every detail so brightly that I have watched a small drift of smoke rising from a corner of the building without taking my eyes from his.

We have been trying to reconstruct exactly what happened. All around Yale-in-China there are small buildings built on the European model, with gabled roofs and rose gardens. They are untouched; the grass is still green in their gardens. On January 1 the Chinese had almost decided to bombard Yale-in-China, knowing that the Japanese could turn the immense hospital into a fortress. When the Chinese made their sorties from the North Gate on the 2nd and 3rd there was serious fighting in the neighborhood of the hospital, but except for a few bullets fired from the windows the Japanese found little use for it. On the night of the third, when they were finally driven away, they set fire to it coldly and methodically. They emptied tins of kerosene on the floors and on the beds and set fire to them with hand grenades; and the walls blazed all night and long into the next day. Into this funeral pyre they threw some of their own dead—and they must have warmed their hands by the flames, for it was bitterly cold that night, according to the Chinese officer who accompanied us. Afterward, having abducted and murdered two or three of the Chinese nurses who were caught between the two fires, and having killed all the patients who could not be removed, they retreated northward.

Bergery wandered through the debris and came back looking paler than I had ever seen him, for he discovered only afterward that he had been walking through the ashes of the dead.

We came home slowly in the gathering dusk, the long clouds drifting over the Hsiang river. We passed old rock gardens, small country houses on the edge of the city which seemed to have heard no sound of bombardment or fighting. Still the soldiers marched down the empty streets; and in this great darkness of dusk the gleam of bayonets was brighter than starlight. We were footsore, and besides had seen so much of destruction that each unharmed house was like an affront. The Chinese colonel, who had stayed in the city throughout the bombardment and the furious counterattacks, kept murmuring to himself, "Not long, not long——" But whether he was referring to our passage across the river or the rumored defeat of the Japanese in a pitched battle on the north bank of the Milo river, we could not tell. We crossed the river in starlight, but when we had reached the other side and we were walking in sand nearly to our knees, the stars went out; and we traveled down the long dark road between the pines seeing only the small guttering candles which the Chinese soldiers lit for us.

And we were grateful for the darkness and the light.

January 7th. Again we set out early in the morning, again we crossed the river at the point of silence, wondering at the redness of the cliffs, the whiteness of the town, and the green trees standing at the foot of the burial mound. The town is becoming familiar to us. We know—or think we know—every street and ruin; we are friends of the water fowl who dive low over the hills; and at the same time we know that we are passengers who will depart for the southwest leaving the blue-clad soldiers alone in possession of the green hills.

But this morning we are provided with donkeys. They are round-barreled, well-fed, and very sleek. At the place where we crossed the river, the donkeys were waiting for us—twenty or thirty of every imaginable color. They frisked their long silky ears and pretended to be the most docile donkeys in the world, but as soon as we mounted them, they showed an extraordinary reluctance to keep still.

The long road led north through every imaginable painting of Chinese scenery. The sun came out, and shone on the small earth temples; it shone on the dead Japanese horse, red and swollen, which lay in a deserted farmyard; it shone on the dead Japanese and Chinese lying by the roadside among the broken, twisted telegraph wires, and on the small lakes with ducks floating on them. The atmosphere was cooler when we came out of the city. Its taste was the taste of an air which has been blown over leagues of rice fields, a taste like cool milk in summer. Here and there the dead lay in small, companionable groups, like lovers. Nearly all the Japanese were naked, stripped of their clothes by the Chinese soldiers, who knew the coldness of the long nights. And so, as we rode in single file through the stone-thatched villages, where everything was silent as the grave, the doors padlocked, the villagers gone, only the fireflies and the neighing donkeys seemed to be truly living. Oh—and the ducks. There were a thousand small green ponds strung like necklaces between these small villages, and there the ducks roamed at will, giving an impression of life to the austere landscape, where frost still glittered and the descending clouds were the same color as the fields.

In the distance we heard guns. We heard them rarely, when the villages acted as sounding boards or when the wind was favorable, a sound which the small green mountains must have deflected into our ears. So we wandered through the tapestry, the hooves of the small donkeys treading delicately and deliberately along the broken road, now less than a foot across, a road which once could have taken a carriage and pair. It was a road raised above the level of the rice fields, but the earth and stones at each side had been removed until there was no more than a thin wall between the reddish-gray fields, and it might have been easier to ride on the plains. Once or twice we saw people, and spoke to them. They had hidden in wells, or in the small fortress-like crests of the hills. And once, when we were completely lost in the tapestry, we saw a man driving a buffalo over the hard flinty earth, making a little dark solid picture in the corner of the landscape—the ploughman, the brown buffalo, and the white steam rising like plumes from their bodies.

On a field near the edge of a small green lake, under the lowering clouds, a heap of charred black bodies lay in confusion. The area of the funeral pyre was about the size of a tennis court, and the bodies lay thickly together. They were black as cinders, shrunken like old charred wood, small sticks of bluish-black charcoal lying in confusion. And beside them, a little way off and nearer the pool, lay two Chinese peasants—father and son. The old man gray and grizzled, the young son handsome still in spite of the crust of blood on his forehead. The funeral pyre had been lit at night; and it seemed certain that the old peasant and his son, who had lived in a house nearby, had been found spying on the Japanese; they were shot, their bodies were thrown in the pool. The rain had fallen toward the end of the ceremony, for in one corner of the field a few bodies remained half-burned, very yellow and black, teeth gaping, heads split open, hands flung out.

It was growing late when we came to the Liuyang river, the air already blue with dusk; and in the darkness of the huddled streets, crowded with peasants and soldiers, our small donkeys allowing no one else to pass, we wandered in a kind of daze. It was warm in the village. Behind a small church the headquarters of the Chinese advance forces resembled headquarters everywhere else. Bare tables,

maps, uniforms, impossibly young soldiers standing guard with blue
bayonets. But though we had left our donkeys in the yard, we could
still feel the thumping motion of their barrel bodies as they rode
across the stone paths; and it was difficult at first to realize that we
were among stone houses and friendly people. Food was set out for
us. We ate ravenously, but we were not sure that we were not dreaming. Throughout the whole journey we had not thought there were
towns.

The commander of the Chinese forces made a speech. He was a
small wiry man with six days' growth of beard; and as he spoke,
rapidly and almost silently, occasionally pointing to the maps on the
wall, it was as though the army itself were speaking, so solemnly and
so quietly did he announce the totals of the dead Japanese and
Chinese, the number of captives, the lists of captured machine guns,
bullets, Samurai swords. He reviewed the merits of the Japanese and
Chinese forces, saying:

> Our merits: (1) Determination on the part of officers and
> men; (2) advantages fully made use of; (3) secret dispositions; (4)
> mobility of our troops; (5) capacity to hold out at strategic points.
> Our weaknesses: (1) Lack of telegraphic communications and
> liaison; (2) lack of guns and tanks.
> Their merits: (1) Better equipment, co-operation between guns
> and air force; (2) courage and refusal to surrender; (3) under-
> standing of terrain.
> Their weaknesses: (1) Tendency to advance without heed to
> menace at sides and rear; (2) failure to hold strategic points; (3) in-
> effective intelligence and reconnaissance; (4) neglect of defense.

But when the speeches were over and the young commander was
walking with us down the steep slope to the river, the battle became
again a part of our lives. It was no longer a thing of statistics, but of
the air we breathed; and the willows on the banks of the green river,
and the great sailless junks which floated us over the sandy beaches,
showed bullet holes at the stern; and there were more bullet holes on
the stone steps.

It was a raw afternoon, the wind coming down from the northeast and the clouds very high. A few starlings rose from a bamboo
coppice. Small boys who had taken part in the fighting were swinging
their legs from the gunwales, smiling now that the enemy was out of
earshot; and the water fowl rose screaming high in the air. There was
nothing in this village on the Liuyang river to distinguish it from a
thousand other villages in Hunan—gray walls, white stone steps, a

few old junks berthed under the green edge of the river. In silence we crossed the river. In silence we walked through the first white strips of evening mist which lay over the banks; and still there was no sign of the war. It was half an hour later when we came to a turn in the river that we saw for the first time in China the effect of enfilading fire. The rice fields were unsown, the earth hard and brittle underfoot; but from the rise of the rice fields down to the sloping sandy beach the dead lay in confusion. They were naked, their bodies very white in the frost, and often they showed no signs of wounds. They lay there in the wintry stillness underneath the mist, perhaps two hundred of them, and we passed in silence, while an immense water wheel continued to revolve and sometimes the white water fowl would perch on the buckets of the wheel, cawing loudly.

The dead were everywhere. A young Chinese sergeant in a sky-blue uniform explained how the Japanese had crossed in the evening when there was a thick mist, and how he had posted guards along the river bank. Suddenly one of the soldiers came running toward him, shouting that the Japanese were coming, and he had ordered him to return and wondered what would happen to him. The telegraph system had broken down. He kept on shouting, "The Japanese are coming," until at last reinforcements arrived in time to stop the steady flow of Japanese from the island, but already many of them had crossed in rubber barges. Throughout the night there was fighting, and for the greater part of the next day. They fought between the high earth ridges between the rice fields; and it was there, below the ridges and along the bank, that the dead lay with their faces turned to heaven, so quiet and harmless now that they were stripped of their uniforms.

Near the river we could hear the tock-tock of mattocks as the peasants built shallow graves. The river flowed silently at our feet, the watermill continually revolving. Empty cartridge cases, blood-stained handkerchiefs, cigarette cartons, little pieces of paper which had been torn and scattered by the wind, a rifle buried in the high grass at the edge of the fields—this was the landscape where they lay. There are moments when the Chinese are proud of their adversaries, and I was surprised when a soldier who cannot have been more than twelve years old came and led me to the body of a Japanese officer whose fingers had been broken and whose teeth were still clenched tightly over five bullets. "He fought to the end," the soldier said. "Look at the bullets in his teeth. We had to cut off his fingers to get at his revolver, so tightly did he hold it." He smiled. It seemed then that the Japanese were an enemy worth fighting, until the memory of the charred funeral pyres and the dead Chinese peasants near the green pool obliterated all sense of pity. But those who were young were still beautiful, and those white bodies, lying among the green tufts of grass like swimmers sleeping after their bath, tormented us throughout the rest of the journey.

The Chinese counterattacked. They forced the Japanese back across the island, where the saplings gave no shelter and the earth was so hard that it resembled brown ice. We walked in silence, hardly daring to think of the blackbirds and the wild dogs who gorged themselves on this unnatural feast; but already many of the bodies had been buried, and there was sadness on the faces of the peasants who leaned on their spades. Even here the dead appeared to be sleeping. At any moment they would rise and plunge into the river; and while the mist hung around them it was easy to imagine that the white breath rose from their lips. They were young soldiers mostly. They had come down from the north without knowing that the Chinese were waiting for them, and so often on their dead faces there was an expression of surprise, the brows uplifted and the mouth parted.

The island had been occupied by the Japanese for a week, yet they left little sign of their occupation except scraps of torn paper which one of the Chinese cavalry officers was attempting to piece together. When three-quarters of the letter had been dovetailed, he read it quietly and then blew the pieces away, complaining that he had no time to read love letters in Japanese; and yet he was strangely moved.

As you left the main track through the saplings, wandering among dead mules and spent cartridge cases, you found everywhere the small evidences of a soldier's intimate life—a blue leather diary, three or four sheets of notepaper covered over with a thin black scrawl which was now illegible, for the heavy dew had run the letters together, a notebook which contained Japanese banknotes, a gold-studded saddle, even a short Japanese sword. And yet, though these things were real, they were less real than the terrible sound of the mattocks and the spades, and the expressionless faces of the peasants who had buried more bodies than they could count, and the terrible watermill which continued to revolve in the half-darkness of the winter afternoon.

We rode over the red hills of Hunan, along the broken pathways, and as night fell the small shuttered homesteads became

smaller, little pools of blackness in the starlight. I have often wondered why farmhouses seem to contract at the approach of night, but
it was easier to understand near the battlefield. Here and there we
noticed small glittering objects in the grass and on the muddy
fields—spent bullets, a Japanese cap, the spectacles of some Japanese
officer crushed underfoot and shining like a small heap of diamonds.

I have forgotten how long it took to go from the Liuyang river to
Changsha. It seemed an eternity. Occasionally we noticed the glitter
of spurs or a Chinese belt, but everything else was muffled for a while
in the thick night. But soon the stars came out, the air was pure and
clean, washed by the starlight and the soft transparency of recent
rains.

January 8th. We heard the rain all night, but when we awoke the sky
was clear, pale blue, with here and there a few patches of deeper
blue. I noticed the same phenomenon when we were coming up the
Hsiang river—in China sometimes deep blue clouds hover over the
heavens.

This morning a Japanese prisoner, captured near the East Gate,
was brought to the house. He sat in the open courtyard in the sunlight, his face very gray and tired, and there was about him an extraordinary air of sorrow, as though he no longer cared to live; but he
was happy to see the sunlight. His name is Kyoshi Kowahara, a
twenty-five-year-old insurance agent from Nagoya. He has a wife and
three children; his father owns a small mill employing eight people.
We clustered around him, while Colonel Liu acted as interpreter,
and occasionally Bergery would say a few words in Japanese, and the
young Japanese would look up, thinking by the tone of his voice that
Bergery was a friend.

Of all the Japanese I have met, he was the only one who impressed me. His sorrow was so deep that he seemed to have much in
common with Bergery. He sat there in his brown coat, his head
bowed, the black hair shaven to the skull and so dark that it resembled a smear of black paint, his hands folded between his knees,
never looking up.

"What regiment do you belong to?" Colonel Liu asked.

"The Sixty-eighth of the Fifth Brigade."

"How much do they pay you?"

"Twelve *yen* a month."

He explained that everything was free—food, transport, uniform.

There was a faint smile on his face. The winter sunlight shone through the bare plum trees, and in a broken voice, the voice of someone who no longer believes even in his own words, he explained that twelve *yen* was sufficient at the base camp for one woman a week or two hundred military cigarettes.

"Women must be cheap in Japan?" Colonel Liu asked, smiling a little; but the soldier said nothing. A cold wind shook the plum trees, and from time to time he would nod his head quickly, as though anxious to finish the conversation.

"Will you shoot me?" he asked.

No one said anything.

After a while he spoke in quick nervous tones about his food, for he had been asked to give a complete list of the food supplied to the Japanese army. He said it consisted of rice, compressed beef, and a kind of powdered sauce; he complained that since the Chinese soldiers had only two meals a day, while the Japanese soldiers had three, he had felt hungry ever since his capture five days before; and shortly afterward, when someone brought sugared rice from the house, he smiled, took the food on his lap, and gazed at it without interest. He was courteous and gentle, and in the end when Colonel Liu gave him the freedom of the garden, he smiled to himself, made the faintest inclination to the correspondents who had crowded around him until it seemed that they were all peering within an inch of his face, and sat cross-legged on the grass facing the red cliffs of Changsha. All afternoon he sat there, so quiet and impassive that it was difficult to believe that in the confused fighting at the East Gate less than a week before, he had attempted to blow himself up with a hand grenade; and when the grenade failed to explode, he quietly surrendered, expecting no mercy.

Later. This evening there was a storm. The rain came down, and the small river which we jumped across this morning is now a torrential stream. The house shakes, there is lightning, and as we wait in the cold, uncomfortable bedrooms for the storm to cease, it is difficult not to think of the soldiers in the rain north of the Milo river. There are winds in Hunan which can break a man's back; there is a fierceness in this earth and a still greater fierceness in the sky, and perhaps this is why the Hunanese are famous for their ferocity.

But when the storm cleared a little we made our way through the muddy roads to a small timber-stacked farm shed near the river, and there among small hand printing presses we toasted the Chinese press at the front line.

Wherever there is an army in China, there is a small printing press. Young soldiers, perhaps twelve years old, lift the lead characters from the boxes where they are arranged in order and insert them carefully in slots on the printing muchine. The characters are so small that they become blinding when you read them; and the ink is so bad that the letters run. Yet the press functions perfectly, the characters are always replaced in their proper order, and three or four hours after the newspaper has been printed a fast automobile takes them to the front line. There are wireless sets on which the news is received, and here and there you will find small portable electric motors.

While the small red-cheeked typesetters worked in the half-darkness, the tables were lit in another side of the room under immense flaring acetylene lamps. Bergery sat next to the Russian correspondent, the *Times* correspondent sat next to the *Ta Kung Pao*. A tremendous feast was set out for us. No one knew where the food had come from. There was white sweet rice, pigeon, duck, innumerable dishes of pork with sweet and sour sauce. There were four kinds of wine and six kinds of fruit—and it was winter, and there was a battle raging less than thirty miles away. The Chinese press kept repeating that they were delighted to have us; and since we had burned our throats with their white wine, and since we had nothing but admiration for them, we were not even amused when the *Daily Express* correspondent began to make a speech, which continued to our amazement for more than an hour, in which he repeated his love for the Chinese and his displeasure at all those who did not love the Chinese people. The Chinese had won a great victory. The evidence of the victory which we had seen was already splashed across the front pages of the leading newspapers of the world, and we were in no mood for what the Chinese call "small speeches." We congratulated him, and carried him home through the storm, while the great winds howled through the pine forest and only the faintest glimmer of lights shone from the house buried in a nest of leaves.

January 9th. All day we have done nothing except stare at the leaden sky. There were plans for further excursions—even as far as the Milo river—but as the day wore on it became clear that no permission would be given us. The air has become colder than ever, the wind breaks up the small pieces of ice on the frosted fields, and the blue magpies still shriek from the black branches. A day of desolate and streaming winds, gray clouds which would be slimy if you could touch them with your fingers, and always this waiting.

I am beginning to understand the life of a journalist. Bergery's patience is something which he has learned by years of partial failure. "And all journalism is failure," he said later this afternoon, before the banquet. "We prepare ourselves to tell the truth, we go into journalism with the one object of telling the truth, as though we were dedicated to the task, and afterward when we look back on the life of constant travel and terrible vicissitudes, it amounts to so little." When we are doing nothing, he lies in bed with his eyes closed. The eyes are heavily lidded, and a single blue vein can be seen throbbing on each lid. He smiles sometimes to himself while he sleeps, but more often his lips are pursed, and seem to be suggesting the eternal nightmare of the journalist who sees so much and can explain so little.

The more I see of Bergery the more I come to the conclusion that in spite of his ancestry, which includes great-grandfathers from three different countries in Europe, he is predominantly the product of New England. Alone of the correspondents he attended the banquet this evening in a formal dress suit.

We had seen General Hsueh Yueh before when, on the verandah of his house some miles away, he showed us the secret documents which had been found on the body of the Japanese Colonel Kato. Three months before the Pacific war broke out, documents from Japanese sources had passed into the possession of the Chinese High Command, and according to General Hsueh Yueh the information had been passed on to the American and British governments. Neither the Americans nor the British had apparently paid very much attention to the documents. He smiled, rubbed his hands, and seemed to be saying, "We are an old race and these young races have still so much to learn." He looked remarkably young, the face of a fourteen-year-old boy, very slim, reddish, with hair turning gray. He smiled frequently. The tables were set for dinner, and he talked to me of Singapore, where he had been in the years before the Kuomintang party assumed power in China. "I was arrested three times in Indochina by the French authorities for the small part I played in helping the Chinese revolutionaries to obtain arms, but I could always find a refuge in Singapore." About the war in Malaya he refused to be drawn out at first, but afterward he said, "If they carry out the scorched-earth policy, the Allies will be victorious." It looked a simple phrase, and we would have dismissed it as a polite irrelevancy if he had not continued: "We have won the war in China, or rather we have prevented the Japanese from assuming complete political power over China, and we have done this simply by employing the scorched-earth policy. This has been our major strategy. We have destroyed China—removed every stone, burned down every farm, torn up every railway track, and we have done this so successfully that the Japanese have already repented of their invasion. They are tired and weary of their invasion." As he said this, we remembered the face of young Kyoshi Kowahara, and his statement that the Japanese army in Yochow had greeted the opening of the Pacific war without enthusiasm: "We knew that it would be a much longer time now before we would see our homes."

General Hsueh Yueh was born in 1893. He was therefore nearly thirty years younger than Dr. Sun Yat-sen, whom he adored with the kind of devotion which is reserved only for the great. In 1918 he graduated with the rank of major from the Kwangtung Military Academy, and he fought under Chen Chi-mei, the uncle of the present minister of education, in the revolutionary battles of the south which made Canton in summer a place of desolation and hopelessness. He was perfectly sure of himself, and his long thin hands would drum on the table with pleasure whenever anyone made a remark which particularly pleased him. Someone mentioned Genji Doihara. His face lit up, he smiled broadly and without the slightest trace of self-satisfaction; but as though he had taken the measure of his opponent and succeeded in beating him away, he said, "Doihara is my particular enemy. We have fought and are still fighting a duel together, but I flatter myself that my weapon—the Chinese army—will outlast his."

In a neighboring room a telephone bell rang. An aide came to announce that the Generalissimo was on the telephone. He excused himself and returned two minutes later, smiling: "The Generalissimo has asked me for the assurance that the foreign war correspondents here are being well treated." We assented gratefully. Throughout the rest of the meal the General ate nothing, but insisted on handing to us on his chopsticks the more savory morsels which he had detected on the immense shining plates lying before us.

January 10th. There should have been ice floes. It was bitterly cold, and we envied the Chinese soldiers in their green-gray caps, for these caps contain two strips of heavy cloth kept in position by a blue and white Kuomintang button, and these strips of cloth can be folded down over their ears. Bergery wore his heavy fur-lined coat, but the rest of us shivered. The gray road, the gray sky lit by occasional streaks of a heavenly blue, the immense stretches of level sand by the river, the small boat plunging in the heavy waves, and slowly Changsha fades away in the distance.

I have been watching it with Bergery from the stern as we roll in the enormous swell. It is still white and ghostly, with river fowl screaming above us. The dead soldier who lay at the foot of the red cliffs is still there, but now there are thin gray puffs of smoke rising from the chimneys. Thousands are returning. We can see them lining up the bank, a black mass of people on the water line waiting for the sampans to take them across. The green island, which stands like a sentinel between Changsha and the opposite shore, is greener than ever under the lowering clouds. We watched the city until it was out of sight, and at last Bergery drew his fur collar higher and whispered, "They will talk about it in all the newspapers of the world, but they will not understand. They will not understand that the Chinese have fought victoriously, while the rest of us have fought only to our shame."

Later. Toward evening we were still running desperately against the current. The engine had broken down, and for a while we drifted northward till a Chinese engineer stripped the engine and put it right. While a thick mist lies outside, and the last cormorants have gone to sleep in the boats, we glide down the mysterious river. Bergery sits with his eyes glued on the window, and suddenly he turns to me and says:

"No other river in the world has had such great poetry written about it. I used to wonder why, since it is not more magnificent than the Yangtse and less terrible than the Yellow river. But its proportions are so good—exactly the right width—and how mysteriously the villages appear to rise above its banks. Chu Yuan is perhaps the greatest Chinese poet, and therefore the greatest poet who has ever lived——" and he began to recite, in the same low-pitched voice which accompanied his recitations as we rode back from the Liuyang river, the song which Chu Yuan addressed to the Lord of the Hsiang River:

With you I wander the Nine Rivers,
The whirlwind and the wave rises.
Floating in a water chariot

With its roof of lotus leaves,
I climb above the K'un Lun mountains
And search eagerly in the four directions.
My spirits wander over the face of the deep.
The day is waning; bemused, I forget my home,
And dream of the furthest reaches of the river.
In an abode of fish scales, in a hall of dragons
Under a purple-shell gateway, in a palace of pearl,
O Spirit, why do you dwell in the waters?
Riding the white tortoise and chasing the spotted fishes,
I wander with you among the small islets,
The melting ice comes swirling down river.
With a gentle bow you turn toward the East
And I accompany you to the south anchorage.
Wave after wave comes to welcome me.
Multitudes of fishes come to bid me farewell.

January 11th. We have slept again at Hsiangtan, in the same hotel, the same terrible bedrooms overlooking the courtyard—everything dark and damp. Rice cauldrons boiling under the black eaves, the red candles and their redder flames. A girl singing in some distant street, and the muted notes of violins. The dust and the dirt and the tremendous swirling shadows which move across the courtyard walls—someone gambling—the tuck-tuck of mahjong tablets—and those momentary quietnesses when the sounds of the night seem to be gathering themselves for the furor ahead.

There is no silence in these small villages. Hsiangtan was at one time the center of the trade in fireworks, but the noise comes from the refugees who have come down from the north to swell this small town. Perhaps I shall never see this town in daylight. We came in the darkness of a late afternoon, and disappeared before sunrise. We are to leave at five o'clock tomorrow morning.

We slept fitfully. There were rats and the continual tramp of feet on the loose floor boards outside; there were sudden squeals like the squeal a rat makes at the moment when the wire trap closes over its neck, and perturbing menacing silences. On his pallet bed of straw and boards near the window Bergery has been reading by candle flame. Of all the correspondents he alone is enjoying himself. "Three thousand years ago life in China was like this," he said happily. "Nothing has changed—straw, wood, broken pieces of porcelain, a cracked mirror. They possessed all these things. And perhaps here, two thousand years ago, in the same room, holding a candle to the same words, another scholar was reading the *Analects* of Confucius."

"And this pleases you?"

"Yes, of course. Why do you look surprised? Everything that suggests the continuity of the past and the present pleases me, for in these ages we are doing everything in our power to destroy the dominance of the past. We believe we are new. Not only in China but all over the world people believe that they are born into a new world. And yet the world is so old, so old—and they have so little reverence for its old age. Think of this room! There must have been a village here three thousand years ago, perhaps five thousand years ago, for the Hsiang river has been navigable since the earliest records of Chinese history. There must have been a hotel here—perhaps it was very little different from this hotel with its square courtyard and overhanging eaves. Think of the people who have slept in this room—scholars, merchants, murderers, prostitutes, courtesans. Emperors have fled in disguise down this river. Kingdoms have been proclaimed from Changsha, and great armies have fled in barges to the north and the south. And perhaps the straw in the bed you are lying on has not been changed for three thousand years, and generations upon generations of people have been born there, and the murderer——"

I fell asleep, dreaming of the eiderdown blanket and the fur cap and the thick underwear I bought this evening. Hsiangtan is cheaper than Chungking, and its narrow black streets are more Chinese than anything I have yet seen in China.

January 12th. We traveled from Chungking by air to Kweilin and then by the Blue Express to Hsiangtan. There was a time when the Blue Express traveled between Peking and Shanghai, and romances were written about the train which the Chinese government preserved from the Japanese only by the greatest use of dexterity. It is a train *de luxe*, with sleeping berths and soft cushions, excellent lavatories and immense windows from which we can look out on the countryside. Painted navy blue, streamlined and efficient, it comprises the only well-built set of carriages left in Chinese hands.

We have been traveling all morning through a bleak countryside. The gray fields are being ploughed, but only rarely do we see the peasants. A damp mist, dripping from the clouds, covers everything; and there are few trees. A short while ago we passed one of the famous five sacred mountains of China. It was not impressive—a small purple mound on the skyline. And no one knows why this mountain should be chosen as one of the five sacred mountains except that it is in the dead center of China.

And so the Chinese countryside flows on, gray and misty, with sedges and small brakes where pheasants are flying, and a few grayish-yellow stone-walled cottages near the winter skyline. There are no soldiers. The land is not dead but sleeping in its winter agony. The river, which gave life to the villages, is far away, and Bergery speaks of the monotony of the small villages in China, where there are often no rivers or streams within fifty miles.

"They live in a perpetual seclusion and have only their ceremonies to keep them together. Or rather, this is their chief glory. When I first came to China, I would ride across the countryside for miles, and suddenly I would alight on a.deserted village. The villagers would be kind to me. They would entertain me, knowing that I was unarmed and friendly and possessed a passionate interest in their customs, and so they would arrange an archery contest or perhaps a boxing match or some swordplay for my benefit. It was only twenty years ago, in the intervals between the civil wars, yet they still kept up the old customs which gave them strength and self-pride. The most handsome youths of the village would be chosen for the archery contests. They would be dressed in their long loose silken robes, and with those splendid bows made of the muscles of bears or heavy-horned cattle, they would perform the contest to music. Then, indeed, I believed I was living in the age of Confucius. Near the green fields and the stone temples these handsome boys would throw out their chests, smile at their bearded fathers, and shoot the plumed arrows. But now——" He gazed out of the window, expecting perhaps to see the sun shining on a green meadow and to hear the cracking of bear sinews as the bows were stretched by the boys. But there was nothing—only the gray mist and a skylark spiraling into the sky.

At Henyang we noticed a hospital train. The sun was shining faintly, and the great doors of the cattle wagons had been thrown open; and there, lying in small heaps on the straw, lay the wounded who had returned from the battle. They were bandaged well, though here and there we noticed a bandage which should have been removed, for there were often yellow stains seeping through the gray bandages. They looked pale and weary, and we wondered how long they had been there, shunted down this small side track on the edge of the railway station.

Henyang is not beautiful, though there are wide roads and a river flows at the bottom of the city. The railway station resembles a provincial railway station in France, all gray stucco and brocade uniforms. But as soon as you leave the railway station you are among broad thoroughfares, small white houses, and then the city no longer reminds you of France but of some delightful village in the south of Poland. There are duck ponds and small lakes. There are promenades beside the river, where in the broiling sunlight which appeared shortly after we arrived, girls were walking in light dresses and old men were sleeping in the shade of chestnut trees. Scattered over the red hills, the city branches out in all directions and seems to resemble nothing so much as a delightful spider's web. The center of the web consists of four streets crowded with shops and beggars and wailing infants who walk about quite naked. Beggars followed us from the moment we left the railway station. They were harmless and said nothing, but continually stretched out their bony arms; and if we refused them, they would go away for a little while, only to return a little later, chastened perhaps but still hopeful.

I shall remember Henyang for the dust and the green hills, and the Japanese airplanes which came over five minutes after we left for Kweilin. At first the driver had not heard that there were airplanes. The train went on, while the airplanes flew low over the town; but a little later we came to a siding, the train roared into silence, shuddered and stopped dead on its tracks, while we staggered out among the low, green grave mounds and wondered how we should return if the train were hit by a bomb. But the warmth was glorious. The sun shone on a small farm of bamboos, on the white-lettered graves, and on the peasants who worked still in the fields, oblivious of the distant thunder of anti-aircraft guns. Spring comes early in Henyang. The bright plowshares flashed in the sun, the peasants called to one another, a small boy brought them porcelain cups containing food. An hour later the train went on again.

Bergery looks puzzled. He gazes at the disappearing landscape and murmurs, "But what is so extraordinary is that for a moment I thought I was in England. I smelt the hay, and heard the cricketers on the fields——" He is still gazing out of the window, his brow furrowed, dreaming of another country on the other side of the earth. "It was like a dream—no, it was not like a dream. The sound of the plowshares in the earth, a child calling, the old mare lumbering under the shade of the coppices, I must have seen something like that many years ago in England. I had forgotten it, and now this small corner of China will remain in my memory as long as I live."

January 13th. There was mist and rain when we came to Kweilin. There was mist and rain before, when we arrived from Chungking on our journey to Changsha, but this time the whole town has changed out of recognition. Ten days ago it resembled a small provincial town in France, the broad streets lined with dusty plane trees, and even the houses and shops were so French that we expected to see French signboards hanging from iron chains. But the signboards are in Chinese, and there are few Frenchmen left in the city. Once Yunnan and Kwangsi were provinces within the French sphere of interest. There were French reading rooms, and returned students from these provinces brought back with them some of the graces and many of the habits of France; and at meetings of the provincial governments it was not unusual to hear French spoken across the council chambers. But they have all disappeared to a small lake in the northeast of the city, where the French community awaits the end of the war, visited occasionally by the provincial Chamber of Commerce, the provincial police, and the old aristocrats who have found in Kweilin safety from the more eager prejudices of the central government.

Even in the rain, there is an atmosphere of leisurely progress in this city. The streets are broad and flat. There are no rocky hills to climb as in Chungking, and the people are calmer and hurry less often than their relatives in the capital. Here on the pavements you will see the most exquisite lace and silverware, four or five cinemas, so many good bookshops that we have lost count. Things are cheaper here than in Chungking. You can buy, for example, an enormous thermos flask, brightly painted and guaranteed to last little short of a lifetime, for seventy dollars. It would cost more than two hundred in Chungking. You can buy innumerable French books, innumerable translations of Chinese stories into English. Until the Pacific war broke out, there was continuous communication between Kweilin and Hongkong, but now the communication has broken and the old city, once the capital of China, seems to be stupefied by the absence of contact with the south. It is not self-sufficient like Chungking. It has none of Chungking's overwhelming majesty. It is simple and a little childish, and perhaps a little afraid of itself and its ancient history. And so, as you walk down the avenues of limes or plane trees, or wander through the damp roads leading to the river, where for the first time you notice the poverty that has spread like a sore over China since the beginning of ages, the city no longer bewitches you; and the first enchantment passes as it passes always when, after meeting a pretty girl, you discover that she is interested only in the artifices of her beauty.

For Kweilin is beautiful, and she knows she is beautiful. For fifteen hundred years artists have traveled down the great trunk roads to paint those incredible mountains. Standing by the bank of the green swirling river, you see the pointed limestone mountains like immense candles raised to heaven. There, in the gray afternoon, you gaze out at a fantastic landscape of cloud and slender gray pillars, like petrified trees, four or five hundred feet high, with a few trees growing on the summits. The earth is flat like a draughtboard, and these mountains rise out of the earth like enormous chessmen, separated from one another by five or six hundred feet of intervening fields, so tall that their summits are sometimes buried in the clouds. I have seen these mountains in Chinese paintings, and did not believe that they could exist. But there they are; and in the shadow of the immense, towering cliffs black-sailed sampans move steadily down the green stream.

January 16th. The Yangtse is still high, a great turbulent white sheet flowing under a thick mist. It is impossible to see the sky or the clouds, and in this whiteness everything dissolves in patches of mist. This morning, as we crossed the river in the motorboat, we saw a small sampan gliding past us, caught up in the current, and three or four small brown figures cowering at the bottom of the boat. There was no expression on their faces; they looked neither backward nor forward. As sometimes happens in a dream, when the figures suddenly lose color and great black spiders' webs begin to dissolve the picture, I had the impression that at any moment a black hand would descend from the clouds and carry them away. Our small motorboat chugged in circles. There was the occasional sound of rocks grating against the iron bottom of the boat; and in the mist the small yellowish-gray sampan was still gliding past us, so slowly that I felt certain that this was a dream. When the sampan was about to disappear from our field of vision, it suddenly stopped and began to sway backward and forward, caught against the rocks, swinging like scissors, until suddenly the roar of the river came to our ears and at that moment the sampan broke in two, spilling the occupants into the white river. For two or three seconds—certainly not more than five seconds—we watched three or four small black heads bobbing up and down against the smooth rock; then they disappeared, following the boat which was already disappearing downstream.

I am told that this happens always in time of floods. The rocks are treacherous, and the current so deceptive that the most skilled boatmen have been known to lose their lives in the Yangtse. The river is quite merciless; and though in some places rocks have been dynamited, and though the masts of sampans can be seen protruding above the river at all seasons, every year the river claims its victims. I am beginning to believe that the Yangtse is a living and breathing thing, a smooth turbulent dragon who never relinquishes her claim on the lives of the Chinese who live on her banks. This morning after we had watched the sampan breaking in two, we were lost in midstream. The mist was as thick as a waterfall. Somewhere a boy was beating a drum on the high rocks, and we heard the continual hooting of automobiles high up on the rocky cliffs of Chungking. We were continually turning in circles, and once we hit a rock with such a sickening crash of plates that we instinctively made ready to dive overboard; but if we had dived, we would have lived for ten seconds—no more. It was half an hour before we reached the other side of the river, we were drenched with mist, and our cigarettes wouldn't light—they were so wet. And as we began to climb the immense reach of steps which leads to the Dragon Gate of Chungking, I looked back and watched the river through a break in the clouds. The river was white and full, swirling along, hurrying, talking to itself in absorbed, intent tones. And the suspicion that it was a dragon, a real dragon with scales and fins and great golden eyes, with an immense lashing tail and huge hairy arms with which it could climb on the shore and engulf everything within sight, became so overpowering that I began to understand why there are more suicides in the river at times of high flood than at any other time.

But at night the river is beautiful beyond words. The little black paddle steamer, with its ghostly oil lamps, lies reflected in the torrent. Armies of cloud march in rank across the sky, obscuring the mountains with their ragged banners, and through the mist you can see the faint silver lights shining on the south bank and the great red puffs of smoke coming from the bamboo flares on the landing stage. Sometimes it may take an hour to cross the river, even in the paddle boat.

But once you have arrived on the rocky shore of the south bank, small boys run forward with plaited yellow bamboo flares, and the smoky red flares shining on the granite steps and on the faces of the passengers are so vivid and so consoling that you forget the tedium of the journey and the loneliness in mid-river, when the paddle boat mills around in a whirlpool or fights against the sheer weight of the current.

January 17th. It is at night that the city wakes into life. The electric lamps in the street are fainter than the stars in Malaya, but the roads are so wet that the light seems to come not from the electric light standard but from a million puddles in the street. We have been in search of Rewi Alley. We found him at last in a small bedroom in the northeast of the city, one of those barren rooms which you reach across interminable rabbit-warren courtyards. There was the usual low Chinese bed, the usual distempered wall, the usual naked lamp throwing down a faint whiteness on the unpolished wooden floor. Rewi Alley looks extraordinarily like T. E. Lawrence, deeply sun-burned, stocky, with immense brown hands, a continual amused expression on his lips. He is short and powerful around the shoulders, with the build of a wrestler.

"I'm going back to the northwest as soon as the papers come through," he said, shivering at the thought of the cold weather which lay before him. "It's so cold in Sian in winter that if you spit at somebody, you can kill him with your spittle—it turns to ice."

We went out into the cold streets, where the shadows revolved on the high walls. Chungking at night is eerie with invisible ghosts, whose pattern of behavior is to darken all exits. Shadows climb out of gutters, stretch black and silver arms from half-open windows. They breed shadows, and you feel as you walk down the deserted streets that they are palpable and malevolent, and covered with sticky gum-like spiders' webs.

He began to talk of the northwest, the million blankets which had been ordered by the Chinese army, the extraordinary sense of co-operation among the peasants. Into the dark night he brought an unsuspected glow of sunlight and physical strength.

"We invented the co-operatives, but the Chinese peasants have made them their own. I've never come across people so willing to work at a trade. They are in love with their tools—they make them with a kind of instinctive love and understanding. Give a Chinese boy the roof of a motor-car, and he will make a lathe. Give him a lathe, and he will not stop until he has made a factory. The million blankets are ready three months before they are due. We started the second million a week ago. But if the Burma Road closes, and we have no gasoline, how are we going to transport them?" He told us about some of the methods of transport which were now being used. "Drums of oil are floated down rivers in Kansu on inflated pigs' skins. Whole armies of coolies are being employed to carry drills to the northern oil fields. These are people living in the Stone Age who carry on their shoulders the whole weight of modern transport.

"Don't forget that this is the fourth year of the war, and they are undernourished and weary beyond endurance. In the old days disease would have swept them away, but they seem to live longer now—perhaps because they have something to fight for. This is a popular war. You realize that the nearer you get to the front line. Hatred for the Japanese has bitten deep in their souls."

He spoke of farmers who would plow their lands by day and make blankets on their looms at night. He was full of a fierce kind of admiration for the people in the north, and it is clear that they love him. He has T. E. Lawrence's trick of being abstracted from the scene while remaining at the center around which everything revolves. In the dark streets, clinging to the walls, he hurled defiance at the dark shadows.

January 19th. The clouds low, the day gray, and the rocks along the road were spitting out dew. I have never known a day which so much resembled the end of the world. Sometimes the smoky mist clears over the Chialing river, and you see far down a glassy pool of bluish-green light with a sampan riding at anchor. Foghorns, boys beating drums on high rocks, the soft slurring sound of the river and the distant roar of automobiles high up on the rock behind us. Ragnarok—the end of the world.

But the mist cleared later in the morning, and though the sky was low, colors began to appear again—a girl's red dress, the green uniform of the postmen, black street lamps, a few yellow leaves. The road winds along at the base of immense sandstone and granite mountains with tombstones decorating the slopes and no forests in sight. The young Chinese who accompanied us explained that the Chinese refuse to allow their dead to be buried in the cities, and every city is surrounded with tombstones. "If you are on your way to a city, you know at once that the city is near when you see the dead." His sepulchral voice was perfectly calculated to disarm us. The automobile splashed through the mud, throwing up great black bow-waves and leaving a black wake, like avenging angels, flying through the air.

National Central University is about twenty miles north of Chungking. It has been savagely bombed, and some of the students and professors have been killed. Among gray open fields, among cedars and yews, the young students lived in small plaster and mortar houses, but the gray choking clouds drifting close to the earth made them look worried and care-worn. The boys wear Sun Yat-sen uniforms and the girls wear blue gowns. Not all of them looked well-fed, and many were pale with weariness; but what was most surprising was their long swinging strides as they walked under the avenues of trees.

Most of the classrooms are small underheated plaster rooms—a blackboard, rows of chairs, nothing else. I imagine the students in Russia in the sixties resembled the students here. They are the elite of the country, the chosen vehicles of the future greatness of China; and therefore they work like Trojans, throwing their whole lives into their work. Their eyesight is bad. At night they work by the light of rapeseed-oil lamps; during the day they work by the light of a weak sun. The impression of terrible responsibility and a perfect acceptance of that responsibility is unalterable; and I have never felt before how greatly I have underestimated the power of reconstruction in China. Those students, some of them so obviously suffering from tuberculosis, belong to a generation which has lived and starved through the war years, and they are determined that the future generation shall not live and starve as they did.

I met a girl student on the campus and spoke to her. She was thin, with a grayness in her skin which spoke of arduous study and perhaps of tuberculosis. Her eyes, very dark, were old, and yet her face was young. She spoke in almost perfect English. She had been a guerrilla in Manchuria. She had been wounded. She came down to Chungking, and then, feeling that the war was not being waged in the capital as it should be waged, she returned to the north. It was only when she was wounded for the second time that she decided to return. She was studying physical chemistry, and hoped one day to be in charge of a factory—it didn't matter what kind of factory as long as it was productive and useful for the country.

"We are all working for China. This is all that we think about. There are students here who believe in communism and others who believe in the party, but we have no time for arguing. We carry on because we believe that above communism or above the party there is always China."

She spoke about her adventures.

"I was sad when I came down. There were so many rich people, and besides I was friendless. When we were fighting, we knew everyone. If we wanted money or arms or bandages, we always found them; but it was more difficult in the capital. I met the Generalissimo. He is so great that I wept for three days because of the terrible tasks which face him. And then too he is very handsome and looks very young. But the terrible tasks! No one else in China has so great a responsibility. I believe in him and pray for him, but not everyone in China is like him. . . . You know I was wounded. We have no hospitals in the north, but hospitals are not necessary. I stayed for three months in Japanese-occupied territory, and though the Japanese passed every day they never found me."

"What do you want to do when the war is over?"

"I shall go back to the north and start a factory in Manchuria. The earth is so rich there—and then I shall marry and have children."

I spent some time in the hydrology department. On the walls there were maps of the Yellow river, the scourge of China; and I was not surprised that most of the students came from the north. There was a young Dutch professor of hydraulics, who spoke about the lives of the students with more hero-worship than I have seen in the eyes of a professor before.

"They live on nothing and they work like madmen," he said. "I gave them an examination a little while ago. One of my best students fainted during the examination. I found that he had been studying for sixty-four hours without stopping, without having any food. He finished the paper—the whole paper—in about half an hour, and then he fainted. This is the kind of thing we are faced with—students who continually sacrifice their health for the sake of knowledge. And yet what use will their knowledge be if they are dead before they practice it?" He was filled with fear for the students. Their food was bad; almost all of them were penniless. There were a few rich Szechuan students, sons of landed proprietors, but the entrance examination was unusually difficult and only the best students were capable of passing. It was the second best university in China,

the best being the Associated Universities in Kunming. He had visited the Associated Universities and wondered why they were less
famous abroad.

"A student will think nothing of traveling from Peking to
Chungking or Kunming. He knows that the best professors are here,
and that the blueprints for the future of China are being made in the
universities. Our professors could obtain well-paid appointments in
the government or in private industries, but they know that the
future of China lies in their hands. Two-thirds of the students here
are taking science subjects, and the minister of education, Dr. Chen
Li-fu, is even attempting to make it difficult for students to study the
humanities. We have enough natural humanists in China, but we
haven't enough scientists. There were more trained hydraulic engineers in China three thousand years ago than there are today. That's
why they are working so desperately hard—to catch up with lost
time."

The professors' dormitory was dark and damp. A long low building, with a corridor leading off into small shuttered bedrooms, each
with its pallet bed and little else. Sometimes whole families lived in
these small rooms, where the rain crept through the broken tiles and
the paper windows fluttered like flags in the chill wind. It was cold. A
mist rose over the Yangtse, and it was impossible to see the river
from the steep cliffs. And here they worked and lived and sometimes
died, not fearing for the future, quietly making plans for a renovated
China, dreaming of the sun among the winter mists, planning steadily and with forethought for the day when the war should be over.

"But they are so tired, you understand," the Dutch professor
told me. "They are weary after four years of war. They have been
bombed, and will be bombed again—National Central University has
seen whole buildings go up in flames. I know the Minister of Education. He is doing everything he can for them, but even so prices are
rising, the rice is not always good rice, and the birth of a new child
may mean ruin to many of them."

He took me to the library. It was getting late, and the students
were already reading by the light of rapeseed oil lamps, each student
with his own green lamp. The students looked cold, but they were
rapt in their books. They looked hungry, but the books carried them
into a strange land—a land where everything was rigorous, scientific,
and perfectly proportioned to its appointed end. All around the small
low building books were crowded; there were books in Chinese, German, French, English—in every known language. And as I walked

around, listening to the hum of whispered breathing, the faces of the young students golden in the light, everyone quiet and intent upon the book before him, it seemed that the whole building was a hive of seething activity. In those young minds a new China was being made.

And then home, in the darkness, the black cliffs shining in the headlamps. The car was crowded with students who wanted to spend the week-end in Chungking. All the while they sang and talked, so charming in their youth and the bright audacity of their conversation that I realized at last why Bergery spoke so often about the young in China. "They will build in faith." "But what if their faith misleads them?" "It doesn't matter—they are the toughest creatures in the world." But in the dark automobile, winding along the rocky road which leads to Chungking, it was difficult to think of them as tough—they were like the young everywhere, who live neither in the past nor in the present but in the refreshing river of the future.

January 20th. I have been to see an official of the ministry of education. Like many other officials I have met in China, he looks extraordinarily young and has the manner of a boy, yet he is over forty. (Bergery said, "Add ten years to the age of any Chinese you meet, and then you will probably be right.") He wore the customary blue Chinese gown, patched and darned, with holes at the elbows. There were thick lenses in his glasses. I asked him what he thought of the future of education.

"It is not a fair question, for I should answer that it has never been brighter. At last we are dealing with education with every ounce of strength. You must understand that in the days of peace, every university could go its own way; but now every university follows the pattern set by the government. You may think this is dangerous, but on the whole the dangers are offset by the advantages. In the old days the universities carried on according to their own lights, but today the common experience is pooled. There is a great hunger sweeping over China—a hunger for education, and there are not enough scholars and too many students—not enough equipment and too few books. We carry on, and the future has never been brighter, but the present is a time of experiment."

He was head of a department in the ministry of education—a department which was struggling with inflated prices and the knowledge that at any moment the last egress from China might be closed.

"If only we could pay our scholars better," he murmured. "You see, we are a country of scholars—and they have always starved. Yet they are the acknowledged leaders of the country. When the guerrilla wars broke out, it was the Chinese professors who were asked to lead the recruits, and sometimes a Chinese professor of philology would be asked to conduct a siege or an attack against a Japanese railway line. It didn't matter whether he knew anything about military matters—he was a scholar, and he was expected to know everything. Professor Wen Chien-kung led the guerrillas in Shansi. Professor Chang Yu-kuang led the guerrillas in Shantung. Professor Yuan Mo-han led the guerrillas in Chahar. And so in all the other provinces where the guerrillas are fighting—the professors are elected to the places of honor and the greatest danger. Of course it is a tradition in China that the professors should be called upon at any moment to conduct military operations, but today we can no longer afford to let them disappear from the schools."

He was gaily optimistic about the fighting in Burma. It was unthinkable to him that China should be cut off from the outside world.

"And if we should be cut off?"

"We shall continue in the old way—we are theoreticians of the moment, and we dare not think more than a few hours ahead."

He spoke of the long journeys of the Chinese students across the interior. Sometimes, caught in a Japanese nest, they had to fight their way out; and usually they were unarmed. The students in Wuhan University at Hankow walked to Kiating in Szechuan in 1938. About a hundred perished on the journey. They were bombed and machine-gunned; they lost the greater part of their scientific equipment but managed to preserve their library almost intact. They lived in a temple where the golden gods shone down from the altars; they were not well fed. . . .

And so, through all this tragic exodus of the Chinese race, through danger and ill health, without medical equipment, often starving, the students came to the southwest. The young official smiled—the gentle, deprecating smile of the cultivated Chinese.

"It was worse in the Sung dynasty, and it was still worse when Confucius was living."

January 23rd. I am surprised when people tell me that Chungking is not beautiful. Even if this viscous gray mist lasted throughout the year, I would still be happy here. "But wait a few more days," they tell me. "Wait until the thought of green fields in spring becomes like a nightmare. In the old days the Chinese loved the mist and the rain, and they would journey from one of the old capitals—Loyang or Sianfu—just to experience the pleasure of walking through the mist and seeing suddenly, high above them, a crag mossy with evergreens. But not now—the poetry has gone, and we curse the mist and the rain and the muddy streets as we curse the Japanese."

At first I hated it. Walking in the evening down the long winding road which leads from the Press Hostel to the center of the town, while automobiles swirled past in the blue mist and the red lamps shone in the valley below, I began to feel so weary of the undifferentiated grayness that I almost wept. The smell of wood oil, the poverty of the beggars, the enormous black automobiles, the swarms of people moving like one person, the riches strewn in all the brightly lit windows and the poverty cowering in the moist alleyways—all these became wearisome beyond endurance. And then suddenly and unexpectedly a child in a blue cotton frock would pass slowly down the street carrying on her back a child who was hardly an inch smaller; and the quick gravity of the child and her perfectly shaped features made life tolerable again. China is rich—too rich—in her children, and yet there is hardly a child who is not graceful and even beautiful. I have seen in Europe—in the ghettos of Cracow, for example—many deformed children, and there are many deformed children in China; but I have never seen a country where the children are so full of vitality. I have seen children, especially the children of rich parents, who looked as though they were dead to the world, without life, the sap no longer flowing through them. But here, even when they are quite silent, the children's faces are filled with the most intense expressions of amusement, enjoyment, or melancholy. "This is because we are so primitive," a young student told me. "Our children are in the Stone Age still." And a little while later he added, "The parents pay no heed to them unless they want them as laborers. They are left to their own resources; the parents go to work, and the other children would starve if the older ones did not tend them. And so they learn early, too early, to fend for themselves. Have you noticed that all our children have the expressions of middle-aged persons?" It was not true. The children had the expressions of children, delighting in their childhood, though it is harder than any childhood anywhere else on the earth.

On the way to the British embassy there is a wasteland where the buildings have been torn down by bombs, a long stretch of yellow mud littered with rubble. According to my student friend, this place was the headquarters of a gang of child robbers and cutthroats. He was extraordinarily bitter about them. "They will do anything for money—they will rob, steal, pilfer, murder." We went there once late at night. Hidden in the remains of a house, the children were playing; and it was true that they were members of a secret society, and perhaps it was true that they robbed a little. They were orphans, and yet for some reason they had no desire to enter an orphanage. Instead, they formed a society and clubbed together. Whatever they earned was placed in a common pool, and once a month they gave themselves up to an evening of leisure. They danced, they made incredibly long speeches, they played cards, smoked cigarettes, and read the newspapers aloud. One child—perhaps he was eight years old—was making an impossibly serious speech when we arrived—an interminable political speech, calling upon them to sacrifice themselves for the country, to devote their lives to the reconstruction of China and many other laudable objects. He was desperately serious and even pompous; and he would never have ceased speaking if the student had not begun to put questions to him. He answered them all with becoming gravity. He was obviously the star attraction, and the other children were a little in awe of him. The candles guttered out. New candles were brought. In the light of the candles the children's faces glowed redly, almost unbearably beautiful. A girl in a bright red dress was calmly feeding a baby with oranges, stuffing them in the small mouth and throwing the peel over her shoulder. And sometimes, when she thought we were not looking, she would take a bite from one of the oranges and eat it swiftly; and then, noticing that we were watching her, she would blush in confusion. The speeches continued. In our honor the children decided to order a bottle of white wine. They did this quite secretly, without telling us, and I am convinced that they made the decision by means of signals which neither of us observed. They poured out the wine in small white porcelain thimble-cups which miraculously appeared; and in return for their hospitality the young student and I were called upon to make speeches.

"How long should I make a speech?" the student asked.

"About half an hour," they answered, "and your friend because he is a foreigner should make one for an hour."

And so they listened, quietly and gravely, while the student exhorted them to serve their country, obey the Three Principles, help the weak, and never pilfer. It was a strange series of commandments, but they cheered ecstatically; and in the corner the babies slept, and the girl in the red print dress still blushed in confusion whenever she saw us watching her. She was beautiful, with enormous black eyes and a long oval face—a child madonna.

"What is so curious is that the most terrible stories are told about them," the student was saying, when we returned. "There is a story that much of the opium smuggling is done by the children, and that they have even killed other children and opened their stomachs and filled the stomachs with opium and arranged immense funeral processions, and the opium has been taken across the river." It cannot be true. All night I was haunted by the dark eyes of the child in a red print frock as Confucius was haunted by the Duke of Chou. There is so much goodness in these waifs of Chungking that I begin to believe again, as I used to believe many years ago, that it would be better if the world were given over to children, and anyone reaching the age of twelve should be painlessly executed. To watch the children of Chungking is an education in expediency and beauty. They live with terrible intensity; at night they lie in small heaps in doorways or underneath the great piles of timber near the river; and yet they do not live for themselves but for each other. And that curious mixture of maturity and childishness in their faces is so beautiful that it sometimes becomes unbearable. At night, in the shadows, sleeping in the cold mist, shivering in their brilliantly colored rags, they dream of the sun.

January 27th. Interminable discussions about East and West, but where is the dividing line? I have lived for years among the Chinese in the South Seas, and though there are acute differences, they are not analyzable and the same differences exist among ourselves. The passion for making distinctions. And yet the Chinese are so like the people of the West that all the geography book definitions fail. I have seen in a book on human geography the statement that the Chinese have thick black hair, almond eyes, small hands, thin bones, and are generally smaller and slighter than the people of the West. Every one of those statements is demonstrably false. Nearly all Chinese children, for example, have light brown hair which grows darker later; many retain brown hair for the rest of their lives and some have hair with a golden hue. I have rarely met a Chinese with almond eyes, though it is true that on the Chinese stage slanting eyes are the characteristics of the gods and of beautiful maidens. That they have small hands in the south is perhaps true, but there are giants in the north; and the northern climate together with *kaoliang* have bred a race which is roughly the same height as Europeans.

To make generalizations about the Chinese people is so dangerous that it should long ago have been regarded as a sin of scholarship or good taste. Their customs and their history are not ours; their ways of regarding life are not ours; and often they have different motives for doing the same things. A Chinese outside China is as assimilative as any foreigner, and I am beginning to believe that there is only one thing which really distinguishes him from the rest of the inhabitants of the world, and that is the Chinese landscape. We are creatures of the landscape. Our minds are shaped according to the countries we have lived in. The mind of an American of the New England coast is like the coast itself, craggy with rocks and bitter with longing for the South; there are great flowering trees in the minds of those who have lived in Oregon, and sunlight broods heavily over the minds of the West Coast. So in China there are precipitations of yellow earth in the brains of the Chinese; there are rocky crags and temples and herd boys blowing pipes and sampans flowing down river in the luminous mist. Our minds are landscapes; and though we would often prefer to forget the landscapes which have given us birth, we can no more escape from their dominance than we can escape from our sins.

February 1st. What is so extraordinary about Bergery is that he has seen everything—everything without exception—and remains the most completely humble person I have ever met. He has been a war correspondent for so long that the sight of blood or the evidence of torture awakens no physical pangs in him; he has killed his own nerves; and yet, by the most terrible concentration of effort, he has been able to recreate in his mind a purely *logical* sensitivity which has nothing in common with the sensitivity of the flesh. His face is heavy, and reminds me sometimes of the face of the central figure of the Elephanta caves—dark, drawn, and terrible. This at least is what I think when he is not present in the room; but when he is there the suspicion of a gaunt bitterness vanishes, the heaviness disappears, the *terribiltà* is nowhere to be seen. Only from the way in which he weighs his words, ponderously dreaming, calculating every nervous twist and fiber of the words which he loves so much, do you realize the background, the long years, the wandering, the knowledge, which is always there, that perhaps the wandering is in vain. He is married, but he never talks about his wife. There are even children, about whom he has spoken only once since we arrived in Chungking. He is completely self-contained and always seems to occupy the least possible amount of space. And sometimes, watching him as he reads the *National Herald,* I have a suspicion that he is not a man who has experienced every war of the last thirty years but a man of the future.

It is impossible to record in writing the *weight* which he gives to words. When he says, "China is the mountain," the words at first mean no more than they appear to mean. Later, the reverberations of the voice suggest endless dissociated meanings, and you begin to imagine a pyramid of meanings only to find later that the meanings he intended to convey included so many more pyramids, each one superimposed on the other, that the effort of keeping pace with him becomes confusing. He loves China with almost the same breathless adoration with which a lover loves his first mistress, and this is perhaps because China was his first mistress and his early formative years were spent in Manchuria. In the cold, windswept valleys of Jehol he first saw the imperial splendors he has been searching for ever since. They left on his mind an impression so absolute that he still regards them, as I regard him, as belonging to the future. And this evening, sucking at his pipe, frowning so that dark brown lines appeared on his brown forehead, he began to talk of the young Chinese he had been seeing in Chungking with exactly the same delight as he talked of Jehol.

"They have come to this stage of the history of their country with a complete knowledge of their future, and it is the first time they have possessed this knowledge. They know they will become a great power, and that just as it took Germany ten years to recover from the war, and Russia fifteen years, they can expect to be great within twenty years of the end of this war. They have planned their future so industriously that they have no time for anything else. They have no time even for recriminations. They have not forgiven Roosevelt for sending scrap iron to Japan; they have not forgiven Churchill for closing the Burma Road. They are dangerous. They are the most dangerous race on the earth. And they are dangerous only because four thousand years of traditions have implanted in them a tolerance and an abiding love of goodness which will one day shock us out of our complacency. A war does not shock people out of their complacency. It increases complacency. But the time will come soon, perhaps very soon, when the example of the Chinese scholars will be the example which we shall all be unconsciously following. Voltaire admired Confucius above all men; yet Voltaire was the father of the French revolution. The coming revolution will be fathered by the Chinese themselves, and perhaps it will be fathered by them without their knowledge and certainly without their permission.

"The revolution will come. It will be a revolution as terrible as any in the world's history; and it will owe its origin to some Chinese scholar, working quietly and in poverty in some remote valley in China, and through him the veils will suddenly be lifted from our eyes and for the first time we shall see clearly. I tell you, China is dangerous for the peace of mind of the world. Imagine China after twenty years of peace. Imagine every small village in the interior with its own electric light, every farmer with his automobile, every rice field with its tractor—and behind all these four thousand years of conscious history. In twenty years a quarter of the human race, having suffered the greatest crimes known to man, suddenly leaps into consciousness of its own strength. Do you think it will have little effect on the rest of the world? Do you think it will sit there, supinely obeying the dictates of the foreign industrialists and allow itself to be exploited by others? Do you imagine that a race which once imagined it possessed the whole world will allow itself to suffer any more indignities?

"But what is so extraordinary and at the same time so understandable is that the Chinese of this generation are determined to set an example to others. *They are the race which has suffered.* Therefore they are determined that the knowledge they have derived from suffering shall not be wasted, and this is true only because the knowledge we derive from suffering is the most precious thing we possess. They have mapped out their future. They have decided to become a great industrial power, and at the same time all that we mean by American industrialism is foreign to them. The scandalous labor conditions of the treaty ports will not return. The scandalous impositions of foreign interest-bearing securities will not return, perhaps because we know already that it is dangerous to place a foreign race at the mercy of the stock market. What Mexico accomplished, China can accomplish with still greater ease. And so for them the future is not dark, but so bright that it is blinding. That is why the young students work through the night by the light of rapeseed-oil lamps. That is why you see on the walls the one word, 'Reconstruction'—a word whose history is as old as the Chou dynasty. Of all the countries in the world I have the greatest hope for China, not because she is numerically stronger than any other country, but because the old traditions have never died and the old books are still read by scholars and soldiers alike. If I could live another twenty years, I would prefer to live them in China; and if I must die, I would prefer to die in China. The greatness of this country is terrifying, and this is what I mean when I say that China is the mountain."

Into the early hours of the morning he was still talking of China, her prodigious history, her incalculable expenditure of treasure, her vast knowledge and incredible patience. But I suspect that Bergery's main argument belongs to the sphere of art, and it is really because China has produced the greatest artists that he believes her to be invincible. When he talks of China, emotion enters so quietly that at first it is a vision. He is still the young lover adoring his first mistress, incapable of finding fault with her and so enamored of her that he would follow her to the ends of the earth.

February 7th. Coming down the Wang Lung Men steps this evening, I had an impression that I was in Elizabethan England. The masts and ratlines were etched against the misty blue river. Half-naked coolies, with immense yellow chests, were carrying casks of cement up the three hundred steps. The masts of ships were flowing past, and the noises of the city came down the stone steps, muted it is true, but still so vibrant that they resembled the calls of the London street vendors. Here, as at Greenwich and Battersea, houses are built on piles. Here at low water small mat-sheds are erected, and by the light of red candles you can buy horseflesh and rice, barley and rice, those yellow chickens which dangle from strings with their entrails hanging out, headless pigs and the bleeding heads of pigs killed only a few moments before. You can sit on a baulk of timber and watch the world passing in the candlelight, and you notice—though you must have noticed it before—that everything looks more beautiful in candlelight, and even the blood dripping from the mess of bones in the pig's neck is resplendent. There in the corner you will notice a teahouse, where thin transparent glasses are filled with bright green tea, and leaning against her husband's shoulder a weary girl who can be no more than seventeen unbuttons her dress and feeds the half-sleeping child on her lap, and you are surprised to notice that in the candlelight the color of her breast is bright gold. Over there is a young merchant who smokes a cigar and plays endlessly with the gold

chain of his watch, and from time to time he looks toward the
blackened roof of the ferry station, sighs and watches for the green
light of the approaching ferry. But the ferry is delayed, and the green
light is still shining in the mist on the farther shore.

Through the teahouse small boys come running with the evening
papers. The papers are dark brown in color and miserably printed,
but their faces shine like apples and their bare shoulders move with
ease and ingenuity among the crowded tables. They cluster round an
old man with a wizened forehead, who holds a long-stemmed pipe to
his mouth, and they wait anxiously and desperately while, from the
folds of his voluminous gray silk gown, he extracts a brown fifty cent
note so frayed that you expect it to fall to powder in his hands. A
blind beggar enters, led by an extraordinarily beautiful girl in pigtails.
He sits down quietly on the only available chair, mutters into the ear
of the girl—for the blind are as secretive as the deaf—and waits for
his tea to be served, and all the while he taps his stick. The waiter
pushes through the dense throng of tables. He is a short man, but
powerfully built, with a heavy mustache and immense antennae consisting of three or four hairs wound together, springing from a rasp-
berry mole. He is bright yellow, not gold, the bright pasty yellow
which you associate with anemia and jaundice, and he is yellow from
the roots of his hair to the creases of his rolling stomach. He lifts the
pewter teapot above his head, and a stream of perfectly white or
silver water pours from a height two feet above the cup, resembling
the trajectory of a silver bullet. He does not smile. He is an autom-
aton. When he hears a voice demanding tea, an incomprehensible
sound is vomited from his mustache, and he makes his way with the
deadly aim and earnestness of a sleepwalker across the room. He has
no preferences. The young prostitute with the oily and ringleted hair
is served almost at the same moment as the famous banker, who was
recently appointed to the highest post in the Stabilisation Board. The
sound of the small teahouse is like an inferno, or like that rumbling
which I am beginning to associate, ever since I first heard it in
Barcelona, with the sound of subterranean dynamos working at full
pressure. There is no pause, or rather a pause is the signal for an
increased volume of sound. And all the while, like a deadly mono-
tone, a half-naked beggar whose legs have been cut off above the
knees and whose sores are still covered with bright green scabs,
whines at the entrance of the shop.

Over the dark misty river the green light of the approaching
paddle steamer comes nearer. You notice it, and at the same moment

fifty other people notice it. They stream out of the tea shop like
viscous lava, flinging decayed notes on the rush tables, pushing and
shouting, the young girls clutching their babies and attempting to
safeguard them from the pressure of the surrounding crowd. The
landing-stage is like a maze, guarded at both ends by policemen with
bayonets and green *papier-mâché* helmets. You struggle down one
side of the maze, and the wave of struggling people pushes you
toward the other. The wooden gates are opened; you throw yourself
down three feet into the utter darkness of the ship's deck, muttering
under your breath at the youths who have jumped over the rails and
taken the only available seats. A small yellow candle burns in a socket
nailed to the iron funnel. Everyone is good-tempered, and everyone is
weary with the day's work; and watching the black water and the
occasional spurts of silver spray which come from the paddlewheels,
admiring the yellow lights of the city as they recede in the distance,
you begin to compose yourself for the struggle ahead. On the farther
shore there are no teahouses; there are small half-naked boys whose
bodies shine bright red in the light of the bamboo torches they hold
in their hands, and steep rocks, and perilous pathways along the
water's edge. You brace yourself for the inevitable shock which comes
when the ship's fenders break against the wooden deck of the floating
stage. You pray humbly and earnestly that the sound of the screaming child will not everlastingly fill your ears, and you admire in the
darkness the curve of a girl's neck and the flowing beard of a scholar.
A boy, with the face of a dryad, offers to take your baggage up the
steep cliffs. You argue with him, but you know that there is so much
charm in his movements and in his smiles that you will inevitably
accept his price; and when the shock comes, and you are climbing the
steps cut out of granite rock, holding a flare in your hand like a blood-
red banner, you know that now as ever you are not in Chungking but
walking at night among the ghosts of Elizabethan England.

February 11th. In a house off Liang Lou K'ou I have met a living
Buddha. He wore a loose Chinese gown and a small black skullcap,
and except for his rosary he resembled any one of a thousand Chinese
you can see in the streets of Chungking. His face was perhaps a little
thinner and a little darker; his eyes were small and very black like
olives, and he smiled with such serenity that it was impossible not to
smile in return. I bowed very low, and it was curious to watch how
the others who were present also bowed low, making a slight genu-

flection. An old Chinese, whose thin frayed white beard resembled a white feather in the wind, seemed to be overcome with emotion, and for a long while he gazed into those burning black eyes. There are, I believe, seven living Buddhas in China, Mongolia, and Tibet, and according to the *hutukhtu* "there are others whose names are not known." The living Buddha spoke a few words of English and smiled happily when he said, "Good morning," although it was already late in the evening. Except that he remained incredibly still, he was not unlike the other Chinese in the room; and his voice was softer and gentler than the other voices. He ate delicately, but with more gusto than I had thought possible in so holy a man; and when he smiled there was a trace of melancholy still in his eyes.

There are still a few rooms in China which are well decorated. The merchants, the landlords who have possessed property in Szechuan for many generations still have enough money to decorate well, and they have exquisite taste. The room was papered in gold; there were comfortable chairs; a wood fire roared cheerfully in the chimney. Servants entered soundlessly, and the curtained lampshade alone was enough to remind us that civilization was present. All the graces of life were visible, and nothing was lacking for our comfort; and yet, and yet the presence of the living Buddha made a mockery of them. So quiet he was, and with such insolence did those dark eyes measure our pretensions. All the time he seemed to be saying, "This is not life, but a mockery of life. The only life is to pray for the sins of the world."

February 13th. Professor Chen suggested that I should interview Dr. Sun Fo, the son of Dr. Sun Yat-sen and obtain his permission for the life of his father, which we are writing—or rather, the life which he will write and I shall revise if revision ever becomes necessary. We received a message from Dr. Sun Fo that he would receive me at his country house just outside Chungking at ten o'clock this morning. I was late. We could not find the house, which is perched on the top of steep hills, and besides the chauffeur insisted on believing that the house we should go to was a house some thirty miles away. It was windy and rainy. A fog crept over the city, and we could hardly see more than a few yards ahead. We climbed the steep hill, and arrived covered in mud.

In a large room, facing the river, with a blue carpet and blue chairs, a room with almost no decoration at all, we talked about the life. Dr. Sun Fo wore a blue suit and looked younger than I had imagined, very alert and at the same time shy and self-effacing. He looked very like the photographs of his father. The telephone bell rang. He disappeared behind the blue curtains and returned some moments later, saying that he had received a telephone call from the Legislative Yuan, of which he is president, but though he would have to leave shortly, there was no urgency—where were we?—oh yes, there was a recent investigation of the Sun ancestry, which tended to prove that the Sun family came from Kansu, where they were known as princes under the Ming emperors. He was not absolutely sure that these investigations offered a complete proof of the history of the family, but they were almost complete.

"In China our ancestral temples are the sources of history," he said. "Our names and often the details of our lives are recorded in the temples, and sometimes these temples are in distant provinces and we may never go to visit them. There may be four or five temples for each family, since each family during the last thousand years has moved across China." He went on to speak about recent researches in his father's life. Much of the material has been lost in the fire at the Commercial Press in Shanghai—"fire" was a euphemism for the deliberate Japanese bombardment—and much more is carefully hidden in Japanese-occupied territory. He was anxious that the life should be written so that men would see him as he was, and he spoke a little wistfully of the complexities of the political career of a man who after being president for a few days deliberately took the road of political exile.

In becoming president of the Legislative Yuan, Dr. Sun Fo had followed his father's choice, for Dr. Sun Yat-sen had insisted that the country should be governed by law and a duly elected parliament possessing the rights of recall and referendum. As president of the Legislative Yuan, he fulfilled the functions of Lord Chief Justice, and yet he looked absurdly young and resembled a scholar who has entered a government organization though he would have preferred to continue his days in a university. In the blue suit, against the blue curtains and the blue carpet, he seemed to bring with him that curious sense of self-effacement which I have noticed so often among Chinese scholars.

February 17th. Coming out of a side street in Liang Lou K'o, where two roads meet high above the cliff edge overlooking the air-

field on the Yangtse, I came face to face with the Generalissimo. He
wore a black *ma-koa* (one of those short, black, patterned coats
which all Chinese wear when they reach the age of scholars) and a
long blue or maroon skirt. His mustache is turning white; his cheekbones are high and sharp, his face thinner and smaller than I had
imagined. He walked gracefully with squared shoulders, and as we
passed he turned to a short fat little man who hobbled at his heels
and said something in a voice so sweet and feminine that I stopped
dead on my tracks and listened for dear life. But afterward there was
silence.

I had seen him before on the famous day when he addressed the
ministry of foreign affairs and upbraided them for being—I have
forgotten their crimes, but I know they were many. It was the day
when Quo Tai-ch'i left the ministry. We were walking along the
road which runs parallel to the river. The ministry of foreign affairs is
a small brown building half buried by the debris of a shattered sky-
scraper, whose broken stumps cling to a ledge of rock twenty feet
away. We were walking through the courtyard when suddenly an
immense automobile drove up, guards jumped out, the doors opened,
the Generalissimo sprang into the car and was driven quickly away.
Muffled in a brown greatcoat, he resembled the figure that I have
always had of him—mysteriously gentle, ruthless, the spirit of the
Han dynasty revived. And then that other day when a fast motorboat
surprised ours and threw up so great a wake that we were half-
drowned, and reclining in the back of this streamlined blue motorboat, smoking a cigarette, wearing a trilby hat and a military overcoat,
the figure we have seen so often larger than life was magically reduced to human proportions.

I have asked K., who knows him well, what he thinks of the
Generalissimo. K. giggled, pulled at his mustache, which he has
grown in imitation of the Generalissimo's, and burst out into a long
hymn of praise.

"But what do you really think of the Generalissimo?" I repeated.
"After all, he has himself deprecated the tendency to treat him as a
god."

"He is a very great man. . . ."

"Yes, I know, but what do you really think of him?"

Half an hour later he told me, "You saw him in that fast motorboat which takes him across the river from one of his houses among
the mountains to the headquarters of the party. The boatman is a
wounded soldier, and sometimes—especially on a moonlit night—the

Generalissimo sings in the boat. I assure you, he sings with especial sweetness, and sometimes they sing a duet, and sometimes Madame Chiang sings. He has a great love of singing." He told me of the German military adviser who lives on the south bank, and who is still paid regularly for his services in the past. "The Generalissimo is the man in China with the longest memory," K. continued. "He never forgets those who have fought him or those who have pleased him. When you meet him, you will be surprised by the depth of light in his eyes. He is great and gentle above all men, more merciful and compassionate. . . ." In another five minutes he was declaiming from the Generalissimo's speeches; and once more it was necessary to ask him to be more definite.

He burst out in surprise: "But don't you regard Churchill as a god?"

"Certainly not. We know all the mistaken interpretations he has read into the life of his distinguished ancestor Marlborough. We know nearly all his faults, and it is possible to criticize them openly in Parliament. We regard him as the best man for the job, and the wisest. But we don't speak about him in hushed voices."

"But we do—we regard Churchill as almost superhuman."

"I think you are foolish and mistaken. Surely we know by now that it is dangerous to think of men as gods."

"It is a danger we have very nearly fallen into," K. admitted. "You must remember that for a long while we possessed German military advisers, and American Methodism has also added to this peculiar attitude of reverence for our leaders. Then too, the party is extremely powerful in China, and there is little or no organized opposition. The party is the seat of all power, all industry, all effort. You must understand that we are grateful to the Generalissimo for everything that he has done for us, and we show our respect by regarding him as almost superhuman. In the political training center, which he has inaugurated for party members, that feeling is perhaps greatest; but it exists among us all, and though it is true that he deprecates it, it is also true that others encourage it. How much does he know? No one knows. A little while ago the *Ta Kung Pao* wrote: "There is a halo of sanctity and silence around the Generalissimo." The newspaper was suspended for three days, the manager made a personal apology, but still no one knows. He is a military leader, the greatest since Tseng Kuo-fan, but we are not sure that he is a great administrator. And so we live and dream of the war, knowing that it is better to be well-led in war and best to have faith in a good man."

It was night, and we were descending the Wang Lung Men steps in the mist. Far away, down river, a small motorboat was throwing up a great white wake. Was it our imagination, or did we really hear the sound of high-pitched singing coming from the boat?

February 28th. They were sowing the winter rye high up in the green hills. Ducks—the brightest-colored ducks imaginable—were wandering over the fields, and the small boy clinging to the buffalo did not shiver in the cold wind which came from the second range of mountains. There were pine trees sighing in the wind, whose leaves are beginning to shine with the color which steel would have if there were any greenness in steel. The small kernels of rye lay in the old man's hand, so plump and white that you would have said they were a small family of white mice if you had seen him gazing at them from a distance. And slowly they began planting. I know nothing of farming; I do not even know the way the seeds are dug into the ground, or how they are reaped, and so I watched him carefully as he rolled his sleeves and dipped his hand in the water. The hand seemed to stay there for a long time. He was bent down, ankle-deep in the soft slimy water in which his blue coat, open at the neck, and his round shining copper head were imperfectly reflected—an old man, but his body was young and lithe, and there was no great pain in bending. The old woman followed him with her basket. He lifted handful after handful from the small bamboo basket, and when at last every inch of the field had been covered, and his hands and his body were splashed with mud, he looked up to the sky and sighed. It was like watching a primitive festival, for at that moment the sun came out through the heavy clouds and for the first time the grey muddy field shone gold in sunlight.

Afterward we followed them to their home, the small brown cottage half-buried among the pines. When they were near the house, they came to a small stone shrine the color of old bread, very brown and no higher than their waists. There were two gods within the shrine. The paint had peeled from their faces, and their gowns, which were once gold, were a still darker brown and pitted by wormholes—as though the gilt bread had been nibbled by mice. The old woman took a red spill from the basket, lighted it, and pressed it in the little mound of gray ash within the shrine. They stood there for some minutes, gazing intently at the impassive gods. Then they went on their way, the old woman swinging her empty basket and the

old man striding forward as though he possessed the whole earth.
And after them came the small naked boy clinging to the horns of
the buffalo, his face bright red and all his body wet and shining from
the rain.

March 2nd. In the house of the American Military Attaché—surely
the warmest and most carefully decorated in Chungking—you sit
round the fire, wine is poured out, the uniformed servants slip past
on noiseless feet. Here is everything you want—good butter, books,
whisky, the choicest wines. An atmosphere of complete repose. You
can hear the radio in another room, and as though from a long way
you can hear someone speaking into the telephone. You look round
the room, the doors are painted white, there are curtains, cushions, a
strip of Chinese embroidery on a table. A long-legged youth is declaiming against the Japanese while leaning comfortably against the
fireside. We have been discussing Changsha, but already the battle is
so remote that we have only the vaguest idea of what we are talking
about. The Philippines, Malaya, Burma—they are present in our
minds, but only as even the most innocent of us are eternally accompanied by ghosts. The ghosts do not raise their voices. The servant in
the white mess jacket enters to announce that dinner is served, and at
that moment the American military attaché announces that he
had himself taken that extraordinary photograph which hangs upon
the walls. It is a photograph of Chungking—in flames. It shows
towering columns of heavy black smoke rising over the city, twenty or
thirty of these columns, and each one nearly a mile high. The shadow
of the smoke lies on the river, which seems to be broken by the
weight of the smoke hanging in the air. It is obviously a bright day,
for where there are no explosions the city is dead white, like powder.
And suddenly, as we all look at the photograph, the defensive
mechanism of our minds crumbles like the smoking, powdery city,
and the ghosts of the Philippines, Malaya, Burma, the islands in the
South Seas raise their voices. All through dinner there is a hush. We
ask polite questions, we discuss for the ten millionth time the differences between American and English words and their meanings, and
we all know that we want to return to the fireplace and the photograph of bombed Chungking.

There is a chill in the air when we return. The fire has gone out.
The photograph seems to be in movement; we can see the flames and

the black smoke-clouds climbing, and we have only to shut our eyes to see the Japanese aviators sweeping in formation over the defenseless city. You can hear the sickening thump of the bombs and the screams which break the silence between the raids, and then in this silence the Military Attaché speaking: "But the most terrible thing of all is not in the picture—people were trying to reach the safety of the south bank; there was a large boat, and the Japanese bombed it. When the Japanese had gone away, there was no boat and no people struggling on the water, there was no sign of wreckage and not even the white trace on the water which shows where bombs have been—*there was nothing at all except their screams.*"

March 7th. We have been to see Dr. Wang Wen-hao, the minister of industrial reorganization. A Dutch friend had given us a letter of introduction, and he begged us on no account to spend longer than a quarter of an hour with the Minister.

The Minister lives in a new house built over the Yangtse, a small white courtyard where a few trees planted in stone vases give an air of the countryside, and around the courtyard are small white buildings. The sun was shining. The river was pure white in the faint morning sun, and this sequestered corner of Chungking began to acquire a charm which I had thought completely lacking in the city, the charm of something small in a city of giants. And the office of the Minister was equally small—hardly larger than my bedroom on the south bank—and there were no decorations except a few maps on the walls. Through the window he could look out at the Yangtse, the small black sampans and the coolies, the black masses of people milling up stone steps—the industrial reorganization of China.

He was a small man with a brown face, deeply suntanned. His lips were thin, his forehead high; his fingers as he laid them on the blackwood table resembled the fingers of scholars, and you expected to find long white nails in golden sheaths. A terrible motor accident some years ago had very nearly broken his skull in two, but there were few signs of injury and the small face turned toward the light possessed an extraordinary calm. He was a scientist, like General Yu Ta-wei, the minister of munitions, but he had thrown himself into the task of Chinese industrial reorganization with something of the passion of a religious enthusiast. Yet he did not look weary. There were hardly any papers on his tables. In his long maroon gown, he looked perfectly at ease, smiling quietly, his hands folded on the table; and as he listened to Bergery's remarks an occasional quiet laugh would break the monotonous voices of the conversation.

Bergery asked him about the effects of the closing of the Burma Road. Dr. Wang Wen-hao laid his hands on the table, palms upward.

"It is disastrous," he said quietly, so quietly that we could barely hear him. "In A.D. 126 the explorer Chang-ch'ien opened the road toward the West. As you know, he crossed the Tarim and the Sogdhana, and visited the kingdom of Samarkand and penetrated into India. Today the road is closed, and for the first time since Chang-ch'ien left China, we we are cut off from the world except for the small supply routes through Russia. The future is dark. We are reorganizing our transport and our industries on the basis of self-sufficiency; but our means are limited and we cannot see far into the future."

He was not optimistic. He complained—not bitterly, but with a kind of proud intolerance, about the British failures in Burma. It was clear that he regarded Burma as the crux of the transport situation, and would have been prepared to sacrifice a province of China rather than let communication with the outside world be interrupted. He pointed to the maps on the wall. He showed us the centers where the greatest production was taking place, and when Bergery asked gently about the oil wells in Kansu, he made it clear that their development was as nothing in comparison with the development of oil wells in Burma. He spoke about the difficulties and the successes of Chinese industry, the extraordinary stratagems to which the Chinese were reduced in an effort to maintain production, and though he believed fully in the recuperative powers of Chinese industry, he was clearly disheartened by recent events in China.

"But we shall go on—we shall send out more and more expeditions to find whatever metals remain in the Chinese earth. We have the scientists and the workmen, and though we are fighting for time. . . ." He shrugged his shoulders. We have already been talking for an hour. He came down the steps to the doorway, looking very slight and extraordinarily young in his maroon gown, and as we shook hands he said, "Have no fear. The mistakes of the past can be rectified, but we can no longer afford to have mistakes in the future." He smiled; and while the car drove off, he stood there waving, and we wondered why so great a man should waste so much time on us.

Almost alone, he had reorganized the basis of Chinese industry. The young students going out to the northwest, the factories along the river or buried among the mountains owed their origin to him, and more than any man except the Generalissimo he was responsible for the continued resistance of the Chinese people.

I remembered the slight figure outlined against the bare branches of trees later in the evening when Bergery was looking across the silver river in the moonlight.

"Did you notice, though he was very short and almost insignificant, there was something so clearly shining in his eyes. They were like the moon. . . ."

I do not know what had come over him. A dog barked. Between the rows of dull trees a fog was ascending. In the rice fields there was all the moisture of plowed lands, the heaviness of labor and growth and grain-bearing, the sweet scents of autumn strangely transformed to winter; one could breathe them only on the bright edges of the world, on the rim of the desert, or in the center of a great kingdom.

March 10th. Last night, returning from Chungking, the boatman took me three miles down stream. It was very late, the moon was covered with clouds and the river so dark that perhaps he was in danger of losing his way. I remember that the small boat moored at last on a sandspit, and there were great rocks high overhead, and it rained dismally, and I heard his oars creaking in the oarlocks long after he had gone away. I climbed along the rocks. I could see nothing except a faint silvery-blue gleam on the river and the lights of Wang Lung Men steps. No boat passed. It was dreary and miserable, and because the sun had been shining in the morning, I had taken no overcoat. I thought of Bergery, sitting up alone in the house, reading or writing by candlelight (for there is no electric light in this small walled house in the country), and I wondered whether he had awakened the servant and whether they were climbing down to the beach to fetch me.

I wandered for hours. It was difficult to see, and the rocks were precipitous. People were sleeping under mat sheds, thin crusts of bamboo ten inches high; and sometimes in the shelter of the rock there were beggars and small children sleeping fitfully. They did not stir as I passed, but I heard them coughing. And then the dogs barked. I had come to the outskirts of a village. I was pursued by the

Furies. They barked and snapped and jumped out of the darkness till
I almost cried out for mercy against these avenging angels of silence.
And still everyone was asleep. At a large walled house at the end of
the village, I knocked on the gate. After a long while an old man
came out, and it seemed to me that I was listening to him for hours
as he hobbled across the cobbles. He opened the gate and raised the
lantern to his eyes and said nothing. He stared into the depths of the
landscape, and sometimes his lips would move, but he said nothing.
He was shivering in the rain, his eyes were wide open, and the little
tassels of his cap gradually filled with rain and turned silver. And so
he stood there, watching the night, long after I had gone.

I slept in the shelter of a gravestone, looking down over the milk-
white mist and the faint rain. There was a small plum tree in front of
me, and though I slept on and off for a few minutes, I was conscious
of the presence of the plum tree all night. I did not dare to touch it.
It was perfect as it stood there, and I wondered whether its flowers
would open with the dawn. But in the dawn the tree was black and
chilly, without buds, and the inscriptions on the gravestone were
unreadable, and I walked back to the small white-walled house in the
hills feeling like someone who had trespassed upon the night. And
even now I can hear the dogs barking, barking, barking. . . .

March 12th. In a few days I shall become a professor in a Chinese
university. Years ago I met a Chinese scholar who spoke of the
universities of Peking as though they alone possessed a passport into
the future. He would describe the laboratories, the lotus pools, the
blue-gowned students, the wealth of books, and the glory of old
Chinese architecture, and he would say, "You are wasting your time
here—you should go to Peking, which will soon be the intellectual
capital of the world. All that is best comes from the universities. And
now——" And then he would go on to talk of the vast plans of
reconstruction which were in the hands of the Chinese universities.
The youths and young girls who came out of them were building a
new life and a new civilization. He had no words to express his
admiration of them. "In my youth we were fearful, we obeyed orders,
we followed the ancient traditions, which were good and just. But
these—these young people, without any traditions—throw themselves upon the world. They are rockets, burning in the night, and
they give so great a flame that I am continually dazzled by them."

March 17th. Four o'clock in the morning. We have been sleeping in a small house facing the Chialing river, and the sounds of the mahjong players could be heard through the walls, and suddenly there were the sounds of cries, sharp orders, a terrible sound like an interminable wailing. The police had come to arrest the mahjong players, and the young poet woke up with a start and rushed outside. When he returned he was pale, and his smooth black hair was covered with glistening globules of rain.

"What happened?"

"The police came to arrest them. I wanted to see it."

"Why?"

"It's interesting, and besides—I want to know everything that goes on. I am trying to write about China. I must see everything."

He spoke of the young girls and the old men mounting the steps in the rain, their hands tied behind their backs with black ropes which had been soaked in tar, and he began to wonder what would happen to them. "They may be able to bribe themselves out, and they looked rich enough to have food provided for them in the prison. But what was terrible—really terrible—was to see an extraordinarily beautiful girl mounting the steps in the rain, with her hands tied behind her back, and the policemen saying coarse things to her. I don't play mahjong but do you know, there is nothing else to do now. All amusements have been stopped. The films are not worth seeing. We are cut off from the world. Everything is so expensive, and now there is only gambling to relieve the monotony of life."

But at four o'clock we went out into the rain. It was pitch dark. We carried torches made of bamboo strips cunningly wound into the shape of hollow turnips, and inside a small greasy red candle burned and spit with a yellow flame. There was a wind, and we had to shelter the lantern with our bodies. As we climbed down the steep steps, the faint candle threw immense flickering shadows on the walls—shadows of beggars and sleeping children, shadows of old women and young girls; and they slept through the rain and the continual beating of hammers from the small shipyard nearby. In the great darkness a small paddleboat lay moored off the landing stage, gaunt and gray, the rain shining a little on the iron roof.

And still we had to wait. We waited for a long time, a solid mass of people all sweating in the rain, while the night thickened and candles flickered continually down the stone steps like will-o'-the-wisps, for we saw the candles, but we could not see the people who carried them. It was more than an hour before a faint watery light began to streak across the sky. We sat on the iron deck of the boat, waiting patiently, listening to the squeal of ungreased wheelbarrows high up on the rocky streets. We began to distinguish the pale faces of our fellow passengers, the little girl holding a hen by the feet so that it continually knocked against the iron deck; the Taoist priest with the face of the medieval mystic and the hair wound into a greased topknot; the babies asleep against blue-veined swollen breasts; the lovers gazing into the darkness and holding hands. The smell of sweat and rust, garbage and stone. And then suddenly, in the cold morning air, the light begins to grow; the white river birds torment us with their screaming; a small boy comes on deck to feed us with salted rice cakes, and the deafening roar of the city begins to grow out of all proportion to the city's size. There are curious intervals when the roar dies down, inexplicable silences, but we have no ears for the city now, we are gazing across the river toward the first jet of sunlight which falls on the white pagoda high up on the cliffside.

And now with the increasing day a mist rises, white and tender as the mist in Chinese paintings, and over the summits of the gray-blue hills a white shaft of sunlight penetrates the clouds; and in this frail sunrise we bathe gratefully, knowing not only that the mysterious Chinese darkness, blacker than ink, has perished, but that all the frozen particles in the air will soon disappear into a faint warmth. Hot tea is poured out. Vegetables are loaded on to the galleys. The steep plates on the deck are thick with rust and curve dangerously as we walk on them, but already a great rumble, like the coughing of a dying man, is making the plates shiver and sending up streams of white smoke and froth at the sides, and already we are setting out—toward the gorges, the gray rocks, the golden sand, and the mysterious small cities. And suddenly, in that curious intoxication of morning which makes China so strangely different from all other countries, we see the gaunt rocks assume fantastic shapes; they are gray lions, purple dragons, and the frail scenery appears to be painted in deep brown and ocher on an interminable blue sheet of silk.

The delicacy of the Chinese scenery is most noticeable in the early morning, when the rocks are still insubstantial and the dreaming air still broods in an enduring sleep. Above us the city towers, washed clean by the night and the rain, and while the sun climbs still higher the granite rocks burn with a kind of luminous flame. And still, though the river hovers in faint pastel colors before us, the city retains the primitive contrasts of black and white. Small rafts are passing us; soon they will be followed by larger rafts consisting of hundreds of logs bound together, and in the center of these rafts small log houses are built and the great yellow sweeping oar rides on the stern, guided by a small boy. But there is little traffic on the river, though thousands of boats, with small red fires burning, are wedged against the shore; and the smoke from the boats is already turning the white city into the colors of the river. Soon the city disappears. We are gliding up the river, silently, hardly disturbing the water fowl; and looking over the rail we see that there are only two or three feet of water in the shallow river. We are gliding away from a dream into another dream; a dream which is eternally repeated in China whenever the sun shines in the early morning.

But the wind coming from the west across the mountains, a wind as cold as ice, brings with it the scent of the graveyards and the dust of the previous day; blows out the patched sails of sampans, and throws up small white columns of foam against the sides of the rocks. It is not a heavy wind; it seems to be bursting out of the restricted spaces of an invisible tunnel and to play fanwise on the water—but it is cold. You take shelter by stepping away from the rail, or by disappearing downstairs, where in a small cabin lined with benches, the portholes gray with mud and dust, people are lying down like so much baggage, and here and there a squat silver Szechuanese pipe, with its long silver stem and box-shaped water bowl, can be heard like the continual sucking sound of water near a well. At first you think they are opium-smokers, so engrossed they are in their pipes; their lids fast closed and their faces screwed into the shape of meditation. But they are not opium-smokers, there are no dancing girls smoking with old men, and though even the children smoke cigarettes and it is not unusual to see a child of three with a cigarette in its mouth, nothing is happening which could offend the most timid spirits.

Upstairs, thousands of things are happening at once. The water fowl are screaming; thousands of sampans with ragged white sails patched with somebody's blue trousers are bearing down on us; the sand is glittering—level reach upon level reach of sand; the fields are changing color—have changed color, for there are no more small knolls of graveyards, and in their place there are great clumps of silver-blue cypresses, green willows, oaks on the horizon, walled houses, and terrible rocks rising like immense teeth from the riverbed. Through all these things, with a clanking of chains and spitting fire and smoke from the funnel, the small paddleboat passes without the least trouble; and the eye painted on the bows does not quiver in the least.

We are deliberately and quite consciously traveling through a dream.
At every moment the landscape changes. Here are fields of winter
rye. They have disappeared. Instead of the immense hill fading into
the sunlight which you noticed a moment ago, there is only a high
white rock carved with Roman figures, to show the height of the tide
in former ages, and a small temple with a gold roof, colonnades, and
a small encircling wall. The temple has gone. You are fighting your
way through steep gorges. You feel like water—you are being poured
through the narrow neck of the gorge and you will find yourself in
the darkness of some dreaming stomach. Nothing of the sort. The
gorges disappear by magic, there are no more hills, and once more
you are basking on level shores of glittering golden sand; and you
watch the man swinging the long colored pole at the bows like someone mesmerized, forgetting that in a moment he will order you off
the boat, for the river is so shallow that she can no longer proceed
with passengers.

We wade ashore through four inches of water. The sunlight
plays on the water; and waving lines play on the curved strakes of the
ship. You notice with a feeling of surprise that the paddleboat is
floating in three and a quarter inches of water, and you ask yourself as
you climb on the rocks what will happen if a gust of wind turns the
boat over. For every year there are accidents on this river; so many
ships have been lost that passengers are officially warned to be fatalis-
tic; and though the sunlight shining mistily on the bamboos and the
cedars shines with a light which seems to be reflected, and though
you have noticed the most extraordinarily colored rocks just beneath
the surface of the river—rocks which are bright green or bright
orange, veiled with velvet moss of all colors—you are sufficiently
conscious that the dream might end at any moment to realize that
there is no safety on Chinese rivers. Do you want evidence? You have
passed seven junks with only their masts and a part of their bows
sticking out of the water. Some of these junks are green with age,
small boys bathe from them, and they have become an accepted part
of the landscape, and even their number does not terrify you in this
mist-frail morning. But while the paddleboat carves its slow passage
between the small rocks and the shelving sand, you are glad you are
on dry land.

As though the scenery were determined to make you believe that
you were dreaming, you notice that there are no seasons. There are
rice and barley, horse-tooth beans, winter rye, green radishes, clusters
of bamboos in all colors ranging from the innocent green of the

young shoots to the stately brown of old age. There is no sunlight; it is all moonlight—with a golden moon. How long it will last you have no idea, and you do not care; the river alone will bear you along through the wondering enchantment of the strangest moonlight you have ever seen.

We sit and talk under the awning, watching the small white temples to the earth gods as they sail past, very white against the green hills. You pay no more attention to the extraordinarily beautiful cedars on the distant hills than to the rafts wheeling in a white millrace or the flicker of the colored pebbles in the river disturbed by the iron paddles. Everything is reduced to the level of a single enchantment; and as the sun grows hotter and the fumes from the funnel crowd down upon you, the enchantment does not lessen—it increases by infinitesimal degrees of prestidigitation. The "perilous seas forlorn" are three and a quarter inches deep, and Ruth is still wandering in tears amid the alien corn under a marble pagoda. But it is the small white temples to the earth gods, and high up on the hills the bright yellow walls surrounding the farmhouses, which attract our attention. There are places where thousands of barges are moored, and other places where the air is sweet with the blue-gray smoke of lime. All along the left bank of the river there are limekilns, where white cliffs of chalk can be seen among the bright green cedars. Small boys hover over the red fires under the brickkilns, and there are so many of these fires that our progress down the river is lit with these incandescent flames. Occasionally there are villages. You recognize them first from the distance by the great sloping wall down which the merchandise of the villagers is slipped into waiting boats. There are coal mines, potteries, basket-makers, innumerable farms, and you have no need to wander in the villages to see the things they manufacture; for everything is prepared for you along the riverbank, and every sampan is being heaped with merchandise before your eyes. The green cedars, the white rocks, and the blue river under the towering skies are things which you know you will remember, even if the strange shapes of the sampans with their high sterns and long sweeper oars did not make it inevitable that you would remember the journey. And meanwhile the birds, great white river gulls with yellow beaks and wings as silver as the wings of herons, coast around the stern of the paddle steamer, where food is being cooked and an enormous copper cauldron is seething with soup. The landscape has changed beyond recognition. It is no longer Chungking, or anything approaching Chungking, and it is only when the haulers come again into view that you realize the hardships of the land. The ship they are drawing is far out in midstream, and they themselves are wading thigh-deep among the loose stones; and though the river is low, there are whirlpools and high rocks in midstream, so that sometimes they have to bend and strain against the thick ropes of palm fiber slung across their chests. A man stands amidships beating a wooden drum, standing on a platform which makes him visible to the world. The long slings are jointed to a sliding crown on the masthead, and when the mast is bending and creaking with the strain, he puffs at his pipe and renews the tattooing on his drum—but it is a different tattoo, sharper and more insistent, and almost like a cry of pain. The haulers wait. They stand there in the water, seeming naked, mopping their sweaty brows and cursing the delay; and then once more they crawl on all fours, resembling otters in a stream, only their heads visible above the level of the glassy river.

I have been watching the haulers for a long while until it seems that I am myself a hauler, wearied beyond endurance by the weight he carries on his back. I am straining fiercely against the current; my feet are bleeding; I am hungry for rest and weary of toil. For ten, twenty, thirty years I have walked along the banks of this river, until I recognize every stone and tuft of grass; and the weals on my shoulders have healed only because they are tired of festering, and even the beauty of the river has no meaning for my eyes. I am sick of the river, and yet I know more of the river than the foreigners who travel on the steamers. I know its changing caprices and the face of its storms, its hollow echoes and its merciless confusion of beauty. I know that it will not pause if I drop dead. I know that there are kites and vultures overhead; and graves on the slopes of the cedar-clothed hills. I know no end to suffering. *Ai-ya! Ai-yee! Ai-ya! Ai-yee! Ai-ya!* . . .

And suddenly, turning among the hills and the ravines, we saw the sun streaming down between high green cliffs, a mist floating lightly on the gorges. We are already in sight of Peipei. The wind turns sharply as we leave the gorge we have been traveling through behind; and coming at last to an estuary, with green hills on one side and a sandy, stony beach on the other, with red-brown houses perched on the granite rocks, and field after field of cedars, we know we have come to the end of the journey. The steamer will go on, but it will leave us at the dock. The sun shines. There are thousands of small booths on the shore, and the deserted river is once more filled with small boats bobbing on the immense glassy wave which our bow sends toward the shore. I have been looking for the university—it is not large, a few small whitewashed buildings facing the village and perched above a sandy cliff. I would not have noticed them if my companion had not pointed them out.

March 18th. Peipei is a small town, consisting of three streets joined together like two letter L's, yet in all Szechuan it is hardly possible to find so many educational institutions. There is an academy of music and ballet, the Kansu Medical College, three or four middle schools, the Sun Yat-sen Institute for the Advancement of Culture and Education, the bureau of the School of Compilation and Translation, the headquarters of the Geological Survey and the Geodetic Survey, a school of science, and three or four other schools, and not far away there is the building where the Legislative Yuan decides upon the laws of China. And yet, when you first come to the village, there is no sign of all these institutes of learning. You see small fields among the mountains, ripening yellow wheat, brown glistening paddies, green seed-beds and vegetable plots climbing the rolling green hills. There are few trees, for here as elsewhere China has been denuded of her trees by the ravages of house-builders; and there are few children. The spring crop of wheat, barley, rapeseed, and peas is being gathered; the horse-head beans are purple; the cabbages are still tender green. You walk down the main road, dusty with a luminous bright dust, passing the ghosts of rickshas whose wheels are patched beyond recognition and whose hoods are ribbons of greasy yellow cloth, and in two minutes you are out in the country. There was a village here in the T'ang dynasty, and perhaps long before; and it is difficult to think that the village can have changed. The same blue-yellow ducks were floating on the ponds, the same sycamores and elms were sheltering the rice fields from the wind, the same goats and pigs and fowls were scrabbling in the mud on the edge of the fields. The air is sweet, as always in places where the river opens after being constricted between high rocks; and though the houses are poor and the peasants look poorer, you are surprised to notice the number of distinguished scholars who walk away from the village street with their cotton bags filled with the purchases they have made in the crumbling shops.

The scholars here are desperately poor. Their loose gowns are patched with ill-matching colors; their shoes are down at heel. A bus roars past, swallowing them up in purple wood-oil vapor, but they do not care. They have been here for years; they have taught in the schools, translated the classics of foreign languages in the Bureau of Translation and Compilation, which was founded more than eighty years ago; and they are still poverty-stricken. Early this morning, when I came out onto the great square facing the river, I saw hundreds of middle-school students exercising in the rain. They formed fours, bent their knees, lunged out with their arms, and ran around the square like young gods, or rather like young goddesses, for afterward I noticed that they were only girls. They wore white trousers and thick woolen sweaters, and they raced with an ease and a grace which I would have thought impossible so near to Chungking. I have seen nothing like this in the capital. Their breaths came in white bursts and the rain fell on their upturned faces, and they looked so young and graceful that for a moment I imagined I was again in Bali. Afterward, they broke ranks and wandered schoolward, their hands deep in their pockets, striding with perfect freedom like goddesses through the rain.

March 19th. It is still raining, and the white walls and gray tiles of the university have turned black as soot. Here the buildings are low and small; the mud lies thick round your ankles; in the cold unheated rooms the students shiver in the wind coming down from the mountain. They look ridiculously young, and yet they do not walk with that extraordinary grace which I saw yesterday on the field. They have come to years of responsibility, and perhaps their studies are harder. There are students from every province of China—the broad cheekbones and broader foreheads of Mongolia, the dark eager faces of Kwangtung in the south, the beautiful ivory pallor which I shall always associate with Soochow, the red cheeks of Hunan, and the solemn beauty of Peking.

I came over in the ferry this morning in the sweeping rain, plunging through mud down the slopes of Peipei, past the enclosed bamboo matting of innumerable sleeping sheds, amazed by the skill of the boatman, who knew every reef and found his way through all the currents. A mist was trembling on the green hills; the gorges on either side were invisible. Alone in the boat with the boy ferryman, I felt like one of those boatmen in Chinese paintings of the Sung dynasty, who find themselves lost amid encircling hills and an encompassing mist, and dream of the lotuses which they could pluck if they were not so busy singing on their lutes. The mist hid everything except a trace of green, and on this smooth wake the exertions of the boy seemed unnecessary and even vulgar, for there was no visible current, and nothing by which we could measure the movement of the boat. We came ashore nearly a mile from the university, and I walked along the riverbank, straining to see the land on the other side. There was no land. The river is rising. Occasionally, very faint, there was a silver gleam like the spin of a coin in the sky.

Inside the classrooms everything was as I had expected it to be. As though determined to make the gray sky disappear, the girl students wore their most colorful gowns, and even the drab blue gowns of the men shone in this dusky twilight. But what was even more delightful was to notice that though they were shivering in the cold, they looked well fed and there was no sign of the grayness of the faces of the people in Chungking. I gave my first lecture, feeling very nervous, wondering whether they could understand a word I said, and watched them as they walked out in the rain with a feeling of elation. In their smooth jawbones and fine eyes there was a keenness which I had not yet noticed in China, and I was delighted at the thought of staying among them. I looked at my watch. It was ten minutes to eight in the morning. I felt that I had spent the whole day either wandering in the mist or talking to students.

March 20th. Nearly all the books in the library were lost when the university moved from Shanghai. I have been browsing in the library while the rain falls in torrents outside. Outside, a few wet pigs, black and steaming, swelter in the rain, and the silence of the room is broken only by the bugles which announce the hours. One of the librarians, who wears a tattered black gown, was the son of a duke who received his dukedom under Yuan Shih-kai. He is a scholar. He looks out timidly through thick eyeglasses at thin rows of books on the shelves and sighs deeply. "You should have seen the library in Shanghai—ah, that was something to talk about." I console myself that there is a complete edition of the *Encyclopedia Britannica,* and if necessary I can read it right through. The rain falls, and in a small room leading off from the library someone is singing in a high fluted voice a Chinese poem about the rain.

March 21st. The sun shone for a while this morning, and I watched huge clouds of smoke rising from the grasses. D. has taken me to see the farms which belong to the university. Pigs and sheep are kept;

there are sheep browsing in the meadows, and the cows are calving. I have been to four universities, but I have never seen a farm so close to the place where scholars study, and the rightness of this arrangement is so pleasant that I can hardly tear myself away from the fields to attend my own lectures. "There are fifty different kinds of citrus plants," D. tells me. "We are experimenting on new kinds of tea leaves; we are making vinegar and preparing plans for increasing the productivity of our fields." He is young, with a high forehead, and though he stoops like a scholar, he walks with quick easy strides through the mud, delighted because I have fallen completely in love with the duck pond and alarmed whenever I show my ignorance of Chinese fruit.

"Oranges came from China—the original 'sun-kist' oranges came from Szechuan, and these lemons——" He crushes the leaves of the lemon trees between his fingers and holds them to his nostrils. "Our lemons are sweeter than yours, and our potatoes are sweeter, and everything is sweeter." He is so pleased with the fruits coming from the Chinese earth that he is almost prepared to swear that olives were first known in China. "At first we wanted to have the agricultural produce in the hands of the students, but they had no time, do you understand, and there was labor trouble, and the students' food is not good enough for hard manual labor, and so we employed local labor. They are not the best material for scientific farming, but what else could we do?" He was annoyed beyond measure when he noticed evidence of blight on the winter cabbages. "They were good a week ago—useless now, except for manure." And all the while he was rubbing the sharp-pointed glistening leaves of the lemon trees between thumb and forefinger, shouting with sheer joy at the productivity of earth.

"Soon the hills will be covered ten feet high with Indian corn; there is nothing so good as a hot Szechuan summer with the Indian corn sprouting so quickly that you can actually watch it growing. And then this part of the world, do you know, is more productive than anywhere in Europe. We have two, and sometimes three crops of rice, and every inch of the land is cultivated." He talked about the hookworm disease which attacks farm laborers who wade knee-deep behind their plows. Their bellies become swollen with the worm, and their legs are distended as though they were suffering from an elephantiasis or varicose veins. "The university is studying it—we are trying to find ways to prevent it. We are experimenting all the time." It was not strange to hear these words. I had heard them before in

Chungking, but here at least they were wholly convincing. This small university, with its pathetically simple and inadequate equipment, is conscious of its own importance and experimenting all the time.

April 4th. I do not know why I have delayed so long in meeting the dean of the faculty of law. He lives in a small house facing the river, which is also the headquarters of the magazine which is edited from the university. More than anyone I have met he resembles the Chinese scholar of my dreams. He is lean and thin-boned, and his hair is turning gray; his fine eyes are continually lit with little dark flames, and he speaks precisely, with a minimum of gestures, as befits a famous lawyer. At one time he was a judge of the Supreme Court under the Peking government. In later years, when he ran a school in Shanghai and lectured at the university, he was counsel for the defense in the Court of the International Settlement when three Chinese gunmen were put on trial for the murder of a Japanese consular official. At that time his life was worth nothing. Threatening messages came from the Japanese, who ordered him to throw up the case. He refused. With a passionate devotion to justice and an equally passionate devotion to his country, he continued to act in their defense.

The small room was colder than any room I have ever been in. Through the concrete floor moisture seeped. There were papers everywhere—bound copies of the magazine he edits reached almost to the ceiling, and there were no other ornaments to the bare room. There were paper windows which were torn to shreds. He wore European clothes which were torn at the elbows, and his shoes were down at the heel; and yet, so great was the impression of pure sincerity and even of majesty which he conveyed that it was only long afterward that I noticed the discomforts of the room.

He spoke about the university with more affection than anyone else. There had been complaints that the university had failed to maintain the standard it reached in Shanghai. Poverty-stricken, it had attempted to remain a private university to the last; but in January this year it was incorporated into the system of national universities endowed by the ministry of education. He had watched the university through all the crises. He had accompanied it overland from Shanghai to Peipei, and he possessed for it the devotion which is reserved only for bachelors who have a passion for learning. But this morning he refused to talk about the history of the university, and spoke instead of the long tragic exodus from the coast. The present Minister of Education had saved it from extinction by giving large sums of money from his own purse in order that the university should be transferred in safety.

"In those days life was cheap, and so was food. We could live comfortably on our salaries, and the students looked well fed. When we came down the Yangtse, we could buy two hundred oranges for two dollars—as many as we could carry away. Today oranges are eight dollars each, and everything else has gone up in proportion. We could manage the university on ten thousand dollars a year; today a university costs the government an unlimited number of millions, for the students are fed free, the professors are paid from government funds, and even the doctors and the medical supplies are paid for by the government." There was no bitterness in his voice. He was happy there, but he was deeply concerned about the professors who possessed large families. "How do they live? No one knows. It is difficult enough for the students, but it is still more difficult for the professors. The President lives in an old farmhouse, where the rain leaks through the roof. In the old days a professor could afford a car; today he is penniless, and at the same time he is supremely happy, because he knows that his job is worthy of him."

He spoke for a short while about his defense of the Chinese in Shanghai. I asked him what happened in the end, but he shrugged his shoulders.

"The judges did not dare to pass sentence, but the Chinese boys were held in prison. We arranged that they should be fed, for as you know in Chinese prisons the feeding arrangements are very primitive. But they disappeared—no one knows what happened to them."

Above all, he liked to talk about the history of the university. Fuhtan University was one of the oldest in China, where the age of universities is still measured by decades. There were universities in the Ch'in dynasty, more than two thousand years ago, but though the ancient traditions have been carried through, the modern Chinese universities prefer to regard themselves as newborn. Dr. Sun Yat-sen had been one of the founders of the universities, but even before the revolution, under a famous Christian scholar, the students had worked for the emancipation of China. Students from Fuhtan had died during the revolution, and it was perhaps for this reason that Sun Yat-sen provided the university with a plot of ground in Shanghai and became an honorary president. At first the university was supported by grants from overseas Chinese; and though its character was now changing, and it was no longer a university dedicated to the sons of businessmen, the tradition of the founders was still visible in the large faculties of finance and economics. The dean of the faculty of law wanted to see it broaden out. He wanted it to become one of the great institutions for scholarship and scientific experiment; and it was clear that he dreamed of little else except the enlargement of the scope of the university.

We walked out into the garden. It was already getting late, and the moon was rising clear over the hills. The Chinese flag had been removed from the flagpole at sundown, and now everything looked bare and deserted. In the river the last sampans were moving to shore. He picked up a small leaf from a plant that grew in profusion on the edge of his small garden.

"It is a sensitive plant," he said. "You touch it, and at once it curls up in fear. We are like that. During this war we have shown that we have tough exteriors and can fight with the best, but underneath this superficial appearance you must realize that we are farmers and scholars—in three generations the scholars become farmers, and three generations later the farmers become scholars. The fabric of Chinese civilization was as delicate as a spider's web; and so you can understand that the death of one man can shock us so much that we grow afraid of the future."

April 7th. Walking up the steep hill behind the village near the university, we looked down at the green rice fields and drum towers, and there in front of us lay the white sails of the sampans rippling in the breeze. They were so white, and they shone with such excitement, clapping their sails and dancing in the wind, that we were for a moment astonished. I have never thought this village was anything but hideous. The narrow streets are covered with stone slabs which are often broken, and sometimes at night your foot slips down into the running filth which creeps below the slabs. The children look diseased; they are thin and pale and underfed. The black pigs, snorting lugubriously in the dark shadows, are as menacing as the filth underfoot, and the shops are tawdry beyond words. Though in Chungking a beneficent government has outlawed the tea shops, there are more tea shops in this village than I have ever been able to count; and new ones grow like mushrooms overnight. But suddenly, standing among the fields and looking over the curved roofs of the houses, the white sails took our breaths away.

China is a place where beauty appears unexpectedly. The proportions of a curving roof, a girl smiling sleepily in a doorway as she whisks the flies away, a child riding a black pig bareback, three old women walking arm-in-arm through a mist-laden field, the clean curve of a plow as it comes dripping from the earth—all these have the quality of everlastingness. If you search for them, you will never find them. They come so suddenly that you are overwhelmed, and they have gone before you can photograph them in your mind.

April 21st. Bergery arrived this morning, having traveled all night by pony along the riverbank. It was very typical of him, but he looked tired—he had been caught in the rain—and the *mafu* was evilly disposed, a one-eyed man with an expression of pure malevolence. Bergery insisted on making the journey, calling the *mafu* by all the names of Eblis; and the *mafu* followed him with surly patience.

I have taken Bergery to see the president of the university, an old man, already a little tired, with the eyes of a young bird. They shook hands, sat down to discuss the future of universities in China, and completely forgot my existence. Bergery looked at the colored maps on the wall. "We shall have buildings here—and here—and here——," the President kept on saying. I have never seen Bergery look so much the child. He asked questions in bad Chinese, and was answered in the most correct and lucid English. Some students came in. Bergery leaped up and made a low bow, which amused the students and set the girls giggling. He was perfectly at ease, and when the President suggested that he should make a speech in the barnlike amphitheater, all wooden beams and boll-weeviled timber, he complied at once, asking only that he should first be allowed to browse through the *Encyclopedia Britannica.*

He made the speech in the afternoon, introducing himself with a few words of apology in Chinese. He spoke of the prospects of peace and the place of the universities after the war. He drew a picture of peace so eloquent that we wondered why the war had not ceased ten years ago, a peace in which students, farmers, and artisans were described as the leaders of the future, a peace in which there would be food enough for all, there would be no beggars, no one would be poor, but on the contrary everyone would be so extremely rich that they would be continually dazed by their good fortune and by the fate which allowed them to be born in the world. It was a speech such as I have rarely heard, for it was passionate and scientific

at once, and at the same time it was prophetic of mercy and redeem-
ing love. The gaunt head on the rostrum, the long face, the dark eyes,
and the unmanageable streaks of gray hair which wound round his
temples fascinated us; and when it was over I was amused to see the
students crowding around him and begging for his autograph.

I can remember very little of the speech. A few isolated phrases
which numbed us with expectation of glory, a few sentences of
impassioned hatred against those who had made this war possible, a
few revelations about the progress of the war which came to us like
the strokes of lightning in a clear sky. And then the extraordinary
hammer blows of the peroration:

> The mania which has descended upon us now belongs to an
> epoch outside history; and we who live in the world and outside
> history must find the road back again to history only by the most
> terrible hardships. You have proved that you are not afraid of hard-
> ships, but I must warn you that what lies before you will be still
> harder. The world is hard; all things—beauty, the grace of children,
> understanding and learning—are hard, harder than you have ever
> imagined. I have not come to make you think the world is easy.
> There is heroism only in combating the enemy, and the enemy lies
> in ourselves, in our love of ease, our tiredness, our terrible weariness
> of our responsibilities. But today the war is almost over, and you will
> have your rewards. Forgotten by the outside world, you will suddenly
> be remembered. You will live in a flowering land, and by your suffer-
> ings you will make yourselves known. So it is in the world. The terrors
> are always followed by peace. The moon shines in the cloud-littered
> sky on the night of the murder. The way is hard, but there is hope
> and perfect beauty to be found on the road. I have only one more
> message—work; love the sun; make small groups of friends among
> yourselves, such groups as can never be broken; meditate.

There was thunderous applause, but I doubt whether anyone
understood what he was saying. Fascinated by the spectacle of a
famous war correspondent, who was only too obviously ill and excited
beyond words by being among Chinese students, they returned his
almost visible adoration, and begged him to stay. He has not yet
decided whether he will remain.

In the evening we talked of his plans. He would like to remain
somewhere near the university, on a high mountain overlooking the
river, surrounded by books, attended by two or three servants and by
bearers who could take him down the mountain whenever he would
like a change of scenery. We have not once mentioned the fact that
he is obviously dying.

April 22nd. He is still behaving like a young child. This evening I found him among the shallows near the river, talking with the students. They were perched in the shadow of the rocks, and while he told them of his adventures, they listened openmouthed. But often he would insist that they should tell him of their adventures, and then the tables would be turned, and he would listen openmouthed to the unsung heroes of the Chinese wars.

In the evening I took him to the village, where there is a school of ballet. I had told him nothing about the invitation I had received. We walked down a lane where the ducks shone in the pools in the red rays of the declining sun; and suddenly, as we passed a grove of alders, the small white stone cattlesheds beside the road burst into music. I cannot explain it otherwise. We were walking quietly, listening to an old woman in the distance who was flogging her pony, when suddenly the air was filled with music from four or five pianos and violins. He was utterly thunderstruck, and so excited that he kept saying, "No, this is nonsense, it can't happen, even in China where miracles are apparently commonplace." Inside the cattlesheds we found a famous Chinese dancer in black tights, surrounded by her pupils. They were all very young, and some of them were extraordinarily beautiful.

"What are they doing?" he asked from the seventh heaven.

"They are practicing a ballet," she answered, and spoke of the ballet school of Kurt Jooss in England, where she had been trained; of Dartington Hall; of Irina Baronova; of the Russian ballet in all its glory and mystery. It seemed so odd to Bergery to find, in a remote village in China, portraits of the women he had seen in the crowded theaters of London, Paris, and New York, and he looked at the photographs on the wall with the weariness of an old man who sees the loves of his youth returning in all their glory. The Chinese children fascinated him. "They have no bones," the ballet mistress said, twirling a great ball of twined wire which apparently demonstrated the positions of the body. "I think we shall make a ballet in China as great as anything produced out of Russia. They come to us very young. We train them in music, painting, and drawing; we have complete control over their lives. They are like nuns dedicated to beauty, and if you come again to China in five years' time you will see the old Yuan theater accompanied by a ballet so splendid that you will wonder how it is that you have never seen such beauty before."

She spoke in the language which Bergery could understand, the somewhat hyperbolic language of the recently converted. She told us that it was by the order of the Generalissimo that music and ballet dancing were being encouraged; that the money on which all the students lived came from the Ministry of Education, for they were all too poor to support themselves. There was a small spindle-legged girl with dark eyes and an oval face who looked exactly like the early portraits of Pavlova. There were three or four small urchins dressed in ribbons who looked as though they were already prepared to take the stage and dance until they dropped dead. It was late when we left. We heard the booming of the drum and the faint music of the violins as we passed down the deserted road.

April 24th, Market Day. In the little village there are three market days a week, but every day is different. There are days when you see immense bluish-white slabs of broken salt and round bamboo trays filled with every variety of yellow beans, melons, grapes, sunflower seeds. There are other days—usually stormy days—when you see only immense heaps of patched clothing, rusted locks, silver toys, herb doctors, dentists, quacks. There are an extraordinary number of quacks, who will tell your fortune and discover your ailments by the most incredible numerology. As we went through the dim-lit cloud-covered streets, we saw an old peasant with his trousers hitched up to his thighs—old, grayish thighs, the color of mud and swollen with hookworm. He looked weary with pain, but when the street doctor pushed a silver needle into his thighs, his face brightened, and it was evident that the pain had gone. There was a little blood, and the doctor wiped it away with some brown paper. A moment later he pushed a needle into another part of the thigh. The needle slipped out and fell in the mud, but he wiped the mud away on his sleeve, blew on it, and once more inserted it into the wound, and once more he brushed away the little flakes of blood with an old torn piece of brown paper. The peasant did not die. An expression of intense happiness came over him; he smiled and shook with happiness, and became still happier when three more needles were inserted into his leg. The sky was downcast, but the little crowd surrounding the street doctor lived in the sunlight.

April 27th. Bergery has decided to visit a temple high up on the mountains. This is not the famous temple on Splendid Cloud Mountain, where the Abbot T'ai Hsu lives with his Buddhist students, but another. It is small and almost inaccessible, but there are three or four farmhouses in the neighborhood, and he expects to be able to get all the food he requires.

We left early in the morning, when the thick vapor still hung over the river, followed by bearers and wandering along the shore, at first on level plains of sand, then clambering over rocks, and then, since the sun was almost unbearable, we took shelter in a grove of mulberry trees. After nearly three miles of walking, we came to the beach where the small covered boats sail for Pei Wen Hsuan and the rocky defiles of the gorges.

It was one of those days when a strong scented wind, coming down river, brings you the scent of orange blossom so keenly that the nostrils can barely withstand the excitement. Bergery was in good humor, joking with the students who had offered to be our guides— and yet not joking, for he possessed too great an admiration for them to let the conversation develop so quickly into laughter. A girl student had crowned him with flowers. Another fetched ripe yellow corncobs from the nearby fields, and as we unwrapped them from the dewy bluish-green leaves, they were so tempting that we began to eat them raw, after brushing them with permanganate of potash. At the bay, where the sunlight shone so brightly on the river and the sand that we were blinded, we paused for a while, taking breath, gazing at the small white orphanage which lay towering high above us on the cliffs; till at last the salt smell of the river and the hurrying sun told us that we must seek shelter in the boats covered with coir matting, and slowly we sailed down to the hot springs.

The springs are not the only hot ones in Szechuan. According to a doctor in Peipei, they have medicinal properties; and as we sailed beneath them, watching them smoke out of the rocks in great falls, we put out our hands and received an unexpected benediction of boiling water. There is perhaps nothing so mysterious as the gorges of a Chinese river. Once in the gorges, you are no longer bewildered, for you find yourself in a green lake shadowed by cliffs of all colors—here blue, here red, here crimson-lake, and there deep orange turning to tawny brown. Ragged trees, their branches sagging outward and their roots climbing out of the rocky subsoil, groan and overshadow the lake, twisting and turning according to the prevalent wind. Here there are no horizons and no sounds. These rocks do not echo; all sounds are muted between them. And in the small village which has grown up among gardens and temples where the hot springs gush out

of the earth, the thick clumps of yellow bamboos add to the silence
only the whispering of the leaves.

Bergery begged the students to sing for him. He lay at the bottom of the boat, fanning himself, gazing up at the immense depths of
bluish-white sky above, so overcome with enjoyment that he forgot to
thank them. We were perfectly content. The river, the cliffs, the
darkening air, the silence, and the thick white spiral clouds of smoke
ascending from the springs; and beyond them the long road to the
mountains. We climbed up the stone steps, passed the open-air bath
where boys were bathing naked, and found ourselves at last in a stone-
flagged garden, among rockeries and small lakes where the lotuses are
in full bloom, the red tips shining like spears and the oily green leaves
filled with quicksilver drops of dew.

There were small stone tables among the whispering elms. A boy
came from a tea house and offered to bring us tea, to the astonishment of the students, who had tried often to have their tea brought
out into the gardens and failed. It was growing late. The sun was
high above us. We had forgotten the time taken to travel down the
river, and soon it was time to climb the mountain or abandon the
journey for the day.

It was Bergery who insisted that we must abandon the journey.
He found a grove of bamboos in the afternoon where we could take
tea, and nearby some limestone caves where you could sit in the cool
shelter of the rock and meditate on the surrounding whiteness. He
found, where the mountain road begins, great blocks of stone on
which the emperor of a certain Han dynasty had caused to be engraved the ascetic features of Buddhist monks. These stones, half
buried among ferns, were known to the students, but they had never
seen them. We wandered through temples, where the folding sunlight cast shadows on the gold Buddhas and on the painted eaves and
ceilings. A temple had been converted into a school. Along the walls
there were hideous posters showing the features of eminent scholars,
and it was surprising to come upon the faces of Napoleon, Genghis
Khan, and Thomas Paine. We listened to the hungry buzz of small
children reciting the sounds of the Chinese characters they were
learning; and when night fell we wandered among the lotus gardens,
listening to the shrill cicadas and the sighing of the bamboos. It was a
night of pure magical expediency, when fireflies wander among wil-
low trees, when the river is silent and yet boats still sail down stream,
a night when the cliffs appear to possess whispering lives and the

small hot streams in the square mossy channels beside the pathways were filled with goldfish.

"It is a night to die in," said Bergery. "Tomorrow we shall go up to my temple."

He was completely happy. All the weariness which comes over people who have stayed for long in Chungking had disappeared, and on his face there was only an expression of perfect content.

April 28th. Before dawn we set out. I remember now only the blue hills we saw at the summit of the first cliffs and the girl in the red dress washing clothes in the mountain stream. It was hot, hotter than I have ever known it in Szechuan, and we walked through rice fields tilted along the slopes, while the water poured through them from the fountains high above our heads. But there was no sign of the peasants. Silence and desolation filled the air, and sometimes there were birds' wings. It was the silence of deep summer, when the earth smells of treacle and the mist still smolders on the ground.

We were carried by bearers. Their naked shoulders grew silver with sweat, and they walked with a kind of dancing motion, so that we were continually being jerked from side to side; and yet this was pleasurable, for it meant that there were moments when we could see the mountains shining clear in the heavy summer. Here there were thick groves of Indian corn, here there were walnut trees; and under the shade of the trees, while the kingfishers dipped overhead, golden and greenish blue, passing the small earth shrines where a few red candles still glittered, we saw the trees growing thicker and thicker toward the summit of the mountain, passing through so many shades of greenness that we lost count and felt dizzy already with the altitude.

"They never told me Szechuan was like this," said Bergery. "After the war we shall have posters in all the railway stations: 'The Highlands of Szechuan beckon you!'—something like that—and the thousands of people who come will never know that we came up the mountains in the silence, before them."

The scenery was magnificent. Wave after wave of ice-blue mountains, the white river smoking below, the sails of the sampans sometimes catching the light, and the silence of high summer with the hummingbirds among the trees, the lakes of rice so still in the heavy morning that they seemed to be caught up in a wave of breathless adoration. And then suddenly the rice fields disappeared: we

were on broad uplands, and there was Bergery shaking his stick at all
the imagined glory of the place, and saying: "If one has to fight wars,
it is better to fight them in China. The attack begins at dawn—no
one knows why, but it always does. And China is the only country in
the world where the dawn is supremely beautiful."

It was late in the afternoon before we reached the temple. We
were high up, the air thin and sweet; and from there we could no
longer see the sampans flickering in the broad sunlight, nor the corrugated iron roofs of the university. The gorges, too, had disappeared.
The small temple of red brick, surrounded by a crenelated grayish-
white wall covered with inscriptions, with small outriding gardens
and pavilions, shone on the very summit of the mountain, with trees
all around disappearing into the gray depths below. A servant came
out, bowing low. They said he was an old monk who had forsaken
the monastery to enjoy the comforts of matrimony, and it was surprising to see the young wife and the small child who played there on
the summit of the mountain.

We had no time to go in. One of the students decided to remain
there for a night, or perhaps for three or four days; but the sun was
already low in the sky and indeed had disappeared beyond the mountains, and even if we hurried it would take two hours before we could
reach the university by the quickest route. For a moment we saw the
dragon gates open, we heard his tremendous laughter as the books at
last burst out of the blue sackcloth bag in which they had been
hauled out of the valley; and then there was silence, broken only by
the double call of the snipe, the hummingbirds, the eagles, and the
curlews.

Halfway down we heard the moaning of panthers in the forest.
Shortly afterward one of the students turned to me and said, "It is
true that the panthers love the heights." Then I knew that Bergery
would be happy. He would study Chinese poetry; he would be visited
by the monks; he would play with the old monk's child; at night he
would listen to the sighing of the pines and the moaning of panthers
in the forests.

May 10th. I have wondered for a long time how the students live.
They are mostly poor, though they are not so poor as the students in
National Central University, which is nearer to Chungking, and
therefore nearer to the smoke and dust of the city. J. has been telling
me how he lives. He writes a few articles for the newspapers; his

poems are being published in the poetry magazines which are springing up in every city and parish; he earns a little more by acting as a
librarian in a small community library in the village; he has a few rich
friends among the students who invite him to sumptuous meals, and
an uncle in Chungking who remembers him occasionally. "But it is
so terribly unfair," he complains. "There are students who are so
poor that they cannot even afford to cross the river. Their clothes are
the clothes they wore before the war. Even a haircut, a notebook, a
pencil may be beyond them. Because their food is bad, they lie out in
the sun, since someone has told them that they can obtain vitamin C
in this manner. Then they get sunburned and have to go to the
hospital. For the very poor students, the fates are utterly unmerciful;
the girls will not pay any attention to them, and they know they are
outcasts. What would you have them do? And even when they have
obtained their degrees, they have little hope of more than a few
hundred dollars a month. Yet they live on the most glorious hopes
that Chinese students have ever had. In two or three years they will
take part in the reconstruction of our country, and they know that
nothing is so important."

It is sometimes difficult, watching the students as they play basketball or as they study late at night under the great timber roof of
the auditorium by the small leaky flames of tung-oil lamps, to realize
how few of them are in good health. I have known a brilliant student
of philosophy who had to leave a few weeks ago because it was only
too evident that he was contaminating his fellow students with
tuberculosis. He did not complain. He spoke of returning fully cured
after the summer, and if will-power alone can cure him, he will
certainly return. When I saw him for the last time he said, "It is
necessary that we should have philosophers, and so I must work and
read and understand all that has been written on philosophy in
China and the West. We must make a bridge between these things,"
he said, and his eyes were feverishly bright. . . .

No, this is impossible. There have been only a few periods in the
world's history when students have sacrificed themselves so completely to learning. The Chinese students of the present generation
are not always brilliant, but those who are brilliant are so great that I
am continually being awed by them. They say that Chinese education has failed to meet the stress of war; and this is partly true, and in
any case it is an inevitable result of the war. The middle schools are
not good because the teachers are underpaid; there are whole

branches of the universities which are bad, and should be uprooted. But here and there, in the most unexpected places, you will find students so talented in their knowledge of science and the humanities, knowing all or nearly all that the West has to offer them, and all or nearly all of what China has given them, that one bows before them. There are professors who are tired, and there are others who have overcome their tiredness; there are students who are sick, and others who have overcome their sickness. And in all of them there is the spirit of an astounding adventure.

May 16th. There was a rumor that old Mother Chao, the leader of the Manchurian guerrillas, is living in our village. I have seen photographs of her, an old wizened woman less than five feet high, with a broad forehead and penetrating dark eyes. Three of her sons had been killed in the border fighting, but she wept only when the youngest and most handsome died. There are students here who have come from Peking and who regard Madame Chao with something of the same adoration with which we regarded Lawrence of Arabia. She was already old when the war broke out. Sickened by the behavior of some of the northern generals, who refused to fight the Japanese, she began a ceaseless war of her own. No Japanese ever found her, for she could disappear with ease among the common people; and more than once she penetrated Peking. There is a story that after a successful attack against an armament depot inside the Forbidden City, the guns were hidden in a house near the North Gate. There were so many guns that at first no one knew how to remove them, until at last Madame Chao decided that her eldest daughter should marry her eldest son. There was a wedding ceremony, and a great cavalcade of painted sedans and chairs was led out through the gates, and though a Japanese soldier tried to kiss the bride, and there were moments when they thought all would be discovered, they set out successfully toward the western hills; and in each chair and every sedan there were guns.

We have wandered all over the western bank of the river, climbing over muddy foothills, slipping and disappearing in the sand. The junks are all piled up against the shore, for it is a gray day, and only the red bell-rope tassels of the ponies and their silver harness gleam under the leaden sky. There are retired generals living near the village, and many concubines, but there is no sign of Madame Chao.

May 25th, A message from the mountain. Early this morning a message came from the mountain that Marshal Feng Yu-hsiang would be pleased if some of the professors from the university would visit him. He lives in a small house surrounded by a wattle fence, not far from the Buddhist monastery which I have never visited, on a mountain range not far from Bergery. According to rumor the small cottage was guarded by the wildest bloodhounds imaginable, and there was half a division of soldiers hiding in the surrounding woods. But we failed to see either the bloodhounds or the soldiers, for today the soldiers were given a holiday and the "Christian General" was prepared to allow himself to be defended by professors.

It was a long journey under the sun, and we were tired when we reached the cottage in time for lunch. The Marshal resembled his portraits; his great round face beamed with pleasure and he walked among the forests in an old gray Sun Yat-sen coat and with a walking stick. He is well over six feet tall, enormously wide, and with the most charming smile I have yet seen in China. He gives the impression of reserves of strength and of the most extraordinary dignity, and at the same time he possesses a quite childish enjoyment of life. We sat down at table, very quiet and dignified, discussing poetry and taking sidelong glances at the porcelain figure of the laughing Buddha on a sideboard which resembled him to perfection. The sun shone. The blue smoke from the kitchen invaded the whitewashed hall, and the murmur of conversation continued in the drowsy afternoon so long that even when everyone else had finished dinner, I was sleepily carving the remains of a chicken on my plate. With the most perfect good manners the Marshal carved an imaginary chicken on his.

We spoke of his battles and the great days of the north. When the southern army under Chiang Kai-shek invaded the northern territory of China, Marshal Feng Yu-hsiang's army was still powerful. There had been times when he might have fought it out, for no other army in China was so well disciplined. Chiang Kai-shek's army contained a sprinkling of excellent officers from the Whampoa Academy, two or three good divisions, and an incredible number of raw recruits who possessed *exactly one bullet each in their gun pouches.* If Feng Yu-hsiang had fought, he would probably have driven the Kuomintang army to the sea, as he had driven the army of Wu Pei-fu to the sea. He did not fight. He became a blood brother of the Generalissimo, the only person in the whole country who can address him as

"ti-ti," or "younger brother." He spoke of the extraordinary venera-
tion he possesses for the Generalissimo, and in halting English he
spoke about the necessity of love.

Somewhere in one of the books of Vincent Sheean there is a
description of a meeting with Feng Yu-hsiang when he was en-
camped in Honan. Feng Yu-hsiang is described as a bloodthirsty
tyrant whose use of Biblical precepts was a sham and a delusion to
outwit his enemies. It is doubtful whether anyone meeting him now
would come to the same conclusion. Feng Yu-hsiang is sixty-five. He
is not ill, but he is loaded with years; and like many Chinese he longs
for the quiet of the monastery. The days of glory are over. He will
deliver speeches whenever he is asked; but in his heart he hates
traveling about in the cloistered silence of an automobile, and only
the dramatic instinct which led him to wear two-foot-high astrakhan
caps in the streets of Peking, so that his appearance could be seen
from a distance, gives him pleasure in these days when speeches no
longer have much meaning for the hard-driven people of China. He
is content in the little wattle hut on the mountain, and likes to quote
the poems of Tao Yuan-ming. When one of the professors asked him
what he wanted above all things, he answered, "Peace."

June 1st. The summer rice must be plowed, and so they work knee-
deep in the black mud, the old peasant, the buffalo, and the peasant's
boy. The buffalo resembles one of those shaggy prehistoric beasts,
mud dripping from his shoulders, the gray muzzle half under water,
only the immense bloodshot yellow eyes sweeping from under the
curved ridge-bones of the forehead. And so they walk round and
round the small field, the black earth turning under the level of the
water in which the perfectly white clouds and the green sheaves of
Indian corn are brilliantly reflected; tirelessly, tirelessly, turning up
the black mud. The boy wears only a pair of blue sweat-soaked shorts
rolled up to the thighs, and he steps beautifully and easily in the
thick mud; but the old peasant is ponderous like the old buffalo. I
have seen the boy in every city of China: he is always the same, lithe
and strong, his face deep red, his round head shaven white and his
small mouth continually pursed for whistling. He walks with little
quick strides, and his lean yellow shoulders have a habit of rowing,
for in his effort to keep up with the other animals in the field, he
must use every muscle. So they wander round the field in the blazing

sunlight, taking no care of the shade, remorselessly turning up the earth, while a warm, sickening smell of summer sweeps up the river and steam rises from the rice lakes down the mountainside.

The slow plodding of the plowman is nightmarish; hour after hour he drives the plow through the mud. Sweat trickles down his bare chest, which is the color of wood which has wasted away in the sunlight; and the white bones shine faintly through the stretched skin. He seems to be unaware of the great heat. A kingfisher dived like a blue bullet across the field. He paid no attention to it; nor did he pay any attention to the sandy curlews on the branches of a banyan. He was content with his field. Sometimes he would pass his hand slowly across his chest, and glance at the boy with an approving eye; but in this terrible heat, the sun nearly vertical, their inky shadows as thick and black as mud, there was no need for words.

Suddenly a miracle happened—or rather. three miracles followed one another without taking breath. From somewhere near the university a white cloud of river fowl rose and scattered in the sky, shining like drops of rain, and suddenly they swung low over this field and alighted on the green banks, where parsley grows and a few lettuce; and they stayed there, wings shivering, perfectly white against the green. A moment later, as they were turning the corner of the field, the plowman lifted the plowshare from the mud; the mud dripped away, and the white blade, beautifully grained and curved, whiter than anything in this landscape except the birds, flashed in the sunlight, so well proportioned and so sharp that it resembled a knife, though made of wood. A little while later, as though weary of circumnavigating the field in the remorseless sun, the boy climbed on the buffalo's back and produced from somewhere in the rolled-up folds of his trousers a small yellow flute, which he played—and immediately, in a scurry of white wings, the birds flew away.

June 8th. The examinations are still going on, the river is still rising, the wind is still sighing through my pine trees, and we decided to rest and go upstream to the Hot Springs. There must be floods in Tibet, for the river rose so much at night that we heard the crackling of houses on the waterfront as they were dashed against the rocks; and the boatmen looked wild-eyed this morning, as though they had spent the night fighting the monster.

The beach was covered with debris and patches of soapy foam, and the field where the gliders sometimes rise twenty feet in the air was sticky with deep mud; and we walked dangerously along the cobblestones, feeling them sink beneath our feet. The boatmen were chary of taking us, and we decided to ride along the ledges of the mountains on the small ponies whose hoofs we sometimes hear at night as they strike flint from the rocks. I chose a pony with a necklace of bells, and all the way to the monastery and the springs I took a perverse pleasure in the music of the bells.

It was already afternoon when we reached the springs. We climbed down into the cool limestone grottoes and drank innumerable cups of boiling tea; and sometimes the students composed poems or sang quietly in the soft melancholy voices which they assume in the heat of the summer afternoons; and then again we descended into the limestone grotto as a preparation for visiting the temple, which is now a library, and where there are trees that sing and Han dynasty copper vases which produce sounds like the quick sigh of violins. We found the singing tree in the courtyard, below the carved steps which lead to an immense plaster statue of the Queen of Heaven. The tree was an elm, three-quarters dead, which would produce only one sound, a low monotonous sound like the withdrawing of the sea. The copper vase was more captivating. It could produce many sounds, and many patterns of water. It was laid reverently on the stone floor, filled with hot water, and the two shining copper handles were vigorously rubbed by all of us. Then dancing patterns appeared on the water, and a soft fluting sound rose and fell according to the strength of our hands or the tricks we played when rubbing the handles. There were patterns like fantails, and others like snow crystals when they are seen through a magnifying glass, and still others resembled the jewels in kaleidoscopes. While the patterns formed in the water, a thin spray from the vase hopped and hovered in our faces.

In the cool of the evening we returned to the bamboo grove and the stone tables and the cups of boiling tea. Darkness came, and the striations on the mountains on the opposite side of the gorges turned purple, and then malachite green, till at last the purple rose again and the mountains seemed to be hollow in the heavy darkness. There were no stars, for the heat of the day was so great that the air was water vapor.

Then the stars came out and grew dim again; we could hear the last of the coal coolies coming down the mountain. There are great depths of coal here, which are brought down mountain trails in wicker baskets slung on men's shoulders, or in the panniers of ponies. The cost of the coal is almost prohibitive: but in a country whose imports have been almost entirely cut off, even prohibitive costs become economical because necessary. And perhaps it was the sound of the coal cobbles falling from the panniers along the granite ledges of the mountain which made the student who was studying mining engineering speak out aloud.

"China is still unexplored. There is tungsten in Hunan, and wolfram farther north, and tremendous loads of limestone and coal in this valley. But what do we know of the vast quantities of minerals which are yet unexplored? They say there are few minerals and little oil in China, but we have only begun to explore the crust of this earth. They used to say that there was marble only in Dali in Yunnan; today we know that there are thirty immense deposits in Yunnan. They used to say that the iron ore in Hunan was of second-grade quality; today we know that there are deposits of the first quality. The government is doing everything to increase our knowledge of minerals. Already there are blueprints for the economic shape of the country after the war. There will be four great ports: one near Shanghai, another at Tzapu, another near Canton, and still another north of Tientsin to take the trade of Manchuria. And from these ports our minerals will travel all over the world. . . . "

The bamboos sighed, and the freshening wind among the pines and the immense cypresses along the mountainside. Water was rippling in the stone fountains among silver mosses shaded by datura plants, and sometimes we heard the voices of the lovers in the limestone grottoes. It was time to descend the stone pathway to the waiting boats; but still we talked about the future of China, the tremendous increase in cultivation which would follow after the war. The four great ports were a vast prize for the undiscovered hinterland: and in our minds' eyes we saw factories rising in deserts, telegraph poles, steel foundries, great blast furnaces spitting red fire against the night skies. China, the last to enter the commercial race, might find herself among the first. The recaptured islands of the Indies would for years replenish her stocks of prime commodities, and with the return of Hongkong and the greater voice which China will have in the affairs of Malaya and the Philippines and Java, there was no end to the prospects lying before her. "We have come to the crossroads," one of the students said. "For thirty years we fought the ghost of our past at the crossroads, but now from beneath the gallows where our dead past swings, we can look clear-eyed on the future. For us, it is more exciting than the future has ever been."

July 19th. We have been climbing up Splendid Cloud Mountain nearly all day. Early in the afternoon we passed through the village of Ch'in-k'an-pei, among white stone houses and immense banyan trees. The sky was molten. The sweltering heat of Szechuan rains down from a small copper-colored sun, sending all the villagers to sleep; and no one walks on the mountains. The red earth between the rice fields shines like a smooth shield. Even Liang Tsong-tai, the poet who is leading me up the mountain, complains of the *quality* of the heat, though he pretends that in his native Kwangtung the sun is stronger.

"The heat here is like a bathhouse—it is all fumes and steam," he complained; but in truth, though the heat is wet, and you feel exactly as though you were in a stifling Turkish bath, there are no fumes, no smoke, no clouds. And inside the houses the old peasants are asleep.

I have no passion for Splendid Cloud Mountain. It is too near, and we see too little of the sunlight because we are surrounded by mountains. The green mountains hem us in on every side. But as we began climbing the mountain, along a paved road where every other stone retained the characters inscribed upon it when it first became a gravestone, out of the dark village into the flooding sunlight, we achieved the exhilaration of people who are sunstruck and who walk for miles in the burning heat because they are unconscious of everything except the blinding radiance of the countryside. Liang Tsong-tai, in his leather sandals, his shorts, and his green shirt, flaunted his magnificent physique, and his bare arms worked like pistons; but already he was tiring and his small eyes looked worried. And so we climbed up, silently, wondering whether we would reach the green heights high above us, taking shelter under the tormented tung-oil trees, whose green berries are beginning to burst into fruit. And slowly we watched the river, which was so wide when we crossed it a few hours ago, disappearing until it was no more than a thin milky line etched among rice fields. To the right glinted the shadows of the fire forests which sweep up to the very summit of the mountain. Behind us lay the nestling villages, the rapids, the rice fields, and the river.

"I can walk for fifty miles," Liang Tsong-tai announced.

I did not doubt it, but I was sick of walking and the bearers who were carrying my luggage were turning pale under the sun.

"This summer I shall walk from Chungking to Kweilin," he announced shortly afterward. I did not doubt it, but I would have preferred to remain silently contemplating the landscape from the frail shadow of a tung-oil tree.

All the way up the slope he spoke of his prowess at walking. It was admirable, but I noticed with satisfaction that he was beginning to breathe heavily. The sun was disappearing behind the opposite mountains. Even then the heat remained. The stone path blistered our feet, and we lost our way once.

"There are villages in China which are forgotten by everyone," Liang Tsong-tai said, "and perhaps this is one of them. T'ao Yuan-ming, a great Chinese poet, once described a fisherman who discovered a village where everyone dressed in the costumes of a preceding dynasty and everyone was happy, but when he went to find the village again it had disappeared. I have known in Kwangtung villages which have never seen the income-tax inspectors, because they are secluded among the mountains. Perhaps this is one of those."

When we turned at right angles, crossing a small stone bridge, the village had disappeared; and perhaps indeed it is one of the secluded villages of China, for I have never seen it again.

It was growing dark. Tall trees grew above our heads. Occasionally a peasant would walk slowly in the quiet of the evening to his farmstead, or a village girl, half-asleep after her long siesta, would take a stroll. But there were few signs of life on the mountain, the trees were growing wild, and we made our way up some precipitous steps, dank with leaves, and found ourselves in an enchanted garden of tombstones and small graying obelisks, the black leaves high overhead. Soon we came to a broad high road, the main road leading to the summit of the mountain. Temple bells were ringing. We heard the beating of a deerskin drum, followed by the reverberating and ominous silence which follows always, as a sign of its accomplishment, the beating of the drum. Then suddenly, long before we had expected to see him, we saw an immense giant, shaped a little like a bear, standing in the middle of the road. He was performing exercises with his feet, according to the rule of Chinese boxers everywhere, kicking an imaginary opponent and laughing at the top of his voice. He had not seen us. It was Marshal Feng Yu-hsiang, once lord of the whole of north China and still one of the leaders of the country.

When we were some distance away, we bowed, but he paid no attention to us. The red earth road shone in the sunset. When at last he saw us, followed by the two bearers, sweating and panting as we climbed the hill, he laughed with all the strength of his immense lungs, a laugh which reverberated in the forest and frightened the birds nesting in the trees, so that they rose in a flurry of white wings.

He wore a blue uniform without medals or any sign of rank. He walked with immense strides, and yet delicately, conscious of his great strength. He was particularly gentle to Liang Tsong-tai, for though Liang was small and muscular, he was no match for the Marshal, who was tormented by the thought of hurting people, even when he shook hands. It was nearly night. He led us to a small pavilion which looked down over bare uplands to the villages in the valley. Under the eaves of the pavilion, in gold on a red board, was the inscription "The Moon-Regarding Pavilion."

The moon rose. Lights shone in the valley. The river disappeared under the shadows of the bank. There were a few monks in black gowns enjoying the spectacle of winged shadows descending on the green valley. Very faintly, like a small white square in the distance, the university collected fragments of the remaining light.

The Marshal was talking of poetry.

"Is it true that the young people in the university still read my poems?" he asked.

Liang answered truthfully, "They read them with great enjoyment, but they are trying to write different kinds of poems."

"My poems are simply poems written by an old soldier," the Marshal continued. "I have no claims to be a poet."

"Yet you have invented something which did not exist until this time," Liang replied. "You have invented a poetry which reflects the feelings of the people."

The Marshal was particularly pleased with the answer. He beamed from his immense height and spoke to the young monk standing by his side, who disappeared and returned some moments later with cups of tea, biscuits, and bread.

The night grew darker. The valley disappeared, and only the white birds sailing slowly over the uplands caught the faint light of a forgotten sun. A pale moon came out, and immediately everyone became excited. The "Moon-Regarding Pavilion" was fulfilling its purpose. We talked in hushed voices, and I noticed the young monk who had been talking to Marshal Feng standing by my side. In the moonlight he was very beautiful. He was not well fed and wore only a thin black gown, and I saw the protruding ridges of his ribs and the shape of the sunken stomach, and his bare feet in sandals shone in the moonlight like his face. He was talking about Buddha and Ananda, the cousin of Buddha, and of how they watched the moonlight riding over Benares; but I forget the story and remember only that he spoke later about T'ai Shu, the abbot who lived in a temple higher up on Splendid Cloud Mountain, and the peace and quietness of the monastery. Later in the evening I learned that the young man had been an airman before he became a monk. After leaving his monastery in Hongkong, he accompanied T'ai Shu to India and obtained the rank of *bhikkhu* or lawgiver; and now, peering through the night, where the shadows were green and gray, he looked too young to sacrifice his life in meditation, and as the moon rose higher over the waves of hills, he seemed suddenly to turn to stone, to become as monumental as the granite hills or the great oak trees, and still he remained young. His dark eyes were vigilant in the night. He listened to Marshal Feng Yu-hsiang discussing poetry with Liang Tsong-tai, and yet he appeared to be abstracted from the scene. The moon came up, a silver ibis in the desolate starless sky. We left the pavilion and walked toward the monastery, hardly talking, for the night was alive with strange visitations of moonlight. Occasionally he would point to one of the open catacombs where monks had once been buried, though like the tombs where Charlemagne's knights were buried in Alyscamps, nothing is left of their bones. Rising above the forest trees the stone stupa containing the bones of the founder of the monastery shone in the moonlight. Occasionally we saw men lurking among the trees—monks perhaps, or soldiers guarding the life of Marshal Feng Yu-hsiang, and once we heard the roar of a leopard in the hills.

Nearly a thousand years ago the monastery was famous. During the T'ang dynasty the famous artist Wu Tao-tzu painted on the walls of the monastery a fresco depicting the pains of Hell, but there is no sign of the fresco at the present day, though the remains of an earlier monastery in rough sandstone, an elephant god who has long since lost his trunk, an urn in the garden, can still be seen.

The young monk was still talking of Ananda. Another monk passed, wearing a yellow robe which fell over his left shoulder, leaving the other bare. Through the deserted lanes beneath the tall trees only the birds and a few wildcats with startling green eyes appeared to disturb the silence. The Marshal's soldiers were looking for us, and we returned to his camp.

Hidden in a grove of bamboos, surrounded by a wattle fence and reached by stone steps, each one of which retained the inscriptions of ancient tombstones, there stood the "Hall of the Empty Heart." Here in the small stockaded courtyard lit by tung-oil lamps, the sol-

diers were busy with tables and chairs. The Marshal had decided to
write a poem in praise of the moon. Paper was brought out, ink slabs
were swilled with water, a boy with a horsehair whisk stood behind
the Marshal and brushed the mosquitoes away. In the silence there
was only the faintly perceptible sound of ink brush and paper.

He waited in silence. The young monk had disappeared to make
arrangements for Liang's stay in the monastery. The Marshal had
unbuttoned his coat. Occasionally he would gaze up at the moon and
start chanting in a deep bass voice. Black letters appeared on the
moonlit page, thick black strokes which were written in so firm a
hand that one expected them to turn into tortoises, rhinoceros horns,
anything you pleased. Tea was brought out, enormous wide handleless bowls sprinkled with what appeared to be silver tea leaves,
though later they were recognizable as chrysanthemum petals. Everything was enormous. The Marshal was enormous, the bowls of tea
were enormous, the characters on the white page, and the bronze
kettle of boiling water—they were all enormous. Once again the
Marshal looked up at the moon in the sky, baying like a wild wolf, his
eyes closed, his great hand still stretched over the table and holding
the poised black brush. The poem was finished. The secretary slipped
it away and carried it into a remote room behind the stockade. And
as we drank and listened to the cicadas, the Marshal of China, who
was born the son of a baker and who assisted the Kuomintang into
power, began to sing again in the wild tempestuous voice which
comes only from the northern plains, a voice so melancholy and so
deep that we began to grow uneasy, afraid that it might be prolonged
and still more afraid that it would assemble the ghosts of the forest
from every side. And swiftly, as though he remembered that we were
tired, he dismissed us and returned to his own room, followed by the
boy who still waved the fly whisk above his head.

July 25th. This heavy mountain air is like wine, and it is only in the
evening, after sunset, when we walk down the lanes carved out of the
mountain, that the excitement of thinking about these people disappears; and then it is perhaps because Feng Yu-hsiang is twenty
times larger than life, and all other thoughts are obliterated.

He carries a swordstick, and at some distance behind us there is
one of his guards. His English is good, and he has a passion for
pointing to things and giving their English names. "A lime tree"—
said very slowly, every syllable clearly pronounced, and afterward a

tremendous burst of laughter which echoes against the rocks. Down below, the river winds swiftly between the gorges, there are villages and hamlets and small men working in distant fields, but they are so small that they resemble children's playthings; and it is easy to imagine that we are in a land of giants.

It is in these hours when we wander among the coppices, speaking of the past and the future, that I have learned most to understand China. Feng Yu-hsiang is not a great dialectician; he knows little enough about Chinese painting or art or calligraphy; he is at heart a recluse, and perhaps he has never entirely believed in the efficacy of his wars. For years he had the best army in China, but he rarely speaks of it; and that serenity which shines from his face is the serenity of the Chinese people when they are at peace. He is China, and like the Chinese he is crafty, ingenuous, melancholy, hardworking, subtle, evasive, dominating, capricious, loving and hating by turns.

This evening he spoke about the campaigns in Burma, where his best generals were lost. He spoke without bitterness, though he clearly believed that the British failed to use the opportunities that were open to them. He asked many questions about Singapore, and mused silently about the collapse of the East Indies. He had not expected it to come so soon. The war of tanks and airplanes is not altogether to his satisfaction. He complains that there was more nobility in the ancient wars; and in his first campaigns the Chinese were still using lances and arquebuses, and bows and arrows were not yet entirely negligible. He has never ridden in a tank or flown in an airplane, which he considers idiotically dangerous; and he thinks longingly of the old days when the villagers obeyed the ritual of the seasons far more than they do now. He is an anachronism, but he is also a portent of the future; for the world must come back to this simple ritual of life before it goes to destruction.

July 26th. Early this morning we went to the monastery. I could not recognize Feng Yu-hsiang in the military uniform, the neatly creased blue uniform, and the flowing blue cape. He wore no medals or insignia, and he says that he has never worn them, perhaps because he is sufficiently aware of his importance in his country's history; but as we strode out under the palms and the silver eucalyptus trees, he looked as though he was about to invade a beleaguered city. We were welcomed at the gates by the *fa-shih*, the doctor of law and the second-in-command of the monastery, a man nearly as tall as the Marshal, wearing only a great orange-colored gown folded like a Greek toga and leaving his left arm bare. There were bows and salutations. Like mice, the little gray monks hurried across the tiled courtyard. Soon the elders of the temple approached down the steps, where the yellow-gold flag of the Buddhist trinity waved in the wind; and behind the carved doors of the temple, we could see the innumerable colored silk curtains which float down from the high-timbered roof.

The heat was appalling. Although it was still early, the sun glittered on the tiles, on the gray, lichen-covered stones, on the painted roofs of the temples, and on the gray-black gowns of the monks. They are all youths. They walk quickly, with the little running steps of people who are not accustomed to cities. They crowd round the Marshal, looking with slightly myopic eyes at the extraordinary giant who has suddenly appeared among them. They crowd into the schoolroom, where he will give an address.

The proceedings are opened with a Buddhist hymn. The abbot smiles from his chair facing the youths, and as he smiles he caresses the silk sleeves of his gown or touches the jade bracelets on his wrist with an expression of benediction. They are an extraordinary couple, the Marshal and the Supreme Abbot T'ai Shu, the Buddhist pope of China, but they have more in common than they perhaps imagine, and they smile at one another from time to time with expressions which do not hide a slight mutual contempt. The Marshal has been known to draw blasphemous ink drawings of monks riding donkeys with their faces turned to the donkeys' tails. He likes the monks, but he finds it difficult sometimes to understand why they are so many and so badly trained from the military point of view.

The prayers and hymns come to an end. The crossed flags of China and the Kuomintang party on the dais gather the sunlight. The monks cheer his opening sentence, in which he says truthfully that he is delighted to be among them, reminding them that they have shared melons together in the Moon-Regarding Pavilion half a mile away. And then he continues, his voice rising and falling with the precision of a trained actor, speaking of China and the unity of China, the accomplishments of the war, the necessity of loyalty to the Generalissimo, the continual awareness which is necessary if the war is to be won. The monks have a place in this scheme of things. Unlike the monks of a previous generation, they are well educated. They have a function to perform, and they must never forget that their learning must be put into the hands of the unlearned farmers and artisans. He tells them stories of the Generalissimo. He recounts his own adventures. We have entirely forgotten that he was once the military leader of the whole of north China. He is a country gentleman who has come to visit the monks living on a nearby estate. And then, when it is all over, when the Supreme Abbot has begged him to enjoy a vegetable lunch and when he has refused, we wander out into the sunlight, while the birds chatter in the enormous oaks which range in countless tiers above our heads.

We have returned to the Hall of the Empty Heart. The military tunic is removed. In shorts and singlet and bare legs, we sit down to our northern meal. But first there are certain sacred obligations to be remembered. The macaroni must be stirred and mixed with a liberal sprinkling of pepper. The onions, which are enormous and colored with deep veins of purple, must be solemnly chewed, for he believes quite rightly that they serve as a preventative to a whole series of deadly illnesses, including gout and tuberculosis. He must also exercise his legs, for at the age of sixty-five there is a great temptation to grow fat; and so he rises from the table, leans one immense, powerful arm on the trunk of a great bamboo and begins to swing his legs backward and forward, gazing up at the blue pigeons and the rice swallows who are unaccountably lingering in the branches. This accomplished, he sits down to his meal. We are entirely alone. The guard of honor, and even one of the cooks, has accepted the invitation of the monks to dinner. The sun shines. We are driven from one patch of shade to another, for the sun is entirely overhead. After dinner he does his boxing exercises, and a small boy from the orphanage comes to present still another pound of blue-red juicy grapes, which are bathed in permanganate of potash and eaten with relish. Some books are brought out. He writes a poem, chanting the tones in a monotonous high-pitched voice; and all the while he is gazing at the fluffy white clouds overhead and their dark blue shadows on the folds of the hills. There is quiet and contentment. Lazily he turns over the pages of a book—a book which possesses a peculiar significance because it is the only present he has ever accepted. It is a book printed and painted by hand in the Ming dynasty, showing green reeds, swallowtails, birds perched in the sedge of a lake, innumerable colored birds, painted so freshly that it is almost impossible to believe that it is many hundreds of years old. The birds glitter on the pages, flash their wings, cheep, and fly away. And when the last page of the book has been turned, he walks slowly upon the stone pathway, where the inscriptions of ancient graves may still be seen, and disappears into the remote recesses of the wattle cottage.

The afternoon is prolonged into an interminable silence. A white-tailed egret perches on the sunken milestone in the road. From the distance you can hear the drumming of temple bells. A flock of white birds, rising from the distant rice fields, flickers in the sun with so blinding a light that we are dazed. Very faintly in the river we can see the steamer coming from Chungking.

July 29th. Mysterious visitors arrive. They come early in the morning, which is the only time that the journey from the gorge is tolerable; they come with leather cases, and in the cool silence of the Marshal's bedroom their low voices can be heard like the murmur of a distant stream.

This evening the visitors were no longer mysterious. We sat in the courtyard of beaten earth, while the chickens scuffled in the dust and the only sound came from the flickering of the horsehair fan which the orderly waved over the Marshal's bald head. We spoke in English. We discussed the future, the Japanese, the arming of the Chinese armies, the terrible lack of equipment and food among the Chinese soldiers.

I asked him what he thought the Chinese would do to the Japanese.

He answered at once: "We shall leave them alone; we cannot contaminate ourselves with such vermin. We shall punish a few, but the rest have been misled; they are poor people, and we should sympathize with them." And then, a little later, laughing gently: "We will take Tojo round China in a cage. The amusements of the Chinese peasants are not so great that we can afford to miss this." He had a horror of monarchy in the East. When I suggested timidly that the Ch'ing emperors had in the early years of the dynasty deserved well of the country, he very nearly exploded. "No monarchy! No monarchy! We Chinese have finished with monarchs forever." And then again: "We are not slaves." He said this in a tone of terrible indignation. "The Japanese thought we—the Chinese—could be made into slaves. How is it possible? How is it possible that they thought such a thing? We are not slaves. We fought the revolution to free ourselves from slavery. Did they think we fought the revolution for fun?" His contempt for Pu Yi, who was for four years in his power, is terrific. "A little man, a very little man—did he think he could rule China?" It was amusing to think of the diminutive Pu Yi and the giant Marshal together.

"I have never seen the Emperor. Why should I see him? What business is it of mine to see the Emperor? Should I bow before him?" He made a mock bow and burst out laughing. Really, there were things that were incomprehensible, and one of the most incomprehensible was that the Ch'ing emperors had held China in fief for so many years. "No, never, never, *never* will there be an emperor again in China."

We discussed peace terms. With enemies, according to Chinese custom, there are only two methods of behavior. One could deal with them harshly by extermination, or one could leave them alone in their shame. He said that the Japanese were beyond everything else stupid and should be dealt with as stupid children. They should be punished; but to remove them from the fair land of China seemed punishment enough. "We have to rebuild China; we cannot afford to waste so much time on the little dwarfs."

The sun went out at last. The visitors, who are among the highest in the land, disappeared, and we were left to the dust and the softly waving bamboos. After dinner he began to sing, while puffs of smoke rose from the freshly made tea and the fly whisk still flashed menacingly above his shaven head. In the moonlight the deep-throated songs coming from the immense chest had a curiously hypnotic quality; and the great round copper-colored head itself seemed to be suspended in space. He sang for half an hour, an interminable song of huntsmen on the Mongolian frontiers; then suddenly and without saying a word he went to bed. For long afterward I heard the voice and saw the copper-colored head bellowing at the moon.

August 2nd. We climbed down the mountain early this morning. Sometimes when I looked down these hills, it seemed impossible to believe that there was any life in the valley. The mountain air, or the excitement of living in these heights, has given me an extraordinary sense of isolation, an isolation *which contains everything.* On the heights everything is clear, even in the darkest weather.

This morning, coming down the hill into the warm blue aqueous air of the valley, surrounded by an armed bodyguard (for we had left the Marshal defenseless in his eyrie), I began to believe for the first time that I was really suffering from tuberculosis. A white heron rose over the marshy rice fields—a real heron, rising slowly, with a tremendous wide flapping of wings, shining silver in the low sun, poised interminably over the yellow blades of rice. It flapped its wings, but did not move, and it was so beautiful that it left a taste of some terrible sweetness on my mouth. Still, still, unmoving, yet moving, rising gracefully and falling again, yet unmoving, seen against the clear blue sky and the gray uprush of the mountains, it hung there for eternal deserts of time. And did not move. And did move. Even when some prisoners, shackled and bound with iron rope, were pushed roughly past us on the dusty road, it still shone there, an image of permanence while the world flowed through my hands. I have never seen anything to compare with its beauty.

August 4th. I have been again to the hospital, but the film is still wet and it is difficult to see the marks of lesions, if there are any. This is the second film, and it seems identical to the first. The doctor was enthusiastic about sulphanilamide. Three years ago nearly all his patients suffering from pneumonia died. "It is the disease which attacks our soldiers most. When you are undernourished, when you are fighting and sweating and living in the open, pneumonia comes so naturally that we become accustomed to the symptoms. A million people have died in China of pneumonia since the war, and they still die of pneumonia; and it is no longer necessary." He spoke of the National Health Committee, which was doing excellent work, though there was inefficiency there as elsewhere. But on the subject of the local sale of drugs, he was violent in the extreme. "On the coast our doctors were among the best in the world, but what is so tragic is that they have succumbed to the general atmosphere. They do not heal. They think only of money." He shook his head sadly. "They have forgotten their training, and those who should be the first to help their country are among the last."

August 6th. It is in the evening that the heat becomes terrible. Shops shut early, but the doors are left wide open, or rather they are removed from their frames and laid on the pavement. The doors become beds. Everyone who possesses a right over a portion of Chungking's pavement sleeps out of doors. In the evening a thick treacly

soup of heat exudes from the walls and the earth. Now is the opportunity. It comes out, exactly like a sticky treacle, creeping over the
almost naked bodies in the road.

There is more gambling, more crime, more debauchery in the
heat of summer than in the wet cold of winter. The spirit of man is
defenseless against the grueling heat; and he can only pray and hope
against the murder he may commit, or the murder that may be
committed against him. Tempers are easily frayed. All afternoon an
old woman was screaming in the courtyard; in a small shop near the
river a girl with a hatchet was explaining volubly why she had murdered her husband. He was not murdered, but he was gravely injured;
and the blood ran in streams from the crown of his head.

Where will it end? We do not know. The heat gathers like a
crouching lion and springs upon us unawares.

August 10th. In Chungking there are all the modern conveniences,
though some of them are in an unrecognizable form. There are tall
buildings, there are even elevators, there are black shining limousines,
there are flower-vendors, dairies, steamships, contractors, government
officials, bank clerks. And now suddenly a new convenience has
appeared—every street has its ice-cream shop. There is an ice-cream
shop in the street I am living in. In small rooms, painted blue, with
electric fans whirring pleasantly, in a temperature of 80° we drink
iced lemonade. Oranges and lemons are plentiful in the province of
Szechuan, but they ripen in winter and the price has gone shooting
up through the last three days. On Monday an orangeade cost fifteen
dollars; on Tuesday it was twenty; on Thursday it was thirty. So does
everything rise, and we sit in corners discussing the inflation.

"It has come to stay," C. announces, with a worried look in his
eyes. He has just bought thirteen hundred electric fans and proposes
to hoard them. "What else can I do? We are all hoarders now—the
banks are the greatest hoarders of all. The government cannot stop it.
It must go on, because it is in the nature of things." It seems an
unsatisfactory explanation, and we discuss the history of prices in
China during the last few years. "When I first came to Szechuan, the
peasants distrusted us—we were 'down-river men,' meaning that we
were not Szechuanese and deserved in their eyes no better fate than
the fate they proposed to administer to the Japanese. They did not
like the government. It was better and stronger and more capable
than the provincial government, but the provincial government was

theirs and they felt they possessed a kind of proprietary right over their warlord. The Generalissimo changed this. He is careful in the use of force, but when it is used, it is used effectively."

He thought for a while and then continued: "These things change. When we came, though they distrusted us, they allowed us to buy at reasonable prices. Rents were the same for all. Now there are three rents: a rent for the Szechuanese, a rent for Chinese, and a rent for foreigners. They are not conscious of doing evil. It seems very natural in their eyes, for they regard trade as something holy and secretive, and among themselves they exchange prices by inserting their hands in one another's sleeves and silently telling the prices by squeezing with their fingers on the forearms. But at first—for the first six months—the Chinese prices were very much the same as the Szechuanese prices. We could buy as many oranges as we could carry in a basket for a dollar. Rice was ridiculously cheap. House rent was ten, twenty, or thirty dollars a month—and we thought it excessive. Then they gradually came to realize their power. They knew we were here to stay for many months, and perhaps many weary years. They decided to get rich. They decided that we should pay for our occupation of their territory. The Szechuan gentry decided, at a secret conference, to produce a state of affairs by which the ancient warlords would once again enter their patrimony. They will fail. Even with the help of the secret societies they will fail. They are in league with the banks, and they will deliberately raise prices so that the soldiers, the officials, and the professors will find life difficult. The soldiers, the officials, and the professors will go away and never want to return if they succeed; and then perhaps purple poppy flowers will once more grow over their fields. But they have forgotten one thing. They have forgotten the Generalissimo. They have forgotten his army and his air force, and above all they have forgotten that in every province except Szechuan and Yunnan men have forgotten their ancient acrimonies and a national consciousness has been born as never before."

I do not know how much to believe of all this, but there is certainly some animosity between the Szechuanese and the "downriver men." Meanwhile the fans are whirring pleasantly, and an extraordinarily beautiful girl in a print frock comes to take away our glasses.

August 15th. The atmosphere has changed since I was here last. In February and March we were afraid. We were afraid not of Japanese airplanes but of the defeat of armies. It is a time which the Chinese already call "the time of the collapse of armies," and while the Philippines, Malaya, the Dutch East Indies, and Burma were falling, there was an air of hysteria over Chungking. We lived in a double-darkness, for the fog also covered everything. During those early days of defeat, we spoke much about the ABCD front—America, Britain, China, and the Dutch. Now we talk less about ABCD, perhaps because we have come to believe that God helps those who help themselves. It is extraordinary to realize that we are isolated, almost completely isolated from the rest of the world. A few camel trains descend through the northwest from Russia, a few airplanes arrive from Calcutta—and this is all. We are at the mercy of ourselves; we cannot expect help for many months; we are separated by vast oceans and unclimbable mountains and great deserts from our nearest allies. *And this isolation has proved a strength.*

The portraits of the allied leaders, which are to be seen in nearly all the cafés, have grown old and dusty with age; we no longer refer so trustingly to the co-operation of the allies, though we know it will come. But how long? No one knows. And simply because no one knows, the best among us have decided to tighten their belts still another notch and fight it out again. The spirit of the Doomed Battalion has returned.

August 21st. Night! We have been walking through the streets under a full moon, looking down at the half-naked corpses that lie on the pavements. In the moonlight their faces are touched with green, their arms thin and heavily veined; their legs are sprawled out across the pavement. There are old men and young girls, and sometimes small boys nestle in the arms of the old men and babies crouch over the breasts of the girls. Some are so nearly naked that at first they seem to be naked, and others tear off their clothes as the night advances. For they are not corpses, and it is only the stillness of the hot night which gives them the appearance of corpses—that, and the expressionless faces of those who sleep heavily.

For during these hot nights, if we sleep at all, we sleep heavily, like drunken men. We are drunk with the heat, which shrivels the palm trees and throws a great cloth of mist over the roaring river. The river is the only sound you hear at night. The river is rising. Already it is turning brick yellow, though the Chialing river is still blue—and there is a wavy line drawn across the Chialing where the two rivers meet. No thunder. The night roars: in every sleep there are great roaring waves—the sound of the sleepers as they breathe heavily.

More corpses; more stretches of moonlit, white road; more naked children who have crawled out in the middle of the road, where there is more wind and the moon is brighter. Still they lie like corpses—some face downward, some gazing blindly at the brilliant circle of the shimmering moon, some leaning against the walls like dolls carelessly thrown away, and you expect to see eyes made of buttons and the stuffing coming out of their stomachs. And still the night goes on, not changing, heavily breathing, with roaring waves of sleep coming from the slumberers.

Heaven help those who are sick tonight! The heat sucks all energy away. From the steaming foreheads of the dead comes a thin vapor like a spirit. Occasionally you see people walking in the streets, treading carefully among the corpses. Here and there you will come upon the sounds of activity. In a small room off the Street of the Seven Stars, there is a cotton mill. Pale-faced girls, having wound the thread on the bobbins, draw it up tightly across the slotted frames of laurel wood. Through a chink in the shutters, you see them bending over the frames, hear the soft clink and shuttle of the woof, smell the heavy smell of wet cotton. The carders are still working, and the lovely humming sound of the wire which beats the cotton into a kind of white silk fit for our pillows and embroidered eiderdowns can be heard in the deserted lanes. But not many people are working, though the lights shine from every house. The Chinese have a passion for sleeping in the electric light; and at other times of the year they sleep easily. The moist damp shadows creep along the wall—an old beggar with a tuft of silver beard, blind and led by a remarkably beautiful boy who looks as though he has stepped out of an Italian picture. There is a green flute, a long-handled pipe and a small tobacco case shaped like a walnut hanging from his belt. The blind do not sleep. The shadows come out into the glare of a concentrated battery of electric lamps; and the light is so bright that even the blind man knows he is in the presence of a mystery, and sighs, and would sit in this curious glow which filters through his broken eyes, but the boy leads him on. The thumping of the stick on the stone road awakes no one. In all Chungking there are no sounds like the faltering steps of the blind on a hot moonlight night.

And then the dawn. A gray funnel of yellow appears over the hills, and a few trucks creep out of the silence of the caves of rock and begin to move toward the heights overlooking the city. But now the full horror of the heat is upon us, for many have died during this night. "Lend a light! Lend a light!" A small coffin is brought out on to the street, and we make way for it as one might make way for a triumphal procession. "He died during the night," someone mutters, and at the same time we see the small boy, with arms like matchsticks, who lies against the wall. No one has covered him with matting. The sun catches the small, pinched, starved, and blue-white features, and he seems to be smiling. "Lend a light! Lend a light!"

September 6th. We have been wandering over the steep hills of Peipei, wondering what lay beyond. The mountains above the gorges are so high that daylight comes here only for a few hours, when the sun hangs directly overhead; but there was no sun today, and already we are on the verge of winter. There is no autumn in Szechuan. The dead leaves fall from the trees, the streets are thick with mud, the gray awnings over the shops sag in the heavy wind, and there is no hope in the face of the land. Or rather there is immense and permanent hope, but we are like people imprisoned in the gray weather, not knowing where to turn.

We had crossed the range of granite hills which lies above the river. We had come to villages whose existence I had never suspected, villages where there were no rivers, and where the old men sitting out-of-doors seem never to have heard of that majestic river which flows at the feet of the university. Here the water comes up through wells or small silver mountain streams the color of leaping salmon. And though they are only seven or eight miles away from the Chialing, they live in a world of their own, with customs which are different from ours, and even their faces are sterner, stronger, redder than ours. C. has been speaking about the forced immigration which took place at the end of the Ming dynasty. "Once, when we first came to this place, we went out over the hills and came to a village buried among great cliffs of rock and great forests. It was a village in which even the headman was ignorant about the war. They knew nothing; they lived entirely remote from the world. And though, by some magical means, they were aware that the Ch'ing emperor was no longer in power, they still burned incense before his portrait and carried on the ceremonies of ancient times. They had not heard of Chiang Kai-shek, though they had heard vague rumors of an uprising in the north. When the first revolutionary armies penetrated Szechuan, the elders of this small village forbade people to leave. They were afraid of the warlords, afraid of having to pay taxes sixty years in advance. And so they grew up happily, separated from the rest of the world, perfectly content—for their fields produced good rice, good wine, and good herbs. They had everything they wanted. Why should they enter the world?" But everything had changed now. It was a village like other villages, with its soldiers in blue-gray uniform, its shrines to the earth god, its wine shop where wine is poured out of great casks bound with flax and lacquer, and there was even an officer who lived in a small house on which the twelve-rayed white sun of the Kuomintang shone against a sky-blue background. In only one thing did it differ from other villages. Before the shrine of the earth god there were no candles—there were bronze vases filled with flowers.

September 7th. This evening, after classes, we walked out across the fields again, crossing the mountain road where the mud-stained ponies come with their great bamboo panniers of coal dust and charcoal. It was late, but we wandered off into the darkness, for the sun had been shining and we were happy to wander in the moonlit night.

C. has been trying to find a house for me. We found a beautiful house, surrounded by an enormous spiked wall, overlooking a mountain stream and a clump of bamboos. There were partridges and perfectly white egrets wading in the pool, a few stone tablets dating from the latter part of the Sung dynasty. It is impossible to imagine a lovelier place in summer, or a more desolate one in winter. Today it looked at its best—the waving bamboos, the egrets, the deep pool, the houses banked against the mountainside in the distance, and the forest of pines running along the contours of the mountains. In the moonlight the house looked like the house which all scholars dream of possessing. In such a house Tao Yuan-ming had composed his elegies; in such a house Su Tung-p'o composed his odes.

But we wandered on along the mountain path, and decided to return only when it was very late. Unfortunately, we took a shortcut down the muddy bank, and coming past the courtyard of a timber-roofed house set in a grove of alders, we discovered ourselves surrounded by armed men and barking wolfhounds. Rifles were pointed at us; the dogs leaped at our throats. We were glad we had taken short sticks with us, for undoubtedly they saved our lives. We were examined roughly by men who looked as though they were bored and therefore would take the greatest pleasure in cutting our throats. But at last, our pockets having been searched and our bodies roughly handled, we were allowed to go on—saved only by the metallic badge which bears the name of the university and which we wear on the lapels of our coats.

"What kind of house is it?" I asked. "Is this the headquarters of a military station, or have we come upon a band of thieves?"

C. shook his head sadly. At first he refused to tell me, but at last he admitted: "The house belongs to one of the great banks. They are hoarding cloth, waiting for the price to go up, when they will sell it on the market. Probably there are a million million dollars' worth of cloth stored in the house."

September 9th. I have been to see the mayor in the hope of finding a house. He is a short man with a face of dull leather and small eyes; but he holds himself with great dignity and carries on the lapels of his coat the emblem of a silver greyhound, which means that he has been appointed the mayor of a *hsien,* the autonomous or nearly autonomous unit of Chinese civil administration. We have been talking in the mayor's parlor, where the rifles are stacked in rows and gendarmes enter from time to time to lay reports on the blackwood table. China is still in the state of "military tutelage" according to the principles set out by Sun Yat-sen; and the effect of the military is visible in nearly every detail of civil administration.

We talk about the past, when the mountains surrounding this village were infested with bandits. The mayor's brother had marched against them less than ten years ago and executed them out of hand. They were deserters from one or other of the warring armies that swept back and forth through Szechuan.

"It is not all over yet," the mayor said, gazing up at the ceiling and blowing out great puffs of tobacco. "There are still a few bandits, and we punish them mercilessly." He spoke about the last bombardment of Peipei, which occurred when Lin Yutang was living in this village. "We had to build everything up again, re-establish everything. There was no panic. There are many ills in the neighborhood, and many shelters; but everything had to be built up from the beginning. This is what is heart-rending." He was proud of his administration and prouder still that the Generalissimo had come often to inspect his plans. "Peipei is a model village," he explained. "The government proposes to carry out experiments, which may later be copied by other villages throughout the land. There are so many centers of learning here, and we are not far from the headquarters of the legislative assembly and the ministry of education. Experiments in education, in civic health, in the training of the young. . . ." The list was endless. "But we are not satisfied; we shall never be satisfied until everybody in this village has enough to eat and has the best medical care."

He is a good mayor, but his problems are almost insoluble. There is heart-rending poverty here. On the clay banks of the rivers there are people who live under mat shed roofs like beasts, and the haulers who come up river, leaving behind them a trail of blood from lungs or chafed ankles, are in no better plight. And prices are mounting, mounting. But at night, as we crossed the river, seeing the banked smoke fires of the furnace, the chimneys of the mills, and the lights burning in the dynamo house on the water's edge, we felt that he had reason to be proud.

September 13th. I have crossed the river in the mist wondering how the boatmen could find their way among the rocks, for there are rocks everywhere and the river is low. There is no rule for the river; one day low, one day high; and the changes are so sudden that you may see the small mat sheds by the river's edge wandering down stream in a soapy yellow froth five minutes after the river has risen. But by good luck this morning we drifted down stream and came to earth at the foot of the village.

This little village, with its two muddy streets and great banyan trees, is a paradise in summer, and we are able to forget the coal coolies who come panting down the mountain. But in winter it is impossible to forget them. They are half-naked, their bodies covered with soot, and there are red weals in their black bellies which shine like jewels; and even in this cold wind they sweat under the weight of their bamboo baskets filled with coal. They come in straggling groups past the watchtower on the slopes, treading deep in mud, sullen, footsore, with expressions of agony on their black faces; and they have lost all patience and care nothing if they collide with you, smothering you in the black dust of coal.

But the mist is beautiful, and when I see them coming through the hovering shapes of mist which hang over the village, they seem to have come from some other world, in which mist and darkness are thoroughly understandable. They pant and whistle as they run the last remaining stages of their race, the coal dust dripping from the baskets, the dogs howling at their heels, inhuman in their agony, their eyes like red ink splashed on a black page, their bodies trembling in the heat and cold. So in this wilderness they come to the waiting boats.

There are epics to be written of the workers of China. The story of the tin mines of Kochu in Yunnan is still untold; the story of the North-West must remain for another generation. Here we have only the haulers and the coal coolies, and today both of them have been shining dimly through the mist, invisible until they are a few paces away from you, and simply because they disappear so easily in the mist they seem to be as free as the crested sandpipers who swoop low over the river. These are the people who have made China. They have altered the shapes of rivers and the contours of mountains; it is by their agony and sweat that we live. And therefore we accord them the reverence we offer to all laborers who starve by the wayside.

September 17th. A messenger came down the mountain this morning to remind me that the Requiem would be sung in the monastery in the evening. With the messenger came a large folio bound in brown covers—a present from the abbot. The book contained the Chinese text of the Requiem, which is supposed to have been composed by the Sung dynasty poet Su Tung-p'o. I spent the morning poring over the book with one of our poets. There are whole sentences in the Requiem which he cannot understand, whole sentences of Sanskrit written in Chinese characters according to the sound; and he guesses wildly at these strangely un-Chinese sounds. Best of all, the book contains illustrations of the positions of the hands to be assumed during the ceremony. They are like the hands you find in Indian sculptures, long and without bones. But where I saw swans and towers, sudden gardens and stairways, Yang Chih-sing saw tempests and sunrise. You can read anything you please into the expression of the hands.

Later. I reached the monastery long before the ceremony began. Bergery was there, with a white spaniel and three or four small urchins he had picked up on the road. In the bare, tiled refectory, the monks came on slippered feet to see whether we were comfortable, and spoke of the ceremony in hushed voices, wondering perhaps whether it was right that a foreigner should be admitted.

The sun had long ago disappeared, and when at last the ceremony began by the light of butter lamps and a few incongruous pale blue acetylene lamps, we had forgotten the events of the day; for a Chinese temple is made for the night. We seemed to have been living among the silken curtains of the temple for all eternity, and only the distant barking of Bergery's spaniel suggested a world outside.

At the head of an immense table the presiding priest took his position. He was dressed in a flowing red robe, the color of brick dust, squared and patterned according to no known law; and on his head he wore the five-faced Buddha crown on which little embroidered figures of Buddha standing upright in the attitude of blessing shone in the blue and yellow light. Down the sides of the white table priests sat bowed over their instruments, the psalm books open, their hands playing lightly on the strings. They were all young. Unlike the presiding priest, they wore their customary black gowns. And suddenly, while the wind fluttered the hanging curtains, the priest began to intone, and his fingers would describe the paradises to which the soul of the dead man had gone.

Even when they had finished singing these psalms the ceremony was not over. The small bells were ringing, the monk with the Buddha crown was folding and unfolding his beautiful hands, while the robes of the monks continually swayed softly; and slowly, but with ever increasing momentum, the singing gained power and authority, rose higher, became piercingly sweet or suddenly subdued to a whisper—a whisper which could be heard, as the deerskin drum is heard, twenty miles away. A few monks prayed on the bamboo fiber hassocks on the tiled floor, but those who sat at the table were not praying, and seemed indeed to be whispering to the ghosts of the dead. The aged monk at the head of the table removed his crown, his colored robes were taken from him by a serving boy; and in his dark robe he continued to sing. A curious chased dish was placed before him. I was told it was a model of Mount Sumeru, on which the earth is suspended. The cakes on the table glittered in the pale blue flares of the acetylene lamps, and a small vase, perfectly white, was suddenly added to the unaccountable riches on the table. With this vase, by running his finger lightly around its rim, the priest blessed the food, and still singing, he began to throw crumbs of rice into the air. This was the food of the dead, who were present in the air and perhaps hiding behind the softly falling scarves which hung from the roof beams. And still they sang, playing on conches and horns and flutes, their long bony fingers strumming the strings of violins. They were no longer conscious of the world. The priest was lost in abstraction and gazed with half-closed eyes at the shape of Mount Sumeru inlaid with silver. The white vase shone, and the singing continued to the end. Finally, more showers of rice were thrown to the waiting dead, voices were rising higher and higher, and still there was no sign that the music would come to a conclusion. Suddenly, as though in the middle of a theme, it ended; and at that moment we knew that we had seen the shadow of paradise before our eyes.

The horror began when we went to bed. In one of the large rooms on the wing of the monastery, there lived a former governor of Peking, who amused himself in defeat by counting his beads and writing elegantly on white paper the poems he had composed in his youth. There were two or three beds in the room, and the former governor was kind enough to supply biscuits. I shall remember this night for a long time. The sense of horror and loneliness began when he started talking of Peking. There was a single rush light. The walls were crumbling, the bamboo laths showing through the plaster, and I suppose the immense shadows we threw on the wall had something to do with it Occasionally we heard "the wave of the pines," the soft sound made by the higher branches of the pines in the mountain wind, and then—still more occasionally—the hollow, vibrating tunelessness of the deerskin drum. It was still dark and cloudy; strange shapes began to form outside the windows; the wind began to tear through the thin paper panes. The governor, in his blue silk gown, walked up and down the room.

"It could have been saved, it could have been saved," he kept repeating. "If the capital had been Peking, and not Nanking—"

We sympathized with him. We ate his biscuits. We purred gently when he explained how he had increased the amenities of Peking, which the Japanese are now tearing to pieces; and when he spoke of the huge ferroconcrete buildings which were being erected on the outskirts of Peking, we sighed contemplatively and wondered whether anything would be left when at last we arrived. In 1937 he had lost his kingdom. Too proud to ask the central government for help, he lived in the monastery, perfectly content, growing fatter each day, and each day a few more wrinkles appeared on his brows. Occasionally he was solaced by the presence of his daughter, who was allowed to remain in the monastery against all the rules of the order.

Bergery had known Peking in the days of her glory. He lived quietly in a small house inside the Forbidden City, planting stone-white magnolias and carefully tending three or four shoots of rhododendrons specially imported from Yunnan. He had had a heart attack as a result of following the Abyssinian war, and he lived very quietly and secretly. He had met the Governor occasionally, and they began to talk about Peking as lovers will sometimes talk of their discarded mistresses. And so they continued, while the mosquitoes chirred in the yellow-washed room, and occasionally a flake of plaster would fall from the walls.

There was something terrible in this conversation of vanished glories. They would say, "Do you remember Prince Tao Belah in the summer after Wu Pei-fu ran away and left everything to Feng Yu-hsiang? That was the summer of the great drought." It was like a nightmare. First one, then the other, would begin a flow of reminiscences, each one more sickly than the one which preceded it, till I had a vision of Peking in all its glory suddenly falling into powder and leaving no more evidence of its existence than a few stones. I remembered Xanadu. It has been discovered at last, but not by the Chinese. Japanese archeologists have unearthed four or five enormous stones, a few inscriptions, the black hollows in the earth where wood has lain. Now there were only black-beetles and rubble. . . . "I never had time to count my art treasures," the Governor was saying, and when Bergery asked him whether they were safely buried, he almost burst into tears.

When we went to bed, it was long past midnight. The sky had cleared, and the mosquitoes delighted in the warmth. It was as though millions of mosquitoes had suddenly entered the room, whirring their black wings and drowning the sounds of voices. At night the sound of someone chewing biscuits can be pure horror. So it was now, in the silence that followed the last of these terrible memories; and when the rush lamp was put out, and we went to sleep under beautifully embroidered silk quilts, the night became more intolerable than ever, for we were all dreaming of the vanished glories of the past. It was then that the horror began, or perhaps it was a quarter of an hour later, a horror which made us sick to death, and showed our worn faces the next morning like the faces of people who are about to be executed, or have been executed already.

I do not know why bedbugs in Chinese monasteries are worse than bedbugs in Chinese hotels. I only know it is so. They lived in the blankets, in the thin seams of brocade, even inside the silk covering; but at night they swarmed over us. In the morning they would die, but they made the very best use of the hours that remained to them, and they crept under our pajamas and made sleep impossible, and life no longer desirable. They were quite remorseless, and they were quite impossible to find. All through that night, while the deerskin drum could be heard beating at intervals, they assaulted us from every direction, and though sometimes we would catch them, and a small silken bladder of blood would be squashed between our fingertips, they had nearly always escaped when we searched for them. They have gone before you feel the scratching pain. They raise horrible red blisters on your flesh, they jump easily from one end of your body to the other, they slip between your fingers, they crowd in your hair and walk solemnly over your face, producing the most comical and the most terribly unexpected lumps on lips, nose, ears, and eyelids. And you fight them all night, with never a moment's rest, until you are exhausted and you lie back, surrendering to them, but then they climb all over you and once again you begin the unequal contest. You no longer have the feeling that you are fighting an animal smaller than a fingernail. You are Beowulf fighting with Grendel. Not one animal, but a million animals, and all of them have hairy arms, and all of them bite. I cursed and groaned, and shortly afterward I heard Bergery and the Governor groaning, and the rustle of the quilts, and sometimes one of them would get up, walk to the window, and return slowly to bed. The beds were against three sides of the wall. A faint moon rose, and the mosquito nets shone like white ghosts floating above the bodies of my friends. They said nothing. All night, there was this interminable terror, and when dawn came, we were fast asleep and the bedbugs were having the time of their lives.

A monk came in when the sun was high in the sky with a message from the abbot, and some flowers which he had gathered with his own hands in the garden. We dressed and shaved slowly. There were weals on my shoulders and a red road across my chest and stomach. One of Bergery's eyes had swollen to an enormous size. Only the Governor of Peking was apparently untouched, but he looked weary beyond endurance, pale, no longer fretful, but as though the life had been washed out of his dark, bruised eyes. We went out into the garden, where the white mist settled still on the flowers, and the most heavenly blue sky brooded over the temple eaves.

"The Requiem for the dead . . . ," Bergery murmured, thinking of what had happened the night before; and looking at his swollen eyelid, the size and color of a small red pear, I burst out laughing. The abbot was coming to meet us. In one hand, carefully and tenderly, he held an enormous fan.

September 23rd. One of those days in autumn when a thick white mist like flakes of ice settles on the river, and you know that there will be no clouds and the sun will shine on the fields of winter barley. I walked out in the mist, seeing the gray trees intangible in all this whiteness, the sun above burning a great hole in the white cloud overhead like a hayrick on fire. Then one by one the houses on the opposite shore appeared, very bright, like the whites of eyes, and the river below, golden in the faint sunrise, like a mouth. The illusion of watching the apparition of some beloved face with clearly defined features continued for perhaps five minutes, but at last even this illusion disappeared in a moment which was still more miraculous—the mist dissolved, there was a liquefaction of blood, and suddenly the blue river, the yellow gorges, and the immense sky swung out of the mist, trembling with dew, glittering with a thousand points of liquid light, so vivid that you could almost hear the clash of cymbals as the whole earth danced into life.

And then in the evening another miracle. Crossing the river at night, under a faint moon. A few naked haulers were still wading knee-deep in the river, dragging the long hemp ropes attached to the masts of the sampans, their bronze bodies shining in the faint moonlight. Some trick of the light made them appear larger than they were, so that they resembled archaic gods on their way to perform a sacrifice. But there was still another miracle in store. High up on the beach great balks of timber which had floated up during the floods lay motionless and quiet. The moon came out, and I remember that at that moment the naked haulers looked smaller than ever, for they threw small black shadows; but the young poet Yao Pen, who was by my side, pointed to the great white balks of timber shining in the moonlight and whispered: "The bones of the earth." And for a brief moment it seemed as though they were indeed the bones of the earth, huge, terrifying, monstrously enlarged by the moonlight. And I remember I thought, "If they perish, the earth also will perish," but later, as we walked across the deserted beach I remembered that in the morning I had seen the young earth dancing in all her finery, and it seemed curious and strange that we should have seen her in such differing disguises at such short intervals of time. Tomorrow, perhaps, there will be clouds over the whole sky, and we shall not see the earth at all.

September 30th. A long procession forming in the town. A gray day. No clouds, but a kind of gray pall over the sky like lead or like brains after they have lain for a few hours on a battlefield. There were puddles everywhere—perhaps it rained in the night. A soldier in an old brown uniform, beating a drum, and the procession very silent and still, as though not walking but gliding—a procession in a dream. I followed it down to the river, thinking it was part of the autumn sacrifices, though I should have known by the expression of the faces that it was something still more important than a sacrifice to the gods. A few boys were shouting, someone was weeping, and somewhere in the center of the crowd a man was moaning and complaining in a tired voice. At first I did not see him, but when we were halfway down to the beach I heard many voices complaining and noticed that they came from a group of four men, naked to the waist, their hands tied with rough cord behind their backs. Their bodies were not brown like the bodies of the peasants, but pearl-white and thin, the flesh touching the white prominent bones. They seemed to be drugged. Suddenly I thought, "Yes, this is a Buddhist ceremony. They are going to offer a sacrifice to the river." We were very near the beach. One of the men, shorter than the others, with a great hairy black mole just below his underlip, was struggling and attempting to break the cords which bound his wrists. From time to time he shouted, or rather barked, in a voice which was halfway between a cough and the bark of a sheep dog, "I am not guilty! I am not guilty!" And immediately afterward he cursed and sat down on the stones, refusing to get up. The soldiers wore black and carried shining carbines. They lifted him up very tenderly. He was no longer cursing. In a kind of dull stupor, walking a little behind the others, occasionally throwing up his head, his mouth twitching nervously, he followed them to the river's edge. Then the crowd was told to move away, and only the children continued to speak excitedly, pulling faces and jeering at the condemned men. The river seemed to be still, and suddenly the wind dropped out of the immense white sail of a sampan in midstream.

We waited. We did not know why we waited. It was like watching a play. The soldiers stood at attention. The prisoners also stood at attention. The soldiers moved away, and the prisoners edged a little toward the river—but I have no idea what happened afterward. I think I noticed first the scent of powder, not acrid, but slightly sweet, and then a little later the gasp of astonishment and fear and understanding which ran through the crowd, and long after that the sounds of the rifle shots. I turned away. There was some sound of moaning, and then a long silence. When we were perhaps fifty yards away, we heard the sound of scuffling, and that was the most terrible, for there were no voices, only the slither of stones and human bodies and no cries of pain.

In the city there are already notices saying that three famous bandits and a murderer were executed by order of the mayor. The orders had been prepared beforehand, but the ink was still wet and running a little on the paper.

October 7th. No sun. There will be a few days of sunshine before March, but not many. Here at least it is better. In Chungking there are gasoline fumes, rain, yellow rock: there is no sign of grass.

I have been writing here, between bouts of sickness, the first chapters of the long story of China which will probably be called "Love and Peace." I began it in the summer, only a short while ago; but already it is winter. At night, after classes, in the deserted hotel bedroom, among rats and lice, it will be written.

Perhaps it is true that one writes best in illness and filth. These small unwashed cubicles in the hotel are the home of red-bellied rats who nest in the bathrooms under the great earthenware tubs. Occasionally the bath boy will throw boiling water over them. They do not die. Scalded, their bellies turn bright pink. There are more rats in this village than I ever dreamed possible.

October 9th. With my students I went to the hot springs. The lotuses and the willows are dead. Only a few leaves of the lotuses emerge above the silent pools. Above us the mountain was shrouded with mist. No sky, no sun.

October 12th. Jaundice. Fainted twice in the street, and was carried home. I looked in the mirror. Quite yellow, and deep blue rings under the eyes. A feeling of weakness, but how exciting the moment when you fall asleep and all this weakness disappears. Suddenly strong, you go running after dreams.

October 27th. No clouds, or rather clouds everywhere. No sky, no sun.

1943

April 15th. Winter has passed, and spring comes round again. The small flakes of ice in the rice fields vanished, the heavy red mud of Szechuan changed inexplicably to dull yellow and green, and once more the sails of the sampans going up stream are white. This winter was like the travel of an airplane through heavy clouds; no sign of the sun, and often we were freezing around small charcoal fires. There were tunnels of gray air through which we tried to find our way; but it was all unnecessary. If we had had patience, we should not have complained.

I am less sorry for the students and professors than for the farmers. Even in the winter fog, they plowed knee-deep through their rice fields. The swollen hookworm veins of their legs grew larger; under their immense straw helmets they seemed to be bowed down to the earth, and you saw them in the distance, moving slowly against the ashen gray of the fields where no plants could yet be seen; and as they walked homeward they did not sing. All through the winter I thought of that journey to Kweilin, when suddenly the white towers and pinnacles of the place shone through the mist as we approached; and of the wealth of that city which is so much wealthier than ours. There you could buy pig skins, ivories, tiger skins, small lacquer Buddhas; there were shops full of jewelry and still more shops full of bales of cloth. We are poorer here. There is less wealth in Szechuan, for communication is difficult; and in these outlying villages, communication is almost impossible.

But spring has come! There was a day when the mist disappeared so dramatically that one feels it will never return. There are good auguries, too. On Chinese New Year, there was snow for the second year in succession, and we feel sure that the war will end soon. New buildings are going up on the university campus. Even in the village, there are signs of returning prosperity; but perhaps it is only because there are more men smoking their long pipes in the tea shops, and more girls in light costumes walking under the alders.

Already there have been air raids or air alarms, but we face them with more confidence because we have seen the sun.

April 19th. I have been to attend a meeting at the Legislative Council, which occupies a building some distance away from here. I had already met Dr. Sun Fo, but I was still more impressed by him today. He wore a brown maroon gown, and as he stood in front of the portrait of his father there seemed to be such an extraordinary likeness that it was as though Sun Yat-sen had come to life again. Something of the same thing happened when I saw him before; and it was curious to see the miracle repeated.

There were more than two hundred members of the Legislative Council present. They were men from all walks of life: farmers, scholars, merchants, editors, writers. They were of all ages and of all classes. They had not been elected, but were chosen partly by the government and partly by Dr. Sun Fo himself, and though the election is undemocratic, it has given a fairly representative body of legislators to China.

I asked T. K. Chuan, the editor of *Tien Hsia*, whether it would ever be possible to have a purely democratic system in a country of nearly five hundred million inhabitants. He is himself a member of the Legislative Council, though he has made few speeches. "It is not entirely representative," he admitted, "but every kind of opinion is represented on the council. We have members representing the occupied part of China, members representing labor, others representing capital; there are members representing the government, and other members representing the universities and research institutes. It is like England—in wartime a thoroughly representative legislative chamber is impossible." There was one sense, however, in which he admitted that the Council was totally unrepresentative—there was only one woman in it. "She is the woman with the greatest responsibility in the world," I suggested. "She carries on her shoulders the weight of nearly three hundred million other women." He laughed; and when, a little while later, we met the extremely attractive representative of three hundred million women, it was difficult to think of that tremendous responsibility reposing on her slight shoulders.

The legislators meet in an old farmhouse so securely buried among the forests that no airman will ever be able to find them. There were reading rooms, offices, a library as large as the university library; there were small rest rooms where the legislators could dream in comfort of the effects of their laws; everywhere there was a feeling of activity. The legislators admitted there were difficulties. A large part of the functions of the Legislative Council had been taken over by the Supreme Military Defense Council. Government departments introduced their own laws, and sometimes these laws conflicted with those introduced by other departments. There were three or four officials who spent their whole time attempting to codify the laws. Still worse, the laws of the realm could be promulgated, but no one could be certain that they would be carried out. The voices in the assembly rose to a hum. A bill on the control of medicines was being passed. The legislators were leaning forward, intently listening to the young doctor who was speaking. There were a few people talking in subdued voices at the back of the hall, but everyone else was listening. The bill was passed. On the dais, with the photograph of Dr. Sun Yat-sen below the crossed flags of the Republic, Dr. Sun Fo was sitting at a table covered with a red cloth. The meeting came to an end. Dr. Sun Fo passed through the gangway, and came out into the courtyard, among the stone elephants and ancient lions and the fig trees. Another meeting of the Legislative Council was finished.

Afterward, we lunched with Dr. Sun Fo in a small wooden house high up on the spur of the mountains. It was raining; the forests were thick with damp and smoky vapor; down below, the rice fields glittered in the faint sun. Servants came to take our coats, policemen inspected us carefully; but inside the dining room, by the warm fire, while the pictures and scrolls gazed down from the walls, a magnificent host in a maroon gown answered questions without pause. We talked about the scrolls written by the famous poet Su Tung-p'o of the Sung dynasty which hung on the walls, and Dr. Sun Fo discussed those characters which he admired best.

A Chinese scroll is often a work of art, every detail of the calligraphy worthy of the attention of the connoisseur, for the art of the calligrapher lies in minute details. Most difficult of all are the characters which seem the easiest, the characters which have only a few strokes and those, too, which are most commonly repeated.

April 23rd. In the courtyard the children have been screaming all afternoon. They are poor and undernourished, their skins are pale blue, and neither their father nor their mother pays much attention to them. They live in the house near the gate, which lies over a cesspool where the rats congregate from the four corners of the earth. And so they screamed. There was no reason for their screaming. Or rather they screamed because they were ill and undernourished, because their skins were blue, because there were lice in their hair, because they were sick of suffering. It is a sound which can be heard often in China, and only one sound is worse—the sound of a woman screaming.

T. says that all this will end as soon as sanitation comes to this village. But when will sanitation come to this village? Night soil is used on the fields, and every morning as I come across the river, I see the open casks of night soil as they are taken to the fields. In Peipei the soil pipes are buried underground. Here in the village there are open drains, where the rats crawl and the green flies hover in clouds. The children cry because their intestines and skins are sick with disease; and only the strongest survive.

"We have proved," says T. sadly, "the theory of the survival of the fittest. Only the fittest could survive the agony of Chinese life." He smiles wearily. "There is even a department of sanitation at the university, but what can we do against the vested interest of open drains? It will be a long time before they disappear."

The child is still screaming. It is impossible to work, or even to think. The terrible cold quivering voice of the child is only a response to suffering; but as soon as I have told myself this, I know that it is no longer true. There are good nurses and good doctors in China; the pity is that there are not enough of them.

April 24th. The school doctor has opened a small surgery halfway up the hill, and on the door of the surgery there is a notice: "Those who cannot afford to pay the doctor's fee will be treated free of charge."

There is nothing else, but for this and for many other things the university has taken him to its heart.

"I put the notice up because I saw three-quarters of the village suffering from disease. They must be treated, and it's so easy to treat them. A little scabies, a little goiter, a few—but they are very many—unhealed wounds. They allow their wounds to go on. They see an herb doctor or an acupuncturist, and expect them to cure everything; but the herb doctor can cure only a few things, and there are fewer still which can be cured by the acupuncturist." He sighed, for he knew that the villagers would be suspicious, and then he added in that quiet voice which I have come to know so well, "If you see anyone who is sick, send him to me."

He is still young, and soon the whole village will be flocking to him. His wife, whom he married only a short while ago, is a trained midwife. He comes from a Christian medical university on the coast, and knows his job better than most, and in his quiet manner and in the extraordinary *certainty* of his treatment, I have never met a doctor so impressive.

The university has on its staff a Chinese herb doctor, a short, bald, wiry man whose knowledge of herbs, of Chinese boxing, of building houses, of half a dozen other things is equally impressive. If you have toothache, he will give you an herb which will soothe it in five minutes. For complicated ailments, he will take your pulse; and he swears that there are eighty-four gradations of the pulse beat which can be readily discerned by the trained doctor. He believes in animal magnetism, and can by sheer will and force of character induce an electric current into your arms. Last year he made out a long prescription of Chinese herbs to cure my jaundice. The medicine was bitter and had the consistency of black syrup; it contained the dried legs of frogs and the skin of field mice; but the jaundice disappeared after three days and has never returned.

The problem of Chinese and European medicine will never be solved, for the Chinese believe firmly in their herbs. Their *materia medica* has been tested out for four thousand years; and though it has been found wanting in some things, in others it has admirably served its purpose.

"I do not claim to cure everything," he said. "I do not claim to cure cancer, but I think it would be good if Western and Chinese medicine were studied together—and perhaps too we should study Indian medicine seriously. The Harvard Yenching Institute has been studying Chinese medicine, and finding the most extraordinary similarities between the use of Chinese and Western drugs. There is the bark of a tree which grows in Szechuan; we have used it for centuries against fevers, but it is only recently that the bark has been analyzed and found to have nearly all the properties we associate with quinine. There are many other curious similarities. . . . "

My tooth was aching. I bit on the herb, and in three minutes the ache had gone.

April 28th. All round the university there have been growing up little tea houses and restaurants. Yesterday there was a plot of broken ground where chickens wandered and a few broken bottles lay scattered over the earth. Today there is a thriving restaurant, quite new—with new lamp brackets, new stools, new tables, even new china bowls. In a few days all this newness will have vanished. Soon the bowls from which we eat *pei tsei, mien,* and *tsou-k'an* will be chipped at the edges, and the girl in the bright blue gown who serves us will no longer look young; for though one can become rich by owning a restaurant, the sulfurous kitchens take toll of health.

Six months ago the girl was young, and there was an adorable sparkle in her golden-black eyes. Today she is middle-aged; her hair falls in wisps over her forehead; her gown is unbuttoned, and she no longer cares for her appearance. It is true that her husband bullies her, but the kitchen, where the dead chickens hang on strings, bullies her more. One of the students, who loves her with an entirely platonic love, has decided to set fire to the restaurant to preserve her beauty, and we half wish him success.

There are restaurants in the village where the cooks have salaries at least eight times the salaries of the professors. The world is becoming a place where people eat; for the main task is to preserve one's strength till after the war. But the food is getting poorer and more adulterated every day, rents are going up, and one thinks twice before buying such elementary things as candles. The students who have worked so long by the dim light of candles or rapeseed-oil lamps are already showing signs of great strain. And still the prices go up and no one knows where it will end.

May 18th. Malaria has come. The sun-baked earth, the festering pools, the low tide, and the heavy white sulfurous mist which descends upon the river at night and lifts only with the coming of the sun, the green lakes of the rice fields, and the weakness that comes from dysentery—for we all suffer from dysentery nowadays—have combined to send a wave of malaria through the university. Flies in millions congregate around our desks. Bedbugs climb under the mosquito nets, crawl over your body at night, and mount toward the apex of the net in the morning; and though you catch them, there are twenty again the next day.

We have taken our beds to the duck pond and soaked them in the green messy water, and though the bamboo looks clean now and the ducks flying over our bamboo beds are beautiful beyond words, the bedbugs remain. We tried an experiment this afternoon. We poured boiling hot water over the beds. This killed the bedbugs, but sickened us, for the water turned red with blood. We have tried everything. We have taken our beds to the river, praying that the fast-flowing current will take the bugs with them downstream. But the bugs are tenacious, and perfectly happy in the interstices of the wooden bedframes. They are the color of the wood and no eye can see them.

The legs of the students are covered with weals. Kept awake in the night, they are sleepy during the day. They have no rest from the insects, and since each insect carries poison they have no certainty that they will come through the summer unharmed. At high noon we are so weak that we lie gasping on our beds.

June 6th. At the foot of Splendid Cloud Mountain there is a small village of huddled roofs and great banyan trees called Chin-k'an-pei. Somewhere in this region is the Peking mining syndicate, but rather more important than any syndicates are the small houses covered with vines and approached only by long avenues where a few distinguished scholars have retired. This afternoon we called on an old scholar who is famous because in a book of a hundred pages published more than thirty years ago he made a reasonable attempt to synthesize the philosophies of Taoism, Confucianism, and Buddhism.

It was one of the smallest houses I have ever seen, a single room which he used as bedroom and study. He wore an old tattered gown and a gray patched skullcap; yet he was not poor. He was absorbed in his studies—those studies which would lead him in another ten years if he survived to write another small book of perhaps eighty pages on the religion of the Chinese. He was thin-boned, and had once been tall. His skin seemed paper-thin in the light coming from the paper windows. His white beard, like his clothes, was torn in places; but the great jade ring on his wrist, his courtly manners, his sharp beaked nose, and the small black eyes peering from behind heavy lead-colored spectacles suggested an enormous capacity for sustained thought. We talked about his first work—that small pamphlet which had changed a little the opinions of the scholars ever since.

"But scholarship is dying," he said. "The old order is dying—that is true. Yet scholarship is so precious in itself and as an example to others. In the West you have put your trust in scholars who are scientists, and perhaps that is legitimate; but I would prefer that there should be some good scholars who remain." He apologized for not speaking English perfectly and confessed that he had neither read an English book nor spoken English to anyone for forty years; yet he spoke perfectly. "You have a good few scholars still in the universities—there is a scholar who has studied the Chinese calendar in all its phases, having read eighty thousand books on the subject, in your university. Perhaps he will write a book of three hundred pages, or even of four hundred pages, for all these things are important. People speak too much—speaking is an excuse for not thinking—and they study too little. Before the revolution we thought carefully before we spoke: today we think little, and talk too much. I cannot read the newspapers. There are *speeches*; there are *battles*; there is no *thinking*. In the old days Chinese scholars were chosen by the emperor. On them there was imposed pure trust, and rarely did they misuse the trust. They lived frugally, governed honestly, wrote little, and were content with the world. Our military commanders were scholars, Tu Fu and Su Tung-p'o were scholars and officials—even T'ao Yuan-ming was an official. This was a world in which the behavior of scholars was the hallmark of everyone's existence. Then how could we fail?"

His room was even poorer than the rooms of Chinese scholars in the university; he was talking a language which they alone still understood. There was the table, three or four ivory brushes, a tattered scroll on the wall, a jeweled fly whisk which, since it was high summer, he was occasionally flicking against our clothes; there was the cheesecloth mosquito curtain and the thick-soled slippers under the bed, and here and there on the walls, cut out from the scrolls which he had once possessed and considered insufficiently dignified to grace his bedroom, were *single characters of Chinese*, written boldly and elegantly, with tremendous passion and effrontery. It was as though the calligraphers at the moment of writing had seized the secrets of nature. There were perhaps twenty of these characters written in different styles and at different epochs; and it was clear that the old scholar believed that in the whole history of Chinese calligraphy no characters as good as these had ever been painted. Later, just as we were about to leave, I noticed what appeared to be a bronze umbrella stand behind the door filled with rolled-up scrolls.

It was then that the room became charged with excitement. One could not ask him—even as a favor—to show us the scrolls. One could only hope that he would notice their presence before we had gone. I felt sure that they were good; and they were better than anything I had ever seen before—copies of T'ang dynasty paintings, a painting of a monk, perhaps Bodhidharma, in a red robe, a single curlew on a swinging branch painted in thick monochrome like tempera, some golden birds and some court ladies dancing at the foot of the throne, and four or five other paintings and a few pieces of calligraphy.

"The rain has got at them," he said sadly, pointing to the yellow spots, "but perhaps it is better like this. The world no longer appreciates good painting or good government. The world is covered with high clouds, and we hear only the murmur of the rivers and see nothing clearly. All that is good in China is past; and I am too old to hope for a resurrection."

June 7th. Marshal Feng Yu-hsiang is staying at the hot springs. We walked among the deserted lotus ponds in the rain, while the trees shone like jewels and the great yellow building which clings to the cliff wall shone like a fountain. Suddenly a wounded soldier came limping along the wet road. The Marshal stopped and gazed at him for a long while, with a curious wondering expression in his eyes. When the man came near, the Marshal bowed very low and smiled, and the wounded soldier smiled; then they began to talk in low voices like conspirators dreaming together. The talk went on for a long time. The rain dripped on their shaven heads and on their clothes, and they were entirely unconscious of the rain. When the soldier had gone, the Marshal turned to me and said, "It is curious—I have led many armies to battle, but I have never been wounded. Perhaps I would understand better if I had been wounded."

We went back to the small villa he occupies near the lotus pools. He sat on his bed, joking and laughing, laughing sometimes until tears came to his eyes. Cross-legged on the bed, he no longer looks tall; he is reduced to human proportions until you remember that Buddha sits cross-legged behind the glass walls of his altar. We talked about the poverty of the universities and of the soldiers, who are often terribly underfed; of the thieving and hoarding which are sweeping like a plague over China. He nodded silently. After a while he began to invent new names for all the foreigners he had known in China, for there are thousands of possible names which correspond to the sounds of a foreign name. He roared with laughter, but as we left he remembered the soldier limping along the muddy road and begged us to buy something at the shop which the soldier has opened—"anything, just a trifle, two or three dollars only." We walked out in the rain and at a turning in the road we came to a small shop where biscuits and fans, rolls of towel cloth and inkstones with green inscriptions lay in profusion. The soldier was there, staring at the mist and the river. We talked about the Marshal. "He is so good to me, so good to me——," the soldier kept on saying, and his eyes filled with tears.

There is no point in this story. People *are* good to each other; people do weep and greet each other courteously in the rain. There is a lack of sophistication in the Chinese character at its best which is dangerously near to the most complete imaginable sophistication. There are people who say that the Marshal must be incredibly sophisticated and that his simplicity is a disguise, the disguise of a robber baron. It may be true. There is no judgment of these things. But J., who came with me, said afterward the only words which have any meaning: "They were walking in the rain, they bowed to one another, and afterward they wept for the misery of the world."

June 9th. I go around this campus like a ghost. I know every pebble, every flower bed, every mud-brick building by heart. I know where the crocuses are planted, and where the sensitive plant ends; I know the cow barns, the sheepfolds, the piggeries, the place where the white eagles come to bask in the sun. I know all this as I know my own childhood; and it is quite certain that I shall leave at the end of this term and go to Kunming. I have not told Bergery. He will complain of being left alone; and if I ask him, as I shall, to accompany me to Kunming, he will say, "I am perfectly happy on my mountain. Go and sow your wild oats in Kunming (which has a terrible reputation), and leave me in peace." I shall not go in peace,

and it will be so difficult to leave him that I shall go like someone
blinded and amazed.

There are rumors of fighting between government and provincial
troops in Kunming, of bandits and highwaymen on the Kweichow
road, of seventy-two dangerous bends on the road to Kunming. I shall
go, nevertheless, for though I have great loyalty to this university, the
greatest university of all in China is in the southwest.

This evening, as I came across the river and climbed the muddy
hill which leads to the campus, the moon shone on the white flowers
beneath the flagstaff. The flowers shone in a kind of luminous brilliance which I have never seen before—it was half-ghostly and half-
frightening. "We call it," said T., who has not an atom of poetry in
him, "the moon flowers shining in the snow."

I do not know how I can tear myself away from this place. The
small cramped classrooms, the colonnades around the campus, the
muddy road to the library, the long walks along the edge of the river,
the basketball players and the small teashops at the edge of the
field—they are too much a part of my life for me to be away from
them for long. And this moon shining on the ghostly flowerbed
makes it more difficult than ever to depart.

June 15th. Automobiles still come to the hot springs, but God knows
where they get their gasoline. There are sleek black limousines which
look for all the world like streamlined seals. There are women
walking in dresses which seem to have been made only yesterday; and
there are fat profiteers looking like innocent caricatures. But there are
also young girls and boys lying on the grass, and eagles spiraling high
above their heads with bronze-colored wings: there are small boys like
cherubinos and small girls like dolls. There are temples which are
now schools; and as you pass the walls, you hear the zzzzzzz-
mmmmmmm of their continual repetition of the sounds of the
Chinese characters. It is one of the most pleasant sounds in the
world, and not to be forgotten, for it is as continuous as the river, and
sweeter than the song of the golden oriole on the branches of the
willows.

Bergery was waiting for us on the steps of the temple, leaning
against the stone balustrade. Although it was warm he was wearing a
heavy tweed coat, and there were three layers of scarves around his
neck. He did not look ill, for his face was sunburned; but he looked
weak, and his weakness showed in the long thin hands as white as the

stone wall, and the way he spoke. There was an unexpected heaviness in his words; he spoke with a kind of weighty insistence on their value, and sometimes his voice would break almost to tears, a broken cracked voice coming from the great head, from the soft lips, from the blue eyes, from the tangled autumn-colored hair.

It occurred to me then that autumn had come, though it was ripe summer: an autumn of heavily laden branches with downward-sweeping leaves, an autumn of silences. He was still tall, still immense; he still dominated those shining green-roofed temples and green lotus lakes, but he was slowly withdrawing into the shade. There was a museum in the temple behind us. It had been used as a library, and Bergery had objected; but today there were no cheap paperback books on the shelves—there were scrolls, stone lions, griffins, turtles bearing on their backs unicorns of a former age. There were ancient ax-shaped coins green with bronze mildew, and three or four precious examples of T'ang dynasty pottery which had been found in the caves above these rocks. Bergery developed a theory that a great town had once occupied the gorges; but the rocks had crumbled, leaving only the stone slab with its figurines of Taoist priests which can be seen on the rise of the mountain road. The temple at the top of Splendid Cloud Mountain is known to have existed in T'ang times. Surely this was a great place of pilgrimage, and he himself was the last of the pilgrims. Outside on the green lawn an extraordinarily beautiful child was suckling a baby. "There is peace in the gorges," he murmured.

We wandered down toward a small hotel which hangs over the roof of the gorges. From there you can see the blue-sailed sampans slowly moving down stream. We noticed some enormous rafts on which houses had been built; and piled high on the rafts and all round them were bright yellow inflated goatskins.

"This must be the Kansu oil," he said. "They are floating it down from somewhere near the source of the Chialing river."

The oil passed down stream, silently, into the gathering dusk. There were blue shadows under the ginkgo trees, and the girl who had been suckling the baby came into the hotel to rest a little from the last explosions of the summer heat.

"And when it is over, when all this war is over," he said, "people will still come here to rest from the heat. The lovers will hide at night in the limestone caves, and the truly adventurous will climb the mountain to the temple. There are no places in China which are sacred to peace; but there are quiet places where war may be forgotten. The Chinese are accustomed to war; therefore they have made oases of peace, and perhaps all that is great in the culture of China is no more than a terrible reaction to the commonplace of war. After the great wars there have been great painters, great musicians, great dancers. Kublai Khan sent his armies to Szechuan through Yunnan and Kweichow, but the arts of the Yuan dynasty were almost as great as the arts of the Sung. War is not necessary, but war is the revenge which the world takes on itself, while art is the revenge which the artist takes on heaven. For the Chinese the blue sky is the source of all goodness. Let us be satisfied with these simplicities."

He was talking like a prophet, like a man who knows that he cannot live but must make terms with life. He spoke slowly and effortlessly, choosing his words with terrible deliberation. And suddenly he would stop and look at the white gulls floating against the green river, or at the young girl still suckling the child. For him there can have been little difference between them.

"The Chinese have few amusements," he said a little later. "There are no cinemas in the small towns, as there are in America, nor is there electric light, nor is there central heating. All those things that the Americans prize are absent here. The Chinese like heavy furniture, the color of the face of a child in candlelight, the touch of hands, the 'wave of the pines.' Their needs are simpler than ours; and this is only because they are more complex than we shall ever be. They play with their children, and never tire of this play. They are happy only when they are touching one another. If D. H. Lawrence had come to China, he would have found all he was looking for—and he would have found a natural courtesy which is lacking, as it must be lacking, in the Australians or the American Indians. China will grow, but she will retain her sense of touch, her dignity, and her lovely authority. There is shame in China, but it is different from ours. There is love, and that too is different from ours. There are many things which we can never understand, but if we could penetrate to the heart of their shame and their love we should know all the secrets of this land."

Someone began to tell him stories of the Szechuan villages, stories which made our blood curdle at the thought of the untamed rapacity of the peasants. They would skin dogs alive, and let them run loose with their skins hanging between their legs. Sodomy and incest were common on country farms; the haulers were homosexuals; there was no law for the protection of the young, who are made to work as soon as they can stand. These stories produced no effect on

Bergery. He had known China before the revolution; and seeing it now, broken and corrupt, carved up by the Japanese, with an under-fed army and a top-heavy bureaucracy, he was still hopeful, still gazing with those luminous blue eyes toward a future which seemed clearer and more sharply defined to him than to anyone else.

"Why should I give up hope?" he complained. "The villagers are cruel, but life is still more cruel to them. Sometimes I go to see the Abbot T'ai Shu on the temple at the top of the mountain. I am plagued with mosquitoes as I talk with him, but I dare not kill them, for my friend believes that they may be the lives of men who have died. I love all life—even that which is cruel. And if you tell me that a Chinese child works as soon as it can stand, which would you prefer—the pampered American child who has no character until the age of eighteen, or the Chinese peasant boy whose character is en-graved on the lines of his face, a character which will change but which will always preserve the characteristics it possesses at the age of nine? I have no right to speak for China; I have only a right to speak for the love I bear the Chinese."

It grew darker. Lamps were lit. On the green tablecloth faint gray clouds floating over the gorges were reflected; and there were Bergery's great hands, pale to transparency, drumming continually on the cloth.

"Which would you prefer?" he continued. "Would you prefer life to come flowing in all its untrammeled strength, or would you see life as it can be in Brooklyn or Broadway? It is dangerous to dam the springs of life, and this is what the Chinese have never done. They cannot. They *are* life. They have not been poisoned yet with machines. . . . "

"The poison will come," I objected.

"But those who have this tremendous feeling for the pure form of life," he answered, "will transmute the poison into a rare metal. The Russians have done this. The Chinese will do it in even less time. We are apt to think of the four great powers as Britain, America, Russia, and China. Unless we are careful the four great powers will be these, but stated in the reverse order."

"You really believe this?"

"Not entirely. The Chinese with power might realize that the power was useless. They would throw it away in a tremendous fit of laughing. What does a Taoist or a Buddhist or a Confucian do when power falls into his hands?"

A little later he was speaking about the Chinese armies in Changsha.

"In the first round of the war in the Pacific, we all blundered. We blundered tactically and strategically. We knew, and yet we did not know. We thought in our blindness that the war was like all other wars; we had few military attachés to the Chinese in the field. We had no military attachés attached to the Spanish Republican Army. We thought the plans of war had been worked out—a few more tanks, a few more airplanes, nothing else. But war has changed, as life has changed. From now on we shall be in a continual state of change; and only those who are weak and sensitive will be able to adapt themselves to the violent changes of the next fifty years. Change!—the whole world changing before our eyes, revolutions of custom and tradition, the dissolution of the elements and the new elements appearing like the heads of ghosts from the gray porcelain bowl in which all these things are mixed together—the witch's cauldron. There is going to be a time of change so vast that none may escape it. Britain will change out of recognition; once more America will search for her west; Russia will turn east; China will be flanked by great industrial centers on the seacoast and deep in the interior. In the center of the world will be India. Oh, if only we had time to prepare for it! But we have no time, no time——The blueprints we made yesterday are antiquated today. Only those who are wanderers of the spirit will survive.

"The wanderers survive; those who are rooted perish. This is the lesson of history, my friends. The crowns of Athens are given to the victors, but the victors pass on, and soon they have forgotten Athena and Artemis as they chase Bellona in the woods of Etruria. The victors pass on! They are no longer here, though their voice lingers for a little space. They have gone more quickly than the seasons or the fall of a pear. They were here yesterday; you saw their sturdy bronze limbs, but already they are only a memory. Today the victors are the Germans; tomorrow the victors will be the British and the Americans, but the day after tomorrow—— The victors have gone. There were vine leaves in their hair. But there are others who remain—the girl suckling the child, the plowman in his fields. The tradition is in the hands of women. Men have formed no tradition ever, for they are wanderers whether they will or no. Yet they survive, and the women perish." He sighed, and called for some more sweet wine, but though we heard the rattle of bottles in the corner, the wine was long in coming. "I say that we are wanderers, and it is better so. There was truth in this statement until a few moments ago. But now at last, after millenniums, we have come to an earth where wandering is no longer possible. There is no virgin earth left for us, and there is no place where the print of our feet has not been. This is the great revolution. For the first time in the history of the world we must find comfort in ourselves. We cannot escape ourselves. We cannot hide. We can fly in airplanes, travel in steamships, burrow under the Antarctic, but always we shall be accompanied by ghosts of ourselves—our friends. Listen! At the end of this war we shall have known everything. We shall be able to control the tides, climb the highest mountains, bring rain from the skies, grow children perhaps in test tubes. There will be no adventure left for us. What shall we do, we who are so accustomed to adventure? We must find, before it is too late, a worthy task for our lives, and we must find it now, in the middle of the war, in the silence that follows the crash of bombs. There is no time to be lost. And this is why China is important, for her philosophers for the last four thousand years have attempted to define the nobility and love of man. China is more important for her philosophers than for all her armies. She is more important because of her books than for all her swords and machine guns. She is important to us now, at this desperate critical period of her life and ours, only because of her philosophers. . . . "

Bergery was exhausted now. The windows were open, and we looked down at the gorges filling with dark liquid light. In his great tweed coat, muffled in scarves, Bergery was uttering his last testament, and hoping to be heard. We said nothing. In the candlelight the great face seemed larger, more luminous, and more carefree. One by one the scarves had fallen from his throat, and the great fur gloves he laid on the table at the beginning of dinner had been accidentally removed by the maidservant. There was nothing more he wanted to say. There in the gorges the last wild birds were flying over an inky dark sea.

June 20th. I am writing this in the airplane on the way to Chengtu. Small white clouds are rolling among the mountains; a gray-blue mist hovers on the horizon. The small Junker plane rattles in the wind, but we are sailing smoothly and intricately above the blue iceberg mountains. For a while I thought I had seen these blue mountains before, and wondered where. They are not like the bleeding red hills of the cordilleras; they are not white like the Alps, nor greenish-yellow like the foothills of Switzerland in spring. They are blue like the sea, a luminous deep blue, never ending. And these blue mountains of Szechuan, with their regular waves, still seem to be in motion. Unchanging like the sea, and yet forever changing, they climb against the horizon and show the bellies of the waves in the sun.

The scenery has changed. There are fields of yellow rice and small hamlets; a river like a stream of milk. Cool, cool—the air, and underneath us everything is burning in a furnace. And still on the horizon there are waves of blue mountains, exactly like the blue mountains I have seen from Splendid Cloud Mountain. We passed over Peipei and followed the gorges, then turned north toward the great yellow fields and the open hearths; for truly this country is like a furnace, where liquid steel is hardening and the glow from the furnace doors. . . . And there are eagles, buzzards, kites—impossible to count them. The waves of the sea have disappeared. We passed a walled village where the gray cathedral spire climbs up above the red roof tiles. Then once again the mountains, climbing higher and higher. . . .

Chengtu is the walled yellow city in the distance in the middle of a green plain. Utterly unlike Chungking. The earth flat, and springing green, the blue mountains enclosing her, and the great wall dividing only at the presence of a river. The wing dips down. The lemon-shaped airfield, the small red buildings with the same red-rusted drums of oil piled in great pyramids which I saw in Kweilin. The trees are different, the color of the roof tiles is different, there are no rocks as in Chungking—everything as smooth as the palm of the hand. Down, and then up again, as though the pilot knew that we wanted to see the city in its immensity, this city which was once the capital of southern China—*hsiao Peking*—little Peking—the greatest capital of the south. But the walls are broken in places, and the yellow wheat and rice are being gathered, and here and there among the fields are vivid blue and silver streams. It is the country which shines magnificently. The little rubble heap of the yellow town is softened by the shadows of willows, but there are few great streets—a rabbit warren, gray and brown, with nothing to commend it. Mercifully the airport is outside the town.

June 25th. I have been staying on Hwa Shih-pa campus. I have seen nothing so restful since I came to China. Under the broad midsummer sun, the cows graze in the green fields, the jackdaws flourish their wings, and the great curving roofs of the Chinese library reach to heaven. It rained this morning. I walked barefoot over the flooded grass, splashing up silver splinters of rain. There were blue pigeons on the trees and great white clouds fanning the sky. Here, for the first time since I came to China, are university buildings which have the dignity which learning requires. They are heavy and solid; they have not been bombed.

And perhaps, too, it is the quietness which makes this place so peaceful. There is no river at the foot of the steep cliffs; we are outside the wall of the town. I am no longer sharing a damp, concrete-floored room with a coolie, watching the paper windows as they are drenched by the rain. Here are all the comforts of European civilization; and too late, I have decided that it is difficult to live without them. I think of Bergery perched in his small red hut on the cliffside, and then of this warm room, papered white, with a Han dynasty vase on the mantelpiece, paintings, comfortable chairs. I was astounded when I first came here. The trim green hedges, the lotus lakes, the neat houses with their lawns, the young girls playing tennis and the boys lounging in the shade of elms—do these things happen? I had forgotten them, living in a world where poverty was the custom and riches were despised. One cannot live here for long; but for a moment—a *brief* moment—it is right that they should be enjoyed.

The world is far away. We are not in the world. The earth is flat, and this too is important, for ever since I came to China I seem to have been struggling up and downhill. Here you can ride bicycles, and perhaps it is this that is so surprising, for no one would dream of riding bicycles in Chungking. There are thousands of bicycles; nearly every student seems to possess one. There are possessions beyond the dreams of Chungking: everything is dearer; fortunes are being made every day; I am still wondering at the student who told me that he had been given a birthday present by his father, a bicycle costing thirty thousand dollars.

But here at least one can recuperate. The silence of these huge willows, the great block of the campus stretching, it seems, for miles, the bright new hospital buildings, the leper colony, the radio masts—they are all here. There is an atmosphere of applied Christianity, for half the professors on the campus are priests; and yet, behind it all, there is a curious sense of desolation, as though the place had been cut off from the world. A few airplanes, like wisps of hay, fly overhead, but Chengtu is living quietly in its dreams. It will not always be like this.

We lie in the grass, watching the ducks waddling in the pond.

The young student with the tousled hair and the thick eyeglasses is speaking reminiscently of the past:

"I didn't want to come here," he ruminated, "but the standard is lower in the Christian universities at Chengtu than in the national universities. I came down from the north. I was sick. I couldn't make the grade." His voice dropped, as a stream will drop below the level of the earth. "We are not in the war—that's what is so terrifying. We are living like lords, as though the war had never happened." He pointed to the obscenely ugly yellow clock tower, half Chinese, half Western, which rose above a clump of dwarf willows. "The city has been bombed, and the Governor of Szechuan, who lives here, had the foresight to drive some large main streets through the town, but the Japanese do not hate us. They have bombed every other university, but I suppose they think the Christian universities are too scrupulous and too inefficient to be dangerous. Why is it? Our classrooms are good—they are not farm buildings, and yet we do not reach the grade of the other universities. Are we taught badly? We have good scientists, the best agricultural school in China, and the best school of dentistry, and yet the feeling that it is all a waste of effort, leading nowhere, taunts us continually. . . . "

He had wanted to go to the great national university at Kunming, which comprises the three universities of Tsing Hua, Pei Ta, and Nankai. He had dreamed of studying there all the way across the mountains of the north, and when he failed in the examinations, he had contemplated suicide. He regretted now that he had not taken agriculture. Nanking University's agriculture department had been transferred to Chengtu, and he spoke excitedly of Frank Dickenson and Professor Buck, who had between them revolutionized the agriculture of China.

"They are experimenting with everything," he said. "We have cows from test tubes, yes—there are actually cows from test tubes on this campus. They have examined Chinese agriculture thoroughly, and the course in agriculture is not easy: agricultural economics, agricultural statistics, methods of farming—every kind of imaginable course!" He was delighted with the fame of the agriculture department, but the agriculture department was not his own, and though he began to speak of the experiments in the production of tea and cereals in Fuhtan, my old university, it was clear that his heart was set on watching the rise of Chinese agriculture.

We began to talk of human sewage. Even in Chengtu, which is

cleaner than Chungking, there were open sewers, and every morning the coolies came to the houses to collect the sewage for the fields.

"It is one of the things that they have discovered in this university, though the Chinese peasants discovered it many years before. The land grows old. It is necessary that there should be organic nitrates to keep the earth living. There is only one way to do this, and the Chinese and the Mexicans have done it for generations, and even in the Middle Ages the Europeans did it. There is a balance between man and the land: the food he takes from the earth must be returned. They have discovered that without these organic substances, the earth perishes. Once people thought that plants required only inorganic substances—water, carbon dioxide, mineral salts—but we know better now. We do not yet know how plants grow, but gradually, with all the accumulated experience of the Chinese farmers behind us, we are beginning to learn."

We sat there, gazing idly at the blue-green ducks in the pond. Suddenly we looked over our shoulders, and we noticed a small cow, with all the delightful ungainliness of the young, wandering among the hedges. She was white, very silky, and the bones shone through the silk. The student jumped up, delighted beyond words.

"Here she is! She was born in a test tube," he shouted happily. "The first cow in China who was born by artificial insemination."

July 1st. The days pass quietly. Every morning I go to the library and quench my thirst for books. There are five hundred books on China, and I am determined to tear the guts out of them. When I am tired of reading, I dream of the extraordinary vicissitudes of these books, which have traveled halfway across the world until they reach the corner of Tibet, or else I wander upstairs toward the museum, where Tibetan bronzes rub shoulders with T'ang dynasty paintings. There is an atmosphere of quiet and reflection; no dogs are barking, no children are howling. Under a glass case a Tibetan mask no longer looks savage. There is grace and dignity in the attitudes of the Buddha, in the small medallions and the huge bronzes.

July 12th. For some reason, long after the event, we were discussing the bombing of Tokyo. The old Chinese professor in the brocade gown nodded his head vigorously as though he seemed to be in full agreement; but suddenly he began to speak, and I realized for the thousandth time since I came to China that a man who nods his head may be expressing the most profound disagreement.

"I was in Chungking during the bombardment," he said. "I have no wish that the Japanese should share the same fate. Nothing is so terrible, nothing is so remorseless, nothing so revolting to the soul as a bombardment. The soul cannot suffer in peace such indignities. Only now, two years afterward, can I think coolly of what happened, and now I praise God that China for centuries refused to harbor such things. The Chinese knew all about poison gases fifteen centuries ago; we invented an airplane, and quite rightly executed the inventor; we are the only nation which has thought continually of peace. I have no malice against the Japanese, who killed my parents and my brothers. I have pity, but it is not Christian pity, I'm afraid—it is the pity that burns."

He asked me about Barcelona, and since we were drunk with the headiness of the subject I spoke of the girls lying in the mortuary at Barcelona looking as though they were sleeping; of the dead child which Toller and Marthe Huysmann found in the cathedral square; of the soldier who seemed to be bowing to me at Mora de Ebro; of Lister and Modesto and Cisneros and all the unsung heroes of the Spanish war.

"It was a popular war?" he asked.

"Yes, the people rushed the Montaña barracks in Madrid, armed themselves, and killed the traitors."

"And their generals?"

"Their generals were stonemasons, carpenters, musicians like Duran, a few members of the ancient general staff like de Rocca. The president was a doctor."

He smiled then, and pointed to a portrait on the wall.

"So is ours," he answered, "for Sun Yat-sen is permanent president of China." And then softly, lest he should be heard, "What crimes are committed in his name!"

July 29th. A telegram arrived in Chengtu at 6:30 this evening. It was written in Chinese, and under each Chinese character there were penciled code numbers, for the Chinese send telegrams by the most complicated numerical code in the world. It read:

COME QUICKLY BERGERY DYING ASKING FOR YOU BRING DOCTOR

It was signed by "the girl in the red trousers."

July 30th. I am writing this in the crowded bus. There are no seats. We sit precariously on our luggage, struggling against the wind, the rocky road, the sudden lurching, and the violence of the countryside. It is still raining. We have been climbing and winding among steep gray hills, and the great red plains of Chengtu are far behind us. There are small hamlets where peasants crowd over little green wisps of flame; and once or twice we have passed men in ragged uniform, with rifles on their shoulders, and as we scudded past they have turned their backs. The fat girl screamed "bandits." She was probably right, but no one cares, though we go on to discuss the large army of bandits that has been seen around Mount Omei. I curse myself for not having climbed Mount Omei, the most sacred Buddhist mountain in China; I am angry because I have not seen the temple dedicated to Tu Fu, or that other temple, greater and more mysterious, dedicated to the hero of the *Story of the Three Kingdoms*, Chu Ko-liang.

There is nothing to see. The rain pelts the canvas roof of this cattle truck, and we are being bounced inextricably together. A wide pagoda flashes past, so beautiful and still that even the little banker's clerk with the wad of American money which he is going to exchange on the black market in Chungking is awed into silence. In three hours, if we are lucky, we shall reach Niechiang, where sugar is being hoarded by the merchants who are determined to beat the government monopoly. There are sweet cakes there, nougat, crystalized fruit. There is even a hotel. We have passed the wrecks of three buses already. "At Niechiang," said the bus driver, "there are all the comforts of the world. . . . "

August 3rd. Back in Peipei. Temperature 103 degrees. There was an apologetic note from Bergery waiting for me at the hotel. "It was nothing, of course, and you must not be frightened. They all panicked because I was spitting blood, but it's all over now—the last stage of the convalescent. I am up and about again—not very strong, but I feel that the real convalescence is happening now. The girl in the red trousers has just bathed my face, and she has brought a basin of water. 'What shall I do with it?' 'Put your wrists in it.' 'And then?' 'That's all—it is cold water from the fountain. It heals.' I have obeyed her, and soon I felt the cool water springing through my veins. Come when you can. B."

August 4th. The servant came down from the mountain in the early hours of the morning. He was very calm and said very little, except that Bergery was dying, and would I go up. He wore a blue shirt streaked with sweat, and though it was already broad daylight he carried a lantern in which the tung-oil flames still shone in wreaths of black smoke. The sun shone. The river was pale green, and the mountains above us were also green, and even the sky seemed to be tinged with this color. In the heat we staggered up the dusty mountain paths, occasionally resting on tombstones or in the shade of the tung-oil trees. I do not know why it is, but the shade of the sparse tung-oil trees is preferable to that of the pines—cooler and more refreshing. It was past noon when we came to the small temple high up on the spur of the mountain. Smoke came from the roof, and I knew then that he must still be living.

I ran most of the way across the spur of the hill, while the servant grumbled. He had bought some rice, sweet bread, and biscuits in the little village near the hot springs; and now the weight of these things caused him to suffer abominably. He staggered along, breathless and uncomfortable, and I could hear the hiss of his breathing when I passed through the gates of the temple.

Bergery lay in bed, his face very white. The young girl, wearing only red trousers and a thin blue milk-stained blouse, was fanning the flies from his face. All the while he was coughing up blood. He smiled when I came in, waved his hands, and immediately began a fit of coughing. He turned his face away to the wall, where the gilded Buddhas and blue-green frescoes of dancing girls reflected the light. Meanwhile the girl ran away, only to return a few moments later with a basket of enormous blue grapes.

"Everything is happening so quickly now," he complained. "I am losing blood, but that doesn't worry me so much as that I am losing hope."

I told him that we could easily fly him to a sanatorium in India.

"Last year I seriously thought of going to a sanatorium, but the Indians wrecked it. I don't blame them, or rather I think I understand them. In every civilization there is a moment when the people take their revenge upon the machines. It happened with the wreckers in England, and it will happen again with the Germans after this war. I wonder if it is true that the Indians sympathized with the Japanese! I doubt it! They tortured British airmen, they derailed trains, they burned factories; and surely it was nothing more than a sudden, instinctive, and overwhelming hate for the machines. And it is better that it should happen now than later." He looked out through the latticework of gilded doors and smiled at the expanse of blue iceberg-like mountains. After a while he said:

"It is a pity I am dying. I might have been of some use. I have seen more wars than most people, and traveled more, and perhaps felt more, but always I was conscious of the vanity of things. This is what spoiled my life. Once or twice in my life I had power; but I threw it away because I did not believe that power was good, or even that it was necessary. I'm the last of the liberal journalists. Those who came after me were mostly youths, without the ability to think, though they could describe well enough the exteriors of things. In the old days we believed the liberals were descendants of the *homines liberi*, who built the city-states of the Middle Ages and fought against emperors and popes. We believed in the European tradition, but what do people believe in nowadays? We belong to Europe. I was born in New England, but I am still a European—nothing can change that. I cannot escape, even if I wanted to. There is no escape for us. And though we use the word 'destiny' rarely, we know that it is our destiny to remain always good Europeans."

He lay back exhausted. He was sick and ill, but there was still the same extraordinary blue light in his eyes. They were shining now, as he lay back, his head against the monstrous stuffed pillows, his hands spread out in front of him. Against the golden fretwork of the temple and the crumbling gods he looked theatrical; and the blood on the counterpane was surely greasepaint. He was a little conscious of this, and hated it.

"The liberal is the only free man," he continued. "He values life, and yet he is prepared to die for the sake of his freedom; and he orders all those who cherish freedom to strive with their lives not only for the sake of freedom, but against any particular freedom when it destroys the love of life in people's hearts. We have only one aim—that people should love life. *The world is a place where people must learn to play.* I believe that we should adore life, and that it is there only to be adored; and the dance of life is something that truly exists, and without it our lives have no meaning."

The girl was chewing grapes and spitting out the seeds. From time to time Bergery looked at her. There was a curious sympathy between them. She was very young, slender and thin, but graceful in her red trousers. A few chickens came through the open doors. I heard pigs grunting behind the temple, and the sound of mallets in the forest, and all the while I was conscious of Bergery's enormous head and the transparent blue eyes.

"It is more difficult to die when you love freedom. For the Germans it must be easier," he said after a while.

He said once that he wanted to be buried on the mountain top, without coffin or inscription; but he insisted now that he should have a wooden cross. He wanted the monks to celebrate a Buddhist Requiem in his memory, and he wanted to cause no suffering to the girl who attended him. His books were to be returned to his wife after the war—she could dispose of them as she pleased.

It was late in the afternoon when I left. He insisted against all reason on accompanying me to the door. In the sunlight his cheeks looked healthy enough—they were bright red, glowing like some molten metal. As he pointed to the distant mountains shining in the ruby sunset, his hands looked vigorous and I noticed that they were more beautiful than when I had seen them last. He must have noticed how I gazed at his hands, for he said:

"You remember the hands of the priest in the monastery who conducted the Requiem? There was perfection of grace in those hands, surely. One can adore with one's hands more easily than with one's knees, and surely the hands are the most beautiful things in our body. Look at the hands—the proportions of all four fingers, their sizes, the way they speak of the experiences which each one of us has undergone. . . . "

Even then, like a good host in a Chinese house, he insisted on accompanying me a little farther, past the temple gate, past the crumbling stucco gargoyles, past the great stone vase, the datura trees, and the small shrine to the earth god, where the weather-beaten goddess resembled to an extraordinary degree one of the queens on the Royal Porch at Chartres.

"The earth god," he smiled. "The Chinese are so sensible, for there is no other god it is so necessary to propitiate."

For the last time he spoke of his plan, when he recovered, of settling down in one of the valleys of Szechuan with a few kindred spirits. They would build an oasis in the middle of war, and like the Chinese they would defend themselves behind high crenelated walls. . . . They would cultivate the earth and carve on the high mountains all the poems that best deserved to be remembered. "We must carve them so deeply that even if the barbarians should one day pass by the foot of the mountains, they would have no time to obliterate them. Whatever happens, our traditions must be preserved. Our cathedrals can go, our most historic monuments can be destroyed by German bombs, but God help us if we forget our great poets. And if everything should perish, a traveler a thousand years hence would find these poems inscribed in a strange language on our mountains, and from these poems he would be able to reconstruct the whole of the European tradition. And what does it matter? In a thousand years' time we shall all be of one race. We shall have Chinese eyes and black hair; we shall be slimmer and shorter than we are now; we shall be more graceful in our movements. The East and the West are already in the melting pot in Malaya and the Indies. How long will it last? No one knows, but certainly it cannot be more than a thousand years. And then perhaps, since we shall be all of the same blood, there will be peace."

He was silent, then, for a long time, gazing down at the blue valley, the mountains like icebergs and the mist. I knew he would have liked to descend the mountain. The girl in the red trousers was shivering. She held him by the hand and begged him to return to the temple, for a rainy wind was coming up.

"It is dark down there," he said. "There is more sunlight on the mountains, and I would prefer you not to make the journey."

"I must give my lectures tomorrow," I objected.

The sun was setting. It caught the golden fretwork of the temple gates and the lamps of hollow glass swinging from the temple beams. I went down the slope. After a few moments I looked back. Bergery was still standing there, his shoulders shaking with the terrible force of his paroxysms of coughing. I shall not see him alive again.

August 10th. I feel certain that Bergery died on the night I left him, but no news has come from the temple. And this is perhaps as it should be. He is one of those who prefer to disappear, one of those who have a passion for hiding behind the screens which life so often and so generously provides. This is not his first death. He had died many times, not only in the sense that he has been reported dead in the newspapers. I remember a railway accident in Germany when the train flew off the rails and together we went up and down the ranks of the overturned carriages, pulling out here an arm, there a foot, there the head of some old man who had perished in his sleep. All the while there was an extraordinary impassivity on Bergery's face. There are men who, because they cannot stand the sight of blood, become surgeons. Such a man was my friend Auguste Souchy, the

leader of the anarchists in Spain, who was credited with the assassina-
tion of more reactionaries than any other anarchist; and yet he lived
simply in Paris, with his wife, in an attic of the rue Boileau. He who
hated murder practiced it because it seemed to him a necessary right,
and because he believed that the reactionaries were stifling the life of
the young. In the same way Bergery, because he believed in freedom,
gave himself no opportunity of practicing it. When Hitler complained against the reports of British and American journalists in
Europe, Bergery laughed sardonically in his face: "It is the first time
we have been credited with good sense." He learned languages as
other men read books. He was determined that in whatever part of
the world he should be sent, he would be able to make his way. He
was often tempted to write books, but he always refused. "I belong to
the moment of time. The man who writes books has perhaps a year
or a century of fame, but it is the moment with all its complexities
which baffles and fascinates me." He was generous and suffered fools
gladly, especially those who, like St. Francis, were fools of God. He
loved priests, old women, the canals of Bruges, tapestries, the Louvre
at night, and the British Museum on a hot August day, when the
galleries are crowded with school children. He loved everything that
was European; and believing that Crete was the beginning of our
civilization, he regretted that he was not sent to Crete during the
invasion. "Everything in Europe comes from Babylon and Crete."
And so he is dead. It will make little difference to the world, yet
thousands of people will have been subtly altered by his presence. He
was forty-nine. He looked younger. In his handshake there was still
the vigor of youth, and his eyes were bright and blue like the Swiss
lakes. Only the two red patches on his face, which gave him the
appearance of an actor who has forgotten to wash away the greasepaint, spoke of his sufferings. Perhaps his sufferings were not great,
but he bore them with the patience and delight of youth. "To die
without suffering," he once said, "that is the greatest imaginable
horror."

August 12th. Bergery died two days ago. He did not die on the night
when I went up the hill. The servant came this morning, before
dawn, when the sky was still shining with stars. He told me that
Bergery had asked to be brought out in the open, on a bed, and he
spent the night gazing at the stars with his eyes wide open. The
servant, who watched him all night, said there was so much

confidence in his expression and so much sweetness in his smile that it was difficult to believe he was dying. The wind blew. The "wave of the pines" on the mountain tops, like the sighing of waves in Irish bays, can make men mad or content according to their ear for music; and so I was not surprised when the servant told me that Bergery was quite calm, as though in a deep trance, except when the wind blew through the pines, and then it was as though he had seen the high gods, for he would smile happily and begin to sing in tune with the wind.

All the way up the mountain I tried to reconstruct in my imagination the circumstances of his death, but as usual, when I try to reconstruct these things consciously, the circumstances are quite otherwise than my imagination would foretell. I imagined that the bed would still be outside the small temple. I imagined that he would still be gazing at the stars. I imagined the girl in the red trousers fanning the flies from his face. I found none of these things. The girl had been sent away. Bergery lay inside the temple, near the altar, and there were nuns and monks praying at the foot of his bed. Nor was the sun shining. It was gray and misty, and everything seemed about to dissolve into decay. A great unpainted wooden coffin lay near the door. He had asked to be buried without a coffin, but the whole monastery had followed the coffin the day before—it was one of the high-shouldered Chinese coffins which are sometimes painted bright blue and decorated with gold-leaf patterns of flying birds. It was quite empty, except for the cock which was tied to a cord and which sometimes perched on the great lionlike shoulders of the coffin. They were praying and beating bells. A young monk, who had only recently entered the monastery and whose bare shaven head showed the bright red weals of the incense which had been burned into the skin, stood alone without speaking or praying at the head of the bed. He was handsome beyond any monks I had seen on these mountains, and it was clear that Bergery had taken a special liking to him. The praying came to an end shortly after I arrived. There was mist on the mountains—great patches of mist which swirled past the doors of the small temple, hiding the pines and sometimes opening to reveal a faint light shining in the valley below. One would look through tunnels of clear air, seeing the river flowing sedately below; and then the mist shrouded everything, and you could see no more than a few inches ahead. He had given orders that he should be buried on a great scarp of the mountain looking over the river, and there we carried him in the late forenoon, the monks supporting the coffin on their shoulders. Even the Abbot T'ai Shu, the reverend holiness to

whom all Chinese Buddhists look for support, accompanied the
procession down the hill, waving the mist away with his fan. It was
bitterly cold, but the grave had been dug already, and the hard earth
shone silver at its sides. It was not a deep grave. I was thankful for
that, but I wondered whether the heavy coffin, so close to the edge of
the cliff, might not topple into the river two thousand feet below. I
think he would have liked the idea, and I thought of the coffin
careering blindly into the river, Bergery himself standing upright with
arms outstretched and *flowing* like a mountain stream. There was
only the briefest ceremony. Bareheaded, the monks stood around,
and the utterly sickening sound of earth falling on the wooden coffin
lid was muted by a sudden wind which waved through the pines. I
recited the prayers of burial according to the Church of England. I
had not noticed until that moment the small dark Taoist priest with
the oiled topknot in his hair and the burning eyes, but he too recited
a prayer; and then there were the chants of the monks. A few mountain flowers were strewn over the grave. On the small cross someone
had inscribed his name in Chinese and the date of his death, and
underneath were the words, "He loved China." Kneeling down in
the hard mud, I wrote in pencil on the wood:

> *Near here died Johann Sebastian Karl Bergery*
> *on August 10th 1943, aged 49.*
> *He loved men, and strove for peace.*

August 13th. There is no longer any reason why I should stay. I have
been invited to join the Southwestern Associated University at
Kunming, and I have already given my resignation. I cannot live in a
place which is haunted by Bergery. And there is so little sun in
Szechuan, and the mountains hide the sky, and there is fever on all
these marshlands. Every time I look up at the mountains, I expect to
see Bergery coming down; and that black scarp of rock which looks
over the river already seems to be falling. Bergery should never have
come here—I have told myself this twenty times a day for the last ten
days. He could have lived in the *provençal* sunlight of Kunming; and
there, interpreting the East to the West, he might have brought
himself an even greater fame. He was not famous while he lived only
because he had no desire for fame. Now that he is dead, he will
become famous as certainly as the moon rises in the sky. He left
papers and letters behind. There was one to his wife from which I
have made here a short extract: "You wrote to me in Paris, saying

that the child was ill. I flew over, and you wept because I did not stay. But, Mary, other children were ill—millions of children, and I had to serve them. A journalist must always be traveling away from the things he loves. You did not know—you could not know—that for me to live in Paris and enjoy everything that was so beautiful was itself mortally dangerous. Forgive me. I am a wanderer. I should never have married. I was too restless to learn how to be silent by your side. Woman loves; man suffers—perhaps that is why women always want to possess too much, and men make war. . . . "

August 19th. The last few days in Chungking. No clouds, the sun very hot; and the dust-laden streets like furnaces. Perhaps we shall go tomorrow—no one knows. I have been wandering in the center of the city, unable to resist the sun, and this afternoon I went down to the foreshore to watch the sampans. There was no wind; the white ships crept downstream like white caterpillars, so fat they were and so slowly they moved. There are places even here where boys bathe, though the river is the color of a yellow cloth soaked in water. The small black ferryboats wander like water beetles on the yellow river, and above them the sky arches, terribly high and remote, shaped like a parabola. I lay flat on my back on a rock while the dragonflies flew out of the river, and it was strange to think of them arising from this muddy stream. Some more children came to bathe, slipping out of their dusty rags, and immediately they lost their air of urchins and became like gods, shining yellow in the water; and their black matted hair on their foreheads gave them the appearance of having stepped out of a Chinese play. They were splendid. They swam seriously, chased after dragonflies, whispered among themselves, and formed wild plots in an effort to catch something bright red which was floating on the surface of the water. Through half-closed eyes I watch them from the big slab of rock where I lay. I could hear the waters thundering, the cries of the children, the red dragonflies whirring in the bright blue sky; I could feel the heat simmering downward from the heavens. I did not see all that the children were doing. They had divided into two groups. They were swimming into places where I thought the river was dangerous, but in the heat and the shadow of the rocks I did not move. There they were, the two white lines of childish heads and arms and buttocks on the grayish-yellow river— two arrowheads pointing toward the small bright red object floating on the river. And someone reached out a perfectly white childish arm and lifted the limp red thing high above her head, squealing with delight. I thought they had found something of value, a piece of cloth perhaps, and when they returned they all clustered around the young girl who held the thing to her breast, and they whispered excitedly, and spoke of it with tenderness and great interest. She laid it in the sand, in the shadow of the rock where I lay, while the sun bathed my face and steam rose from the shoulders of the naked children, and suddenly I looked down and saw them squatting in a ring, grave-faced, looking at the damp red body of a small rat, whose skin had been eaten by the fishes in the river. But for them it was not a rat, nor was there any blood soaking in the sand. It was something mysterious and beautiful, which they watched gravely and tenderly; for the sun dried it, the white tendons became firm, and sometimes the limp red legs would twitch under the impact of the strong sunlight. The voices of the children playing with the dead rat made me immensely happy, for they seemed to come from a world I have long forgotten, a world where everything is interesting and beautiful. They stood up. They dressed slowly in their patched rags of blue cloth, and they carried the rat tenderly in their hands toward the city.

August 25th. I have been to say good-bye to Sir Frederick Eggleston, the Australian ambassador. He lives on a cliff edge overlooking the Chialing river, in an enormous brown stucco house; and all day long military trucks thunder past his house. We came up the steep circling roads in his car, which was surmounted by a wreath of flowers perhaps ten feet long, for later in the day he proposed to place the wreath on the tomb of Dr. Lin Sen, the president of China who has just died. All the small children and all the blue-coated soldiers (who are not very different from children) gaped as we passed, for though they are accustomed to see cars, it is rare to see a car crowned with lilies.

Of all the ambassadors in China, Sir Frederick Eggleston is the most popular. He lives quietly in his great house, rarely going out, surrounded by Chinese paintings, quietly performing those acts of friendship and understanding which are more important in China than diplomacy. You will find professors and merchants sitting at his table; an official of the Kuomintang will be discussing the paintings of the Wei dynasty with a little schoolmistress; and when the wine is served on a silver platter and the ambassador is beaming quietly at the young soldier, who is arguing about the iniquities of the Burma campaign, you have a feeling that the civilization of our forefathers has been restored and the sweat and dirt of Chungking forgotten. In this great room, with the blue carpet, the rows of bookcases, and the black head of a bronze Indian prince gleaming from the wall, perspectives become sharper and understanding is enriched by the quiet splendor of a balanced mind. He sits there in a great chair, one gouty foot stretched forward, and behind him like a curtain all the yellow smoke and dust of Chungking rise into the air. He is courteous to the young scholar who sits tongue-tied in the corner; and he is apt to show the merchant who has been speaking grandiloquently of the fortunes he has made and will still make that he prefers the company of scholars to those of money-makers. He is simple and sincere, and perhaps it is his pure sincerity which makes him so beloved to the Chinese.

I do not know why it is, but the rooms of the wise have an increasing light. There is a splendor in this room which I have seen nowhere else in Chungking. Some blue flowers in a silver vase, the painting of a horse over a fireplace, the little blackwood tables, the silent footsteps of well-trained servants conspire together to make an atmosphere where no one feels at a loss. The courage we have lost in the sweltering heat of a Chungking summer is restored to us, and we begin to feel once more the singing of the blood in our veins.

August 28th. We leave in three days. T. is still collecting "tickets." He must obtain authorization from Garrison Headquarters, the Foreign Office, the Transport Bureau, and half a dozen more. He is terribly afraid of forgetting one out of the many authorizations that we must possess before we go south. He is being sent down on an official mission, the car is an official car, and the gasoline is being paid for by the government; but my presence in the car makes it fifty times more difficult. I have had three photographs taken, but I must have three more. I must have my visa countersigned by the police and may have to pay duty on my baggage. Most of my luggage consists of books, but T. thinks they will have to be left at the customs stations until the police have passed them.

"Why? Dangerous thoughts?"

"Good heavens, no! But there is nothing about books on the list of dutiable articles, and they will want to make sure."

In the heat we are both beginning to become surly and bad-tempered.

"It will be worse in Kunming. You are on a plateau a mile high, your blood runs thin, and you lose your temper on the slightest occasion. You will be near murder so often that it will become commonplace, and you will be in a country where murder is very common. The tribesmen will murder you for a dollar and think nothing of it. We may be held up by bandits—there are at least three large groups of organized bandits between Kweiyang and Kunming. Are you good at shooting?"

"No."

"You will have to learn. If you see anyone with a gun on the road, shoot. There are also wild animals."

"There were leopards at Peipei. They are quite tame. They would feed out of my hand."

"The trouble with you is that you are not taking the journey seriously. Before 1927 there was no road across Kweichow—nothing but mule tracks. Well, the peasants still believe that they own the place, and if we have a breakdown on a dark night, they will think. . . ."

"The car will disappear and we shall have to walk?"

"You will not walk. You will be kidnaped. You may be spared, but I shall not, because I am an official in the Chinese government."

"Do they hate the Chinese government?"

"No, but they don't always recognize it. They believe the country belongs to them."

He talked about the Miao race who once ruled over a great empire in the southwest; but they possessed no written records and it is impossible to recreate their history. As in Hunan, they were dispossessed at the end of the Ming dynasty and their territory was given to the soldiers. They have a great love for bright colors, and they could hide themselves well in their mountain fortresses, and even today there are Miaos who live on the summits of high mountains, dreaming of the day when the plains will once more belong to them. They are tin-miners, silver-miners, farmers, peasants, mechanics, and they have a fine sense of loyalty to their own race and they will murder you for the pleasure of murdering a stranger. The Miaos and the Lolos of the southwest make excellent churchmen, for they have a passion for community singing. You will like them."

I wondered whether I should like them, or whether it was pos-

sible to like them, but he said no more. He has gone to police
headquarters in the hope of finding still another "ticket."

September 1st. Early in the morning, when it was still dusk, we
climbed into the car and began the long journey to Kunming. The
streets were deserted and swept clean by the night's rain. Chungking
at dawn is all whiteness. The great towering buildings of the government offices in the winding streets looked as though they were built
of marble or ice; and the silence was like a benediction, so cool and
pure that we felt we were traveling far away from the towns. The
birds were chirping, small boys were sleepily climbing the streets toward the newspaper offices, and a few girls crowded around the wells.
There are wells everywhere in Chungking, but you notice them only
in the morning. I have passed through the busy streets in the afternoon, thinking that all the water came from the river, for the streets
were full of water-carriers splashing great black slabs of water on the
dusty pavements; but high up, by Liang Lou K'ou and in many dusty
side streets, the small metal-rimmed wells sparkle at dawn. Then they
are forgotten, or perhaps they are hidden from the eyes of strangers.
Now the dawn was coming quickly, a blinding whiteness streaked
with saffron, and soon the heat would be climbing up the stiff white
molten sky, and soon we would be racing through the countryside,
under the pines.

September 8th. At An-ning, on the way to Kunming. We visited the
mayor of An-ning, a man with some kindness in his eyes, although he
was one of those who took his duties seriously. He told us that there
would be an execution later in the morning. It appeared that an
opium smoker, who had been warned three times, had exhausted the
patience of the mayor, who proposed to execute him as a warning to
others.

There was a band, firecrackers were being exploded, small boys
ran cheering along the streets, and the extraordinary procession
turned out of the long street into the center of the town. We could
not find the opium smoker. It was impossible to believe that the
opium smoker was the man dressed up in a clown's costume, a long
white silk costume into which strips of violently colored silk had been
inserted. He was quite young, with a small mustache, very pale and
disheveled. The small boys cheered him, the band played and some-

times stones would be thrown at him, and then he would glance over his shoulder with an expression of agonized annoyance. There were soldiers at the head of the procession. They walked grimly, almost silently, while the crowds cheered from the balconies and the bugles sounded from the drum tower.

We did not follow the procession to the end. The opium-smoker's face had been painted white, or perhaps he was pale with the effort of avoiding the stones. He stumbled along, his hands free, his silk gown billowing in the wind. He looked bewildered, and it was clear that a benevolent town council had given him rice wine before he left the prison. He would turn around suddenly, making little appealing gestures to the children, who can have known little about his fate, though they repeated over and over again, "Shoot, shoot, shoot!" as though it was the most amusing thing in the world. And then, ten minutes later, silence descended over the whole village and we heard the bark of rifles, followed by the winged sound of a single shot. The opium smoker was dead. The village resumed its normal life.

As we sit on the edge of our beds, listening to the soldiers who are unrolling their blankets along the covered terrace downstairs, an extraordinary thing happens. A light shines through the torn paper windows and suddenly the door opens, and a girl enters, followed by an old woman holding a lamp. The girl is beautiful, dressed in green and red silk; her face is powdered dead-white, the arching forehead shadowed by the black mass of oiled hair, and the eyebrows delicately curved. In the flickering light of the two lamps she looks like someone out of a fairy tale. Standing against the wheeling shadows of the wall, perfectly still, smiling a little, showing teeth like pearls and hands like lotuses, she waits for the moment when the old hag behind her will open her toothless mouth and begin bargaining. We both stare at the girl, caught up in the wings of her overwhelming beauty, conscious that the dark night is a wave that has thrown her against these inhospitable shores. The old woman opens her mouth. A settled silence descends upon the courtyard. The girl moves a little toward the bed, her silk dress flickering in the lamplight, moving so gracefully that she resembles an apparition; and suddenly the silence is broken and T. escapes from his dream, waves his arms and says in an unnaturally loud voice: "Pu hao, pu hao," over and over again. The girl disappears, and all through the tormented night I can hear T. sighing, and in the morning he looks pale and disheveled. . . .

September 9th. Always the soldiers. Soldiers everywhere. Soldiers climbing down the red earth gullies between the ricefields, soldiers drinking at the wells, soldiers marching in long serpentine columns over the dusty roads, in the rain, in the bright sunshine, in the shadow of the wings of clouds. I have seen more soldiers on the road than I have ever seen before. There are soldiers who walk proudly, and others who stumble along, as though oppressed by some invisible force; there are soldiers who seem to be running, and others who stand still like beggars in the hot sunshine, showing their scars.

Here and there we come across a few roads where there are no soldiers, but the impression of an interminable stream is inescapable. The colonels ride on white chargers with red saddlebags, the rank and file follow with the guns, the mortars, the machine guns which have been assembled on the backs of mules. There are guns camouflaged under leaves, and more guns painted over in bright green and yellow, so that they will be invisible in the Burmese forests. Already we are in Yunnan. The earth rises. Great mountains with pointed peaks lie before us, gray and green in the shadowed watery light; and still the soldiers march among the rice fields, still they slake their thirst at the village wells, but as we go farther the small blue waterproof bags of rice which they wear slung over their shoulders like bandoleers are becoming pathetically thinner; and their lines too are thinning out, and more and more of them are hobbling in the dust and the mud.

As the car approaches they scatter to the side of the road. They smile as we pass, throw out their hands with their thumbs pointed upward and shout, *"Ding hao!"* and for a moment, at the thought of this car speeding toward the south, their faces shine with amused envy and delight. We are carrying four soldiers at the back of the car. They came up to us in An-ning, saluted smartly and asked—no, they did not ask, but seemed to be praying that a miracle might happen and that all their days of marching would be over. And sitting there, they look at the eternal slow lines of soldiers passing up the serpentine roads with a kind of tenderness, a kind of maternal solicitude, as though they were saying, "Another car will come, don't worry, everything will turn out right in the end."

All afternoon it has rained, and the great cliffs and bastions of the southwestern plateau lie before us covered in the greenish tallow of rain. We climb through mountain passes, only to descend toward the same river again. We count the milestones, the small white bridges, our pulses—and it seems that all are the same. The mountains have sheer cliffs, and high up in the cliffs, unreachable by man, are small black caves. And the trees bend in the wind, and the red road coils like a snake along the immense sloping breasts of the mountains. When shall we reach the end? There are only villages, sheltered under lime trees and scrub oaks, where cigarettes and perhaps rice are sold—certainly nothing else.

The soldiers flash past. The peasants look up from the fields, weighed down by the burden of rain. The gray sky against the patchwork of innumerable spear-shaped mountains has a luminosity which dazzles us; yet there is grayness everywhere. From the summit of a great mountain we watched the soldiers on both sides. They paled into the distance, their sun hats shining red in the rain. They stumbled forward, covered in mud, groping blindly through the rain, weary beyond endurance, their blue coats dyed black by the poisonous rain, more weary than any men I have seen anywhere; and as they passed they smiled, threw out their hands, and shouted, "*Ding hao!*"

T. has been watching them with a kind of abstracted air, as though he cannot believe entirely in their existence, or as though he feels foolish, and suddenly his face turns quite white and he looks away at the little gray and white birds who make sudden shallow dives among the mulberry trees. And then in a voice like a groan, while the armies pass in their interminable columns: "O God, for how many thousands of years must the sons of our farmers die on the frontiers?"

September 12th. The sun very high, shining among the small lakes and trees and the white bridges; everywhere the scent of limes. I had forgotten the great stone wall around the city, and this morning, as we drove out toward the Burma Road, we watched the sunlight gliding slowly over the purple shadows of the wall. The wall is at least forty feet high; there are great drumtowers at the gates and stone pathways leading from the rice fields outside, and the stone pathways are full of a jostling crowd of peasants whose dresses are brighter than anything I have ever imagined in China. There are herds of brown cows, innumerable horses and donkeys, gaily decorated carts. Slender girls carry the water pails up the steep streets, for even here the streets are inclined at an angle. The houses are painted in all the colors of the rainbow: yellow houses, pale red houses, brown houses. There are houses facing the small lakeside palaces, and sometimes, as we pass down the streets, a small door opens on to a courtyard filled with a blaze of red flowers.

At night the lights shine in the streets, the record players blare, American and British officers ride through the streets in jeeps, and there is so much wealth of rippling silks and silver and porcelain that we feel that we have come to another country altogether. And yet the city is not beautiful. Seen from the air it resembled a toy palace, surrounded by glistening lakes; but the small dark evil-smelling alleyways are the same as the alleyways in Chungking, and there is nothing to distinguish this city from thousands of other cities except its wealth and its position among the mountain lakes. Disappointed and at the same time elated, we walk through the crowded streets, where the ricksha-pullers, in an effort to avoid the stream of automobiles, drive close to the curbs, and where the unshaded electric lights blind our eyes. Hungry and covered in dust, we turn down a dark side street. A signboard, engraved in Arabic characters a foot high, reminds us that within living memory there was a Mohammedan revolt in Kunming. The food stalls are brilliantly lighted. There are naked electric bulbs everywhere; and the men squatting behind their baskets of flaming oranges, or the great crinkled yellow oranges which are unlike those I have tasted anywhere else, look up as you pass with an extraordinary sense of possession. They do not care whether you buy. In this dark side street, dark only in comparison with the brilliantly illuminated main streets, the oranges glow with hidden fire, and from time to time someone sprinkles water over them, so that they dazzle like rubies.

Even here, away from the noise of the main streets, there are crowds of people. Throngs of young men in European clothes saunter down the street; there are beggars in networks of rags, old women with silver pins in their hair, young girls in Chinese gowns, white, cherry-red, blue, or in short flowered skirts and small black coats, heavily scented, rouged, with blue eyelids and hair so glossy that it shines silver in the light of the electric lamps. And always the distant noise of the streets, a thunderous roar in the background, a feeling of vitality which I have known in no other city in China, of movement, sudden startling movement, the whole city caught up in a great wave of audible excitement. And suddenly, passing a dark lane, an old woman stands wailing in a courtyard, beating her breasts, tearing her hair, her face outlined in the light of the small window lamps, and we pause for a moment, listening to the high screams of hunger or despair which rise from the courtyard, but the noise of the city

drowns her voice and once more we are lost in the brightly lit crowds
on the side streets. . . .

September 13th. "The beggars, the beggars!" T. complained this
morning, when we went down into the center of the city after daybreak. It was very cool and fresh, the sky bright blue with milky
streamers. A few rickshas trundled slowly up the long steep roads, the
flapping rubber wheels of the rickshas licking the cobbled roads.
Small donkeys stood tethered to the houses. In a few moments men
came out of the houses with great wooden casks shaped like bathtubs,
which they solemnly hoisted on to the backs of the donkeys; and as
we passed, we knew that it was human manure destined for the
country. But it was the beggars, who crouched still sleeping in the
doorways, who attracted our attention. They were covered in filth,
their legs red with sores, their bodies emaciated. They slept and
shivered in the cold wind, and they lay in positions which I would
have thought it impossible for the human body to assume. The sun
rose, shining on the gold letters of the memorial arch, on the yellow
streamers flooding down from windows, on the gray and green tiles of
a Confucian temple, and on the green rags of the beggars. They were
all young—some were boys. Sometimes they huddled together for
warmth, their naked arms linked together, tormented by hunger even
in their sleep, for their mouths would open and close again, exactly
like the mouths of fishes. Girls passed them, walking swiftly uphill to
the government offices, wearing blue gowns. The beggars slept until
the golden sunlight fell at last into the doorways, and then at last
they woke up, picked up their grimy rice bowls, and staggered toward
the shelter of some trees.

In the center of the city there was a roar of traffic. Automobiles,
trucks, jeeps, buffalo carts, small gray asses wound their way with a
deafening roar toward the airfield, or toward the remaining stretches
of the Burma Road. And still, among the great crowds of people on
the pavement, you could distinguish the beggars, who wandered aim-
lessly through the great throngs, with their staves and their rice
bowls, and it was difficult to think that they had once been the
richest people in China.

September 14th. The university stands outside the walls of the city,
where the red hills rise to the north and groves of cedars stand among

the graves. The small mud buildings between the high mud walls have been bombed; and the sparrows and blue magpies noisily chirping among the limes, the automobiles throwing up great pillars of dust along the road, the screaming children in the gutters, and the soldiers busily felling trees have no power to disturb the silence which lies within the mud walls. As you walk through the gates, past the barefoot soldier who stands on guard, an extraordinary impression of silence comes to you. There are small lakes and pools, grass-grown, with green briars and the yellow flags of banana leaves near the walls, and beyond them, high above your head, in the distance, stretch the gray-green mountains under a transparent sky. There is nothing to indicate that this is the greatest university in China except the letters carved in black on a sheet of oak above the doorway; nothing to suggest that those students in blue gowns sitting under the shade of the trees or leaning against the mud walls in the silence of the autumn heat are the future legislators of China. The mud huts are smaller and uglier than cow sheds; the great tiled library, like a ruined barn, would be out of place in a small Norfolk farm. And yet there is no feeling of poverty. Blue-coated soldiers—the guards of the university—work in the fields. A white mare ambles through the deserted rows of lettuce. A professor walks across the yellow pathways in a tattered gown, which was once blue and is now the color of the blue-white dawn, so often has it been washed in the waters of the green lake. Though he is deep in thought, his eyes are bright and his thin face is curiously handsome, and you think you have seen him before, perhaps in some great congregation of ministers of state, until you remember that the man you were thinking of died many years before—a great general who saved the empire against the rebellion of the Taipings. The professor is a descendant of the general. He carries one of the greatest names in China, and his shoes are down at the heel and his gown is frayed at the edges. He is known for his great sweetness and his kindness to students, who worship him, forgetting his fame and remembering only that he preserves the virtues of the great Chinese scholars.

For this is a place where scholarship rules. All that made China great, her arts, her calligraphy, her understanding, her philosophy, her logic, her benevolence, and her wisdom are consecrated here. For thousands of miles the students and professors journeyed to the southwest from the northeast. They suffered incalculable hardships. The books, which they had removed even before the outbreak of the war, were lost during the bombardment of Chungking. Stupidity?

Malice? Inefficiency? No one knows. They were lost at a time when great universities could not afford to lose books, and they were never replaced. But mud buildings can be replaced. They, too, were destroyed when a flight of Japanese airplanes made this university a target for their bombs, but a few days later coolies dug out the red mud on the campus and built new cow sheds for the students.

Walk through the ill-kept garden, which has all the charm of the gardens you see in Chinese villages, past the flagpole and the library and the students poring over the bulletin boards to the blue-painted tower behind the university. From there you can see the tin roofs shining softly under the blue sky, the magpies wheeling above the roofs, the blue-gowned students, and the professors, who wear often gowns of a darker color. From there the university seems so small that you could almost put it in your pocket—a few small fields of red earth, a small lake half-covered with brambles, a few students and professors. Some of the students are bare-legged, for in Yunnan the late autumn is warm; some are dark brown, and some are pale with disease. You can tell those who are sick by the way they walk, slowly, as though they were afraid of expending their energy; and you notice, too, that there is only a very small sports field, with two basketball posts, for on the kind of diet which men live on here sport is a luxury which strains the lungs and fills the stomach with questions it is incapable of answering. From the small blue-painted tower with the curving roof you can see the fields outside, those fields which seem to stretch to infinity with their humps of graves. There are graves everywhere, for we are outside the city walls; and it is here that the kingdom of the dead begins. And perhaps it is right that this home of scholarship, where the blueprints of the future of China are being planned, should be built on dead men's graves, for at once as we enter these walls we are conscious of the great weight of the past, of time flowing like a refreshing river, of youth and old age.

Walk down the hill, past the soldiers sleeping in the sun, the torn blue shirts waving on the clotheslines, the dogs sleeping in the great heat, their soft white bellies gently pulsating, past the blue lilacs and the dreaming boy whose book lies open on his lap, and wander through the library, under the great roof. There are not many books, though a few have been sent recently from American and British universities—far too few for their self-respect if they knew to what desperate straits the Chinese universities were thrown by their lack. Wander among the dusty shelves, the chairs piled high with periodicals, the old mildewed gazetteers and *China Yearbooks* and the

green-coated *Encyclopedia Britannicas,* and then ask yourself how a
university can exist with so rare a collection of books. Look at the
title pages. There is hardly a single book printed later than 1936.
Look at the dust and the rats and the much-handled Chinese books,
which look as though they will fall to pieces with a breath of wind,
and then look out of the windows at the boys and girls who have the
future of China in their hands. They are learning in a hard school.
They have understood sorrow. They know retreat. But even here,
where books and laboratory equipment should be plentiful, where
the most modern scientific papers should be piling in abundance on
the shelves, there is almost nothing. The librarian comes to the
shelves. You notice that he took away a Japanese book on physical
chemistry: and you wonder: "There are people here who understand
all languages, who have before them the task of creating a new country out of the miseries of the past, and they have almost nothing on
which to feed their minds." A rat scurries through the dry dust of the
rotting wainscoting, but outside in the fields the dreaming boy still
pores over the dog-eared book.

A gong sounds. A pillar of metal hangs from a gallows, and every
hour a servant comes and strikes it with an iron hammer. It is a
sound not unlike cathedral bells, pulsating with intervals of silence
across the green fields and filling the air with wings, each note floating through the air like a globe of bronze. And immediately the
students begin to troop out of the cow sheds, blue gowns rustling in
the breeze which comes down from the high mountains. It wakes the
dogs and the old white mare ambling through the lettuce leaves, this
wind that comes from the north and bears with it the scent of the
gorse and pines on the mountains. And while the students, with their
books under their arms, walk hurriedly toward the kitchens, where
they will be given a bowl of rice, a few vegetables, and almost no
meat at all, you can still hear the deep-throated sound of the gong
and you can still hear the wind among the cypresses. It is nearly five
o'clock. The sun is going down, and as we pass the small mud dormitories, where the students sleep, the frail red sun flames on the mosquito nets and on the face of the boy who lies in bed, sweating with
typhus and his unfulfilled dreams.

You walk out through the gates toward the chemistry laboratories; you peer through the broken windows at a few test tubes, and
your heart begins to sink at the thought of all the unredeemed poverty in this land which will one day be among the richest in the
world. Perhaps this is the last generation of Chinese students who

will have to face poverty. There is so much eagerness in those faces
which you pass in the gathering dusk, so much sickness, so many who
walk in thin clothes, for the evenings are cold, though the mornings
are like mornings in the hot deserts, and you wonder how many will
survive into the years.

"But what they dread most," T. was saying, "is typhus. It is not
the pain and suffering which they dread—though the pain and suffering are great enough—but they dread the expense. The hospitals
charge seven thousand dollars for a single case of typhus. Translate
that into sterling or dollars, and then work out how the students can
get the money, when their homes may be in the northwest under
Japanese occupation, their fathers dead, and their farms plowed
under. They dread other diseases, but typhus in Kunming is the worst
of diseases. You have a sick headache; the next morning you have a
raging fever, and as you try to combat the fever, your heart begins to
weaken under the strain—and it is all due to rats. There are more rats
than people in Kunming. They lie dead on the streets, and no one
troubles to collect them; but mercifully a cool wind comes down
from the mountains."

The wind was playing on the tin roofs of the small hospital
inside the south campus; it threw the starlings in the air and suddenly
caught the gray wings of an ancient eagle who had been fluttering
downwind with her head deeply embedded in her shoulders. She flew
down, the great black eyes shining, and settled on a broken wall,
whence she gazed at the world about her. There were small rats
playing at the foot of the wall, very young and almost white; and
suddenly she swept down, seized a small rat in her talons, and flew up
again, treading on wind, feathers beating like feather dusters, clutching the wriggling rat, and then perched on a high lime tree, silent as a
ghost. Suddenly an extraordinary thing happened—she began to wave
her head wildly from side to side, the feathers half-opened, and suddenly the small rat escaped from her talons, dropped forty feet, and a
few moments later we saw the rat running swiftly across the road.

"You see, they are magical rats," T. complained gently. "What
can we do against them when even the eagles are incapable of dealing
with them?"

He sighed. We walked back to the city, passing the green lake
where a few children were boating, crossing the white camelback
bridge which shone like marble, until we reached the house where we
are staying. It must be unlike any other house in the world. A famous
general built a theater in the early days of the Republic, painted it

blue and green, and wrote with his own hand many inscriptions on the walls and pillars. The balconies have been boarded up; the green room has been divided by wooden planks, and even the aisles have become small cubicles where the most famous professors live, dream, and write of the flowering future. Here in this great hall, the roof falling in, the ghosts of the actors and actresses of the past still present in the air, they live out their lives without any splendor except the splendor of scholarship, forgotten by the world as in a grave.

September 15th. I do not think it is possible to have more respect for the Chinese professors than I have now. This evening we sat on the slopes overlooking the lake, one of the professors began to speak in a quiet, low voice of the long journey from Peking to Changsha and then to Kunming. From where we sat we could see the small boats in the lake, the schoolgirls crossing the camelback bridge, the scented limes and the yellow stucco buildings perched like cliffs high above us; and greenish-white herons rose from the marshes, and the jackdaws cawed in the maples behind our backs. And all the while, like a musical accompaniment to the shifting illumination of the lakes, the quiet level voice continued:

"We removed most of our books before the Japanese came to Peking, but many of them were destroyed in Chungking and a few more have been destroyed in the bombardments here. In the science laboratories we are still using test tubes which were sent down from Peking eight years ago. For a while we could still buy books from abroad. We would send down special messengers to Hanoi, and sometimes we would get the books, and sometimes we would fail; for it was always necessary to bribe the Indochinese officials and we rarely had enough money to bribe them as much as they would have wanted. In Indochina we first began to feel our loneliness. We had to bribe our way through the customs, and then bribe our way through the railways—there was no end to bribery. And all this was for scholarship!" There was no note of complaint in his voice. For thirty centuries Chinese scholarship has faced difficulties and dangers, and the present wars did little more than accentuate these dangers. "But sometimes I wonder what would happen if we had to march away again. We are exhausted and underfed, and if we set out again we should have to be accompanied by so many coffins that it would be impossible to transport them, and so we should die by the roadside,

and even this is not strange to those who have suffered as much as
the Chinese professors, the students, and the soldiers." He spoke of
Tu Fu, the greatest poet of China, who had also died of starvation by
the wayside during the wars. "You have seen that starvation is very
near to us; you know that we cannot always continue like this, and
you will forgive us if sometimes we speak of these things. There is a
terrible melancholy in the Chinese race. You have noticed it in the
essays written by your students, and you will notice it everywhere in
China as the war goes on. The children crying in the streets, the
women who beat their breasts and lament openly in the streets, the
quarreling ricksha-pullers, and the Chinese poet softly complaining of
the injustices of the times—they come from a single root, the terrible
perplexing melancholy of the Chinese race." He began to sing in a
soft voice in the high falsetto which all Chinese poets employ when
they are singing their poems, and suddenly it seemed to me that all
that melancholy was centered in the young professor whose hands lay
open on his knees and whose shining black hair reflected the leaves of
the cherry tree overhead.

We returned when it was late to the theater near the West
Gate. This is where the greatest scholars of China live. Feng Yu-lan,
the philosopher, will sometimes sweep down from his high perch
above the stage into the darkness of the auditorium, plucking at his
magnificent beard, smiling mysteriously to himself, to be followed a
little later by Chao Hsun-chang, who stoops a little under the weight
of his twenty languages and his vast knowledge of the Mongolian
Horde. Here are descendants of the greatest names in China, who
walk in rags and are as cheerful as it is possible to be in the sixth year
of the war; and there are men whose names are still unknown,
though they are powers to be reckoned with in the future of China.
They live in these boxes of the old theater, or in small bleak cubby-
holes downstairs. They do not complain, though the furniture in the
rooms consists of a bed, a wooden stool, and a blackwood table—
nothing more, though there are mountains of books in all languages
piled in the corners. Sometimes at night, when a rat crawls across my
face or one of the professors is coughing up his lungs, I wake up.
"This is intolerable—we are living like pigs—I shall leave for India
tomorrow." And then, all through the long night, like a battering
ram, the thought returns: "Is this how one of the great nations of the
world treats her scholars? They are ill, like the soldiers. They have
lived for years in a world where mounting prices are tragedies which
we measure by suicides. They live secretly and silently, and no one

comes to help them or even to encourage them. They are dying. They are sacrificing themselves for their ideals, and they know that there is so much corruption in the country that even their ideals are at stake." And then in the morning the sun shines through the green boughs of the cherry trees, the lakes glitter and sparkle, the soft blue sky is filled with small dolphins of cloud, and we know then (though we knew it before) that men can live on air and sunlight and imperishable hopes.

October 15th. *The search for Wu San-kwei.* I have known for some time that at the end of the Ming dynasty in China, Wu San-kwei assumed power in the southwest, but I did not know that he ruled from Kunming, and I did not know that the last Emperor of the Mings was strangled only a few hundred yards from the place where I am living.

Wu San-kwei proclaimed himself governor of Yunnan and Kweichow. From his capital in Kunming, then known as Yunnan-fu, his armies went out in all directions to suppress the tribesmen and to extend his power. He was utterly without remorse, and at one time even thought of extending his power to the north; and with the help of the lieutenant governors of Canton and Fukien, he thought to proclaim himself Emperor. The young Emperor Kang Hsi of the recently formed Manchu dynasty heard of his plans and fought vigorously against them; there was no peace in China during the first thirty years of his reign. Wu San-kwei levied taxes and maintained a court as great as that of the Emperor. He had captured the last Emperor of the Mings as the boy king Yu-lung attempted to escape along the same forest path through which the Chinese armies penetrated into Burma. He was brought back to Kunming with his young wife, and they were strangled at a place not far from here. There is a stone, now covered with the green rags of advertisements, on which his death is proclaimed—a stone set up during the first year of the Republic, saying only that the Emperor Yu-lung offered his life here. His body was taken outside the north wall and thrown to the dogs; and somewhere, though I have not yet seen it, there is another stone commemorating the place where the dogs ate him. As you step out of the North Gate, where the burial mounds seem to rise in waves of blue-green grass to the infinite distance, the atmosphere of death is inescapable. Even today people are buried here in shallow graves, and sometimes they are not even buried but thrown into the great pits under the shadows of the wall. I had thought when I first passed under the barrel-like gate: "A great man has died here and left the memory of his death." Now I know that the last Emperor of the Mings met his fate here at the hands of a traitor.

October 19th. He came up the Burma Road, looking very thin and white, his clothes bleached almost pale yellow by the sun. I have never seen a man so thin. His legs were like sticks and his face was a skull. And he walked very slowly, tottering like a leaf in the wind. God knows where he had come from or where he was going. Sometimes small horse carts come trundling along these roads, under the shade of the pines, and you can see in them the white-faced soldiers who have neither expression nor feeling, for they are ill beyond any hope of recovery. They look out at the low reaches of the mountains, but there is no life in their faces, and their skin is paper-thin and their mouths are no more than small holes. But there was still some life in this soldier who came wearily up the road past the university in the broad sunlight. He wore the thinnest of bamboo shoes, and his clothes too were thin, and you could see the shape of his ribs, and you could imagine the tall youth who had left his farm two years ago, strong in limb, handsome, with the free-swinging gait which all those who are young and healthy in China possess. He was dying. I think he knew he was dying, for he walked slowly and paid no attention to the passing trucks filled with the red rusty corrugated oil drums which speed towards Kweichow; and he paid no attention to the salt carts and the ponies from whose wooden yokes yellow banners fly exactly as they flew two thousand years ago. He was sick and dying, and he was thin, like a ghost.

He went up the road slowly, paying no attention to us, while the green shadows of the trees sometimes covered him from the sunlight. I noticed there was a great tear in his sleeves, and under his sleeves a yellow bandage frayed with age could be seen. He did not go to the huge North Gate, with its bronze doors studded with iron nails. He sat down wearily under a grove of firs, which look out over a great stretch of distant rice fields. There is a railway line, humped graves, a playing field where the cavalry exercise and occasional reviews are held by the governor of the province, but he paid no attention to these things. Wearily, wearily, he buried his head in his hands, sick to death, utterly weary of the long journey in the dusty road. From a distance he did not look like a dying soldier. You did not see his thin arms, and that terrible white face was hidden in a green shade. He did not sigh. He did not speak. He did not ask for a drink of water. He lay on the stone with his head buried in his hands, and perhaps he was dreaming.

Every day hundreds of wounded soldiers are brought on stretchers along this road. Not all are wounded. Some are dying of dysentery, others of malnutrition; all are thin with that thinness which is seen only in China. They come on their stretchers like dead men, for the Chinese when they are ill cover their faces; and you will see a sick child carried in a basket with only his legs showing, and you will be wrong if you think he is dead. Sickness is widespread in China. There are not drugs enough in all the world to cure half the diseases of the Chinese. . . .

And the next day the soldier was still there. He had not moved. He had died perhaps at the moment when he crept to the stone. Only the once-green uniform seemed to be a little yellower, and the arms a little thinner, and the face a little whiter. But around his head thousands of black flies were playing.

November 4th. You can eat anything and buy anything you please in Kunming. There are no coupons, no restrictions, no blackout, no unnecessary laws. You may buy a fur coat and a bottle of champagne; sulfadiazine can be bought in the medical shops; an electric razor, a flowered silk gown, silk stockings, army boots, guns, oil drums of octane gasoline, diamonds. In the little shops near the Ningpo Café everything—everything in the world—may be obtained. Unfortunately they cost money.

There is no city in the world with a higher rate of inflation than Kunming. Here prices may double in a week, and inflation is so common that we no longer gaze with awe-stricken eyes at price tags. Here prices may change more in a day than in a year in America; our scales of value suffer revolutionary changes, and no one murmurs. We are companions of the incredible. We are so accustomed to the impossibility of making our budgets that we have lost the habit of lamentation. The spiral ascends; we watch it with the same sense of fatality as a farmer watches the approach of a whirlwind.

I have been making a comparative list of prices. Two years ago in Chungking I could eat reasonably well for $300 a month. Today I eat less and it costs $3,000 a month. Two years ago one could buy a fountain pen for $30. Today it costs $700. And so with everything else—a pencil costs $80, which is equivalent to a pound sterling or four or five dollars gold. A typewriter costs $150,000, which is equivalent to £2,000. A small house will cost $3,000,000, which is equivalent, at the official exchange rate, to more than £30,000. No one can foretell what the next month will bring in a sudden leap of prices.

November 6th. There was a time when Kunming was almost a French reserve. There are still shops where the Chinese names are transliterated according to the French fashion; there are still places where Kunming is written K'oen-ming, and perhaps there is no harm in it. There are still a few Annamites in the center of the city, and I have seen in the private houses of retired generals ormolu clocks and Sèvres china and Louis XIV chairs and terrible Dianas. Here, in the houses of the retired warloads, provincial France still exists in all her finery. There are thick carpets, marble fireplaces, gold-handled teacups, little blue bags of lavender, marble-topped tables, antimacassars, tapestries showing Ariadne in her web followed by Theseus in armor, and there are great red satin bows at the backs of the chairs, and at any moment you expect the maidservant to enter with a silver tray with rolled-gold handles and thin lace serviettes, and you are surprised when a young man enters in Sun Yat-sen uniform and announces that the noodles are served. The noodles are delicious—little yellow buns filled with sweet and sour sauces—and there is coffee without cream, but with those enormous thin elongated lumps of sugar which you find only in France, Czechoslovakia, and Finland.

There are exceptions among the warlords. There is a young man in Kunming who owns an enormous estate inside the city, and there you may wander for hours among the trees imagining that you are in some distant province with no city in sight. He has a fondness for blood-red camellias and fast cars; his father was one of the greatest revolutionaries of all, for it was he who broke up the power of Yuan Shih-k'ai. He is modern to the last millimeter of his tapering fingertips, and his young wife and children are beautiful as only young Chinese wives and Chinese children can be beautiful. When spring comes he will throw the gardens open to the whole world, for nowhere else in this country of flowers will you see so many camellias, so many magnolias and roses. "I have a feeling of responsibility. I must open the doors—people must come. It is terrible to be surrounded by all this beauty and enjoy it alone." And then too he will send his servant out in the street with a tray of silver blossoms, and everyone who passes will be offered one.

December 1st. Air raid. The siren sounded, and we went out into the street to look up at the dawn-blue sky, whitened by clouds and small puffs of white smoke. It was hot, and the air low down on the lake was misty with haze, so hot indeed that we kept away from the hot walls and walked out in the center of the street. But the sirens were still sounding, the roads were beginning to fill with people and automobiles, and the policemen could be heard high above the voices of the crowds shouting that we should make haste. It was impossible to run. We were caught up in the narrow streets leading to the great barrel-shaped gate, thousands of people streaming in their red, green, and blue motley into the fields outside.

There have been air raids here before. There have been times when the city was left gasping and smoldering and blood ran in torrents in the streets, days of despair and waiting, days of interminable low-flying planes. But today the planes were high, the fighters were out in pursuit, and except for the cloudy puffs of smoke from anti-aircraft batteries and the great black spiral of smoke which rose in the distance, there was no sound of the fighting once you were outside the gate. The heat rained down. The soldiers in their cotton-padded uniforms were sweating and smiling; and as we walked down the valley past the hospital and the green gates, they waited impatiently for the moment when, with heaving shoulders and the help of battering rams, the enormous rusted door with its green copper-studded nails could be closed and padlocked with rusty chains.

We sat under the trees, among the grave mounds, and the bleeding red pits have been dug into the earth for the greater safety of the living; for crouching low in these pits, many lives have been saved, though the rats come and gnaw at your toes and a dead body may be lying in the mud beneath your feet. There were sounds of distant explosions; a small red fighter plane soared among the acacia trees, and we could recognize easily enough the whitened teeth of a red tiger. Then the airplane disappeared behind flying buttresses of granite walls; more explosions, the twittering of birds, and suddenly like a great wave the infectious laughter of children.

The children are in command. They are perfectly at ease; they have completely forgotten the bombardments of two years before. The young girl in the blue print frock has stripped to the waist, the better to feed the hungry child, and her golden shoulders seen through the haze of smoke from her husband's pipe are dazzling in this rarefied air. Her father has come up from the country with two rough-haired goats for sale, and the goats, tethered to his walking stick, browse and graze in the grass at the young girl's feet. Her mother is there, a great fat hulk of a woman, all blubber, shaking with laughter. Children run races. The most unexpected encounters take place. Every grave mound is a throne for the quiet people who have come to spend this holiday in peace.

And the country is so beautiful, and they have never had time to see it before. The veined blue peak of Serpent Mountain gleams above the trees; there are shimmering reaches of rice lakes; a small toy train puffs and blows across the marshland. Horses are neighing, soldiers are marching, men are gazing up at the sky from the battle-mented walls. It is all like a dream, or like a child's toy. And news travels fast—"Fourteen Japanese airplanes have been brought down, and not a single American plane has been lost." This is what one would expect in a child's toy. The gleaming fields, the scarlet-crested woodpeckers, the young girls lying in the grass of the grave mounds, every track and road for miles filled with people lying on the grass. The fields of the blessed! And surely in the fields of the blessed there are little puffs of white smoke in the sky, and red airplanes with tiger's teeth soar over the low-roofed houses.

December 4th, The walls at night. Coming from the university to the city late at night, I saw three miracles. I saw a man carrying a small colt on his back, and then, tiring of its weight, he let it fall to the ground, held the halter, and then ran after it as it galloped gallantly along the dark road. I cannot think why he carried it on his back, and I cannot think why the sound of the bright hoofs galloping along the Burma Road filled me with such delight.

Then I heard a girl singing. She was alone by the side of the road; there was no one else in sight. She wore a blue gown and her hair was smoothed and oiled and parted in the middle. In the faint light she resembled a princess who had appeared to startle me from the enchanted woods. As I passed, she was still singing.

Then I came to the walls, gleaming after rain, the immense craggy walls standing against the blue sky, and above them the craggy walls of the clouds, and above them a pale silver slip of a moon so perfect that I caught my breath.

If you ask which is the greater miracle, I would answer that I understand perfectly why a young girl should sing at the end of a road or why a colt carried on a man's back should suddenly race down a wet, shining road. Those things are understandable, but the walls of China are always inexplicable There were low whitewashed walls at An-ning; there are crumbled walls at Chungking; there are walls which have been broken through at Chengtu; and there are a few scattered bastions of walls at Changsha. But the walls of Kunming are better, for their proportions have been carefully calculated to dissemble their power and to mingle with the landscape; they are clear and sharp; they have battlements and small towers against the skyline; and when it rains they are like a ring of water circumscribing the fairy city.

December 6th, The walls by day. By day, when the sun rises, the walls are pale red, the color of a painted egg shell held to the light. They are almost transparent, though they are twenty feet thick.

I would like to see these walls from a balloon. The revolving shadows, lengthening and diminishing with the curves of light, would frame the city in exactly the same way that the rain-soaked walls frame it at night. The Chinese have known since the beginning of time that the city gods must be propitiated. You must walk warily by the great gates. But now, in the full sunlight of afternoon, the walls gleaming rose red and biscuit brown, hidden here and there by clumps of bamboos and willows, while the golden curving roofs of a few houses higher than the walls stand out against the sky, it is impossible to believe that the walls are evil. These battlemented walls, though here and there you will find vertical slits for machine guns, no longer protect the city from the enemy. A student said: "We should tear them down, use the bricks for houses, and let air into the city." He may be right, though there are better reasons for tearing down these magnificent walls—the gates are narrow, and it is easy to be trapped in the city during air raids. But if the walls go, something of the particular ethos of the Chinese will go with them; and I shall no longer feel protected.

In the evening, when the shadows lengthen and the small white-washed mortuary at the end of the hospital garden has turned black with shadow, and even the little mountain of lime is invisible from the barrel gates, the wall is alive with running flames of light. The last vestiges of sunlight are reflected by these green-blue walls towering high above me. And at night, black as ink, towering higher than ever, the walls come into their own.

December 21st. Coming around the corner of the lake, with the gold and flaring roofs of a small temple behind him, I met Lin Yutang wearing a maroon gown. His face was brown as walnuts, and the silk gown gleamed red and blue like the sea in the evening. He looked perfectly happy. The small intelligent monkey face showed all the excitement of a mystic contemplating the profound secrets of the universe, and he was almost trembling. He was talking in Chinese, and the words "Chung-kuo" would come out in a sudden rush of endearing epithets. He was glad to be back, glad to feel the soil of China under his feet. Meanwhile the blue lake glittered at our feet.

At the party in President Mei Yi-chi's house we talked about the necessity of translations. China is still unknown in the West. We know so little of her past history that we are always in danger of misunderstanding the present; and the present is no more than an aggregate of its past. The greatest Chinese novels and poems remain untranslated; there are no good books proclaiming the virtues of the Chinese, and their ways of thinking, though Lin Yutang's *The Importance of Living* is valuable as an elementary guide. There are no books on the nature of the historical grammar of the Chinese language except Karlgren's. There are four or five great civilizations still existing on the earth, and China, which is perhaps the greatest of all, remains a mystery to us. We must learn or perish, for if we fail to understand one another, there will always be wars.

We were talking on these lines in the great anteroom with its plush sofas, Lin Yutang happy at last to be among scholars. He is half a renegade. He had begun his studies in China with some excellent work on philology and then disappeared to edit comic magazines and write novels. He was an excellent interpreter of China to the West, but he was losing his Chinese roots and it was good to see how easily he was resuming them. He was not the greatest of the distinguished scholars present; he was humble, and a little sad; he smiled wanly when his great success was mentioned, and more than once he said, "I must stay in China—I must stay——" And yet we knew he would return. He had addressed the students on Confucius, begging them to return to the ancient virtues; and the students had disapproved, wondering at the strange interloper from the West who had dared to suggest a revival of ancient and antiquated virtues, for there were other Chinese philosophers who could lead them further along the strange unknown roads of the future. We discussed the translation of *The Dream of the Red Chamber*, the greatest novel that China has produced, and so far untranslated. We discussed his own brilliant translations of *The Travels of Mingliaotse* and a hundred other things. "Nothing has been begun," he said; "we must begin again from the beginning. We have not begun to translate Western books into Chinese, and nothing of any value has been translated from Chinese into the languages of the West." It was a sad meeting. We were powerless. Here, in Kunming, where a thousand great scholars are starving, the work of translation could have begun if there had been funds enough. We could have gone through the great classics one by one and given them a modern dress; we could have displayed the treasures of China to the West and for the first time we could have made the basis of understanding. Alas, there is no basis. China is still a mystery to us, and perhaps we are half-afraid of this mysterious country, which has developed its arts to a perfection which is almost terrifying.

And so we wandered down the roads which lead to the lake, the golden temples, the brilliance, the sky.

1944

January 1st. The year begins with a blaze of sunshine so brilliant that this morning we were dazzled. The cuckoos were calling in the grove of magnolias outside my window, and the dust rose in golden columns in the narrow streets. The Chinese walls, so black and foreboding at night, are green with creepers and red with the rusty edges of bricks. Day breaks like a clarion. In the whole of China there is no place so perfect as this mile-high promontory in Yunnan.

We went out this afternoon with a young Chinese poet. Small boats were scurrying among the islands like a painting; the eagles foundered in the sky like ships which have lost their anchors. And the sky was high, so high that we lost ourselves dreaming of its immensity. "In China we say that the sky is higher in autumn," he said, "but here it is highest at the New Year. You can see through the veils of the sky." He spoke of the Chinese Taoist astronomers who can see the stars in daylight, and of all the curious explorations of the old Chinese philosophers. "The Chinese believed that man had a place in nature, and it was necessary to find this place; and that nature is sacred and must not be disturbed. In the West you believe that nature is the enemy, to be enslaved by your science. It may be so. We cannot tell. But I do know that for generations the Chinese have searched into nature, trying to understand her secrets without despoiling her, and now at last we must become scavengers—despoilers—men of cunning."

It was curious to talk to him beside the green lakes, where the gulls of winter were flying and the black cormorants could be seen flapping lazily from the berthed boats on the sandbanks. There are many, many things in which the Chinese and the West can understand each other; but ultimately there are differences so great and far-reaching—the differences between two civilizations which have survived without in the slightest influencing one another—and I began to wonder whether it would ever be possible to understand the East. "For us heaven and earth are the two poles of our life, and both are timeless. They are outside the world we live in, and yet in it. They are the concepts by which we understand the world, and shall always understand the world, since it is by heaven and earth that we live. And you, how do you live?"

"By youth and love. In the West, ever since the beginning of things these have been our ideas. By youth we capture the world; a youthful god is slain, and from his blood comes our freedom."

"In China our gods are all old, and they are immortal—they are never slain. We have no belief in youth."

He was young himself, and very handsome, with the clean jawbones and the fine glancing eyes of the northern Chinese, and it was curious to think that he placed no trust in youth.

He went on:

"If we could marry the Chinese to the West—what would happen? I often amuse myself with the thought, for it seems that the children of this marriage would have all your faith in youth and all our reverence for immortal things. A race which had all the virtues of the West and of the Chinese. . . ."

"And what if it had all their vices?"

"I had thought of that, but surely their virtues would outweigh their vices—this reverence, and this delight in youth. Do you know, the Chinese have no love for youth. It is the time of sadness still, the time of marriages dictated by the parents, the time for being soldiers. In children and the old the Chinese see beauty and grace."

"And in young women?"

There was no answer. He had had an unfortunate love affair, and a settled sadness, like the sadness which would sometimes descend on Bergery, fell upon him. It was growing dark. The small boats were returning, the fishing seines hooked on the prows of the boats; and the sun glinting on the jagged red gash on the western hills seemed to be bleeding. We walked back through the damp streets, where light still quivered on the walls. The jade-white magnolias were creeping over the high walls of the houses, and in this luminous hour all the fragrance of the world seemed to be contained in them.

January 15th. I have more admiration for the Chinese professors than for almost any other group of men. For six years they had been attempting to uphold the traditional values of Chinese culture, and they have succeeded more brilliantly than anyone dared to believe. They live like Diogenes—wherever there is room for a chair, a table, and a bed. They have few books. They are continually on the verge of starvation, and they are almost completely unconscious of the heroism of their lives. They have traveled across China, from one end of the continent to the other, and today the three greatest universities in China, whose line of descent can be traced back three thousand years, consist of small mud buildings erected on a deserted graveyard. The students and the professors—it is difficult to think of them without emotion, for all that is best in China is crystallized in their presence. They live in small dusty rooms where there are few or no books and where the paper windows have been torn to ribbons by the wind; and here, almost forgotten by the outside world, they prepare themselves for the final battle which must be won after the war.

This afternoon one of the students told me that a girl student was ill and had asked to see me. The day was very hot, and the gulls and rooks were squawking high above the campus in the branches of the lime trees. We walked through the dust of the deserted streets, for it was noon, and no sounds came from the sleeping houses. The student began to talk of his escape from Peking. It had taken him forty days to travel across the whole length of China. He had been luckier than most, for he found willing helpers all along the road. He had stayed for ten days in Lanchow, five days in Chengtu and perhaps a day in Chungking. On the day before he left Peking, he invited a Japanese officer to dinner, and they had made plans to visit the Western Hills on the following Saturday. "It was necessary, you understand," the student said. "There are a few Japanese who are courteous, and even a few who are understanding. They know that they have not long to remain in China and they are prepared to help us to escape or at least not to prevent us. I was sorry for him. I knew he would wait for me, and all the way across occupied China I thought of him waiting there. It seemed so extraordinarily discourteous, and he had never been discourteous to me."

I burst out laughing. It was extraordinary that a Chinese student should pay so much respect to a Japanese officer.

"Oh, they are not as bad as all that. In every group of a hundred Japanese, there is one who is intelligent. It is true that there are forty who are murderers, and perhaps another ten who are soulless officials, mere machines who dedicate themselves to the task of suppressing the Chinese. Then there are ten who are confirmed opium-smokers —they have fallen into the trap they have laid for the Chinese. But there is always *one* who knows that he has not long to remain in Peking, and after the war, of course, no Japanese will be allowed in our city."

He seemed extraordinarily sorry for the Japanese, and I could not help remarking that I had only met one who possessed dignity, and he was a peasant who surrendered at Changsha and possessed the dignity of all peasants.

"The peasants—yes," the student answered. "You see them marching through the streets of Peking. Some of them are bullies and have no idea what they are doing, and those are mostly peasants who have lived near large towns. But the peasants who have been conscripted from the country can be recognized at once. They come to Peking. They are overwhelmed by its beauty. Some Japanese are told that Peking was built by the Japanese, but very few of them believe this. And so they stare at our palaces and gardens, and wonder what they are doing here, seeing the contempt on the faces of the Chinese who are still fighting, and the contempt of the Chinese who are traitors. Wherever they go, they are despised. Wherever they go, they are outnumbered. There is nothing in the whole world quite so horrible as to belong to an army of occupation. They know that they may be murdered at any time, and most of them know that the time is soon coming when they will have to run helter-skelter to the coast. So they bring their *geishas* and pretend to enjoy the scenery, which is so unlike the scenery in Japan that they walk with their mouths open, marveling like lunatics at the beauty of the northern plains and the greatness of Peking."

He had been stopped at a village near the frontier by a bearded Japanese soldier who threatened to kill him if he did not surrender all his valuables. He surrendered them with good grace—a few dollars, a few pieces of jewelry, for there was nothing else. Afterward, when he had surrendered his possessions, the Japanese soldier made a drunken dive at him with a bayonet, and he escaped only because a military car was passing and the Japanese soldier had sense enough to draw himself up at the salute.

"They are trying to demoralize the Chinese, but inevitably they are demoralizing themselves," he explained, and pointed to the blue lake riding among the elm trees; and it was clear that he was still half-living the experiences of his journey.

We walked through dusty lanes where children were playing the same games that they play everywhere in the world. With a sharp stick they cut squares in the dust and marked the squares with magic numbers. Then they jumped or hopped into the squares, squealing with delight. An enormous black pig, the feet fastened to two bamboo rods carried on the shoulders of coolies, swayed and squeaked menacingly as it was carried down the street. The children paid no attention to the pig. Immersed in their game, they shrieked with delight, and it was only when we had passed that they looked up and shouted after us, "Ding hao!" with their thumbs uplifted—the sign with which they greet all foreigners.

"In Peking the children are silent," the student said. "This is partly because there is so little rice and the rice is so badly distributed, and so they are silent with hunger, but it is also because they feel menaced by the Japanese. The Japanese are everywhere. They have a habit of entering houses and prying wherever they are not wanted. They are tactless, and they are especially tactless to children, who understand these things better than grownups."

We were coming to the house of the girl student. Here, as elsewhere in China, there are courtyards within courtyards. You enter an imposing gateway, you cross the tiled courtyard surrounded by low houses, passing through a corridor which leads to another courtyard, and then another, and then another. There is no end to the courtyards in these large houses. Somewhere at the back of the last courtyard, in a small room where the paper windows were slashed to ribbons and the trelliswork patterns of the doors were moldering into powder, the girl student was waiting for us. She was a friend of the boy student and had escaped from Peking at the same time. They had known each other since childhood. She looked weak and ill. She lay on the bed under a coarse blanket, her beautiful black hair bound over her forehead with a red ribbon. Pale and perhaps consumptive, with bright eyes, she gazed now at the student, now at a perfectly white magnolia which shone from a small, cracked vase.

"The journey was so delightful," she said. "I have never seen so much of China."

"Would you like to make the journey again?"

"Of course. It was so good. Lanchow was much more beautiful than I expected, and we spent a whole day wandering round Sian. You have no idea how beautiful China is. We lived in Peking, and thought only Peking was beautiful."

She told me a story of her friend, a girl student, who had murdered a traitor. The traitor had wanted her to be his concubine. At last the girl consented, but she stipulated that every week-end she must be allowed outside the house where the traitor lived. The traitor agreed, but as soon as she entered his household he locked the doors and refused to let her depart. She suffered this quietly for a while, but one evening, when she reminded him of his promise, he consented to let her go on condition that he was allowed to accompany her. She pretended to object. The more she objected, the more the traitor desired to follow her; and at last she took him in a huge black Mercedes car to a rendezvous in the Western Hills. She had expected her friends to be waiting for her, but they had waited many week-ends and now at last they had lost patience. At midnight she turned off the ignition switch and slipped out of the car, leaving the traitor alone in the darkness, and in her hand she carried the blood-stained knife. Then she walked back alone to the house, collected her belongings, and went to hide in a small house inside the Forbidden City—a house which belonged to another traitor, but one who was compassionate toward those who were working for China. The girl went mad. She could not forget the horror of the night in the Western Hills; but even though she was mad, and would sometimes scream out in a loud voice, she was brought back over the Chinese lines and left in the house of one of her relatives, who promised to look after her.

"Soon she is coming here," the girl student smiled, pleased at the thought that her friend might be coming to share the tragically hard life of a student in a Chinese university.

There are many students like the girl who escaped from Peking. They are not unlike students everywhere else, and it is not always possible to recognize those who have escaped from those who have lived all their lives in discreet comfort. The girl student was suffering from tuberculosis, but so many suffer from tuberculosis in China that this in itself is not remarkable. She was beautiful, with a pale oval face, great dark eyes, and masses of dark hair heaped over her forehead; and neither is this remarkable in China, where girl students are nearly always either beautiful or irrepressibly ugly. She spoke with a perfect Peking accent, and her English speech was soft and agreeable.

"Where will it end?" her friend asked, and turning to me, he continued: "You see, we have been so accustomed to murder that we can hardly think of a time when there will be peace. We have outlawed ourselves. We belong to the generation which kills, not to the generation which creates. That is why so many students are leaving Peking in the hope of continuing their education in the southwest. And what is so tragic is that many of us have forgotten all we have learned and have not enough knowledge even to enter the university. What will happen to us after the war?"

I looked around the small bare room. A few boxes, a toothbrush, a cup, a fur coat hanging on the wall; and everywhere the paper was coming from the wall and the rain was soaking through and leaving dark stains. The student had exchanged the luxury of Peking for the squalor of Kunming, where prices are so high that a fortune is necessary to keep a man from starvation; and the girl smiling there, dreaming of the Western Hills and the night on which she had murdered a traitor (for there was little doubt that she had been telling the story of her life), was so beautiful that it seemed as though she had risen through all the generations of Chinese history and no longer belonged to the present age. She was a court beauty in the palace of Huang Ming, the great emperor of the T'angs. She was the Lady of the Hsiang River, who sighed for the poet Chu Yuan. She was China in all its magnificent turmoil and splendor, its humility and sorrowing pride. For surely it is on the battlefields and in the small squalid houses where the future rulers of China are learning their trade that China is most evident. The merchants who have made fortunes out of the miseries of others and all those who have lost their souls in the insensate money-making hysteria which has swept over the country are not to be counted among the great. The great are here. The soldiers, not always well fed, marching down the streets with immense pride, the students in their dusty rooms, the professors in their cellars—they have been forgotten, and those who think of China rarely call them to mind. . . .

I had been thinking in these strains, forgetting the darkness which was coming down and the storm clouds gathering over the western mountains. Outside, the sky was blue, but rent with clouds. Inside the room only the white magnolia in the cracked vase and the girl's pale face shone in the dusky twilight, and they seemed to absorb

the light and glow with a pure flame. The girl smiled and whispered
something to the boy. Soon a small primus stove was burning and we
were drinking the tea she had brought from Peking—a pale green tea
which was like some precious liqueur. We drank the health of the
students who remained behind and those who had reached Kunming,
till at length, when the storm was driving into the courtyard and we
heard the crackle of rain on the tiles, we left and returned to our
homes.

January 19th. I have been dreaming of Bergery. It is difficult to
imagine that he is dead. Even when I was a child, a great head very
much like his startled my nightmares into peace; but what is so
strange is that when I met him for the first time, I did not recognize
him, though I must have known that I had seen him before. Last
night I dreamed of him again. He was walking in the shade of silver
eucalyptus trees, here or in Szechuan, and speaking in a soft voice of
the things we both loved. He began to speak about a journey he
would like to make, from Ceylon to the Himalayas, when the war is
over; and we were together in the dark forests and on the white uplands. "Do you know that in April or March in the Himalayas there
are enormous white butterflies which hurl themselves up the snow
crevices and die in their thousands? Some instinct, like the instinct
which drives the lemmings off the coast of Norway, drives them to
their deaths. Perhaps in the eyes of God our wars are no more than
the flight of the white butterflies in the Himalayas, and perhaps in
his eyes our wars are less beautiful." He spoke for a long time about a
journey in India—a pilgrimage to all the sacred monuments. We
would bathe in the Ganges; we would walk in the deserted halls of
Fatipur Shikri, which Akbar raised and later abandoned; we would
see the caves of Ellora and Ajanta, and walk through the *ghats.* We
would visit Katmandu and stay a night in the village where Buddha
was born. In the forests we would come upon the pud marks of
elephants. . . .

January 20th. On week-ends the American flyers come into the city.
There is a small street, hidden away among the cinemas, where they
gather, striding up and down the streets in heavy furs, though the day
is warm; they are immensely tall, and the Chinese who pass them
have to look up at those fair-haired, gawky youths who stride down

the street like gods. For gods they are. They wear a fortune of leather on their backs, and another fortune of leather on their feet. Our admiration is reserved chiefly for those who carry a Chinese flag and some mysterious inscriptions on their back. They are pilots who may be forced to descend in some deserted place along the Salween river, alone among strangers, and the inscriptions contain advice to the peasants who may find them.

February 4th. Y. told me a story of the great writer Lu Hsun, whom he had known in Peking. Lu Hsun was a small man, and he resembled in every respect a Kiangsi farmer, with a pale waxen face, a drooping black mustache, and eyes that appeared at first to be crafty, and it was only later that you realized that they were wise. Often they would go on pony rides to the Western Hills, and Lu Hsun would keep them laughing uncontrollably by describing the lives of the ponies, and how much more intelligent they were than the men who rode them. But I liked best his stories of how Lu Hsun lived in a small bare room inside Peking (he was teaching at Peking University), and on the walls there were little strips of paper arranged in no particular order. On these strips of paper there was perhaps a single Chinese character, or a whole sentence, and sometimes he would add a few words here and there, and this was how he built his stories together. He worked very slowly. A short story of about thirty pages would take him a whole year; but it would never be forgotten. I like to think of the room with the strips of paper, some on a level with the floor, some high up near the ceiling; and late at night he crawls from his bed, adds a single character of perhaps even a single brushstroke, to the strips near the ceiling, and returns contentedly to bed.

March 20th. Nearly every day the Governor's *mafu* leads a superb white horse down to the parade ground outside the North Gate. There, in a green bowl of grass, surrounded by grave mounds and the low-lying purple hills, with rice fields under water in the distance, the wild colts are playing with their manes streaming and their long silky tails stretched out like shining spears. I do not know any place so peaceful as the green parade-ground in the late afternoon. Usually there are a few thunder-bearing clouds on the horizon; a few idlers are gazing from under the shadow of trees; a coffin of unpainted white boards is being carefully removed through the whitewashed gate at the end of the hospital wall, schoolchildren are playing in the dust, and a few bright airplanes are flying low overhead. But the colts are streaming like the wind in the green bowl, and they alone have the air of *authenticity*. The rest is unreal, terrifying, or irrelevant. And now I remember seeing a Chinese painting of some young colts playing in a field. It was a painting of the Yuan dynasty, and there were such jade-green trees and lake-blue mountains in the distance. Everything was exactly the same, but the Chinese painter had improved on nature by making the horses ten times larger than life, and the small boy sitting at the foot of the almond trees was ten times smaller than life. And yet you did not notice the incongruity. So it is now, while the rose-dappled colts jump invisible hurdles, rub their necks, trot eagerly and capriciously in the tall grass. . . .

March 21st. Our clothes are in rags. There is hardly a single professor and hardly a single student whose clothes are whole. And yet there is no complaint, even though it is beginning to rain continuously. "A man who pays attention to food and clothes can never be a sage," said Confucius. So we wander with holes in our socks and at our elbows, and no one is ashamed.

T. showed me his shirt yesterday. With his coat on, he looked superbly well dressed in comparison with others. But with the coat off you saw a network of holes joined together with pieces of silk and string.

"But you should see me in my best gown," he murmured. "It smells of mothballs, but once a week I take it out and look at it. It is of pure silk, perhaps a hundred years old, for it belonged to my grandfather. No, I have refused to sell it—whatever happens I cling to my gown. When I go to Peking, I shall wear my silk gown. . . ."

March 25th. "But where are we coming to?" T. exclaimed in alarm. He held in his hand a history of the world in two thousand pages in which China is mentioned on perhaps twenty pages. "This is extraordinary. Do you think it is possible that we don't belong to the world? All our arts, all our conquests. . . . And yet they write these things. . . . It is really most extraordinary!"

Sadness and pity glowed on his handsome northern face. "I shall write a book on the history of the world," he said, "and I shall give exactly twenty-five pages to the West. And all those twenty-five pages will be devoted to Jesus Christ."

I am still wondering what he meant by this.

April 4th. On the blue lake the soldiers were hanging out their washing beside the golden pagoda. All around the lake there is a kind of moat, covered with green duckweed, oily with the refuse of years, but the girls come down from their small houses and courtyards buried in dark streets and with their hands they clear a place in the moat and wash their clothes. Afterward, kneeling in the sunlight, they scrub the blue cotton until it shines in the sun.

It was a heavenly day, the sun very high, the pagodas glittering. Every day when I wander round this city I seem to find a new lake. Yesterday, in the public gardens, I found an oval lake among some fir trees; soldiers lay in the long grass, horses were rubbing their necks against the warm rocks, but what struck me as more beautiful than any of these were the three misshapen rocks in the center of the lake. They were pure white and perhaps the height of a small boy. But they were carved so delicately, there were so many shadows, and they possessed so many facets that I began to realize for the first time the terrible affection the Chinese possess for strange rocks. Through the firs a soldier wandered arm in arm with his girl, and it seemed suddenly that this place was entirely removed from life, it was fairyland, it was the Chinese earth. And even when a wounded soldier came down the narrow lanes between the pines, it was still fairyland, because it was still China.

April 9th, Easter. The bells of the churches were ringing this morning. Over the broad sea of blue sky the white gulls which have been hovering for days now made their way across the lake to the low-lying blue mountains in the distance. The sun danced, and you forgot even the coffins which the soldiers carry on their backs, you forgot the heart-rending poverty amid plenty, you forgot the inflation and the painted girls in the black limousines—you saw only this curious high sunlight which is more delicate than anything else on the earth. Here, a mile above sea level, in a small town set beside a blue lake, protected by American airplanes, there is a freedom in the air which I have never known anywhere else.

So we wandered in the afternoon around the blue lake, where boys and girls were rowing in small canoes, past temples where the goldfish abounded in pools, past the Hôtel du Lac, which has been taken over by the Army, past the camelback bridge and the little kiosks which remind you of France. We must have been wandering the whole afternoon, for when we came through the white marble *pai-l'ou* archway, there were already thick clouds in the sky. The famous poet was talking once again of Chou and Han dynasty bronzes.

"It was a time when men loved the earth," he said; "and therefore they reverenced bronze and iron, and made the objects of daily use beautiful. But this time is going. Our temples are defaced with wall paintings by incompetent artists, our sense of style is being destroyed by the inevitable collision with the West. . . . "

"It has not entirely gone," I objected, and spoke of the delicately carved wheelbarrows I had seen on the fields of Changsha, when the peasants were returning to their shattered homes. "After this war a new art will spring up, and a new literature. The Chinese haven't lost their traditional virtues, and even if only a little of the old culture remains it will flower up anew."

We had been walking through the Wen-lin Kai, and this street of battered mud houses and rickety restaurants with the incongruous name of "The Forest of Learning" was smoking with braziers and brilliant with electric lamps. The tea shops were open, crowded with students poring over their books; and sometimes a small cavalcade of cavalry would pass through the muddy road, for it had rained during the previous night, and the mud lay thick on the ground. At the end of the street lay the great West Gate, and beyond it, now separated and alone, but once connected with the fifty-foot wall which surrounded the city, lay another gate, smaller but more imposing in its suggestion of massive power.

The gates of China still seem to me to be more powerful than the most splendid machines. They stand aloof, perfectly proportioned, with flaring roofs, buttresses, immense uncarved bricks facing the walls of earth beneath. All over China the walls of cities have been removed, but the gates remain. And now, in this starlight, the unpainted but once yellow roof straining toward the sky, the sheer slopes of the walls like plummets directed to the heart of the earth, this gate seemed to be possessed with supernatural powers. It was a gate through which no invaders could pass. Solitary and alone, with its crumbling bricks gathering on the slopes and stray horses eating the long grass which grew among the stones, it still possessed the splendor of the ancient dynasties. Black against the sky, towering among the stars, great shoots of clouds winging their way past its flaring roofs, it was a symbol of what China has been and always will be.

December 6th. Even though the sun had set, the waves of the sun beat against the earth, and there was no moon, and the lights had gone out. In some of the shops greasy candlewicks were shining, mirrored against dusky silver; and we had passed the shops selling dragons' eyes, noodles, and boiled eggs in sweet milk. There was an air raid, and the air was hot and moist on our faces. We passed down a side street toward the lake, stepping carefully over oily stones, and in the faint light we could see the old ceremonial China before us—the stone archway, the camelback bridge, the golden-roofed hotel in the middle of the lake now occupied by soldiers. Wen Yi-tuo was saying:

"This is the last wave of the Japanese—they won't have strength for much more. How do I know? Good heavens, when you teach students you know everything. They have relatives everywhere. Students come from Siam, Indochina, Japanese-occupied China, even India. They are coming all the time. So we know better what is going on than the Foreign Offices. The peasants and the businessmen don't panic in the same way—the students never panic, or else we have worked in vain. The thing is to understand that."

"I have faith in the students, but not always in the professors," I said, and then more softly: "And in many of the students I have no faith at all—they will take the jobs which will give them the most money. I wish there was more sense of dedication. It exists, but not always."

He smiled. "What is dedication? To be out on a dark night, and to have faith in China."

I pondered this for a moment; then he explained: "The poor are so wretchedly poor, so inconceivably badly trained, so miserable with the sickness of their souls that they will come and stick a knife in your back for a thousand dollars. You must have some faith to be walking with me now."

It was dark in the side streets, and perhaps the siren had gone off, and we thought we heard the putter of anti-aircraft fire at the airfield. Suddenly a searchlight sprang up, a solid shaft of ivory, the elephant's tusk leaping out against the strange enemy of the sky; then another tusk; and then another, till the whole sky was full of the battle of the elephants, silently probing for the gnat which would soon appear. We heard the gnat rumbling. And then we came to the house, knocked and entered into the large courtyard, lit with the tusked moonlight from the moonless sky. A marble lion, chipped, looked up at us, looking like an inflated Pekingese in this misty light, and then the putter of anti-aircraft shells came closer; somewhere behind the white tusks were the red sprays of tracer bullets. Wen Yi-tuo was singing softly:

> A woman never knows
> What a good man she's got
> Till after she turns him down. . . .

"Where did you learn that?"

"I was in Chicago," he said, and it seemed strange in this half-darkness, the reddish beard flowing over the patched gown, the eyes sparkling.

I think we were on edge, because the Japanese were still close—they said Kweiyang was in flames, but no one knew for certain—and then he knocked on the door and we were blinded by the sultry smoking candles. The house belonged to a professor of French who knew Gide and Valéry; there were photographs, great shelves of bookcases, laboriously transported from Peking. Clean-faced, somber, with unshaved cheeks which seemed greenish-blue in this light, the professor came to welcome us. Then two generals, in full uniform, came out of the glare of the candles. I recognized a young poet, with glasses, the face withdrawn, a modern Buddha. They said Lo Lung-chi might arrive, but no one knew whether he would arrive for certain. There were perhaps twenty or thirty professors, no students. The servant girl brought in cups of hot tea, the leaves spinning on the surface of the water. Wen Yi-tuo rubbed his hands. We could hear the distant rumble of airplanes through the paper windows, and the courtyard outside was brighter than the candles.

Wen Yi-tuo said: "It's odd how one talks quietly during an air raid. Do we think the Japanese can hear?"

There were prints on the wall, scrolls, uncomfortable cushions, bamboo chairs. The French professor's wife came in wearing a slit skirt, walking delicately only in the places where there was a carpet, because she was going to have a baby. The conversation was desultory, and then Wen Yi-tuo stroked his beard more dramatically than ever and said: "Are you waiting for me, or am I waiting for you, gentlemen?" and I wondered why he spoke in English.

He went on, for they had suddenly become silent: "There is nothing exciting. We want to bring out a new paper. It will be about art—about the things we stand for. We have invited you because we want your help."

At any other time in the world's history, the statement would have meant little; but it meant a great deal tonight. We are being attacked by the Japanese; we are blockaded; the government has openly deplored the activities of this university, in spite of the fact that Lienta is the greatest university in China; we are the seat of a provincial government which is fighting against the Kuomintang, we are the headquarters of the largest American force in China; the students are openly demanding arms to beat off the attacks of the Japanese against the university, knowing that they will attack the university and destroy it before they destroy anything else, as Nankai University was destroyed in the past. Even if there was not one word of politics in the paper, it would have implicit in it an attack on the government. The legendary qualities for which the university stands, only because it harbors the greatest intelligence of China—these will be the subjects of the paper, for here we have men who have studied abroad and yet retain a consciousness of the value of Chinese civilization for itself, seeing themselves more clearly than the uneducated soldiers or the bureaucrats see themselves.

Wen Yi-tuo went on: "We have reason to believe we can have our own paper. I want suggestions for the title, if you agree. I would like to know your views. I won't tell you of the urgency of the matter. Things are happening—it is unnecessary to go into details—which cry out for our voices." And then he was silent, and we heard the patter of anti-aircraft shells against a neighboring roof.

More tea was brought. They were all talking at once, discussing it among themselves, the two generals leaning forward like children who have been allowed to stay up and hear their parents talking.

The lights went on suddenly; we all blinked; and it was odd, then, to notice how the color was drained out of the faces of the impoverished professors by the electric light. In the candle flames they looked better, the redness in the faces showing, but in electric light all the shabbiness of five years of exile came to the fore.

They went on talking about the details of the paper. Wen Yi-tuo was asked to be editor-in-chief. Will there be articles on politics?

There is some dissent, but gradually this disappears. Who will write them? Will they be signed, or anonymous? Will each professor take it in turn? There are so many things that must be said, so much cruelty that must be stamped down, so much justice that must be invoked. And who will print it, and will it come out every week or every fortnight or every month, and how far will it represent the Democratic League and how far will it have a policy of its own? But the Democratic League has almost no policy, except the traditional liberalism of the Chinese scholar; they will build up their policy from the beginning, against all the nonsensical insults of Kuomintang tutelage—how long must the Chinese be under a reign of tutelage?—and against all private interests which insist that scholars shall have no right to speak, though traditionally they alone have the right to speak on all occasions. Essentially, it will be a paper representing the university. But how much of the university? How many of the professors are wise enough to realize that they have a part to play? Some, very few of the professors, are paid agents of the Kuomintang, editing Kuomintang newspapers, transposing all errors into the justice of a cause, bitterly conscious of their errors, yet hiding them. And so it goes on, backwards and forwards, conversation weaving through the cigarette smoke, the birth of a new paper. Wen Yi-tuo rubs his hands and puffs at his pipe, the same bulbous pipe that has long since turned his beard the color of tobacco. He counts the number of people present. "Twenty-seven." Then he nods, the tremendous headshake, and says: "It's enough to start a revolution." Everyone smiles. More tea is brought in. An hour later, in the darkness, for there is no moon and no light in these dark streets behind the lake, we go out.

Someone said: "Have you thought of a title for the newspaper?" Wen Yi-tuo laughs: "It will be the Awakening of China, or China Awake—something like that. Well, it's time."

Then we go out in small groups, back to our dormitories, hearing the plump rats squealing across the road, past the lake now empty of lovers, empty of all things, even of elephant tusks. It is three years since the Pacific war broke out.

December 15th. Chiang Shih-ro takes almost no part in politics, yet he remains among the greatest of the scholars here. It is perfectly possible to be a great scholar and at the same time to be disinterested in politics, on one condition: that the man should by his example give freely his criticism of the turmoil around us. And this Chiang Shih-ro does to perfection.

He is more sturdy than Wen Yi-tuo, more brusque, the brain less complex and passionate. He was educated in America, England, and France; and seems to have learned most from France—certainly he speaks of France with greater affection. He lived in poverty and hope; now at last he has been given a small house in a garden full of camellias, a perfect setting for a sociologist. Once he lived in a house outside the city, in the "bad lands." There, because the landlord wanted someone else capable of paying higher rent to take over the house, and he refused to leave for three weeks, he was beaten over the head by the landlord's hired thugs. He complains gently: "There is no law in this country," or still more gently: "Where have we come to, with our great civilization? Are we becoming animals?" He will talk for hours about the dying soldiers we see all day, the mismanaged hospitals, the corruption that hurts him as though it were a wound on his own body; and by loving him, one learns to love China. More and more I believe that the best remains in the more upright scholars, but what is disturbing is that so many professors have thrown in their lot with a government that possesses secret prisons; and very rarely nowadays do the professors talk of this great university as "a bulwark of democracy." But the students talk of it.

Wen Yi-tuo and Chiang Shih-ro are the two most popular professors. They are popular because their learning is profound, and also because of the example they set to others—fearless and ashamed, with no bitterness and great love for their country. While they are here, I shall stay. If they went away, I would feel that the main pillars of the university had gone—there would only be the threats from the government, the carefully rendered attacks by the Chen brothers on all that the university stands for. I would prefer Lienta to be bombed, as Nankai University was bombed than that it should become the center of a reaction. And yet every day the reaction gains in strength, and an uneducated militarist government pretends to give orders to the scholars. Wen Yi-tuo said this morning: "Oh God, if only the government had been to school. . . . "

December 21st. They were talking of the rape of Nanking. There were three students, two of them girls. One wore her hair in pigtails, yet she looked older than the others, with a long mouth, thick lips and heavy eyebrows. She moved gracefully, and I have noticed that

she seems to move cautiously, often looking back over her shoulder
even when she is on the campus. I remembered, too, that she was not
a very good student, her essays were singularly sentimental and I
think I have read altogether eight of her essays in which she describes
her native village in Shensi. The Communists are there now, and it
may be that like all students from Communist-occupied areas she is
continually under suspicion. The other girl was eighteen, incredibly
beautiful, looking more Spanish than Chinese, her face red and her
body unbelievably lithe under the blue gown. The boy was a young
engineer from Fukien, handsome in a pale way, without much expression in his face, and he possessed a singularly determined desire
to please.

"The rape of Nanking was nothing," the girl with the heavy
eyebrows said. "Oh, it was terrible enough. No one expected it. The
Japanese said nothing would happen, and the people foolishly believed them. But in Shensi, if they come to a village before the
villagers know they are there, then it is truly terrible."

I thought she wouldn't want to talk about it, for she must have
known much about these places, yet she went on:

"I was fourteen—they came very early in the morning. I was
sleeping, and suddenly my grandfather came to where I was sleeping
and whispered: 'Don't say anything, don't speak,' and he put a handkerchief over my face and carried me quickly to the tunnel. There
was an escape tunnel near the wall. He dropped me down—about ten
feet, and I remember I groaned, and at that moment there was a
tremendous hammering on the door. I thought my sisters were in the
tunnel, but there was no one else except me. I could hear everything
that was going on.

"I could hear things, but I couldn't understand them. The Japanese talked such bad Chinese. I heard the sound of wood breaking
and then screams—they were my elder sister's screams. And then she
was begging for life. There was no sound from the other sister. I
thought she was safe. There were only my two sisters, grandfather
and grandmother—mother had died, and my father was in the army.
But the screams went on. She was fifteen, and at fifteen you know
how to scream loudest. I heard my grandfather's voice, very low and
muttering, and then a shot and a great gasp of pain, and I knew it
was my grandfather's voice, and still the screams went on. I wanted
to get out of the tunnel. I could hear the floor boards creaking
rhythmically, now a creak, then another creak, and sometimes laughter, and once I heard a bottle being broken. Once, too, they threw a

heavy lead weight down into the tunnel, but I was hiding under the shelter of boards and they did not see me.

"I went to sleep at last. The air's bad there, and you sleep a long time in tunnels. When I woke up it was night. There was no sound from the Japanese. I climbed up the tunnel. My grandfather was dead, shot through the temple. My sister was lying naked on the floor with blood all over her legs; she was alive and shaking her head from side to side like a madwoman, and there was no sign of my other sister. I started to whimper, she woke up and I helped to dress her, but she was very sick; and you could hear the sounds of people weeping in the next village. We never found my other sister. What was strange was that even when the Japanese were defeated, the girls would hardly ever go out of their houses, they had all been raped and they did not want to see each other. They preferred only to speak to old men."

December 24th. Wen Yi-tuo was saying: "The revolt of Asia has assumed unimaginable proportions, and this time it has come to stay. We are tired to death of hearing what the West has to say about our revolt—they cannot understand us. We are revolting against our own feudal past and against the future the West offers us. We are nationalists who are prepared to throw overboard our eastern nationalism at the first sign of federation. There will be large federations in the East. Asia for the Asiatics! Certainly this will come, but it will not come with any overlordship from Japan, nor from Russia—it will come of our own will, because we desire to be free. The Chinese Communists are Chinese first, Communists later—it would be the greatest mistake to underestimate the nationalism of the Communists. In its more intense form the nationalism of the Kuomintang is only one more example of the disease, telling us nothing of the patient, the boil erupting and the sickness increasing. The important thing is that we know so little about nationalism that we are prepared to squander it in exchange for an understanding with other countries."

He went on: "Tell them that what is happening in Asia is a huge sociological experiment, and we shall never understand the present situation in Asia unless we realize that the peasants are sick of their insecurity, sick of their helplessness, sick of their lack of political consciousness; the young peasants are trying in every way they can to understand what is happening around them. You will see it in the army, where they ask questions fearlessly of their officers; you will see

that they are reading more newspapers than ever, and they are trying
in every way to discover why they are fighting. Their loyalties are
small; their greatest loyalty is loyalty to their villages, their wives and
children. Never have they been so badly treated, never have they
suffered so much. Please do not believe that the peasants are patient.
In ten years they will have political consciousness on a scale that has
been absent from China for over two thousand years. Then, when
they have political consciousness, things will begin to change—a
change which will grow up from this generation and owe its origin to
the circumstances of the war."

I asked him about the newspaper. He said they had found a
printing press, they had even obtained a permit from the governor,
and if one printing press was raided, they would find another easily.
The first number of the paper had been announced and would come
out in three or four days. There would be some trouble, of course.
The paper was liberal and democratic. Simply because it was these
things, the government would attempt to prove that it was Communist. "We cannot write one word against this atrociously corrupt
government without being accused of being Communist." He smiled,
and then he said: "You know—this government cannot go on much
longer. There has been so much crime in its name," and then suddenly, as though he was still following the same line of thought,
speaking in the same voice, he said: "I am following your Mr.
Churchill. There is nothing—not even poetry—so delightful as painting. In painting one can forget everything—everything without
exception."

December 27th. She was a girl student, wearing a jade necklace, and
I think I have mentioned her before in this diary. Even now, though
she will soon be married, she can hardly be more than eighteen, very
lithe and slender, with blue-black hair and cherry-red cheeks, walking
with an animal grace which is common among the peasant girls but
rare among students. She had been a murderer. Once when I asked
her about it, she very naturally burst out crying; but this evening the
whole story came out, not from her, but from a boy who had taken
part in it.

"What you must understand is that in the early days of the war,
terrorism against the traitors was unorganized, and the bravest of
the terrorists were the young students from middle schools. Perhaps
they were brave because it never occurred to them that they might be

arrested, or perhaps they were more cunning—knowing they were young and the police were sympathetic sometimes, they preferred to do the killing rather than allow others, who would be tortured. At that time Chen Ti-kung was the salt collector in Tientsin. We knew he was working with the Japanese, and this in itself was not perhaps sufficient, for thousands of people were working with the Japanese. What made him dangerous was that he was in a position of great responsibility, very close to the Japanese general staff, and he had given orders for the arrests of some Chinese.

"It was decided to murder him. Someone said, 'Oh, we must kill him—it is intolerable that we should breathe the same air with him.' So it was decided. We followed his movements, and we bought guns and ammunition through our house servants. You ask them to buy something, and without batting an eyelid they will always obey if you have the money. They said we could buy three revolvers for thirty-five dollars. We gave them thirty-five dollars, and they bought us six revolvers. We were ready then. We would send guards to wait outside his official mansion, and we would spend hours in the ice-cream shop mapping out his movements, so that we knew at every hour of the day or night exactly where he was.

"Then one of the students saw his car outside a theater which was showing *Gunga Din*. We had seen the film, and we remembered that toward the end there is a prolonged burst of gunfire between the English soldiers and the tribesmen. This gave us time. We telephoned to all the other students to come, and mapped out a plan of campaign. The campaign was very simple. All of us were to enter the theater armed, and all of us were to try to shoot Chen Ti-kung when there was fighting on the screen. It was as simple as that.

"But it was very dark inside the theater and we couldn't find him. Then K. decided there was only one thing to do. You know that on the side of the screen in China there is another oblong screen where the speech appears in Chinese words. One of the students went to the theater telephone and called up the manager. Would he please insert into the slide the announcement that Mr. Chen Ti-kung was urgently wanted in the manager's office. The student spoke as though he was speaking from the salt commissioner's own office. The manager complied. The slide was put on. Still no one came to the manager's office, but it was noticed that a man in the third row had half reached out of his seat. His wife had pulled him back. We couldn't be quite sure whether this was our man. We telephoned the manager's office again, asking that a more urgent notice should be

thrown on the screen. We were lucky, because at the moment when
he rose from his seat there was a fusillade of machine gunning on the
screen. Three of us shot at him. The back of his head was blown off.
His guards began firing. The whole place was in confusion. One of
the girl students found herself trapped into a corner by a foreigner—a
Swede. She brought the butt-end of her revolver down on his head,
and they say he was killed—he had a very thin skull. Half the audience was struggling to get away, and this helped us, because all the
students managed to escape; and we were not so stupid as to throw
our revolvers away—they would come in useful afterwards. I remember the smoke and the fumes and the film still going on, and then
two minutes later we were out in the sunshine. The Japanese never
found us. They arrested hundreds of people. If they had looked in
the ice-cream shop, they would have found us eating ice cream."

1945

January 1st. All things are hungry: the earth is hungry for rain, the moon for the tides, the sun for color, and the young for each other. And then, this evening, sitting down to the table for dinner, seeing the white porcelain bowl hungry for the goldfish painted on her.

January 4th. Amazed, as always, by the differences between the thought of East and West. The Chinese love the sun so much that when they make paintings there are no shadows—everything is seen at high noon. No Chinese would say, with Sir Thomas Browne: "For the world, I count it not an inn, but an hospital; and a place not to live, but to die in." Hence their industry, their tireless enjoyment of life, even the worst forms of life. Hence, too, and this is more important, their delight in human intercourse, their belief that nothing is of greater importance, their regard for the family with all its attendant evils. I remember once coming across a river in Szechuan with the poet Liang Tsong-tai at sunset and being delighted because a student called from the bank a line of Liang's poetry: "Our happiness is to ride in the setting sun." I thought the sentiment was Chinese, but even in the later ages of the T'ang dynasty, when poets were obsessed with "the tears dripped by candles," no Chinese could have spoken in this way without having lived in Europe; and Liang Tsong-tai is essentially a Frenchman writing in his mother tongue. The Chinese have no love for shadows. For them life remains simple, a thing that obeys the seasons and refuses obedience to anything else. They have not the depth or complexity of the Indians, who are in love with darkness; they are the children of high noon, seeing everything clearly against the burning sun.

January 8th. I have never met anyone so dedicated to scholarship as C. He has a devotion that is almost frightening, he spends nearly every hour of the day on his books, dreams of books, dreams of calligraphy, dreams of the university. He deserves the assistant professorship which has just been given to him, but precisely because he is a scholar he is beginning to be afraid of his responsibilities.

"In the first place it is highly unlikely that I shall be able to wake up in time for the seven o'clock classes. The landlady will wake me, there is an alarm clock, I have asked the student next door to wake me, but think what would happen if the landlady were ill, or the student somewhere else, or the alarm clock failed to go off. I am at the mercy of my surroundings. There is a man upstairs who scrapes with his hob-nailed boots on the floor—I cannot work when he is there. Or the wind blows through the paper windows—impossible to work. Or someone comes to see me. I go to sleep, I wake up, I read, I write. I have come to the stage when the only thing that matters is books; I can defend this belief; there is surely nothing so important as producing perhaps a few poems, a few pages of good criticism, and yet it is a terribly empty life."

I suggested it would be good to fall in love.

He thought for a while. "Yes, it would be good, but try to imagine a young Chinese scholar falling in love when he knows everything about it from books. There will be nothing new. It's terrible. I know everything, and I have suffered nothing except the wind and the hob-nailed boots."

January 9th. Tso Tsung-tang, the imperial minister during the Ch'ing Dynasty, was asked by Sir Robert Hart what he thought of Western influence in China. He answered: "You are all too anxious to awake us and start us on a new road, and you will do it; but you will regret it, for once awakened and started, we shall move faster and farther than you think; much faster than you want." But is it true? We have heard so often that China absorbs everything—customs, ways of thinking, peoples and even whole cultures. We are reminded that the Chinese are the oldest nation on the earth, but are they? Like every other race, they are a medley of all races, with here a face that is essentially Turkish, there a face that comes from Burma. China is not homogeneous: each province has its own culture, its own way of looking at things, and none of them has understood or absorbed the West except in the most superficial way. The whale can swallow everything except the West, but the West sticks in its mouth and will not be absorbed without a revolution; and it may happen that the whale, with the West in its mouth, may die of hunger.

Helplessly, in the last two years, and mostly in the last six months, we have watched China or rather the Chinese government incapable of solving the simplest problems. There is resolution, but nothing with which to resolve. The government is run by a single family; the old classic virtue of family affection has become unalloyed nepotism; the best are hindered; the merchants unbelievably corrupt. All this has happened at the time when the country could least afford the luxury of the old virtues. Efficiency is at a discount. In the greatest days of our danger, there is a supreme carelessness over the fate of the people. In the days of the Chou dynasty Po-yi dwelt on the shores of the North Sea and waited for the world to grow clean. But we cannot wait any longer.

January 10th. The fantastic confidence that the Americans have in the Generalissimo. . . . But why? I have no confidence in him. I have no confidence in one man, and least of all have I confidence in dictatorship. The dictators are like Egyptian statues, so much larger than life that we assume they are permanent and all-knowing. But does he know that for the seven hundred millionth time a soldier has come up the Burma Road to die in rags and filthiness, his body like a bone, wracked with malaria, with pus coming out of his eye socket and moving so slowly that he seems to be someone moving through a nightmare more terrible than any invented in this war. "We have ten million soldiers," an official told me, when I complained that these men from Burma should not be left to die. "Does it matter about one soldier?"

No, it doesn't matter. In the long run there will be no changes in China because he has been abandoned. The land will still be the same, the people will be the same, countless millions will still be born, there will still be smoke from the chimneys and the fields will still be reaped. But when it happens that officialdom is utterly divorced from the people, when the food of soldiers is taken from them by their officers, when the people have no more confidence in those who have raised themselves to power, when nepotism and corruption are the rule and the best are starving, how can I praise an incompetent government and pretend to admire it? In this country I admire only one thing: the overwhelming greatness of the people who have suffered too long.

January 19th. The fear has gone. Though the Japanese are still near, and more airfields are being blown up by Americans who are retreating through the incompetence of the leadership of the Chinese army, for some reason we are no longer afraid. We know in our bones that the Japanese have lost the war. They can build their railway from Singapore to Peking, but we know that the railway will never help them to defend their continental empire. The fear went as suddenly as it came. It may come again, but it will never come with the same force or authenticity. We felt in December that the Japanese could do with us as they pleased. With ten more men at the right place they might have thrust down to Kunming; with another ten men they might have thrust through Szechuan; but they failed to take advantage of the masterly inaction of the Chinese. The Chinese peasants and soldiers are blameless. They did what they could and died by the hundreds of thousands. But for those who led them, for the merchants who filled up their automobiles and made plans to escape to Kansu—but what would be the good of escaping to Kansu when the rest of China had fallen?—for the unthinking and the unspirited, and the careless above all, there should be no mercy. Nor will there be any mercy in the hearts of those who fled from Kwei-lin.

We know that the people can stand intolerable strains, we know that there is in them an unyielding strength, but these things give us no comfort. It has become a *cliché* that the Chinese can bear everything without complaint. It is true that they do not complain. They have learned over the centuries that complaint leads nowhere—there is no one to complain to. But what if they should ever find someone or something to whom they could complain? What if they, the most democratic of all people in their daily behavior, should find a government *responsible to them?* (Then the prizes of government would be less, the responsibilities almost intolerable, but at least there would be an end to their silence, and their unendurable sufferings.)

January 29th. This morning there was news from Yenan. To those who have never heard of Yenan it must mean nothing at all, but to us it was an event of astonishing importance. There is a vast area of China which to us is called simply Yenan. We hear little about it, and of the little we hear we are immensely critical; but gradually, out of the welter of criticism and propaganda, we have formed a picture which cannot wholly be wrong. There is another government in China which exerts vast powers. It has said to the peasants that the livelihood of the peasants is all that matters, and all other problems are small, even insignificant, in comparison with their livelihood. And in this the majority of the professors and the students are in perfect agreement, without being in the least Communist. Also, we know that they have been fighting vigorously, with inadequate equipment, we know that there have been full-scale battles against the Japanese in which the Communists won. We know this; we know little more. Because we accept this, and secretly praise the Communists, it would be absurd to call us Communists. We are lost. We cannot go on with the authoritarian government we have. We cannot endure for one moment the thought of the secret police continuing into the peace. We are weary beyond words of rule by the military governors. The Generalissimo has outlived his usefulness. For a while he represented the forces of good will; now he represents the forces of evil. It is as simple as that. And yet we do not want the Communists in power. We want only that this war should be fought to an end, and afterwards there should be a government of no party, no affiliations, no beliefs except the belief that China shall disappear, for nothing is so dangerous as the name, and in its place there shall be only "the Chinese people."

The message from Yenan was brief: "We are well. J. was captured by the Japanese. There has been tremendous fighting."

February 1st. At last we have left the theater where we have lived for a year and a half. A few, but not many of the best professors of this university will remain, cooped up in the shallow theater boxes looking down on a stage where there is nothing at all except bare boards. We were lucky to have lived there at all: there are places infinitely worse. It was never uncomfortable. The misery will wear off. We shall forget the dirt, the falling plaster, and the broken tiles; we shall forget that we never dared invite anybody to see us; we shall forget the mud and the smells of Peimenkai, the half-open graves outside the North Gate, for next to us there was one of the most amazingly beautiful gardens in Kunming and not far away was the Green Lake and twenty minutes' walk away lay the university.

The oddest of all things is that we are going to live in the house of a Russian vodka manufacturer, where the smell of vodka hangs in the air, where the great brown jars lie in rows downstairs and GIs come roaring in at all times of the day and night for their vodka poured into gasoline tanks. Nothing could be more different from the theater than this wide-open spacious courtyard, with its pale red poinsettias and the faintly bittersweet smell of vodka, which must surely be among the most pleasant of all smells.

I have turned traitor. It cannot be helped. I did not even fight against it. When the offer came, I accepted it eagerly. I have spent four years with the professors, and of those four years one and a half were spent in conditions which made the t.b. worse, so that the little calcined spots in the lung opened and bled, and I lived too long in a state of tubercular excitement. I confess I am grateful for it. There are things I would never have dreamed of without t.b., and since everyone around me was suffering from the same disease, I learned to understand them better. The spots have healed now, as we expected they would—we are six thousand feet above sea level, the air is clear, and there is an enchantment in Yunnan, where the streets are filthy beyond words, which cures all disease. The theater was dangerous: cold, damp, insufferably oppressive with the high walls all round it. I comfort myself by saying that we can now at last entertain guests.

But there is the Russian landlord and vodka manufacturer to be dealt with, a huge man with a keen brain and a ferocious temper. He lives in a world which is not unlike my tubercular world last year, incessantly stimulated by vast quantities of vodka, a giant who has stepped straight out of Dostoievsky, ruthless in his determination to make a fortune, suffering from a disease of the spleen, impatient of all restraint and five times larger than life. His father was a station master in Manchuria. He will talk at the drop of a hat of the great forest and the great cold. For him Manchuria is not a part of China, but Yellow Russia—Zhelto-Rossiya. He has the utmost conceivable contempt for the Chinese when he is drunk, and the greatest admiration for their business abilities when he is sober. He took me into a corner of the courtyard this evening. "They're always playing tricks with me. Look at that." *That* was one of the bamboo-covered cases in which crude potato alcohol is brought to the factory before being distilled. He kicked it. A false bottom fell out. "It's always happening. God damn them. They don't know what's good for them." Then he grinned like a child. "But I always find it out."

He has a peasant delight in life, and the quickest brain I have ever known—no nobility of manner, but a kind of desperate good temper. He puts a whole bottle of vodka on the table. "Drink as much as you like. You'll have a clear head in the morning. It's not like whisky—the crude oils have been taken out. Well, what the hell are you waiting for?" He drank down half a bottle, for a moment his face clouded and he looked tired, then suddenly his face resumed its normal appearance of benevolent savagery. "Why don't you drink it? It won't hurt you. You're weak. Do you have to give a lecture in the morning?" I nodded. "All right, take it easy." There is a hammering at the outer gate. "The GIs have come. They can bloody well wait. I'm not going to open the door for them. I like them, but I am going to have my privacy. I'm a merchant. It's not the kind of thing I wanted to be, but I'm a merchant and even a merchant has the right to have some time of his own." There are moments when he looks almost crafty, when you realize there is some deep-seated passion of remonstration in him. He wanted to be a scholar. He has an excellent mechanical brain. He was a White Russian, but it was inhumanly difficult for a White Russian to receive any university education. He wanted it beyond anything he has ever wanted since, but from the very beginning he was cursed with his insecurity and had to struggle for money. For a while he managed a third-rate boardinghouse in Chungking. He opened a restaurant. Then early last year he came down to Kunming on business and discovered there was room for a vodka factory. He bought this building from a retired Yunnanese general who lives nearby, still retaining his old bodyguard. He refuses to go out at night. He has explained very carefully that he must keep his money in American dollars under the mattress, and he dare not leave the house. He distrusts his servants, probably for good reasons. He is supremely dictatorial and cares less than nothing for the opinions of others; but he gives a curious impression of goodness. I realize we have fallen from the frying pan into the fire. He has suggested very gently that sometimes there may be a little drunkenness at parties—nothing very special—a little breaking of glasses. Does the professor mind? The professor, looking at the wide space of the courtyard, is secretly delighted. "And then of course there are my Russian friends. They are terribly talkative. They like to pick quarrels, and sometimes the GIs are troublesome. You are sure you won't mind?" I nod vehemently. "Like hell you don't mind. You wait and see," he said darkly. All the while the hammering at the door continued.

It is going to be a game of wits. He cannot "place" me, but it is not in the least difficult to place him, for he comes straight out of a Russian novel. He has the goodness, the occasional cunning, the delight in losing himself in drunkenness, the fierce casual temper of one of the characters of Dostoievsky's novels. Above all there is the goodness. Tonight, half an hour ago, he was playing Russian love songs on his mandolin. It was utterly delightful. More and more vodka bottles appeared on the tables. The large room downstairs, with its tapestries on the walls, its inverted paper umbrellas for lampshades, its hideous furniture which he designed, the flowers and the tablecloths became a scene of magic. We were in Russia, or rather we were in Zhelto-Rossiya in a small house among the forests. He sang endlessly. He needed no audience, and it was a good voice, even when he was hopelessly drunk, and he had a perfect sense of time. "I used to play the trumpet at Shanghai," he whispered. "Do you know what I would like? To be rich enough to have a large house and a private orchestra. I could shout to the *chef d'orchestre* and say, 'Play this,' and by God they would play it, and then I'd throw some coins at them. I don't want to be a damned merchant. Yes, that's what I'd like." There is nothing in the least outrageous in his desire for a private orchestra; it is the reverse of all his sufferings, the dream of his childhood, which has almost come true and yet has not come true—there is a lurking suspicion in his eyes that it will all fade into nothing and leave him, a young poverty-stricken boy somewhere in one of the coastal ports of China.

February 8th, A strange story. K. told me the story yesterday evening, while we were sipping brandy. He has been with the Americans in Burma, and yet when you look at him, the pale egg-white skin and almost feminine lips, it is impossible to imagine him as a soldier.

"I was a liaison officer, and so I came to know both sides of the conflict, for there was a very real and at times bitter conflict between the Chinese and the Americans. It was not so at higher levels, though there was conflict again at the highest levels of all. The Americans were tough. They were the finest soldiers imaginable, but they had no patience with our old-fashioned generals, whose armies were often paper armies—that is, perhaps a quarter of the troops on the roll had no existence at all except to provide lists of names, and for each of these names there would be a certain amount of payment from the central government. And then another quarter perhaps were dying or suffering from sickness, and of the remaining half perhaps not more than a quarter were active combatants—the rest were officers, servants, orderlies, foragers, stray boys who had joined because they had nothing else to do.

"The army in those days was under the direction of General Wei Li-huang, but the strategy was largely in the hands of the Americans. The final decisions were usually made by the Americans. In general the Chinese were perfectly content that this should be so, but among some of the minor generals there was a great deal of criticism.

"One of these generals, who belonged to the old school, believed in charms. He gave charms to his officers—it was, of course, unnecessary to give charms to his soldiers, but occasionally he would order the priest who accompanied him to make sacrificial offerings. The priest was theoretically a Taoist priest, who wore an oiled topknot and a long black gown. He was usually barefoot, and though he ate sometimes with the general, it was quite clear that the general despised him. Whenever there were visiting officers, the priest was put away.

"I was a major in the army commanded by this general. The colonel befriended me, and we made various plans by which the soldiers could be given better blankets—you know how thin a Chinese soldier's blanket is—and we did everything we could to improve their lot, even to the extent of depriving the general of some of his proceeds from the War Department. We made it clear that we were determined that the soldiers should have a new deal. We improved their pay—partly out of our own pockets, partly out of the commanding general's; and we arranged that their rewards for capturing enemy rifles, flags, swords, and so on should be increased. The Chinese soldier lives for these things. He will attack a redoubt with astonishing bravery simply for the sake of the rifles he captures, and for which we pay a few dollars. He has no final loyalty to China; his final loyalty is to his commanding officer. And usually it is the young commanding officers on the field who win battles and try very often to improve the lot of the soldiers.

"We had been teaching the soldiers to read one afternoon—it was a few days before the coming battle, we were resting just outside some farmhouses. Then the general came along in a sedan chair. There were two sedan chairs, and in the second was the Taoist priest. The priest stepped out and stood by the general while he made a speech—the perfectly normal and inevitable speech, imitating the Generalissimo's voice and accents, about our duty to the country, our passionate desire to rid the country of the Japanese, and the need for the most implicit discipline. We noticed that the Taoist priest was smiling and stroking his beard and was behaving with unusual familiarity with the general, even occasionally winking at him. The general smiled and asked my soldiers whether they were prepared to die for China. The soldiers answered in chorus, the general went on with his speech. At the end there was a short silence, and suddenly the general repeated in a much graver voice whether we were prepared to die for China. All those who were prepared to die for China were ordered to step forward. All stepped forward. The general smiled to the Taoist and was about to step back in the sedan chair when an idea occurred to him. He smiled gravely, contemplated the soldiers for a long time, rubbed his cheek, and said: 'This is very interesting, but as a test of your loyalty to your general I have one more question to ask. Who will sacrifice his life for me?'

"You would have expected perhaps that all the soldiers would have stepped forward, but in fact there was silence. No one answered. If they had known what was about to happen, and if there had been time for them to discuss the inevitable consequences, they would have stepped forward faster than they had ever stepped forward before—they would have rushed the general and perhaps killed him, and they might even have killed the Taoist priest. Instead, they stayed where they were. After a while a curious fluttering movement occurred—there was indecision—there was a kind of deep-rooted tantalizing uncertainty—no one knew what to do. The general—and this is what made matters worse—continued to stroke his chin, looking at them, saying nothing, making curious movements of his hands toward the Taoist priest. And the uncertainty of the soldiers deepened with their increasing boredom, for they had no idea what to do or what was demanded of them, or of their consciences, except that they should stay where they were in order to avoid the most terrible catastrophe.

"Death is not so bad as boredom and uncertainty. A soldier, after being asleep all night, lying on the wet ground, covered only with his thin cotton uniform and his thinner blanket, fights because the nights and the days are an infinity of boredom. We engage battle at dawn, at the moment when boredom has reached its maximum, and more often than not we exchange battle at the moment before dawn, when the interminable boredom has reached a point of excruciating intensity. We fight, then, not for our country, but because we are lonely beyond words, because nothing is left to us, because it seems to us at that moment that life can no longer be endured unless we make a noise, run, shout, and murder.

"For perhaps five minutes the soldiers stood there. I assure you there are times when five minutes are endless. And then suddenly and unaccountably, from various places, soldiers stepped forward tentatively, not knowing what they were doing, unable to stand quite still, saluting the general, but not in the usual way—they saluted him as though they were saluting someone they had seen in dreams. They were like people dazed. There were cries from the soldiers at the back: 'Don't move! Come back!' It was like when you throw a stone into a pool. You notice the same thing sometimes in crowds—an inexplicable uneasiness which slowly accumulates and pervades the whole crowd—not panic, but the heights and depths of uneasiness.

"We knew, I think, what would happen; but we couldn't foresee how it would happen. Five had stepped forward from the front rank—five people standing alone in deathly stillness. The general asked: 'You are prepared to die for me?' There was no answer, but they threw up their heads in the manner which means in the East either a deliberate 'yes' or 'no.' Then, walking slowly down the line, pausing before each one, he shot those five who were prepared to die for him. A pause, and then he said: 'Dismiss,' and that was all.

"But in a sense it was only the beginning. There was no sign of revolt; there were not even the faintest mutterings. The general returned to his sedan chair accompanied by the Taoist priest and smiled at the soldiers, showing his teeth. Perhaps he would be alive now if he hadn't smiled at them; but there was so much triumph in his smile that the soldiers immediately understood that he had scored a victory over them and they had lost 'face.' The most extraordinary thing was the way he remained there, offering no resistance at all

when they suddenly rushed toward him. I could not see the general. I
had no desire to see the general. I remember wondering how he would
die, and what would happen to the soldiers who were responsible,
and whether we would all be court-martialed, and shot out of hand.
But we were not court-martialed, and the general died because they
trampled him underfoot, trampled to death by these young farm boys
who wore only the lightest of cotton slippers."

February 16th. To remember always the things the Taoists wor-
shipped: clouds, floating duckweed, the moss at the foot of rocks, the
valleys where no one ever enters, the peach blossom gardens and the
short stalk of a rose.

To remember the three greatest desires of the Chinese: to live
long, to be unhindered, and to see the light at the bottom of the
well.

But how in God's name, and at this hour of the world's history,
to follow those counsels when we are faced with such despair?

February 18th, The secret police. There seems to be no way out.
We live, in this age of nightmare, with the secret police all around
us. A student has disappeared. No one knows where he has gone, or
whether he will ever return; no one doubts that he has been spirited
away by the secret police. There can have been no trial, there are
even very good grounds for believing that the student who has disappeared has been mistaken for someone else.

You can see them sometimes hovering around the university
gates, men with lawless and broken faces, the excreta of prisons, the
refuse of this civilization which is in danger of making us all refuse,
men with American guns in their pockets and a price on their heads.
It is easy enough to understand why they are there. Of all places in
China this university is the most glorious, because it is dedicated to
democratic government, and believes in democracy, not knowing
what democracy will bring China, because it has never been practiced. One of the presidents of this university has called it "the
bulwark of democracy." Probably he was wrong to use these words,
for ever since then we have been conscious of being disliked. Universities, democracy—the two words most disliked by the soldiers who
are in power. And what is so ghastly is that one can do nothing,
absolutely nothing, to convince anyone outside China that this is

true, that we live from hand to mouth, not knowing what further onslaughts on freedom are in store for us. I said once, and still believe, that whatever is good and new in China will come from the universities, and whatever is bad will always come from the soldiers; the longer I stay, the more evidently true it becomes, for the soldiers have no understanding of the problems of the country, the merchants have even less, and least of all in the future government of this country will the officials have any sense of what is due, since they more than any others have grown to despise the peasants. The peasants and the scholars can be despised, yet they remain.

The voice of the Chinese people is not yet heard abroad. We are confused and shamed by the picture that has been drawn of heroic China. No one speaks authoritatively for China abroad. The chaos is all round us. By the barest margin the Japanese failed to capture Kweichow and Szechuan, and no one is blamed, and no one will ever be blamed, because history will be written by the official historians. But at least there must be a footnote to describe the misery under which one lives with secret police and racketeers in power. And perhaps there should be another footnote which will say that in spite of all this, there was a heroism vaster than anything we can imagine.

February 19th. A few days ago the great scholar Wen Yi-tuo traveled with some students to see the prehistoric forest two hundred miles to the south. He has come back with his drawings, but he is thin and pale, suffering from typhus.

We know he will recover, but it is impossible to describe the fear that overwhelmed us. We cannot—dare not—think of what will happen without him. I know no one else who is so perfectly representative of Chinese culture. Sometimes when I pass the mud hut in the campus where he lectures, seeing the crowds of students who stand outside listening at the windows, I am more than ever conscious of my inadequacy. I think of his reddish beard, the young stocky body in the blue gown, the amazingly sharp eyes, the fire and depth of his voice. I remember the first day I met him, a muddy cloudy day in September when it seemed that the whole street was falling into decay, and yet suddenly made living by his presence. At least three professors have died since I have been here, and there is no reason why, on his pitifully small income, he should be able to resist the disease.

I do not know anyone else in this university who carries such quiet authority. There are moments when his voice becomes deeply passionate, his anger ripens, the grim, relentless smile becomes almost terrifyingly cold, and he will talk quietly of the corruption in the country and the responsibility of the students in the face of corruption. One thinks of people who are pure flame; he is the purest I have ever known. And everything has fitted in: the years when he half starved in Chicago, learning to paint, the years of the civil wars, when he said he became almost insane, seeing the burnt villages and the dead peasants, and knowing that he was powerless to help them. The years when he took part in the renascent movement of poetry, and those other years when he decided to reexamine with all the artifices of modern scholarship the basic interpretation of the Chinese classics. The years of study over the Chou dynasty bronzes, and early inscriptions, seeing the vigorous life in these ancient testimonies of an earlier and better China, and being puzzled by them, and trying desperately to understand the impulses that brought them to the light. The years of suffering and near starvation when he carved seals at night and taught in middle schools for a few extra dollars, and always the quietness and nobility of a prince among men. I asked him once whether he would ever go into parliament, if there was a parliament in this country. "Yes, but it's better to live like this. We are nearer the heart of the people. I have taught a few middle-school students to love Chinese literature and adore freedom."

This afternoon, seeing him pale-faced and sad, leaning on a stick, shivering a little with the memory of how nearly typhus had stricken him down, I wondered how much reserve of strength there was in him, and in the others. Surely there must come a time when they will have no reserves left at all! And this saddens me more than anything else, because I cannot conceive that China will be worth living in when the best scholars have perished in the cold.

February 26th. Wen Yi-tuo was thumping the table: "Human dignity demands that men should not live in fear of the secret police. This above all! Those who employ the secret police are the traitors—there are no other traitors compared with these. We cannot breathe this air. The police should be open and undisguised, unarmed. We are fighting for our liberties. Must we have them poisoned at the source?"

I am afraid it is only too true. The secret police is everywhere among the students, even perhaps among the professors there are one or two, and though we know their names and they have been persuaded into silence, how can we be sure that others will not appear? And what is far more worrying is that every Chinese officer I have spoken to has nothing but the most bitter contempt for the universities. . . .

March 3rd. Just before he died Lu Hsun wrote a short essay called "The Dark Night." He wrote: "There was a time not very long ago when a prisoner condemned to death was led through the busy highway, and he was allowed to protest in the loudest voice against his condemnation, he could say the vilest things against his judges, he could tell the story of his brave deeds and demonstrate his courage in the face of death. At the moment when he was about to be executed, the spectators would applaud. When I was young, I thought the practice was barbarous and cruel. As I grow older, it seems to me that the rulers of the past were courageous and supremely confident of their power in permitting these things to happen. And perhaps it showed that the rulers were showing their kindness and even benevolence to the condemned man. But nowadays this no longer happens."

March 13th. I have been looking again, with a sense of curious bewilderment, at the small sandstone statue of Buddha with his attendants which stands in my room. It was modeled by some priestly craftsman in the Liang dynasty nearly fifteen hundred years ago. Less than a foot square, it has a cool concentrated devotion in its archaic forms; we could not carve like this today, because we could not believe in the depths of meaning that are contrived in the folds of the gown, in the aureoles, and in the kneeling boys. The faces are not Chinese, but they have about them an expression so nearly Chinese that it is easy enough to believe they were modeled on the faces of men from central Asia who had come for many years into contact with Chinese power. The attendants wear the same slippers which we wear today, but their gowns are simpler than modern Chinese gowns and more like those worn in Japan. There is the *bodhi* tree springing from the lotus leaf, and Buddha holds in his hands a gift of fruit— perhaps Buddha is already the goddess Kwan-yin and the fruit is a peach. Here, fashioned in Chinese Turkestan or somewhere in the south, Buddha has been caught and photographed at one of the moments of his pilgrimage and change. Once he was Apollo. He traveled through India, wearing many disguises, and when at last the portrait of him reached the later T'ang dynasty, he was already a princess from the West—in his long pilgrimage he had changed even his sex, so that today my barber still has on his walls a portrait of a willowy girl holding peaches and wearing the silks of earlier dynasties. But what is most amazing is that I noticed for the first time today, on this Buddha carved so long ago, there is incised on the bare chest the sign of the swastika, the wheel turning as the sun turns, the sign of the Nazis, which the Buddhists employed as a sign of blessedness.

So the thing has suddenly sprung into the light and become contemporary. The small carved votive tablet is still fulfilling the purpose which was announced in the inscription, an inscription which never fails to move me because the floods and calamities of the Great Liang dynasty are the same as ours. Here it is:

> *In the fourth year, and on the third day of the second moon, in the reign period Tien Chien, of the great Liang Dynasty, the one who believes, Meng Chi-kung and his sons, Chen Chi and Chen Yeh, on behalf of the whole family who have so often met with calamities, faithfully promised this votive offering. They have now completed their task. They hope that the dead members of the family will enter the Three Orders, and that the living will soon abandon the Eight Calamities and pass through the gate of bitterness.*

Almost it has the brevity of the Greek Anthology; in their own terms, and using the necessary words, nothing could be simpler; and in our own day how many echoes there are to the hope that we shall "pass through the gate of bitterness."

April 7th. I met him first half an hour after he had jumped by parachute from an airplane over Kunming, a huge young American, larger than life, with close-cropped hair and a German name. He said: "The thing you have to do is just go limp. Don't fight against it. Just let yourself fall." He was so heavy that they had to give him an outsize parachute; his clothes fitted tight on him, and you thought he would burst out of them; he smiled gently, and looking at these powerful shoulders, you understood why he was afraid of his own strength. I saw him rarely. He disappeared for months on end, mysteriously traveling behind Chinese lines or through the heart of Japanese country. He came back yesterday. He had been on two missions, one in Burma and another in Fukien. On each of the missions he went with millions of Chinese dollars, with tommy guns and high explosives and an interpreter, for he knew no Chinese, and he would tell the story of his adventures very quietly, without quite believing what had happened, thinking of his wife and his ranch, or of the gangsters he had once known in Cleveland. "The worst moment was in Kachin country. I was going alone—nearly alone, and we knew the Kachins were near us. We felt them. We were walking down a forest path in single file, and sometimes we saw the glint of their knives, but there was no sound. We had gone on for a long time, and then we came upon three Chinese soldiers—but the soldiers were headless. We knew what had happened. The Kachins had cut off each head with a single blow of their long *daos*.

"There was nothing we could do. We went on more carefully— that's all, and then some time in the evening we came upon a Kachin village. It was clear that they distrusted us, but they knew I was an American, and this puzzled them—they did not know whether they were allowed to kill the Chinese who were with me. They stood there, with their arms folded, the long knives at their sides, and they said they were pleased to see us, and they looked up and down at me, and they could not make me out—they are small fellows, though very proud. They kept on looking at me like that. I didn't like it. They came and felt my muscles, and I wondered whether they had decided to put me in a cauldron and see whether I was worth eating. But they didn't boil me alive—they asked me instead whether I was prepared to fight with their three strongest men. I nodded. There wasn't much else I could do. So they took us into their tribal temple, and all over the rafters there were heads stuck on nails, and some of them looked very new. I knew a lot about the head-hunters by this time; I was beginning to be afraid. They have guns and they are good at firing them. If I won the fight over their three strongest men, they would probably kill me; and if I lost I would be killed anyway. It was six of one and half a dozen of the other.

"It was getting dark, and we stripped and fought, and all the while I was expecting a *dao* to cut off my head, or perhaps they would simply fire at me. I was unprotected, and I liked them. They must have sensed it. I knew they were cowards. They don't fear guns, but they fear hand grenades, and they can't make out 'stringers,' which are small things like pencils that shoot about fifteen yards. Well, I won. It was a near thing, but the three strongest men were down on the ground, and for some reason they did not kill me; they gave me embroidered cloth and showed me the path to the next village. I was frightened as hell. It was dark. I set off with the others, and we had gone fifty yards down the road when there was a burst of machine guns firing at us. Odd kind of freaks. I suppose they had a passion for changing their minds."

He spoke about other things: how nearly all the mayors in the Japanese-occupied villages were pro-Chungking. He would go there and find that they knew he was coming, and everything was prepared. There would be feasts for him, the mayor would sometimes present him with one of the mayoral concubines, and once he had helped some Chinese to capture a company of Japanese. The Japanese had plundered and raped; mercy toward others had never occurred to them, but when they saw the American they threw themselves down on their knees. "It was indescribably squalid. They were weeping and shivering with fear. The Chinese pointed out the man who had done most harm, the man who had murdered and raped his way through this small backwater of China. It was this man who was kneeling before me. I lifted him up by the neck and slowly squeezed the life out of him. . . ."

June 2nd, The Japanese prisoners. They came last night in lorries down the Burma Road, but I have only just seen them. It was dusk when we went along to the school and found them there in that huge, walled garden more than half a mile long. In the dusk they looked ragged and miserable, gray shapes huddled over bundles, sitting cross-legged on the earth, with the Chinese guards standing over them with fixed bayonets gleaming in the faint light. Gradually it was possible to distinguish the men from the women, but only because the women had more clothes. They said nothing. They did not complain. Someone was knocking in a post, and soon there were ten or twelve posts round that small huddled group in the dark, and then the barbed wire was uncoiled, and bent nails were hammered into the wood to support the barbed wire, and still the prisoners huddled there, paying no attention to what was happening, not lost in their thoughts, but numbed by the darkness and the encroaching circle of people who were watching them. Then someone lit a light, and the barbed wire shone silver—two silver rings surrounding the faces of the prisoners, which were no longer gray in the darkness but bright crimson. And what was so extraordinary and delightful was that in that moment they did not look like prisoners, they came to life, they sprang out of the earth fully armed with the colors of sunlight, and though they were encircled with silver chains, they escaped from their prison.

June 5th. I am sure there is nothing quite like the Chinese lavatory. On those bare smeared boards with small round holes in them, you crouch with your trousers round your ankles over a green cesspool which is slowly crawling with fat, sluggish silver worms. It is not entirely unpleasant; the difficulty for the foreigner is to keep your balance, because the board is very narrow and there is danger that you will fall into a ten-foot depth of that green-moiling stuff, and you will never come out of it. I suspect that there are three or four bodies in the cesspool where I go every day. I know there are dead rats, for they sometimes float to surface; by the time they reach the surface they are very brightly colored indeed. The wonder lies in the color of the pool, green and silver—the brown miraculously obliterated. There are bubbles on the surface and rats, very dark rats, with bodies as long as your forearm, come prowling round the edges of the pool; and so we squat there, looking for all the world like Buddhas, while the board creaks and only a half-inch thickness of wood separates us from the worms waiting below.

There is, of course, no sanitation in these backwoods of China; we live by virtue of the antitoxins in our bodies, and we only just live. The precarious balance between health and disease is maintained by luck: every day I see rickshas passing down the streets with some dead body or someone hidden in wrapped counterpanes on his way to hospital. These beautifully bright, silver-encrusted latrines are the home of a devil even more forbidding than the Japanese, and far more long-lived; and what is terrifying is that the Chinese seem to have come to terms with the devil, vast numbers of them possess the required antitoxins in their bodies and somehow manage to survive. But in a country where dead rats lie festering in every street, and the drains are clogged, and in the very best of houses the latrine opens into a stream which is no more than ten yards from the house well, the miracle is that anyone survives at all. When the war is over, China will need first, I suppose, railroad engineers; but secondly, and of more lasting importance, will be good sanitary engineers.

June 7th. I cannot believe this story, but I know it must be true. J. tells me that last Sunday he was walking in the neighborhood of a lake near Chenggung, about fifteen miles from here. It was late in the afternoon. He had seen the lake, which is a kind of crystalline green in color, transparent, very cold and, though small, infinitely more to his liking than the Green Neck Lake in the city or the vast lake which lies beneath the Western Hills outside. "And then I saw two soldiers carrying a pannier. They were walking against the sunlight, and I noticed in the pannier there was a soldier. I hardly paid any attention to them. There are so many sick soldiers in China, and they are so often carried in panniers. The sun was going, and they looked huge against the skyline. I forgot about them for a while, but when I looked again they were not far from where they were before, and the pannier was being set down, and the soldier was screaming—not very loudly, but at least he was screaming. Then, and this was worse, I saw the two soldiers take spades from the pannier and they began to dig a grave. I thought: 'They are going to execute him, but the strange thing is that I have seen many soldiers and many men being led out to execution, but they never scream.' So I went a little closer. The grave was being dug slowly, and the voice of the soldier in the pannier was growing louder. It was like a girl screaming softly: probably he was half-gagged. And then the most extraordinary, the most terrible thing happened. They took the soldier out and laid him in the grave, and all the time he was screaming in that faint, weak voice of his. There was nothing I could do. The grave was stamped down, perhaps it had taken altogether hardly ten minutes, for the earth is soft in these places and the soldier's hands must have been tied behind his back. And then, walking very quickly, the two soldiers returned with the empty pannier swinging between them.

"I spoke to them a little later; they told me the soldier was ill and dying, and their captain had ordered them to take him to the hills. This was the expression they used—'take him to the hills.' They obeyed. They could only obey, though they said they deeply regretted it, and perhaps if there had been good doctors he might have recovered." I had it on the tip of my tongue to ask J. why he did not hurry to the soldier's rescue, though I must have known that the grave-diggers were armed. As he told the story his face was dead white. "There was nothing," he said, "there was absolutely nothing that could be done!"

June 12th. The floods have come. All over the field outside my window there is the cloud-reflecting mirror. Yesterday it was messy with pools and ruts of water; today, entirely submerged, it is a brighter blue than the sky. Going along the Burma Road this morning, I saw a cabbage field under water. Three naked children were running through the lanes between the cabbage fields, kicking up showers of silver water. What was surprising was their fat father, with a belly like a bronze bell, wearing a pair of green drawers, was swimming in the cabbage field on his back and at the same time towing a kite which was the same color as his drawers and was probably made of the same material. He looked perfectly, idiotically happy.

July 21st. Nearly all Chinese houses are surrounded by high walls, and living in them you feel like a bluebottle continually buzzing at the panes, or else you feel like a prisoner sentenced to eternal banishment. And somehow, though the Chinese have a passion for space and are never happier than when contemplating the vast regions of their land, they are content in their houses where the stone courtyard, the rockeries, the stunted plants in the marble urns give no impression of space at all, but only a kind of mechanical imitation, very artificial like a dress which preserves them from the nakedness of their land. Sometimes I feel that the Chinese who have wandered over their northern deserts for so many centuries delight in this self-imposed imprisonment, feeling that at last they, the most insecure of people, are secure: they have built these high walls and artificial gardens to protect themselves, and also perhaps their sensibilities have been sharpened to the point where they must take refuge in themselves. There, behind monstrous clifflike walls, the sounds and smells of the countryside and the marketplace disappear, and you walk in perennial quiet.

But this afternoon the quietness was broken by two beggars who came into the courtyard and loudly demanded money. There was nothing complaining about their voices. They stood there in the courtyard, stridently demanding money and refusing to leave; and this has never happened before. There are beggars who sit in the roadway, creeping with lice, with festering wounds, hag-ridden by sores that burst open with a pressure of the fingers as you approach; but though these beggars looked weak, they were whole. I gave them some money, because it was impossible to read while they were there, and the high walls echoed and reechoed their sharp menacing voices. After they had gone R. said: "It is even worse than you can imagine, because the beggars' and the thieves' guilds are inseparable; they have seen that you are prepared to give, and now they will watch the house carefully." I thought it nonsense till I went out later in the evening and saw one of the beggars crouched just outside the gate, and there was the second one, surrounded by three or four more, on the opposite side of the road facing us. They were waiting.

July 25th. There was a famous Chinese scholar so poor that he could not afford oil and worked by the light coming through a pin hole, from his neighbor's room. Sometimes it seems that all our scholars are like this, and we dread what will happen when one of them dies—we cannot afford coffins. Only very occasionally can we afford a feast; we save up for it like maniacs, forgetting to buy shoes for our children and for ourselves. There is a dreariness in this poverty which defeats us all: the university has managed to borrow enough money to buy a small group of houses, has even designed them and built them. The walls are paper-thin: you can hear the man thinking next door, and it is impossible to work. Or rather, one can work, but rarely give of one's best, because there are only two rooms in these cottages and a small kitchen. There are some professors with five or six children; they exist in these two rooms, but I have never understood how they manage to live.

Last week the wife of one of the professors died: students and friends and professors came together and provided the fantastic sum which will allow her to be buried decently. And what of the rest—the soldiers, the beggars, the pedlars? It is inconceivable that they can raise enough to buy coffins. Yet this week I have seen a funeral that must have cost millions. There was a carved lacquer coffin, there were multitudes of flowers, the place where the man died was decorated from the street to the roof with enormous colored ribbons and paper flowers, and at least five hundred monks took part in the funeral procession. The costliest candles were lit, the mourners did not wear white sackcloth but white silk, and when the funeral procession at last came into view, it was as though a fairground was suddenly displayed before our eyes. It was monstrous, and yet it was perfectly understandable—the cost was defrayed by the local government for a deceased official.

July 29th, Opium. I have taken opium five times, and for some ridiculous reason it has never had the slightest effect—not even a headache. I am hopelessly ashamed of this. There are so many visions which are denied to me, so many colors I have never seen, so many *houris* and *devadasis* and golden mountains and vast landscapes which will always be concealed from me. The man who smokes opium downstairs, lying on a bare wooden board, with the long jade pipe and the oil flame that seems to be burning in a glass inkwell— does he have visions? I doubt it. He is fat and greasy, and hoards sewing machines—there are perhaps a hundred in the house; and it is impossible to imagine that he has enough imagination to have anything more than the drifting contentment of the opium-smoker. I have seen him at night as I pass through the main gate, his eyes closed, his lips pursed together, his bleary face in no contentment whatsoever, but seems only to be angry. Little clouds of blue smoke come from the pipe, he fidgets with the ivory bowl, he sometimes speaks to himself. Dogs snap in the courtyard. He does not hear them, and when his children start yelling in their perpetual night-mares, he doesn't hear them either. Deafness perhaps, a delightful waving contentment, as of one riding a boat in a calm sea, but not visions. Opium costs a fortune even here; perhaps he spends ten thousand dollars a day for three or four hours of opium dreaming. It might be worth it if there were really visions, if Ezekiel and Revela-tions could descend in a whiff of pipe smoke, if one could see—really see—the vision that André Malraux describes in *La Condition Humaine* of the gray lotus pond and the boat drifting through it, the two waves coming from the boat seeming to enclose the whole universe.

August 1st. But when we came out, no one was waiting for us. The air was very green and pure, the grave mounds were little green hills among the flooded cloud-reflecting fields and there were no dogs barking over buried bones. The storm had swept everything clean, the white pagoda in the distance shone with a ghostly luminousness, and there was no sign of anybody else. Now, late at night, thinking of it, it seems to me that this is the landscape I shall remember, a landscape that has become a part of me, bare and green, stripped almost to the bone, leaving only the faint green paint which you could scratch off with a fingernail. And then I remember that a little while later someone came across the fields in the light of the setting sun, a girl with a green bodice and a great red skirt, her hair smoothed till it shone silver, with pearl earrings, and she wore red shoes with little tongues that rose up over the heels; and walked like a queen. She was not Chinese. She belonged to one of the primitive tribes who live in the mountains, suffer from goiter, burn wood to charcoal, and fight tenaciously against the revenue officers. They are unconquered still, and sometimes you will see a girl who has the bearing of the unconquered: so clean, so much a part of the landscape, so continually *there*. And at night, thinking of these things, China becomes ever stranger: you think of the faces you see, which are not Chinese, the faces of men who have come down from the Tibetan mountains, from Lichiang and elsewhere; the faces of the Burmese; the boy in the bathhouse who has a negro strain in his blood; the students from the north who walk like heroes out of a mediaeval tapestry. There is not one China, and China is not even a geographical expression, but always a state of mind. I have lived among the Chinese for more than six years, and I know now no more than I knew when I was a child. It is still a country of pagodas, of women who are formed unlike the women of other countries, with slim shoulders, slim waists and small feet whose sound you can recognize so easily on the cobblestones; a country of poets and wanderers; of drunkards and devils; of immense wealth and intolerable beauty and terrible depravity. And it does not exist, it is not real—I have only to close my eyes in the small bedroom with the night light burning away the ghosts, and I am again eight years old, and I am again dreaming of marrying the daughter of the prime minister of China. I can take you down a small narrow street, where you can smell opium and where you will see a man with matted black hair falling down to his waist, holding a tremendous bronze-shafted spear shaped like a trident, with cabalistic signs woven into his helmet, wearing a patched gown of beaver skins and waving a human thigh bone in tune with his songs. And if you do not believe this, I can take you to the emerald lake where the camel-back bridge is perfectly reflected in the still green water and sparrows hop on the lotus leaves, and there is a silence like the silence of dreams. And I tell you that China is haunted with her own beauty, which is reckless, as her people are reckless, and at the same time I will tell you that China does not exist, it is something out of a fairy tale.

August 3rd. The childhood visions of China always return—in colors, in people dying, in the heady winds, in the towering clouds, in the grace of the green-clothed women working in the rice fields in the rain. But this morning it came with a sudden startling vividness: an old gnarled peasant woman sitting on the curb with the golden jaw bone of a dragon on her knees, and all around her baskets heaped high with flowers.

J., who flew over the Himalayas last night, complained of the bitter cold, but he said the mountains were gleaming blue-white under moonlight, and the great plains of snow gleamed like shelving white sand.

"There was the shadow of the airplane beneath us, and really it was beautiful. The airplane went in a straight line, but the shadow leaped up the cliffs of the mountains and down again." He paused for a while. "It is so odd. From the beginning China seems to have been geographically set apart from the world. The Gobi Desert, the Tien-shan mountains in the north-west, the forests of Burma, and then the Himalayas. As though, even now, she was not part of the world, but another planet altogether." He had been running across the air field, and he was breathing with difficulty, for the air is rare on these heights a mile above sea level. "But the shadow of the airplane. You ought to have seen that. The shadow didn't give a damn for the mountains. It just went up and down."

August 5th. The strain of being a professor in wartime China. I have known professors who have suffered a kind of madness, a sudden blackout, a terrible dark hopelessness resulting from eight years of war. There are moments when the bare mud-floored cow sheds on the campus where we teach fill me with an ungovernable horror, and I want to tear them down, for they seem to cry out: "This is a degradation so great that only the Chinese would accept it." And seeing the black limousines passing with the wives of generals on their way to mah-jongg parties, the horror returns. But afterwards I know that it is best to accept them as they are, and surely there is something symbolical in this great university fashioned out of a few mud huts on a leveled graveyard, within a stone's throw of the place where the last emperor of the Mings was garotted and tortured to death. For with the death of the last emperor of the Mings the old China died, and from this burial mound the new China will be born.

August 7th. I have been amusing myself all day translating *The Book of Odes*, where all that is finest in Chinese poetry reaches a kind of

perfection I know in no other poetry. There is an intensity in this
early poetry that defies analysis, a freshness that is like morning light
and a sense of gracefulness and piety that comes strangely on our
sophisticated senses. Sometimes I have the feeling that this is the
only real poetry, and that everything that has been written since then
is only a variation on the same themes. What is curious is the tremendous and I think conscious use of sexual symbols. The white
ponies, the white towers, the rocks, and the muddy streams are the
necessary implements of the Chinese poetic imagination. Poetry in
The Book of Odes is stripped to the skin: it is not stripped to the
bone. There is a nakedness about it which is purely sensuous: no
hardness, nor any luxuriance, only the rhythmical statement so keenly
expressed that it seems to hurl itself from the printed page and
assume the form of singing. It is not folk poetry, but the poetry of
enchanted experience. And always against the background of the
earthly paradise. You can see those paintings of the earthly paradise
in nearly every book of Chinese paintings: a few russet-colored
mountains, a few clouds, a temple in the background, and in the
foreground there are the lovers walking sedately along enchanted
pathways overlooking a river where children are playing and old men
are drinking. In a corner an old man in blue robes is playing on his
pipe, and somewhere in the remote distance there is always a white
horse or a white heron. It is the landscape of the earliest Gobelins
tapestries: quiet, suffused with the light of a sun that casts no shadows, and strangely familiar. There is one love-poem particularly
which pleased me:

> *Pure is the white pony,*
> *Feeding on the young shoots in my stack-yard.*
> *Keep him hobbled, keep him bridled.*
> *Let him stay through all mornings.*
> *So may my lover*
> *Here take his ease.*

> *Pure is the white pony,*
> *Feeding on the bean sprouts in my stack-yard.*
> *Keep him hobbled, keep him bridled.*
> *Let him stay through all evenings.*
> *So may my lover*
> *Here have his peace.*

> *Pure is the white pony*
> *Who comes to me swiftly,*

Like a duke, like a marquis.
Let us enjoy ourselves utterly.
Let us prolong our love-making,
Let us take our ease.

Pure is the white pony
Who lies in the empty valley
With a bundle of fresh hay.
He is like a piece of jade;
But do not be as rare as gold or jade.
Do not go from my heart.

August 10th. I was working at night, and there was a tremendous
roar of spluttering firecrackers outside. The firecrackers went on and
on, and the smell came over the high wall of the house—an astrin-
gent smell like ammonia and rotten wood. But it was the end of the
war.

It was raining, but nobody cared. The streets were filled with
people shouting, singing *Ting Hao* at the top of their voices, the
wet red flags of the republic hung from the houses, the jeep headlights swayed across the narrow streets and fell—now on a child
cowering in the rain, now on an old scholar who was busily trying to
mend his umbrella, now on two lovers in one of the dank alleyways,
and it seemed perfectly right that the silver gleam of the headlights
should pick out these three people sheltering from the rain. Children
were crying. The firecrackers were exploding in all directions. People
threw them down from upper windows, and from doorways: they
were scattered from jeeps, and always after the explosions there was a
dull thud of feet as people tried to avoid them. And then we huddled
through the dark streets in a jeep to the British Military Mission.
The young lieutenant said: "I told the colonel the bloody war was
over. I kicked at his door. I said, 'The bloody war's over,' but he only
grunted and snored like a pig."

And then the ride home with the radio we had borrowed from
the mission, and someone throwing a string of crackers into the jeep,
which exploded all around us, blinding us, and the rain shining on
the flooded river, and the people still milling and singing and shouting *Ting Hao* and not quite sure why they were shouting, and the
older shopkeepers looking sorrowfully from their doorways, knowing
that the army would go away and they would be ruined, and the
young still throwing crackers and sobbing, and the rain falling stead-

ily like a warning. And late at night, waiting for the news to come
through and thinking of the long trek home to the coast . . .

August 18th. The war is over. They say it is over, but so far there is
no sign of it. Kunming is the same, the streets are the same, the
shopkeepers are still cheating, there is continual rain, the price of
foodstuffs has gone up, the dollar rate has sunk suddenly and inexplicably to a quarter of what it was last week, the censorship is still
imposed, the soldiers still look hungry, and it is all foul and miserable
until you think of the university, the scholars, the painters, the poets,
and the writers who seem to live in another world: a world of infinite
gentleness and compassion, and so little power.

J. is trying to leave for Peking immediately. Last night I walked
with him through the dark streets to the airport. A rat scuttled across
the road, a girl screamed, the green and red taillights of an airplane
broke through the overcast sky, and suddenly—it was four o'clock in
the morning—the great white pillar of a searchlight sprang up from
one of the airfields and all over the city there was a white flower of
winter frost reflected from the clouds.

It was amazing then how the city sprang into life, the dust and
dirt peeled away, the darkness evaporated. Under this thin coating of
ice everything looked supernatural. Caught in this winter glare, the
city seemed made of frozen glass. Nothing moved. There were no
more screams. In this dazzling whiteness, the city took on the shape
of a Chinese palace in a fairy tale. And then the searchlight went out,
withdrawn into the earth, sucked out of the clouds, and nothing
remained but the black damp walls towering above us.

There, in the early morning, the beggars slept limply under sod-
den mats, motionless, heaped upon one another like logs. All the way
down to the center of the city there were these beggars, cowering in
doorways, young boys and old men, their skins not brown or white,
but the color of brown paper that has been soaked in mud. We
stepped over them carefully and came out at last into the main street,
which was silent and deserted, and then, O God, suddenly the sun
came through, the beggars awoke and rubbed their eyes, a mist rose,
the creek was jade-green and the birds began to sing from the boughs
of the plum trees.

August 28th. From the Street of the Snail-Skin down to the Street of
the Flowery Mountain the three American soldiers came lurching

through the night, followed by the most delighted horde of snot-nosed children I have ever seen. They were no more than happily drunk. They took off their hats, they bowed, they made incredible speeches, they clapped their hands, they leaned languorously on one another, and then after a few moments they would tire of the happy, screaming children and pretend to be chasing them. A pretty girl passed. They bowed very ceremoniously. A beggar looked at them wonderingly until they removed all the bank notes from their pockets and threw them in the air; then the beggar was lost in the melee of screaming children.

And so they went on, right down to the heart of the city, singing and dancing a little and pausing outside the shops to bow their acknowledgments to the customers, holding up the traffic and some-times bawling at the top of their voices. "Disgusting," said the American colonel. Wen Yi-tuo was there, beaming and stuttering with excitement. "Please tell me, Colonel, how can they be disgusting when they make the hearts of the children glad?" And all night he has been talking about this new American invasion of China, which is far, far more important than the Flying Fortresses overhead.

September 4th. His feet were bare, full of bruises, and the toe-nails were bleeding, and he came up the long dusty road past the university like any one of those ghosts of soldiers returning along the Burma Road who have been tormenting us simply by their terrible presence. He had the thin little red cross sewn to his padded blue coat which has been bleached to the lightest cerulean blue by the sun, and a face like a brown skull. God knows how many miles he has traveled! He has probably had malignant malaria; he has slept in ditches with the thinnest of army blankets; he has been press-ganged from his farm; he has been to hospital; the army has now forgotten him, and in a few days he will die and no one will care very much, for his letters never reached home and perhaps he has forgotten that he ever had a home.

His home now is a little cave in the clay by the side of the banked road. He has put up some shreds of matting to protect him from the rain, he has a ragged paper umbrella and a straw hat, he has made a fire—there are smears of black ashes, and something that may be a kettle; there are some more shreds of bamboo matting on which he probably sleeps; there is nothing else. It is almost a grave. And he is monstrously thin and dying, his eyes sunk so deep in the sockets that he seems already to be retreating from the world which has used him so hardly. It was all unnecessary. He could have stayed on his farm, he could have grown tall and possessed a family and seen the rice grow, but he will not raise a family and he will never see the rice grow again. I try to think of how he looks at the world from the vantage point of his cave. He has long since passed through disillusion and despair. He knows, as we do not know, that there comes a time when the sun fades from the sky, when all this monstrous business of trying to feed oneself in a sparse world is a terrible weight on the spirit, when there is nothing but cold moonlight and fields. He hates being watched. When you die, it is best to die alone and invisible. Then very carefully he squats in the shelter of his cave, collects a few sticks together, lights a fire and warms his hands, though the sun is shining outside.

I remember the way the flames glowed on his face and the way he thrust out his bony hands and the smile as he warmed himself: the last comfort of all men is a flame. I remember how he sank wearily back on his heels with his shoulders against the clay, and the delightful idiot smile of contentment as he rubbed his hands together, I remember the small leaping flame. And I know that he will not be there tomorrow, they will have found his body and thrown it in a ditch; but tomorrow, and the day after that, and the day after that, and perhaps forever, there will come from Burma these sallow-cheeked boys with gaping wounds and faces like skulls who will see the city of Kunming and not dare to penetrate through the gates.

Death haunts the North Gate. There are these gray-green burial mounds right up to the first range of hills. The university campus is only a small square stamped and flattened out of these mounds, which have sometimes fallen in. Here and there are a few pillars, commemorating people whose names have long since vanished; the crows perch on them, and sharpen their beaks on the plinths, and ponies wander among them, and not far from here an Emperor was murdered and almost in the same place executions take place today, and there are the skulls of horses and dogs and men in the open graves.

September 16th. The war is over, I told myself, coming through the dusty streets, where a few beggars were whining, a few snot-nosed children were playing with a dead rat, whose soft grey belly was slashed with the most vivid and most beautiful red, but is it over? Are people happier? Where are the processions and the anthems which

Bergery spoke about? Where are the girls with flowers in their hair? Where are the singers? Where are the hymns of thanksgiving?

I doubt very much whether anything has changed in Kunming. The same beggars haunt the streets, the same starving soldiers come up the Burma Road, the same merchants ride in their black limousines, there is the same heart-rending corruption, the same misery, the same unease. The streets are a little dirtier and shabbier than when the Americans were here in full force; the banks are a little more flourishing; there are more canned goods on the market than ever. A merchant told me this morning: "Well, this is the beginning of the end—we made a pack of money while the war lasted, but now we are ruined." I hope he is ruined. We pay for these things too much in sweat and weariness to care very much about the fate of the Chinese merchants.

There were shoddy enough things during the war in this lovely land. There were officers who kept back the food of their soldiers, there were the hoarding merchants who stored up immense reserves of rice, waiting for the day when want was so great that men would desire it at any price, forgetting that in this country rice is only another name for blood; there were officials who looked on; there were screams of torture from the police stations; there were bodies in ditches; there were soldiers dying on the roads. Kunming will live for a little while longer on its inflated paper currency, but soon the merchants and the bankers will have to look elsewhere—they will follow the whores to the coast. The whores have gone already. I went down the Chin Pi Lu this evening, and only one little brazen tart came out of the shadows, lifting her skirt and saying: "One push— how much?"

There are things in this country I would prefer not to look at. There are terrible diseases: some of them spiritual diseases—and this is worse. There has always been this starvation in China, but is there any reason why it should continue? The land is rich enough, God knows. The people have the richest cultural heritage of the world. There are all the graces and refinements of life imaginable, and yet the art of government is forgotten, and the family still remains—that hard-bitten symbol of the desire to keep everything within the narrow precincts of a single house. So corruption mounts up, since the family grows bigger and more exacting as wealth increases; seventh cousin must have his job, in spite of the fact that he is incompetent and has learned a few vices from abroad—he must have his girls, his cigarettes, his cinemas, his opium pipe, his nights in the dancing halls.

We'll put him in the bank. Excellent. A vice-presidency? No, not good enough for that; we'll give him a stool, and as long as he puts in an appearance for a few hours in the morning, we'll give him a fat monthly pay check, for after all, is he not in the family? And so it goes on, the vicious and ever-expanding circles of nepotism, which seems to affect all business, all government in this desperately beautiful land.

Up to the battle of Nanking, there was the most tremendous enthusiasm for the war and for the government—a spiritual fire swept over the country, China would arise, the real revolution would be formed on the comradeship of war; men starved and walked threadbare the whole length of China and cheered themselves with the thought of their sufferings, for out of their sufferings and the dead bodies in the Yangtse they thought they would make a new kingdom of their own. But you cannot make kingdoms out of sufferings. There comes a time when sufferings become so long-drawn that the body cries out for opiates, and the opiates were all there—a fortune, a job in the government, a sinecure somewhere. You could squeeze in if you tried hard enough, and if you were merciless enough. The Japanese were a long way away. It didn't matter much, and you could salve your soul on Monday mornings by bowing three times to the portrait of Dr. Sun Yat-sen, who said: "The revolution is not yet accomplished." The revolution could wait for another day. It was raining, they were utterly miserable, they were cut off from the outside world, life was short and the things you wanted most were still coming in from Shanghai, but at exorbitant prices. But the people were still starving. Must they starve to the end of time?

September 17th. Wen Yi-tuo was sick in bed, lying under the heavy silk embroidered quilt—the bed too big for him, so that his little brown face seemed lost in it.

"The trouble is that we haven't won the war," he said. "The Americans won it for us—or rather a few German, French, Scandinavian, British, and American scientists with all the wealth of America behind them. The wealth of America! The old Portuguese and Spanish kings thought it lay in the gold of the Indies and in China; they said there was wealth beyond the vision of men to imagine; but there is no wealth in the Indies now and China is poor." He was digressing, but he came back a moment later: "We haven't won the war—the Americans won it with the Manhattan Project, but the Chinese will kick the Japanese in the shins and puff out their chests, yet they know, and we know, that we have done nothing to deserve the end of the war. The tactics were wrong from the beginning—it is always dangerous to take flight to Szechuan. And now we dare hardly face the Japanese for shame of our imaginary conquest." He paused and sipped the mulberry-colored water on the table. "This is what I thought a moment ago," he went on, "but all conquests are imaginary, so there is perhaps little harm in it. We destroy nothing by destroying. The Japanese are beaten to their knees, but never has any nation been so terribly beaten as the Chinese. We learned our weaknesses—pray God we may profit by them."

I began to tell him how I bridle every time I see soldiers. Anachronisms, meaningless now that we wage war with invisible weapons, a little tiresome in that they still remained with all their privileges, bearing weapons—rifles slung over shoulders, detestable little green hand grenades swinging from their belts—all the nonsense of uniforms and salutes and the hint of death all around them. "I see them every morning," I complained, "outside my window— drilling, marching, running round in circles, scaling mountains—the mountains are perhaps ten feet high and the officer wields a white baton and orders them to charge up the mountain at the peril of their lives. What are they training for? Civil war? I doubt whether we will fight national wars with soldiers any more. It's all so damnedly absurd—why can't they go back to their farms?"

He sighed: "There is civil war in China now, isn't there?"

"Yes."

"How long do you think it will last?" he asked.

"Just a few months—until the Americans crack down on them. It's too monstrous—it is so shameful to fight a civil war after the conclusion of this war. Really, civil war is unimaginable—too great a shame."

"Yes," he said, "it's too great a shame, it's unimaginable, but it exists—the merchants have made their money and they want to hold their power, and the soldiers want something to do—the officers don't want to feel useless. Oh, this pride. You are quite right, of course. They have no feeling of shame. The military profession is an honorable profession—or rather, it would be honorable if it did not deal with murder. An American soldier came to say good-by to me. He was going home. He said he was sick of the war—every time he sees a man he is unconsciously looking for ways to murder him: a jab in the groin, an elbow around his neck, some way of killing him. He said he wanted to go home and get back to a farm. 'That's where I belong. Never been on a farm before, but I know that's the only place left for me.' And he said: 'Have a girl and some kids and get away from it all.' It's easier to kill than to get a girl. It's so much easier to throw a hand grenade than to care for children and watch after them. We need women in the government now—by God we need women now. We need people who can smack the faces of the soldiers and tell them they belong to a dishonorable trade, even though their trade is sometimes necessary. There is no difference between a soldier and a hangman—a hangman is necessary, and so is a soldier, but there is no honor in it, though there is bravery. We can learn from women and children—see how terribly children recoil from death, yet we are hardened to it."

The dinner was brought in, and I was allowed to have a glass of his mulberry-colored medicine, which turned out to be wine. There were huge pillows—Chinese pillows are sometimes as huge as those you see on Hungarian bridal beds—and he half tilted himself from the bed, stroked his untidy beard and gazed out of the windows, for the bamboo curtains had been lifted and he could look across the darkening garden, full of bamboos and convolvulus. There were a few stars, though the moon was down. At the end of the garden some soldiers were playing shuttlecock. It was clear that he wanted to go on with the argument, but I wondered whether he was well enough—and besides, it was no longer an argument, we agreed with each other too often, so that it was difficult to sharpen our minds on differences.

September 26th. Why, when, where, and how I shall leave China, I do not know; but I am beginning to suspect that it will be soon. The rumors—they are surely more substantial than rumors—of the civil war sicken me. That there should be civil war at such a time and under such desperate conditions as we are living in terrifies me. Wen Yi-tuo talks of his shame, while the students and the more daring professors (for not all professors are daring) openly proclaim their horror. Who is responsible—the Kuomintang or the Communists? There are rumors that Chiang Kai-shek is quietly preparing with American support for a five-year war against the Communists. China has not covered herself in glory in this war, but that she should follow the path of the Gadarene swine is sickening beyond words.

September 27th. K. came, very mouselike, wearing a loose blue gown, not very clean. He looked as though he had not slept, and he was unshaved. He said he had to go away, one of his friends was in prison and somehow he would have to get enough money to feed him. I asked: why?—don't they feed prisoners? He shook his head. His friend was a democrat who sometimes bitterly assailed the dictatorial policies of the Kuomintang. Well, they had arrested him in some remote country village, where he was unknown, where no law has ever penetrated since the end of the Ch'ing dynasty, where the village magistrate wielded absolute power. Probably the boy had been followed by the secret police, and there he was—a stone cell, a few village louts with Mausers to guard him, and he would have to pay for his food, otherwise they would forget about him. He had managed to smuggle a letter out, God knows how, and he wanted fabulous sums of money for his bare existence, he wanted someone to invoke *habeas corpus* and he wanted to have a fair trial. "Will he get them?" "No—he will get the money, some of it, as much as I can raise—we'll try to bribe the guards or the village magistrate, and see what happens. It's difficult. If you offer too much, they'll keep him there and torture him so that we shall offer more. They know all the tricks—they have had three thousand years of this miserable village dictatorship with some illiterate fool acting as magistrate, possessing powers of life and death over the young boys, and sometimes over the young girls. The village magistrate is god, first because he is the magistrate and secondly because he is the recruiting agent. He can send boys to the front. He can be bribed not to send them. I wish we could have some village government—all power to the farmers and the farm-laborers, not this damned illiterate dictatorship."

It would take him probably a week to get to the village; he had written a letter—it might get through, or it might make things worse, he didn't know. There were blue rings round his eyes and a kind of hopelessness, for he would do everything to save his friend and friendship between these boys goes deeper than it does in the West—the unbreakable bond is not broken even in death. I gave him some money. He looked shabby and sick as he went out into the stone courtyard under the poinsettias, but when we came out into the sunlight he braced up. "I'll get him out somehow," he said. "One shouldn't be allowed to die on that stone floor simply for being a democrat."

It must have been a coincidence, for that same evening another boy came and sat on the edge of the bed, the chairs and tables so littered with books that there was no other place for him. We talked desultorily about Chinese poetry, for he has written many good poems, and sometimes even in English he writes with a startling sense of our imagery. And then suddenly, when it was getting dark and the books were beginning to be swallowed up in the shadows, their presence no longer so dangerous, he showed me a poem of four lines which he said his brother had written. They were terrible lines. They could only have been written by somebody in mortal fear and terrible longing for death, so cold and knifelike they were. I remember reading in some Paris newspaper the lines written by a boy on the night before he was guillotined for murdering his sweetheart, and I told my friend how similar they were: the same poignancy which went beyond the limits of all human feeling. You will see the same thing, too, in some of the last poems of the German poet Friedrich Hölderlin, and sometimes it occurs in Shakespeare; and once or twice it breaks through the gold and silver-greens of the T'ang poets, the wet red open mouth of the beast.

We talked then for a little while about poetry and how sometimes it will seize upon the ultimate blood-red things of the universe: when the stars crack: when loneliness becomes a skull: the poet describing simply how the abyss yawns. The boy smiled wearily. He was not handsome, but he had a high northern forehead, and his mother had come from the tribes; he was unstable, like all those who have the mixed blood of south and north, but he possessed quite extraordinary intelligence. And just as we were leaving, he said quietly: "The poem was written by my brother on the night before his execution at Hankow. They executed him as a Communist, but he wasn't a Communist."

October 2nd. Yesterday the American soldiers were kept in barracks; there are rumors that Chinese soldiers have been attacking the hostels. A few jeeps go around the city bristling with guns, and wherever an American soldier appears he has a tommy-gun at his belt or a rifle slung over his shoulder. And yet there seems to be no reason for it. It seems impossible to imagine that the local Yunnanese forces could attack the Americans. Banditry? Yes, the country still has bandits, but will bandits attack the Americans? I doubt it.

We live on the edge of an earthquake. The stay of the Americans in Kunming has had one curious result—as they pull out, thousands of Chinese will find themselves without jobs. The better and luckier ones will probably follow the Americans to the coast; the others, accustomed to high wages, will be footloose in this city where you cannot live unless you are paid in millions. A municipal officer told me there have been more murders since the end of the war than at any time in human memory. Life is cheaper now. God knows how many jeeps, how many tommy-guns have been stolen from the American depots—a colonel told me that eighty-nine jeeps disappeared in a single year. Everyone knows who has them, they even know where they are, but the new possessors are so highly placed that they are beyond the judgment of the courts; and the judges can be bribed, so it would be useless to bring them to court.

A nasty story. A GI found a Chinese trying to steal the chain-guard of his jeep. "So I socked him on the cheek and smashed his jaw and kicked him a bit, but Christ Almighty, it's better than sending him to the Chinese police—they'd have killed him. And they don't try the water treatment either."

October 4th, Civil war. It will take some time to see this day in its proper perspective. It might even be better to leave it out—I can no longer trust myself to speak calmly of bloodshed. I have such a horror of violence now that I can hardly bear the sight of soldiers, and now they are everywhere. They are swarming all over the city with their V armbands, their sleepy faces, their trigger-hungry fingers, their idiotic blank obedient faces.

This morning I was awakened by the sound of firecrackers. I thought they were firecrackers. It was a lovely day, blue sky, small puffs of blue cloud. Something was wrong, and I must have realized unconsciously that they were not firecrackers, and there was no subdued murmur of people and lorries and funeral processions in the streets—that murmur which comes through the high walls of my courtyard and gives a faint quivering life to everything. Then the firecrackers stopped, then they went on again. One of my windows looks out over an immense field, and at the end of the field there is the Burma Road. There was no traffic on the road. A few soldiers in the field were busily digging a grave.

I have said before that I do not like soldiers; and so I try not to look out of the window in the early morning when they do their idiotic exercises. I prefer this field later in the morning, when the mist has lifted and the ponies are rolling in the grass and small boys play tag and the shopgirls slip away from their counters and saunter beside the muddy pool; or when for some reason which I have never attempted to discover some women come with bales of blue cloth and slowly unroll them and let them dry in the sun. But now there were only the soldiers with their short-handled picks digging a grave in the sun.

The machine gun was brought out later. A very beautiful machine gun, nicely oiled and glinting, with three little legs and a nasty snout pointing in the direction of the Great West Gate. You can see the gate from here with its scalloped flaring roof above the trees, the small machine gun and the great gate in the distance. The soldiers lay down behind the machine gun. They were waiting for something to happen, but nothing happened, there were no more fireworks. I went out into the street, and there was another very beautiful machine gun at the corner, though for some reason it was hooded with white sackcloth. There was dead silence. There were some soldiers huddled in the doorways. They looked tired, and they carried submachine guns, and the street was empty except for the soldiers.

I went back and asked the *amah* whether there was enough food in the house—it might last for a few days, and we seemed to be in the line of fire. There was almost no food, but she did not complain of this. She said bitterly: "If it's civil war, then the pedlars will starve." I asked why. "They can only just live on their earnings, and they must get about in the streets." She spoke very simply: she had seen many civil wars. It was absurd to stay in the house, and so I took a young student who is also staying here and we went in search of an officer. The firecrackers had begun again, but they were a long way away, and there was a sudden crackling of a mortar, but that was nearer. We ducked into shelter. Seeing us, the broad-faced soldiers were smiling and rubbing their hands.

I asked them what they were doing. Fifth Army. They had been there since two o'clock in the morning. Much fighting? They didn't know. Could we go into the city? No, they had their orders, no one was to pass, no one at all. And if we did pass? They were very sorry, but they would have to shoot. And then someone came running up to say that an officer was expected soon, and perhaps we would be allowed to go into the city under escort.

The streets looked so curiously bare. A shutter would open, a face would appear, very drawn and tense, and then the shutter would be closed again. There was no traffic from the East Gate in spite of the fact that it was one of the main arteries into the city. It was this silence that hurt most, and the shutters opening, and the presence of those soldiers with their rolled gray-blue blankets, their pistols, their hand grenades, rifles and trenching tools, just waiting there in the doorways. By now we had counted three jeeps moving along the Burma Road. The soldiers looked very tired. They said there had been fighting at the North Gate, and more fighting still at the Great East Gate.

And then it began to grow clear: the city was under some kind of siege. . . .

It will be difficult to catch up with this diary. Things are moving so very fast, and it is all so very mysterious. There is a siege. This much is certain. The governor is still in the great ochre-colored palace overlooking the lake, and the soldiers of the Fifth Army are all round the lake firing at the palace with machine guns, and there is a Mitchell bomber circling over the palace. American airplanes are still landing on the airstrip and taking off again, there are no American soldiers on the streets, but in all the alleyways and in all the shop doorways there are the drab-clothed, trigger-happy soldiers of the Fifth Army. But I must try to begin from the beginning.

We waited for about half an hour till the escort arrived, two young Hunanese with red cheeks and with four green hand-grenades hanging from their belts. I gathered that they did not relish the idea of taking us to the Little East Gate: there were snipers somewhere, and there were crackling sounds coming from inside the city. There is a wide road which leads down to the quays with shops on each side of the road, and for some reason we did not walk along the pavement but marched down the center of the road, and I remember I kept on looking up at the windows for snipers. It was like Changsha; the shutters closed, the people inside pretending not to exist, the dead silence and the echoes of our shoes on the cobblestones. "It's all over now," the Hunanese boy said, laughing nervously, but just as he spoke there was the sound of firing inside the city.

There were a few people on the streets, and we thought it might be true that the war was over. There were these young soldiers from Hunan and Honan at all the street corners, armed with hand grenades, Mausers, and rifles, and all wore a white bandage with a badly printed V in red on their arms. We noticed they were looking toward the end of the long street; they looked sullen and determined; but there was no firing. We walked up the street past the stone pillboxes; and then we noticed that the machine guns were pointed directly toward the center of the city. What was surprising was that when we came to the end of the street there was another pillbox filled with young Yunnanese soldiers wearing French helmets, and their machine guns were pointed toward the gate we had come from.

We knew then that the resistance was continuing; that the Fifth Army was a Nationalist army sent to demand the surrender of the Yunnanese troops: though there cannot be many, since most of the Yunnanese armies are in Indochina. We tried to get around the lake, but they refused to let us pass. It was odd to be stopped everywhere in this bright autumn sunshine, odd to see the silhouettes of soldiers on the rising banks beside the lake, and odder still to hear the crackle of Bren guns directed at the governor's palace.

Later in the afternoon we managed to get to the North Gate by taking shelter along the city wall. There were soldiers everywhere, small groups of people heatedly discussing what had happened; once, there were bloodstains. The Hunanese boys are trigger-happy, but pasted on the walls are notices saying that if they kill a foreigner, they and their whole families will be wiped out by military order—so, for the moment at least we are safe.

There is a curfew. They said it was at nine, but apparently it was at six, for when we came through the streets in the dusk we were stopped. We went on a little while later. On the Street of the Forest of Learning a mortar exploded just as we reached the house of the president of the university; and then there was rifle fire down the whole length of the street. It looked like those photographs of St. Petersburg taken in 1917—the gray dusk, the people staggering to shelter, the way men hug the walls when there is street-fighting. Heaven knows where the firing came from—probably from the drum tower of the gate. And then all night there were sounds of firing, not occasionally, but continuously, sometimes so close that we heard the bullets nipping through the trees.

October 5th. Some students have been slightly wounded by stray bullets. There seems to have been a short heavy engagement in the hills behind the university. Fourteen mortars were thrown at the North Gate yesterday morning. This is not comic opera: there is too much fear, and there has been fighting all night along the Street of the Forest of Learning, and along the Street of the Flowery Mountain. J. said he counted eleven bodies early this morning. I asked him what the devil he was doing counting them. "There is a daylight truce," he said. "There is only firing at night—and that's better. You can throw off a hell of a number of rounds without hitting anything." But a child was wounded seriously inside the Great East Gate this morning.

There are rumors that Lu Shen-tzu, the second son of the Governor Yung Lun, is coming from Chaotung, about two hundred miles to the northwest, to relieve the city. But the Yunnanese troops in the province are miserably few, though well disciplined. There is only one regiment of gendarmery, one brigade of field artillery and one or two regiments of soldiers. It seems improbable that they will be able to hold out.

October 6th. In the still bright air the sound of rifle shots like the dull patter of cricket bats at the nets: no smoke, nor any explosions, but at night they whine and roar and crackle among the trees. What is odd is that the streets look so normal during the day. There are the soldiers with the arm bands, which had a great blood-red W today—those who did not change them soon enough were shot out of hand, so that the Fifth Army lost apparently over eighty soldiers this morning.

Last night we again mistook the time of the curfew: everyone was so certain that it was nine o'clock. So we wandered down by the wall in the pitch darkness, and when we came to the Little East Gate someone lunged out of the shadows and said: "Put your hands up," and searched my pockets. He was tired and trigger-happy and carried a submachine gun. It was not pleasant, and it became worse later when we were told that we could pass unhindered out of the Little East Gate and found ourselves stopped by shadows at every turn, the road deserted and seeming in the faint light so broad that we were lost in it. We walked down the center of the road, afraid they would shoot at shadows creeping along the wall.

October 7th. I walked all over the north part of the city, and found tanks in the great field outside the North Gate. The tanks have machine guns mounted on the turrets, and some small guns are shelling the governor's palace over the walls. There are bullet marks on the British consulate, there are wires on the ground all leading to Heilungtang where General Tu Li-ming has his headquarters and from where he is operating against the governor, who is still preparing to hold out in his palace. Shops are open all day, but at the first faint approach of dusk, everything is shuttered, for the soldiers of the Fifth Army are ordered to shoot anything that moves after curfew.

October 8th. I have been to the American Red Cross, where L. tells me that in the long courtyard outside the military hospital perhaps a quarter of a million bullets have been fired without anyone being hurt: they have been firing backwards and forwards between the street and the hospital for three nights, and only the statue of the former governor has been chipped. Yet hundreds have been killed, and according to all reports I have read, prisoners are executed without mercy.

October 9th. T.V. Soong has arrived, and Governor Lung Yun has surrendered and flown to Chungking. The war is over, but is it over? The Yunnanese have fled to the hills or gone into disguise. Lu Shen-tzu's forces never reached the city: they were decimated some forty miles away, and it was apparently when Lung Yun heard of the fate of the relief column that he decided to surrender. He might have fought it out from the palace indefinitely, or at least until the bombers came, but he can have had little hope of being successful. If it is over, I shall remember the hollow tock-tock of bullet echoes among the grave mounds, the long dreary nights returning home, seeing shadows and being stopped everywhere; I shall remember the bloodstains and the chips of plaster and a green lake ringed round with guns while Nationalist soldiers fired at a castle on a yellow hill.

October 25th, A Chinese hand. The post office was horribly dirty. There was a little tin of rice paste attached to a string, and everyone was dipping his fingers in it to stick the stamps on the envelopes. We were crowded and huddled there, a sweating, hot mass of silent humanity, and the little window through which we peered had a shutter which threatened to bang down at any moment, for the people inside were hard pressed. I hated it. I hated the soldiers dressed in ragged cotton-lined uniforms who were all crowding so urgently, so preposterously urgently, against the window; they were suffocating the girl by my side; they had probably already killed the baby who was wrapped in a red silk shawl on her back; they were evil-smelling, drab, and unhealthy, and I didn't want to look at them. And then suddenly, on the little counter made fetid with traces of rice paste, I saw the hand. It was so perfect that you wanted to take a knife, cut it off and keep it for ever. The fingers were finely tapered, delicate, and intense, quivering with life, dark brown, shining a little; and though they were quivering, they were in repose. It was like a little brown sleek animal sitting there: somewhere in its shadow there were eyes, and there was a heart beating in the palms, and perhaps—why not?—it had lungs, sexual organs, mouth, and nostrils. And so it remained there, almost a small brown animal curled up and waiting patiently for the moment when food would be dropped in its mouth, so delicate and fragile a thing that you wanted to stroke it, or even put it in a cage. There were faint blue veins and curious whorled knuckles: the silky brown fingers were longer than any I have ever seen. And then I looked up and saw the snot-nosed, ragged-mouthed soldier, with the clipped hair and the eczema and the unshaved beard, as uncouth and horrible a spectacle as any in the army; and yet it is not in the least puzzling that this lice-infested descendant of coolies and princes should have been the owner of these hands, for nearly all Chinese hands seem to possess this delicacy and intensity, this quivering life of their own.

October 28th. He was probably a survivor of the Yunnanese guards who fought against the Fifth Army, but it was impossible to think of this as he was brought out of the Great West Gate on his way to the burial mounds. He was tall and wore military uniform; his hands were tied behind his back with a ridiculously thin piece of string which trailed behind him, caught up in the hands of a young soldier who carried a rifle on his shoulder. There were three other soldiers similarly armed, and there was also an officer with a long black coat which dragged at his heels. It was evident that he was being led out to die; his face was desperately gray, without life, already remote from the world, the eyes unseeing, and the lips set in a broken quivering line. And he walked on, very fast, as though to make up for lost time, leading this procession on the end of a string, going down an old alleyway where there is an empty shrine to the forgotten gods of the place: and it was impossible to believe that he was not leading them, for he walked in front of them and possessed the utterly passionless

and exhausted expression of a man who has seen everything and
knows everything, and is therefore appointed to be a leader of men.
Five minutes later he knelt on the ground and the top of his head
was blown off, and now at night the crows are screaming over him
and the dogs are drinking his blood.

November 7th. Not well. The worrying thing is that when the body
drops, the spirit drops too. The world cannot possibly be as bad as I
painted it this afternoon—going down the street where the mud is a
slimy three-inch thick black jelly for fifty yards, though the sun was
shining, and the jelly remains forever, because the sanitation in this
city is almost nonexistent. I do not know how people survive among
these unrunning drains, squelching cesspools, dead rats, dead bodies
everywhere. Because I have a headache, and probably typhus, it
seems worse: the dead rat gnawed by the dogs assumes elephantine
proportions—it would have been a dead rat yesterday, and rather
beautiful, but today it is a mountainous suppuration of diseased and
running flesh.

November 20th. Convalescence is also a fever, but so much quieter.
Almost impossible to imagine that I have ever been happier. Lying in
bed and looking at the sunlight on the great twisted eucalyptus tree
in the garden, and the hawks wheeling; even when they shoot the
anti-typhus serum into my arm, even the great snaky green feces after
constipation, even the sudden screams at night echoing along interminable corridors, the pure physical sensation of just being alive.
Everything is *received.*

Illness is a kind of blessing. The motor was wound up, and it
would have gone on at the same terrific pace and burnt itself out.
The real trouble was that I had not the faintest idea what typhus was
like, did not suspect that it began with that shattering sickening
headache, and was in any case too drowsy to know what was happening. The temperature mounts up, but you are completely unconscious
of having a high temperature—the human body can live only within
such narrow ranges of temperature. R. says the doctor came and said:
"You'll have to rush him to hospital—it looks very serious." But it
never looked serious to the patient. He was too weak and drowsy to
care and he was mechanically immune from fear—something hap-

pens that blots out fear, there is none of the sterilized excitement I remember with tuberculosis, when you do fear, fear terribly, simply because life becomes so amazingly beautiful. (The lungs rather than the heart are the source of life: the biologists say that life began at the sea's margin—the waves of air beating against the lungs' shore.) And then, too, mercifully and for some reason that must spring from the same causes as sleep, absolutely no sense of the passing of time. The days were continuous, not broken up by hours and minutes—the sun wheeling around, not pausing at nightfall, the sense of the most perfect and delicate continuity.

There was the eucalyptus tree and the changing shadows on the wall and for some reason that I shall probably never discover, a girl skiing in Norway and moving tremendously fast down the snow plains and the Malay girl who was dark and walked very slowly in a gold headdress. What surprises me now is that they were somehow interchangeable and must have come from the same source. No desire for them, only delight in watching them; and being able to summon them at any time I pleased, just as the branches of the tree could assume any shape I pleased—a horseman on the topmost bough, a grinning old Taoist monk somewhere below. And it was so easy to color those shadows on the walls with small villages, boys playing leapfrog, old mountains.

On the night after reaching the hospital, I thought it was over and I didn't care; I might not have thought it was over if they hadn't carried me on a stretcher. That was the worst, and the small white-washed bedroom looked so shuttered. But in the morning the sun came through the window, the leaves of the eucalyptus tree were jade, and some birds hopped on the window sill—it was as simple as that. And then slowly, in little spurts, the strength coming back, though the food was appalling, and the sensation that something in the air around was flooding my body: not healing, simply this incessant quiet *receiving*.

Convalescence is the best. The little spurts become more numerous, and for some reason they feel terribly like the liquefaction of blood—the solid core melting. Sun-bathing is dangerous. The clouds come so very suddenly, and then it becomes bitterly cold for a few minutes until the clouds pass away. I do not know how these thin clouds can suck so much heat from the sky, but they do. And going to bed early and waking early, things I shall never do unless mercifully I become ill again.

November 25th. Well enough to get up and give a party. The electric light went out again, and I was pleased in spite of the impossible cost of candles. There were two young poets and a philologist, their faces ruddy in candlelight, sitting below the Chinese painting of Tien Kuan, which they detested; it is a bad painting, but there is so much crimson, so much jade-green and gold that I shall never part with it; and against this background, with the smoking candle flames drawing the health onto the surface of their faces, they looked bronzed and much younger. Wen Yi-tuo came later with a small bunch of flowers, but the candlelight withered them away—I must try to find out why flowers lose their colors in candlelight, while everything else grows richer. The texture and sheen of his blue silk patterned gown was perfect. And then, afterwards in another room, interminable discussions on politics. R.'s story of the cook in a Peking house who absented himself each night and uncoupled some Japanese railway lines, which the Japanese always replaced in the morning. Wen Yi-tuo said: "If only the Chinese could employ their skill in destruction to purposes of reconstruction, but we are the greatest destroyers in the world: there is probably no other race so efficient at sapping the spirit of its enemies. The Japanese possessed mechanical skill, but they possessed almost nothing at all of our sophistication. So young, and we are so old." He has a real pity for the Japanese, whom he regards as children; and at the same time he has the greatest reverence for some Japanese scholars. "I hope they are protected—so many of them understand us, and they are the only race that does." I asked him how this squared with his former statement that the Japanese were young and the Chinese old. He smiled and answered: "My grandson understands me better than my wife."

The hair-raising stories of corruption and the activities of the secret police cannot all be untrue. "Surely," said Wen Yi-tuo, "the people should have power to investigate the private fortunes of the members of the government. We know the private fortunes of the Communist leaders—probably five dollars each." He has never been so bitter, and he is especially bitter against some of the professors who applaud the Kuomintang Party, saying that it is the duty of the scholars at all times to refrain from political action. I objected: "To say nothing may be treason." "No," he answered. "To say nothing at such a time and place is to applaud the good and condemn the evil." And again later: "The scholars must be above politics at this time. The people may invite them into the government, but at least, when we are showing ourselves so inept, they should remain pure. I am ashamed that in this victory, which we have done nothing to deserve, we are both feudal and fascist—nothing has changed." I objected again: "The Chinese do deserve this victory." "Yes," he answered, "but no party deserves this victory, no millionaire deserves this victory, no official deserves this victory. The peasants, yes, but not the officials." He is not well. He spoke so bitterly sometimes, and with such passion, that I was half afraid; yet there is never any contempt in his voice, he speaks quietly or simply bows his head; and at such moments in the candlelight he was more eloquent than ever.

At nine o'clock we heard a burst of gunfire from the direction of the university. I said: "It is probably someone throwing crackers," though I was almost certain that it was small-arms fire. Wen Yi-tuo said: "How long have you been in China? Four years, and you do not know the sound of gunfire?" There were a few more bursts later. I was pretty sure they were gunfire by this time, and it seemed puzzling till the poet said that there were hundreds of Yunnanese troops in the mountains. "They are living on the land," he said. "They dare not come into the city—they will be executed. The worst of it is that the new government has photographs and details about every member of the Yunnanese forces, and it may be years before the last man is exterminated." Wen Yi-tuo said: "We are manufacturing bandits because we show men no mercy," and told a terrible story of having seen about a hundred bound Yunnanese soldiers taken out of the North Gate to die. "I didn't care a fig for the Yunnanese government—it was as corrupt as the others, but I do care for these boys, there was no reason why they should die. Some of them were tribesmen. They were loyal to Lung Yun, because Lung Yun was a tribesman himself, but their loyalty was not a crime." And just as he was going he said: "A student has told me that he has overheard General Ho, the new commander of the garrison headquarters, saying that nothing would please him more than that I should suffer an accident. Well, let them do their worst. If they kill young boys for no reason at all, boys who are not dangerous, because they are the wealth and strength of our country, there is no reason why they should not also kill the scholars, who have no wealth and little enough strength to offer." He said this sadly, without vainglory.

The electric light was still off when they left, and I led them to the corner of the street with three candles in a candelabra, and remember the light on Wen Yi-tuo's gown. He refused to take a ricksha, though there were a few rickshas about; and now I do not know whether he will ever reach home.

November 26th. The sounds of firing last night came from soldiers of the Fifth Army shooting over the heads of the students. This does not make sense. It is intolerable and unbelievable that the students should be fired on in this way by the orders of the garrison commander and with the intention—the very clear intention—of terrorizing the students in the greatest university of China. Have they gone mad?

I am writing this in bed, because I caught a cold when I went out into the street last night and I have not yet recovered from typhus. No one knows what will happen next. There are rumors that the great clash between the militarists and the civilians will come at any moment—have the militarists decided to liquidate the university? It looks very much like it.

Later in the afternoon some students came, and two professors. They are aghast at what has happened, and yet they are perfectly unafraid, they know they have no weapons against the militarists, they know that they are completely at the mercy of the militarists, and if the militarists liquidate the university, it may be months before the outside world ever hears of it. What was strange was that they spoke very quietly about the events last night, and so very simply. This happened, they said; someone has evidently gone mad, but madness is epidemic in this country—we are still fighting the Communists—haven't they the sense to realize that we must have peace?—above everything else, peace, a breathing-space, a few hours and days and months of rest, the country so terribly weary and all except the very few are so terribly poor. Peace—peace—it was only when they mentioned this beloved word that they raised their voices a little.

During the last month I have been too ill to understand what was happening, and I was so sick of the thought of the civil war that I paid little attention to it, hoping it would pass; but it has not passed; it is still here, and the students are tormented by the thought that they have responsibilities toward their country. There was very little they could do, but they could call a mass meeting: the sounds of firing last night were directed at the mass-meeting they had called in the Lienta campus. The student spoke very quietly, in a hushed voice, exactly as though he was describing a murder, though no one has been murdered. "It was a perfectly orderly meeting," he said. "We had asked four professors to address us on the subject of the civil war, and we invited the students of the middle-schools to listen. It was a dark cold night, and the campus was lit by electric lights from inside the school buildings. There is a plinth just in front of the library, and it was from there that the professors spoke. They had a microphone, so that all the students could listen to them—there were perhaps three thousand students altogether sitting on the grass around the stone plinth, perhaps more, I don't know, it was impossible to count them because it was so dark. We had very carefully chosen the professors who would speak to us—two were members of the Kuomintang, one belonged to the Democratic League, and the fourth was independent. Not one of the professors was a Communist: all of them were famous and responsible people, who would weigh their words carefully.

"It was dark. The first speaker, Dr. Chen Tuan-shen, spoke in a very low voice, saying that the time was ripe for a coalition government. He said it was the greatest mistake, the greatest imaginable mistake, for China at this time to embark on a civil war, the danger of the civil war extending over the whole length and breadth of China was so great, the effects on the life and economy of the nation so unpredictable, the losses in manpower and natural wealth so terrible, that every effort must be made to stop this war at once—a war which could only bring shame on China. He spoke like this for half an hour; it was about seven o'clock; and then the first shots were heard coming from the grave mounds behind the university. No one was frightened. A few shots could be explained. A soldier playing the fool, or an execution—though an execution would be unlikely at night. Dr. Chen Tuan-shen is a member of the Kuomintang Party and a member of the People's Political Council—it was inconceivable that anyone would dare to interrupt his speech by firing. And then a little while later it came again, closer this time, and lower; what was strange was that the firing now seemed to be deliberately punctuating those passages in his speech where he attacked the government for making no efforts toward peace with the Communists. Whenever he mentioned the coalition government there was firing. And then gradually the firing died down, and we thought perhaps that someone was playing the fool and the meeting would be allowed to carry on without further interruption.

"And it did carry on without further interruption for some time. Dr. Chen finished his speech, and he was followed by Dr. Wu Chi-yuan, who is a right-wing member of the Kuomintang. No shots were fired during his speech. It must have been about eight o'clock when Dr. Fei Shao-tung, who is an internationally-known sociologist, mounted the platform and began in a voice so low that we could hardly hear him. He began by saying: 'I have been wondering why I should come to speak to you in the darkness tonight, but above everything else I want peace——' At the word 'peace' firing began again. This time there was no doubt that the firing was intentional. They were firing from beyond the walls of the university, and we could see the bullets streaking above us, and sometimes they clattered against the slate roof of the library—they were coming lower and lower, and we ducked our heads. The electric lights went out, and the microphone became dead. Dr. Fei then raised his voice and said: 'I beg you to have no fear—I must raise my voice above the sound of the bullets.' We clapped when he said this, and then the firing became louder than ever, somewhere in the darkness a trench mortar went off, and the machine guns opened out at full burst. But he went on. They were firing only a few inches above his head, but he went on. Sometimes there would be a little wave of fear among the students, but we realized we were trapped, we could not move, we had to keep our heads down, if we stood up we would probably be shot, and Dr. Fei kept on speaking, in spite of the fact that his microphone was dead and sometimes we could hardly hear what he was saying. A loud-speaker from somewhere outside ordered in the name of the provincial government an immediate cessation of the meeting—this, in spite of the fact that free speech and free assembly were solemnly granted to the nation some weeks before. We paid no attention to the loud-speaker. Someone found an acetylene lamp, and the meeting continued.

"Then an extraordinary thing happened. Out of the darkness there suddenly emerged a man wearing dark glasses and a blue gown escorted by thirty or forty young men. He came up to the rostrum and shouted: 'I am just an ordinary man—a *lao pai hsing*—and I have heard that this university is the home of democracy in China, and I want to speak to you.' There was some discussion about whether he should be heard—he looked so much like a secret service agent, and it was curious that when he appeared there were no more sounds of firing. It was decided to let him speak for ten minutes. He mounted the rostrum and delivered a savage attack on the Communists whom he described as bandits and cutthroats. He said that China had fought the Japanese for eight years; now we must have a united country; and the way to have a united country was to destroy utterly the bandits and cutthroats in our midst—in his opinion, as a common man, it was nonsense to call this a civil war—it was simply an attempt by a legally constituted government to put an end to a few scattered bandits who were of no importance whatsoever. He finished his statement, came off the rostrum, and was immediately set upon by the thirty or forty people who had accompanied him, all crying: 'Beat him! Beat him!'

"This was really extraordinary! His own aides were beating him, pretending in the darkness to be students, and the students had to rescue him. For a few moments the place was in an uproar, for the students now saw perfectly well what was happening and knew that at any moment the firing would begin again, but this time lower. A few students took the man who called himself Mr. Wang to the main gates of the university and left him there; and they were careful not to hurt him. And one by one the others who had accompanied him went out.

"That's all. There was one more speaker—Dr. Pan Pa-kwei, of the Democratic League. There was another wave of shooting, and though he spoke for some time, about nine o'clock it was decided to abandon the meeting. The continual bursts of machine-gun fire and mortars were getting on our nerves; it was coming from all directions, and no one knew when the angle of fire would be lowered—we could hear the bullets whistling over our heads. In any case, the main purpose of the meeting had been accomplished. We had heard what they had to say, and we were in general agreement that the civil war must come to an end, and we had decided to telegraph to the Generalissimo and to Mr. Mao Tse-tung urging them to put a stop to the civil war for the sake of the nation. Then we slowly went out through the great gates, only to find that a machine gun was directed against us in the road and the gates of the city were shut.

"That was perhaps the worst moment, because the thirty or forty men who accompanied Mr. Wang were waiting for us in the street and trying to create trouble. Only a very few students had torches. It was dark, there was no moon, and there were soldiers all along the road leading down from the North Gate. We could see them in the darkness, we knew they had been firing at us and there was nothing we could do. They told us the city gates were closed—no one knew why—and many of us were compelled to stay outside the walls all through the bitterly cold night. There were hundreds of female students, and we were desperately afraid of what might happen to them if they stayed out among all those soldiers. Some of us managed to get through a small gate. A professor in Yunnan University was knifed on his way home—not a deep wound, but still he was knifed, and he was probably only saved from death by the fact that it was so dark that the man who wanted to kill him could not see him. And in any case he was a perfectly innocent and respectable professor, who had taken no part in the meeting and was probably mistaken for someone else."

This is the story: it seems perfectly incredible, but it happened. It may be happening in every university and high school in China. Lienta is the greatest university in the country, a huge complex comprising Peking, Tsinghua, and Nankai Universities, and free speech is at the mercy of soldiers and no one knows what will happen next.

December 1st, Murder of the Students. Four students are dead.

I do not know their names, and perhaps their names do not matter. They were young, and they committed no crime; they were killed by hand grenades; not one of them died outright—they lingered for a few hours, but by six o'clock this evening they were all dead.

It is difficult to understand what happened—there are so many conflicting rumors, and there may be many things we shall never understand. I shall try to describe this thing simply, as it has been told to me.

Many things happened this morning. Between eleven and twelve o'clock three universities—the Sino-French University, Yunnan University, and Lienta—were attacked. The Engineering College at the center of the city was also attacked, but no details of the attack have come through except that some thugs beat up a professor who was experimenting with a galvanometer and accused him of communicating to Yenan with the galvanometer, which they smashed with their fists. There may be more dead in the city: there are certainly about twenty wounded, some of them seriously. The attacks appear to have been careful and concerted, and this time the thugs were armed.

First, all the furniture in the Sino-French University was smashed; then an effort was made to break through the gates of Yunnan University, which is only a few hundred yards away. They succeeded in breaking through the gates, but they did not succeed in entering the university, which must be reached by steep flights of steps, and therefore can be defended. They then went along the long road which leads to the Great West Gate—the Street of the Forest of Learning. They entered a middle-school and smashed up the furniture there. They went out through the Great West Gate and stormed the Teachers' Training College, and when they had finished storming the college, three students were dying from the splinters of a hand grenade two of them had thrown. One was a girl. At about the same time, between two and three hundred soldiers came down the road past the University of Lienta. They marched up and down outside the campus, and one of them was about to throw a hand grenade, when one of the professors interfered; the hand grenade was thrown wild and, instead of killing the hundreds of students inside the campus, it killed a young music teacher who had come to have a haircut at the university.

"They had clubs and sticks and stones in their pockets, and some had hand grenades," S. told me. "I was there—we could see them coming, and we knew what they were coming for. They tore down the notices on the walls—notices in praise of democracy—and they began to try to get into the university by forcing the gates. One or two did get in, and we held them prisoners. The battle went on for nearly two hours, and we never knew if reinforcements were coming up, and we never knew how long the battle would last. Three times they attacked the gates, and each time an officer blew his whistle—it was all so military. And then, when we were taking the wounded to hospital, the soldiers were still there with clubs and poles, and sometimes they robbed the people who were carrying the wounded to hospital; and what was worse than anything was that they frightened the doctors and nurses away from the hospital, so·that there was no one who could care for the wounded."

He does not know how long it will last, or whether it will ever end. Is this the climax, or just the beginning? He has the long narrow face of a northerner, and he came into my room while I was in bed, saying: "They've started killing! Now we know where we are!" And now in the university library, late at night, some of the dead are lying on camp beds, and candles are burning, and young students are crying, and they will remain awake all night. "We're going to guard the university. We'll have guards at the gate with baseball clubs, and we'll examine everyone who enters. They've killed a girl and three boys—do they expect they can do that with impunity? This afternoon General Kuan Lin-seng, the garrison commander, came along in his car and spoke to us. We were completely silent. He said he would punish the criminals, but who were the criminals? Gangs of soldiers are marching through the city assaulting all the schools and all the

people in the schools—does he think he can do that with impunity?"
He was livid with rage and excitement, and kept mixing up Chinese
and English.

December 2nd. It would hardly be possible to imagine a more beautiful day: the campus flooded with young people in blue gowns, the sky
blue, the blue flag flying at half mast. The library has changed beyond recognition. Where there were tables and stools and catalogues
there is nothing: they have been swept away, and in their place there
are only the two camp beds, the two dead boys covered up to the
chest with blankets, their heads bandaged and their faces like wax.
There are heaped flowers on the blankets and a terrible sullen silence
reigns over the library, which has never looked so bare.

Coffins have arrived. The doors of the library are flanked with
those immense redwood coffins, and already on the campus there are
evergreen arches bearing the four characters for "freedom" and "democracy"—nothing more.

Later. The ceremony this afternoon was frightening, and perhaps
most frightening because it was simple. There were no longer the
tremendous blue skies of the morning: mist, gray mist, and scurrying
clouds came from over the burial mounds, and there was a wind like
a knife. I have never known a day so full of foreboding. The students
came, not only from the university but from all the middle schools
around, and they stayed there, singing songs or mostly silent: while
the preparations were made.

The four dead lay on the camp beds in the library. The girl
looked incredibly beautiful, all hint of sorrow and pain had disappeared. There were oranges and flowers on the blankets. There were
young students cleaning up the wounds and bandaging the heads of
the dead; and all so quietly and with such desperate earnestness, as
though almost they were accustomed to these things. The girl students from the middle-schools sang songs with a heartbreaking slow
mournfulness, songs that never seemed to end; and meanwhile it
grew colder. The coffins were laid beneath the evergreen arches: the
coffins were red and gaping like wounds. Until perhaps four o'clock
the bodies remained in the library, so we waited outside in an endless
monotony of expectancy, the air growing colder every moment. All
the students wore small black oblongs on their arms or on their coats.

There were rumors that even the encoffining ceremony would be considered by the local authorities as an assembly that must be broken up; but though we half expected the soldiers, none came. There was the mother of Li Liu-lien, one of the students who has been killed; there were students who had known the dead and whose lips were quivering. Inside the library the air was thick with blood and death, but on the campus there was only this waiting expectancy.

And then they came out, one by one, the camp beds with the bodies lying on them carried by young stretcher-bearers with white lint bandaged over their nostrils. They came very slowly. There was whimpering, but only once was there screaming, and that was when the boy's mother recognized him at the moment when he was being lifted into the coffin; and she ran wildly across the campus toward him. Her screaming turned us all into ice, but the ice grew harder when we noticed the wet red stains on the camp bed so thick that it was as though all the blood had been drained out of him, and gleaming in the faint light. Quilts were first thrown carefully into the coffins; the bodies were laid in them. And then there was singing, and firecrackers exploded, and the sky grew grayer.

December 3rd. The dead were Pan Yen, a girl student of the Teachers' Training College attached to Lienta; Yu Tsai, a young music-teacher at the Nanching Normal School; a boy from the Teachers' Training College; and another from an engineering school. The students say now that they are determined to take the coffins through the city; they are determined to be avenged; they are determined that there shall be democracy and freedom in this country. "You have the right to free assembly," General Kuan Lin-seng is reported to have said, "and I have the right to shoot." These may not be his exact words, but something very similar has been said, and these murders have been committed. The students are heartbroken, and hardly care what happens to them.

I have been reading the student proclamations: "We have no weapons but the righteousness of our cause." "The civil war must end—we have eight years of war to recover from." "We are drifting into fascism, into the rule of the mob, into the rule of the secret police with hand grenades." "Men of good will all over the world, help us to end the civil war, help us to have democracy and freedom."

We have been to see the garrison commander in the hope that we can find some solution to the affair: he has promised to see us tomorrow. Meanwhile there are rumors that two—some say, three—have been arrested for the murder and will be immediately put on trial by the military authorities; but if, as the students say, it was the military who condoned and even committed these crimes, there is not much hope that we shall learn anything from the trial.

December 4th. This morning, between 10:30 and 1:00, an American professor and myself went to see General Kuan Lin-seng, the garrison commander, in the desperate hope that some method may be found to get the secret police off the streets during the funeral procession. I think we have failed. He has told us nothing that we did not know before, but there are places where he has clarified the issue and once he admitted brutally, and in a kind of terror for the consequences, that he possessed no power.

The interview took place in a small room upstairs, with a blue tablecloth and a few wooden chairs. There were scrolls on the wall and little tables for the tea glasses: he sat at the end of the long table facing the door opening on the courtyard. The garrison commander has a bulldog face, heavy eyebrows, a thickset squat man with large hands which he placed on the tablecloth. When his adjutants came in, he told them gruffly: "Go away—can't you see I am talking with foreigners?"

He began by opening the *Central Daily News* and pointing to an article by his chief of staff, which appeared in this morning's edition. This in itself was not surprising, but he insisted that the account given by his chief of staff contained the whole truth of the events that led up to the tragedy and he seemed in some way so dependent upon the chief of staff's views that it was impossible to resist the fear that the chief of staff may have known far more about the truth of the situation than the garrison commander himself. General Kuan Lin-seng said: "I will speak from the heart—the whole truth," and said he was glad we had come so that foreigners might learn the truth rather than the garbled versions that have apparently already appeared abroad. He said he had the greatest respect for the students, he had been a student at Whampoa Academy himself, he would never allow his soldiers to commit any crimes against the students and he had done everything in his power to prevent the murders, but at that moment his voice dropped and he seemed confused. He then went on to describe the events leading up to the murders. He said —we had not heard this, for we had not read the newspaper—that Yenan broadcast at 6:30 on the night of November 23rd the statement that the university would come out on strike and that a university strike committee had already been formed. He was extremely bitter against the Communists and said that everyone knew there were Communists in the university; at this point K. interrupted him and asked how many. "Not many, but they are very powerful and have weapons. We have learned this from our own agents inside the university." He then accused some of the professors of being behind the movement and several times mentioned Dr. Chen Tuan-shen, saying once that Dr. Chen was a Communist in Kuomintang clothing, a statement that was surprising, for this distinguished economist was a member of the People's Political Council, and had often represented China abroad. And then he went on to say in the most matter-of-fact voice that something like a revolution had been planned, and only by great good fortune had disaster been avoided. "We knew that after the meeting there would be processions through the city, public buildings would be attacked, and foreigners would be assaulted." This was surprising, and the statement became more surprising a few minutes later when he added to the first statement: "They wanted the cover of a dark night for their evil deeds." We were asked to believe that the students were intending to use hidden stores of ammunition; they would burn the public buildings: they would create disorder everywhere.

What was strange was that in spite of his knowledge he had taken no measures to prevent these disorders except for sending ten or fifteen plain-clothes men to attend the meeting. He insisted that the shooting was against bandits, and not against students. The students had stated that they heard the bullets whining over their heads. General Kuan laughed a little and said: "I have been a soldier long enough to know that you cannot hear bullets whining over your head—they make no sound at all." This did not, of course, explain the explosion of the mortars, and I have heard bullets whining over my head in Spain. "When I heard that there was firing against bandits in the neighborhood of the university, I ordered my soldiers to withdraw." "Where were you?" "Here."

It was at this point that General Kuan spoke of the disorders among the students. They were Communists, they were armed, and they were disorderly. A certain Mr. Wang had entered the meeting and asked for the privilege of speaking to the students. After some delay he was allowed to speak, but afterwards he was beaten up by the students—this was shocking, for it proved that the university was not a democratic body. The son of his chief of staff had been beaten at the same time. One of us, I have forgotten whom, thereupon asked General Kuan whether the man who had attended the meeting could be traced, since the students had published their belief that he was a secret agent sent either by General Kuan himself or by the Kuomintang Chairman Li Chung-huang. General Kuan dismissed the matter briefly by saying that it would be too difficult to find him. But a moment later he said that the firing the students heard came from blank shots fired by a student called Ho Chung in an effort to create disorder; and it was not possible to ask him how, in a crowd of perhaps 4,000 students, his secret agents had recognized a solitary student in the darkness. We were not there to probe his story, even though the story appeared at all times incredible: we were there to discover whether something could be done to prevent further murders.

A little while later he went on to say how frightened he had been at the thought of the disorders following the meeting—he had referred to this already, but the full horror of the event was so disturbing that he repeated: "They wanted it to be dark, so that they could use fire and hand grenades." There was nothing we could say. The thought of the university students proclaiming a revolution from Kunming was not one we could accept: the night was bitterly cold, and by all accounts the meeting was perfectly orderly. General Kuan said bitterly: "On the 26th of November, the day following the deaths of the students, the students posted up on the walls of the city proclamations against the civil war and asking for a coalition government, and various other things—the withdrawal of Hurley and Wedemeyer, freedom of speech, and freedom of assembly. These proclamations were an incitement to the people——"

K. said: "I understand that freedom of speech and freedom of assembly have already been granted by the central government."

"This is true, but we were faced with terrible responsibilities, and it was necessary for us to act in order to safeguard the peace. Remember, we knew from our agents that the students were armed. We knew that they were asking the factories to come out on strike, asking the farmers not to pay taxes, asking the other schools to come out on strike. They were disturbing the social order. Anyone who criticized their proclamations and speeches was immediately set upon and beaten. The headmasters of some middle-schools asked me to send soldiers to protect their schools. I did not dare to send them. It might create disorder. Even officers have been beaten by the students. There are pamphlets actually insulting the Generalissimo. The students set upon one officer and beat him with stones, but the good students still want to return to their classes, and they have organized an antistrike committee to help young people to return to their classes."

About the attack on Lienta he said:

"Three hundred officer-cadets were simply marching to barracks down the road outside the university. They were unarmed—even their barracks are unarmed. A hand grenade was thrown out of the school, over the wall, and it was thrown by somebody who didn't know how to throw it—the pin wasn't pulled out. One of the cadets picked it up, but was prevented from throwing it back into the school by an officer." This was all: no mention was made of the young schoolteacher who had been killed.

It seemed that the general had no desire to discuss immediately the attack on the Teachers' Training College, for at this point he referred to the trial that had taken place on the previous day. He said sadly that he had invited the students to send representatives, but the students refused; he had also sent invitations to Dr. Yeh Chih-sing and Professor Tsa Liang-tsao, but neither of them had attended, and the two jurists were present from the university on their own responsibility. He said bitterly: "Dr. Yeh and Professor Tsa must have known they would be found in the wrong. There was much evidence to prove that the hand grenade was thrown from inside the university, and they were afraid to face the evidence." We said that the students claimed that the soldiers passed up and down outside the university, deliberately provoking the students with insults and striking down the posters on the walls outside. "This is a mistake—they simply passed down the road, and the students flung mud at them, and stones, and one of them threw a hand grenade. Why should these students say that the soldiers threw a hand grenade? If I wanted to attack the students, would I use only one hand grenade?"

It was getting late. A servant came and brought more tea, visitors were being dismissed peremptorily and the general was getting into his stride. The introduction was over, and soon we should come to the main incident of that tragic day, but before he came to that, the general said: "You must believe that we have never had the slightest intention of hurting the students—all this has happened because there are dissident elements in the university who have nothing to lose by the deaths of some of the students."

He explained the murders very briefly. It was true that some officers had taken part in the scramble outside the Teachers' Training College on the previous day, November 30th. It was true that some of them returned the following day for revenge. It was true that the men who were arrested and put up for trial were former soldiers, but it was a long time since they were dismissed from the Army and at the time they were wearing ordinary clothes. He said that the men who threw the hand grenades had been arrested and already condemned—they had received the hand grenades from a certain Mr. Chiang Kai whom the police were now searching for. And this was all—he could throw no more light on the murders but asked us to read the official report of the trial and to pay particular attention to the statement written by his chief of staff.

He then went on to explain that after the murders he had done everything possible to safeguard the place; he had himself gone to the university. "The students welcomed and surrounded me, and asked me questions and I promised that the students who behaved need fear no more occurrences of this kind, and I said that the criminals would be punished according to law. I did not sleep that night. I was in constant conference with my advisers. I addressed the school authorities and told them that it was not a student strike, but an effort to create as much bloodshed as possible. I went to the university again the next morning, but this time the students did not treat me as well as before; it was evident that dissident elements had aroused them against me: the day before they greeted me with their hearts, but now they were ordered to attack me." And then he went on to attack the students for allowing the dead bodies to remain unburied—"This is being done deliberately by the students: they leave the bodies there, with the evil smell, and this is done just to inflame the students." This last statement was incorrect, for I had seen the bodies being nailed into the coffins.

I said: "Did you know that the murder of the girl took place under particularly revolting circumstances—she was wounded by hand grenades, then knifed or bayoneted in the stomach and breasts, and then jumped upon."

"No, I didn't know this," he answered, but did not seem very shocked.

All this had been introductory to the main purpose, which was to devise some method by which the murders (for it was impossible to believe that they were not deliberate murders) should be stopped. We had no power. We were not delegated by the university, and the delegates sent by the university had failed to find him three days before; the students refused to see him, or to send messages to him, believing that he was the murderer. We were not convinced that he was the murderer. He was a soldier, and he said repeatedly that he would never allow his soldiers to attack students: in this he was convincing, or nearly convincing. He hated Communists furiously, and it was curious that he should pointedly have stated that one of the crimes committed by the students was that they insulted the Generalissimo. They had not insulted the Generalissimo: they had called for an end to the civil war which the Generalissimo was pursuing. They were not loyal, as he was loyal, to the Generalissimo, and I believe that in his eyes this was their greatest crime—he had not fired on the students, but he had allowed his soldiers to be used by others, by Kuomintang Chairman Li Chung-huang or by the agents of General Tai Li, the head of the secret police. The more we spoke to him, the more innocent he appeared; but there were moments when the innocence was almost too childlike to be credible. We asked him whether, if the students held the funeral procession, he would personally protect them.

He said: "If they hold a procession, tragic things may happen, but I guarantee that my secret agents and my soldiers will not be on the streets. The soldiers would be afraid to go near a procession of this kind."

"Are there any other secret police?"

"Yes—the secret police of the former Governor Li Chung-huang. They are not under my control."

Then he said: "I am in contact with Chungking continually. I inform the Generalissimo about these matters three times a day and receive his orders. He has said that everything must be settled peacefully."

"This means that the responsibility and blame are all yours?"

He looked hurt and miserable, banged his fist on the table, and almost shouted: "Yes, no one understands the terrible position I am in. All the blame falls on me." Shortly after this outburst he said: "I am outnumbered. There are others as well as me. For my part I will do everything I can to prevent further disturbance, but——"

The implications were growing clearer. There were others behind the scenes, more powerful. Who were they? There was the Governor Lu Han, who was installed in office on the day of the murder, a general who had only recently returned from Indochina, a man who was known to share some of the liberal views of his half-brother, General Yung Lun, who had been recalled to Chungking as a result of the civil war. General Lu Han was in a delicate situation, and it was difficult to believe that he wanted to see bloodshed with all its unavoidable and unpredictable consequences so early during his tenure of office. There was Chairman Li Chung-huang, who retained the office of municipal affairs and wielded enormous powers by reason of his connection with the party. There may have been others.

But if General Kuan Lin-seng was, as he said, outnumbered, there remained some hope that a person of high ministerial rank could be brought down from Chungking, a man with such power that he could order the secret police off the streets and allow the procession to move unhindered. T. V. Soong had flown down when Lung Yun was removed. Why could not some responsible minister be invited down? The matter was serious and involved public feeling in America and England, where sooner or later men would be aghast that soldiers had thrown hand grenades at students for no other reason than that they disagreed with the government's desire for a civil war.

I asked whether I could fly up to Chungking on a Chinese army plane: I knew Dr. Sun Fo, the son of Dr. Sun Yat-sen, and Marshal Feng Yu-hsiang, and thought I could induce them to use their influence to send down an emissary with complete powers. "But they are not powerful," he objected. "They are not powerful enough." He looked frightened. We discussed the possibility at some length, but it seemed that only the Generalissimo had power to settle the matter, and since it was only too certain that the Generalissimo had been misinformed, it was too late to ask him to send down someone with plenipotentiary powers to overrule any decisions which might be made by the governor, the former governor, or the dark shadow, whoever he was and whoever he represented, who might order the throwing of the next bomb. General Kuan had almost acquiesced to this plan, when the telephone bell rang: when he returned, he said: "It is impossible—I am the representative of Chungking. This cannot be done."

By this time I was feeling feverish and exhausted. There seemed to be nothing, nothing at all, that could be done; and there was no assurance that the secret police could be removed from the streets, for though we believed, or half believed, that General Kuan was in mortal terror of further incidents, there remained the former governor and the invisible presence of perhaps some other power. He asked us to convey to the students a request that he should be told when the procession would take place and offered to provide a guard of honor. And then we went out into the blazing sunshine, across the lake toward the arched stone gate leading to the city. His green car followed us, and he jumped out and begged my companion not to reveal anything he had said.

December 7th. It is useless to go on rumors, and there are so many. I can understand why the students are wild with horror and determined to take the coffins through the city; and they hardly care what happens to them. The garrison commander has insisted that there must be no more meetings, the local press is still gagged, there is absolutely no evidence that a factual report of the murders has reached Chungking.

I am so sick to death of all this bloodshed. At any moment the students may take the coffins through the streets, and there is nothing on earth that will prevent an *agent provocateur* from throwing another grenade. I have been to see the strike committee. I have begged them to postpone the procession for at least a few more days, and they listen very politely, but they say the students are determined. This is the greatest university in China: if they do not assert their rights for freedom now, no other university in China will achieve them. They have their martyrs still.

There is a curious sullen temper among them. They are still half-dazed with shock. There are still blood-red posters on the wall openly attacking General Kuan Lin-seng and Chairman Li Chung-huang of a deliberate murder. There are student guards at the gates of all the universities with baseball bats in their hands, there are notices on every wall shouting out for freedom of assembly, for freedom of publication, for *habeas corpus*, for a coalition government, for democracy; there is still a strike; there is still the feeling that we are on the edge of the abyss. A minor official has come down from the ministry of education, but he has no power over the local garrison command or the provincial government. There are rumors, which may be true, that General Kuan is prepared to hand in his resignation. Fu Ssu-nien, the chancellor of Peking University, has arrived. He saw General Kuan three days ago and said bluntly: "I was your friend up to this moment, but now you are no longer my friend— these students are like my own children to me," and walked out in a

towering hatred for this military despotism, for though General Kuan
may not be responsible for the murders, he is responsible for peace
and order and could probably have prevented the bloodshed.

December 9th. H. has asked whether I would like to read the biographies of the four people who were killed. I did not want to read
them. They seemed, when they were lying on the camp beds in the
library, so very much like other students, a little frail and thin and
not very well fed. I could not imagine that their biographies told
more than any biographies of students taken at random. I said something to this effect to H., who was almost angry. He said bitterly: "If
they had wanted to kill the best, they have succeeded. A girl from
one of the oldest families in China, a young music teacher passionately in love with music, the only son of a poor peasant, and a boy
who was so representative that no one can say more of him than that
he liked sports and worked hard. Is it fate? If you threw a hand
grenade at random among the students on the campus, would they
have killed such good people? All four of them were poor. Not one
was a radical. I have spoken to people who knew them, and they
always say: 'It is better if they had killed us—we are not so good.' "

When he was gone, he still seemed to be in my room, the young
Honanese with the hair falling across his forehead. He looked ill and
pale. I doubt whether he has slept much or eaten much since the
murders; and there was so much decision on his young face that I am
beginning to have greater hope for China. The miracle may happen.
The pressure of the schools may prevent the two governments from
carrying out the civil war, for even now the scholars of China wield
invisible powers. Confucius said: "It may be that one has to give
one's life in order to achieve goodness." He has translated for me the
biographies of the dead students.

PAN YEN

She was born twenty-eight years ago in the small feudal city of Suichow. She belonged to an old family that had been declining for
some time, yet it still retained a position of importance. She was
brought up according to the old-fashioned custom of her family, and
so for seventeen years she passed her life inside the house. At that
time modern thoughts were beginning to fill people's minds, and Pan

Yen recognized the deep importance of being well educated in order to achieve a responsible position in society. She was determined to be educated, but coming from such a family it was almost impossible for her to enter school. She was learning her lessons privately from her cousin, and in the winter of 1934, as a result of hard work, she entered a junior middle school. I must point out that for a girl to enter a middle school after never having studied in a primary school was no easy thing. She requested her parents' permission to join the school, and in the end she succeeded. Meanwhile she employed all her influence to allow other girls from her family to enter school. So, with her help, I too was allowed to join the school the next year.

She finished the three-year course of junior high in two and a half years; then she took the entrance examination for the Girls' Normal School. It was very unfortunate that war swept over the country before she could enter the school. She was not the kind of person who would willingly submit to fate and remain enslaved at home; and so, being deprived of her chance to study, she entered the army.

One cold night in winter I came across her at a railway station. She had joined the Eleventh Army. Fully equipped, she stood there waiting for the train to go to Suichow, where a battle was about to take place. Except for the journey from Suichow to Su in Anhuei, she went on foot all the way from Su to Huangch'uan in Honan, passing through Hankow and Ichang, fighting against sickness and disease as well as the enemy, always going by night. She had joined the army, and she was determined to be always the last to retreat. She was undaunted by danger and found comfort in it.

In the winter of 1938 she arrived at Ichang with no other belongings but the thin uniform she was wearing. I do not know what happened to her during that winter. The next time I heard of her she had joined a girl's middle school, but she stayed there only a year—not because she did not want to study, but because she wanted to study too much, and this was not a school where studying could be done profitably.

She arrived in Chungking in the winter of 1940. She entered school, but in the end months of poverty and misfortune made her give up. Then for four years she kept on struggling, and at last she gained her aim and joined the Teachers' Training College. Once again she could study—but now she has gone. She has gone before us all.

HSUN CHI-CHUNG

He was a boy of only seventeen, a student of Kunghua Technical School, and strongly built, fond of sport and writing. He had considerable ability at these things and was very good natured and liked by his teachers and schoolmates.

His parents were deeply grieved by the loss of their son, yet they plainly understand the significance of their loss. His elder brother, also a student, heard of the death of the boy while he was making speeches in the street. He rushed to the side of his dead brother and swore to take vengeance on the murderers.

Hsun's death indeed was glorious. When the Teachers' Training College was being attacked, and the students there were outnumbered, they were forced to retreat to the Technical College and summon aid. He at once gathered some of his schoolmates together, and with a large club in his hand led the party against the thugs. The shrapnel from the grenade pierced his skull; he died four hours later in hospital.

LI LIU-LIEN

Li Liu-lien was eighteen years old, a native of Chekiang. I met him first in 1942 in the Provincial Sichung Middle School in Sikong Province. He was studying in the school because his father had some business there. He was well known for being an assiduous student.

Some time later he left Sichung and wandered over the country with his father. He was born in Shantung. Since the beginning of the war, he was always traveling from place to place, yet he remained an innocent boy. He entered the Teachers' Training College of Lienta in 1945; it was there that we met again. We lived in the same room, studied together, and played together. He only lived for his studies and had almost no feeling for politics.

The shooting on the night of November 25th aroused his deepest anguish. He spent all his time working with the strike committee. About noon, on December 1st, sixty or seventy armed ruffians broke into the Teachers' Training College. The students all took refuge in the adjoining Kunghua Technical School by forcing their way through the windows. They were provoked by the sight of the ruffians wantonly destroying the school furniture. Five or six students immediately rushed to prevent them. Li Liu-lien was among them.

After the hand grenade exploded, he fell at the gate, all covered with blood. He was carried to hospital by the other students, but he died on the way.

YU TSAI

He was so gentle, so kindhearted, and so quiet, yet his body was sturdy. I met him for the first time three months ago at Nanching Middle School. He was fond of weeping, but never for his own sake. Once he wept for a whole night after talking with a friend who had given up all hope. He did not behave like this out of cowardice, but because he loved men.

He was born into a wealthy Shanghai family—a family without warmth or liveliness. When the war broke out, he left his home and went to Chungking with a small sum of money which he secured by selling the only thing he possessed—a bicycle. On his way he took part in all kinds of war work, being especially attached to work for refugee children. In Chungking he joined the army, for a while he was conductor of a ferry. He refused to receive any money from home but provided money for his friends when they were badly in need.

Six months before he died, he returned from India. His father sent for him to take care of the family property. He refused and advised his father not to worry about money.

He was twenty-four, and he was born in Hanyuan, in Chekiang. He had graduated from a normal school in Chungking, majoring in music. He was a member of the Kuomintang Party. When he died, he was a music-teacher in Nanching Middle School.

He praised the passionate spirit of Beethoven but deeply regretted the silence of Goethe.

December 11th. The vice-minister of education came two days ago, a tall man with buck teeth, wearing a dark blue patterned gown and a black *makua*. We went to see him last night to see whether he could throw any light on what is happening, but he seems to know even less about the affair than we do. He complained that the Communist newspapers in Chungking had complete reports of the murder, but no other newspapers had them. "It proves that the Communists are behind it," he said. But does it? Doesn't it prove rather that no other newspapers will print it?

He has seen the Generalissimo, who said: "Something is

wrong—very wrong. I give you complete powers to settle the matter."
The vice-minister insists that he has plenipotentiary powers, but do
these powers extend over the local military or even the local Kuomintang office? Kuan Lin-seng has been recalled; a new general has taken
his place. The vice-minister said: "Our attitude toward the matter is
very cold—cold." We asked him what he meant by this, for surely
the seriousness of the attacks was realized in Chungking, but he
evaded the issue by saying that he was sent down only to find facts.
What was strange was his continual denial about the censorship.
Theoretically, free speech and free assembly had been granted by the
government, but he insisted that the local government had overriding
powers. "So the provincial government can override the central government when it pleases?" But to this he only answered: "There are
conditions in China which cannot be compared with conditions
abroad." He admitted that it was likely that the provincial government had used its overriding powers to prevent messages being sent
out, but the messages had come out all the same—the news was
printed in Chungking, Chengtu, and Shanghai, and very probably it
has already reached America and Hong Kong. "But the important
thing is to keep cold—keep cold."

It seemed odd. We were very cold indeed: impossible to tell
whether he has power, or has been sent only on a fact-finding com-
mission. He seemed not to understand the seriousness of the situation that tolerated these murders, and said: "General Kuan Lin-seng
talks too much—he is a good soldier, but not a good diplomat." But
we do not need diplomats, and General Kuan did at least speak
openly of the things he knew; though he seemed to know less than
anyone else.

"The funeral procession may be held by the students," K. said.
"Is there any way in which bloodshed can be avoided?" and he
spoke for a while on the terrible effect further bloodshed would have
in foreign academic circles. "Such things have happened in Nazi
Germany—inconceivable that they should be allowed to happen in
China." The thrust hit home. The vice-minister began to growl about
the enemies of China. "They try to hit us with everything they
have—there are enemies everywhere," and since he evidently included
us among the enemies, this seemed the strangest of all. He had spent
the first night of his arrival with a general connected with the garrison command: there had been objections. He thought it might be
possible to stay in a bank tonight. And so we left him, two hours later
in the deserted courtyard, a tall man who seemed not to know which

way the world was going, who possessed power of a kind and yet hesitated to use it, afraid of his responsibilities, afraid of the deaths of the students, the only man connected with the universities who had access to the highest quarters; and it seemed impossible to believe that he would be able to add anything or take anything from a situation which had grown above our heads and enclosed us all.

December 12th. It is a time of rumors, of strange whispered threats, of still stranger silences. The students and the provincial government are fighting a war of nerves. The censorship is stronger than ever; three hundred more censors have suddenly been enrolled. On the surface everything is quiet, the students are no longer molested, they even make speeches in the center of the city calling for an end to the civil war. Yet you are conscious all the while that there is terror in the silence, though the silence in the university library, where all the coffins are, is deeper.

December 13th. Confucius said: "The true knight must have broad shoulders and a stout heart, for his burden is heavy and he has a long journey to go. For goodness is the burden he has taken upon himself. Only with death does this journey end: then must we not grant that he has far to go."

And surely the students are doing no more than echoing these words when they announced so courageously in their proclamations: *Death we are not afraid of, for we are assisting a new China to come to birth.*

December 19th. The weight of this murder is like lead. We forget it for a while, but the memory of it returns, obliterating the memories of other murders. Wen Yi-tuo is griefstricken. He speaks so humbly of the students that one almost forgets his own goodness. There, in the tangled garden, where the convolvuluses were dying, he leaned on his stick and spoke about the students he has known in the past. "They are still among the most complex animals in creation. I remember the time when every student wore long silk gowns and carried a fan and even the boys wore jade bracelets—less than twenty years ago. They played football in those days so delicately that it was like watching a slow-motion film. They have grown taller and sturdier; they have cut themselves adrift from the past, and because they

are even now saturated in Confucian doctrines, they are still drifting."
At that moment a boy student and a girl passed through the garden,
arm in arm. "What will save them is that no one in China is more
than four generations removed from a farmer. They are much
stronger than you think."

December 24th. The strike goes on, the faculty meetings go on,
there have been interviews between the student council and Governor Lu Han, there has been a message from the Generalissimo calling upon the students to return to their classes, but no one knows
whether the students will return.

The campus was flooded with sunshine and has never looked
lovelier. There can be no campus like this. The mud huts shone this
morning like honey in the sun, and the small green lakes among the
vegetable gardens were thick with duckweed; but it is not the campus
which is beautiful—what is beautiful beyond all words at this
moment is still the library which stands like a great crumbling cow-
shed beyond the small lakes. The archway of evergreens has been
removed, and there are no longer any guards at the university gates
with baseball bats to prevent the entrance of *agents provocateurs.*
There is the immense cow shed, and the girls in blue gowns from the
middle schools who are making their way there. Inside the library
there must be at least two thousand funeral scrolls hanging from the
rafters, some on white silk, some on paper, and many of them composed with great heavy black brush strokes; and you wander through
this forest of scrolls until you come to the four black coffins covered
with the red and blue national flag, and on the way you pass the altar
where the enlarged photographs of the dead students gaze down at
you. There is Yu Tsai looking a little like a young prince, with a small
mouth and dreaming eyes; there is Pan Yen who gazes out of her
frame, more mature than the two youngsters beside her, already a
woman, with such stores of character and forthrightness on her
gentle face that one would have thought her worth preserving for the
future of China; there is Li Liu-lien who looks for all the world like a
young football player; there is Hsun Chi-chung who looks almost like
a child. Before the photographs red candles are smoking; oranges and
apples and bottles of wine are heaped on the white tablecloth; there
are joss sticks burning in urns and wreaths of evergreens. And then
you walk on for a little space, and suddenly on the walls you come
across small photographs of Pan Yen: there are photographs of her in

military uniform, playing with children, at picnics, climbing mountains, the inevitable posed photographs of her in a long student's gown, and then there are the other photographs showing her body being placed in a great iron cauldron with the head still showing and the fires burning; and you remember that this happened only two or three hundred yards away, and that the air you breathe contains more of her than you can guess. And somehow it is not terrible—it is as you expect it to be—and those photographs which were taken from her purse contain her whole life, you can understand everything, and she is young China still in all the glory of her young womanhood. So you go slowly around the library, where the funeral scrolls swing gently in the wind and the blue gowns move silently among them, here in the library where there is no longer the musty smell of books: there is only the scent of flowers and of blood. For there on a table against the wall are the clothes they wore when they died, and a campbed with a great oval rust-red stain on it. They were put here deliberately: the students were probably wrong to have done this, for the middle-school children come and gaze at them and even touch them, as others touch holy relics, and go away afraid, realizing that they wear the same kind of clothes and simply by realizing this, they come into so close a contact with the dead that they are like people who have seen visions.

There is no place in China so hallowed as this university library, and there is no greater quietness anywhere else.

1946

January 1st. We break our bread and sleep and wander in the sun, and those are the three best things—and all these we do to perfection in Kunming. If we must add a fourth, there is scholarship; and if there is a fifth, there is love-making; and the sixth is adoring the perfection of this lake a mile above the sea.

So I wrote when I first came to Kunming, but all of it has changed. In those days, with a kind of grim selfishness, we could forget the war, content to live in this cleansing air, to study and to breathe. But things changed so deeply, there is so much terror abroad, and life is held so cheaply, that we are beginning to look at this mountain valley with something of the attitudes of soldiers caught up in a citadel and determined not to surrender, though they starve. We have lost faith completely in Chungking. We had little enough faith, but now it has gone completely. We have not much more faith in Yenan, though we admire much of their program for agrarian reform. What is important is that until October there was freedom in Kunming. No man was killed for uttering "dangerous thoughts." The prisons were nearly empty. There were no armed thugs on the streets. There were desperate ventures—no one knows how many guns, how many jeeps, and how much ammuniton have been stolen from the Americans, but none of these took on the scale of a relentless civil war. There was a time when I first came here when Lienta was among the most glorious things in China; it is glorious still, but something is lacking among the professors, their spirits have been tried too hardly, their suffering has reached breaking point and it is no longer true that Lienta is "the last bulwark of freedom in China." The last bulwark has fallen. The students have not changed; they are as determined as ever that the principles of democracy should survive, but with the exception of a handful of professors, the faculty has thrown in its hand. The students will be forced back to work, are already forced back to work, and the faculty has promised that the murderers will be brought to justice; but everyone knows that the promise is worthless, and the faculty has no power. We must go on from here, but the way seems darker than ever now.

January 2nd. I met Wen Yi-tuo walking gravely through the gardens near the lake. There are goldfish and small temples, and places where you can drink tea under bamboo shelters, and great hawks wheeling overhead. His newspaper has been suspended indefinitely; he will be arrested the moment it appears, if it appears illegally. He has been from one printing press to another, always trailed. He said: "It's the most idiotic thing of all—to know that you are being trailed. It gives you the most damnable impression of your own self-importance." He laughed. "We haven't deserved this—the students haven't deserved it—they will still fight, but somehow they have got into their heads that they must fight in the ancient Chinese way—dramatically, as one fights for lost causes. But these causes are not lost. They say they are going to take the coffins through the city whatever the cost; a hundred thousand children believe this, but it would be better if we had just one good man in the government, or one bad man less." With bent back, walking slowly, he disappeared among the silver trees.

January 7th. This was not the place we had hoped to come to, because we had lost our way, and the dust was getting into our shoes, and there was nowhere to rest. I remember I was frightened because we might have to walk all night, and I feared the yapping of the dogs more than the bandits in the villages, and besides, all the comforting things of evening—the smell of wood smoke, the colors of the fields, the sense of being surrounded by friendly people—all these die away at night. Nothing is so unfriendly as a Chinese night when there is no moon. Night the enemy, and the houses all shuttered, and you couldn't see the pathway, and we were utterly tired of crossing fields, and sometimes L. would stop and say he heard the sound of a pheasant or a barking deer, and I heard nothing, the night enclosing us both so that we were doubly afraid.

There is a shuttered horror at night in China, and I remember that Tu Fu complained about it, and God knows in his wanderings he must have seen these landscapes under a black moon, the dogs like avenging and invisible furies and all the houses darkened so that they look like unfriendly stones. The Chinese are callous—it is better to admit it—they say they must be callous to survive, but the night is more callous still, and we couldn't go on much further. I suppose a rise in the ground hid us from Kunming, but the most extraordinary thing was that there was a heavy mist, and we were not conscious of it, and only knew of it afterwards. And then, quite suddenly, we came to a small village near the gates, where there were dim lights and the smell of dogs and children were playing. Those last moments before we reached the village were almost as terrible as the night last year when we were coming home after curfew and someone with a submachine gun pushed it into my stomach and told me to put my hands up; the night was as calculated and bestial as that.

And then the sudden recovery, the sense that the world was safe, because there was the smell of wood smoke, and sleepy children were playing, and there were rapeseed oil lamps, and money in our pockets to pay for food—sweetened eggs in milk, juicy figs which are called "dragons' eyes," and whole loaves of unleavened bread. And afterwards, coming to Kunming at last, seeing the gate opening like a great white horn leading to the world of dreams.

February 1st. What is Taoism? One hears so much, and one knows that it is characteristically Chinese, and we can learn much by studying those ancient fragmentary texts written more than two thousand years ago. There is a strange sense of irresponsibility in the Chinese, a sense which derives perhaps more from the continual hungers of the people than something intrinsic in their character. They are the world's anarchists, who know that responsibility is often ridiculous and obedience is a shallow simplicity, for they know only too well that laws are man-made and are used by judges to incriminate others. There is no law in China. Habeas corpus goes regularly on the statute book; the imprisonments and the arrests and the political assassinations continue. But this evening I came upon my friend, Dr. Lin Tung-chi's description of the Taoist, which is so important that I shall write it down here:

> Taoism may be defined as romantic individualism. It is the natural and necessary counterpart to the complacent and yielding gregariousness of Confucianism. Come what may, the first prompting of a Taoist is to "debunk," so much folly and bad taste does he see in this all too human world.
>
> One can best describe the workings of this mentality in terms of a curve.
>
> It begins with an ascending movement whereby the discharging energy of debunking is directed outward to the external world until it reaches a point where the fire of debunking turns into a white flame of defiance. It is the moment most supercharged with possibility of action, the juncture at which a Chinese intellectual may most readily turn into a revolutionary if ever his defying mood finds its way to combine with the popular discontent of the age.
>
> A typical Taoist nature does not, however, become a revolutionary as a rule. He does not actually mix with the populace. A proud artist, he stands alone, contemplating no comrades. He, predestinedly, sees a war of one against all and one against everything. And a more exalted and tense frame of mind cannot be imagined.
>
> Yet there is no vent. Totally unable to view the impending battle in terms of practical interests and concrete issues, he is at a loss as to where and to whom to deal his blows. The intensity of his charged feeling, thus blocked, soon recoils upon itself. A mental crisis develops when an involuntary repression compresses the rising temper, which, foundering at this tremulous height, quickly turns into a state of Dionysian drunkenness. The Taoist revolt at this stage takes on the character of emotional self-abandonment. He gives himself up to himself. He no longer defies, he simply disregards. A sort of ecstasy takes place, in which the half-conscious bitterness and the half-felt rapture combine to produce a vent peculiarly Taoist— the devastating laugh of the intoxicated. But this blessed stage cannot last long. A mental numbness born of helpless desperation is foredoomed to come to a *dénouement*—the beginning of the descending curve.
>
> As the effects of intoxication clear away, the last possibility of action disappears. He cannot but question now the worth of it all. "Why excitement and fury?" asks the erstwhile rebel. And he begins to debunk *himself*. With a chuckle he drops the gauntlet and retires into the mountains. The boisterous rebel becomes the saintly recluse. After the tempest, the serene sunset.

I do not know any description of the Chinese mind so honest as this. It says much that has been on my mind for many years, and though not all Chinese are implicated, there is a Taoist irresponsibility in all of them to some smaller or greater extent. There is a sense in which the whole of the Confucian ritual was simply an effort to *invent* order and stability where there was none before.

The more I think of this world with its suppurating and increasing wounds, the more I believe that we need the patience and incisiveness of doctors. The wounds are there. What are needed are swabs, ointment, a long and peaceful convalescence. And just as a doctor needs to know the complete history of the patient, so we need to know all that has happened in the minds of countries in the past. But once the wound has healed, or is healing, the mind of the patient is no longer so important, for he will begin his life again like a man newborn. I like the statement of Lieh Tzu: "The joy of traveling lies in its purposelessness. Others travel to see what they want to see, but I travel simply to see the whole earth perpetually changing. Travels, travels, none can see my travels." Though I like it, I know that it is wrong-headed. We must know where we are going. We cannot afford this detachment and irresponsibility, even in our private lives; and nations can afford it still less. China is awake. Of this there can be no doubt at all. But what a complex awakening! After so many years of slumber, intoxicatedly dreaming of the Celestial Empire, she wakes to find herself at war, her face covered with blood and her eyes still unaccustomed to the light.

March 17th. We had almost forgotten the four bodies of the students lying in the library of the university. Gradually, imperceptibly, we had become accustomed to our library as a mausoleum. The dead were there, in the lacquered red coffins, amid the forest of scrolls, but a new and much smaller library had been formed behind the main library, and so we allowed them to stay there in peace. For weeks peasants have been coming to the university on pilgrimage. They came from all the villages around, they wandered among the scrolls, they watched the nuns chanting and the candles gleaming on the altar, and sometimes they bowed, but more often they simply gazed at the immense portraits of the youngsters who were killed. I believe this is what the students liked—the simplicity of these peasants who came in their coarse blue cloth, quietly reverential, not so much paying tribute as coming to see the place where democracy had been fought for, and where students had been killed.

For some months now a stone tomb has been in process of being built near the foreign languages department. At first there were only heavy cubes of glistening white stone, the masons continually chipping them into shape, so that it was dangerous to pass by them for the flying splinters. Now at last it is ready. There is a great stone wall, six or seven feet high, steps leading up to it, an avenue of saplings, stone railings, and at some future time there will be a stone carving behind it. The university will leave for the north, but the tomb will remain. And they have done it well, very simply, with only the names of the students engraved in the stone and the date of their death.

Late last night they chose today to march through the whole city with the coffins.

I have rarely seen anything so moving as this long procession that seemed to comprise all the students of Kunming. There were school children, there were boys and girls from the technical schools, and there were representatives from all the universities, with banners and muffled drums. The police had disappeared from the streets. The procession started out from the university early in the morning. The whole procession must have been at least two miles long, and it went very slowly, the banners were slit, so that they wouldn't flutter in the wind, and the drums sometimes gave place to muffled trumpets, and there was a tremendous gravity on the faces of the students.

Now, hearing the muffled drums, the tinkling of small bells, and the soft deliberate padding of their shoes on the ground, I remember odd details here and there. A white flower was a sign of the mourners, and under the blazing sky there was the sea of calm faces and the sea of white flowers. I saw a schoolboy wearing a white flower, and when the procession came past, his father, wearing a mottled blue gown, noticed the boy's white flower for the first time, seized it, and crushed it underfoot; and the small boy's hands were jerking uncontrollably. Every two hundred yards tables were set out, with oranges and bottles of wine and incense sticks; and at these tables the processions would pause, the incense sticks were waved over the coffins, but the bottles of wine, the oranges, and all the other fruits remained on the tables. I did not take part in the procession. I saw it only toward the end, when it was coming out of the Small East Gate, and already they were weary, and the coffins were no longer being carried by the students but were hoisted on small carts with rubber tires. The blood-soaked clothes were carried on rickshaws. Hundreds of the long scrolls which have hung for three months in the university library were being held by the students, but the wind had torn them to ribbons by the time I saw them. And always the sound of the muffled drums and the tinkling of bells.

They started out at seven this morning; it was five when they returned to the campus, more weary than they expected to be. They told me that they were never frightened: one obtained an extraordinary sense of security—the same illusory sense of security that accompanies an army on the march.

I went into the library, the immense tiled roof under which we have all worked for so many years; there was nothing now except a great emptiness, the floor boards dirty and here and there were mountains of torn and littered scrolls. Once they had been like a forest—these long, carefully inscribed scrolls hanging down from the ceiling, so close to one another that it was difficult to move among them. Now gradually and slowly the students were surging into the campus, very silent, the weariness showing on their faces, the last sunlight falling on the green mounds. It was a long time before the ceremony began. The crowd stood round the white grave, and one by one the coffins were brought up the steps and laid beside it. Not all the coffins possessed relics of the dead. One possessed only the books and some of the clothes of a girl student, for her body had been burnt not far from here; and this is according to an immemorial Chinese custom that decrees that the things nearest to a dead man may be conserved in his tomb. Unlike the Greeks the Chinese have no reverence for empty tombs.

Wine was sprinkled on the steps, and red incense sticks were waved by a professor, and already the sun was going down and it was beginning to be cold. Bells rang, a song was sung, and then three professors climbed the steps and made short speeches, saying that the students had not died in vain, though afterwards we might think they had died in vain, and freedom and democracy were things worth fighting for. The professors were Wen Yi-tuo, Chen Tuan-sen, and Wu Han. They spoke very simply; there was no rhetoric. Then the names of the students were called out, as though we half expected them to answer from among those present; and then the relatives of the dead students, and some of those who had been close to them, came up the steps and walked round the coffins. Then the coffins were lowered with ropes, and it grew darker. Acetylene lamps began to shine, and we began to see that the coffins had entirely disappeared into the ten-foot holes. It was over now. The workmen would cover the four red coffins with cement, and there would be marble facing, and meanwhile the dusk was growing stronger and we could hardly see one another. Afterward, I remember in the streets outside the university, how gray the shadows were as we drove home in little carts.

It is over, but we have no certainty that this will not happen again; we are at the mercy of men with hand grenades, and until the students find out those who are responsible we shall have no peace. We shall be haunted by this evening and the gray shadows. Not far from here, under nameless graves, lie two former Kuomintang officers who have been put on trial and executed for these murders; but they were not responsible. The search for the murderers must begin again.

March 18th. In Hunan they are selling their children, there is almost no food, men are living on grass roots. The responsibility lies where? It is easy enough to say that it lies on the warmongers and the inefficiency of the transport system, and certainly it does lie heavily on the government which appears to be increasingly detached from the people. But K. said this evening something so frightening and true that I have been disturbed ever since. "In the old days when there were floods, the men who were sent to safeguard the lives of the people were those who were known to have high standards of morality. The Emperor Yu became Emperor only because he was known to be good. The stories of the old Emperors are well known. When the floods came, or when there were ravages in the country, they dedicated themselves to their task; they never visited their wives; they took no care for themselves. Nowadays, when floods come, we open a subscription and collect money and think that by doing this our consciences can be absolved, and even when some wretched official runs away with the money, we still think our consciences are absolved. The ravages that come over China are more terrible than the ravages of atomic bombs."

March 20th. We still dream of the day when the long pilgrimage will be over and we can return to Peking. The books are being packed. There is even a provisional date for our departure—May 4th. But how shall we go? The railway to Mengtzu has been broken by the Japanese. We have discovered that we shall have to walk for seven days through malaria-infested country before we can reach the Indochinese railway. We cannot all fly to Peking. Safest is probably to walk across the whole breadth of China.

But the worst is over. The long exile of these three Chinese universities from Peking is nearly over. We pretend we are "working as usual," but how can you work when nearly all the books are no longer available, and when every time we cross the campus we see it as it will be next year—abandoned and forgotten, with its stone tombs and its fifty cattle sheds in which we have taught for so long.

April 4th. Her pure face has, like the moon, its increases and decreases, its periods of fullness and absences; she is always changing, and some subtle trick of light or dress makes her change always for the better. And this young student, who looks almost Spanish, her cheeks and lips as red as apples, who hurries about with books under her arm and looks after a baby in the intervals of studying philosophy, seems to me in many ways an epitome of the modern Chinese student.

She wrote once in an essay: "I am like a dark glass in a dark room, and the glass is covered with dark cloth. I do not know what is inside." In this she was exactly like all the other students, caught up in the Chinese crisis and hovering between East and West. She belongs, like nearly all Chinese students, to a lost generation that may yet find itself. I say "lost," because they are so convinced that they are lost; but to know that you are lost is the first step to being "found." These students know the odds against them. They know that under present circumstances they can obtain useful employment only if they have friends in the government, that nepotism goes on unchecked, that their resources are small in comparison with the resources of the men who have no love for the things they love. They see the wall around them coming ever closer, and it is only very rarely that they can break through. Where shall we go? What shall we do? What shall we fight for? They know what they want to do, and where they want to go, but simply because this university has the reputation of believing in democracy and a freer system of government, they are made to hesitate—the forces arraigned against them are too great, and though they have not yet lost heart, the time may come when they will be compelled either to silence or to a part in a government that represents none of their ideals.

I think of the girl who looks so Spanish, who reads and sings and

teaches in a middle school and attends lectures and tries to bring up
her baby and says little, because there is little now that can be said,
though she struggles with her books and feels a kind of assurance
when she remembers that she has married a mechanical engineer
from the university—the hope of China lies perhaps more in her
young mechanics than in the others. I think of the young chemist I
know, whose dark sensitive face I shall remember always, and he too
wonders how he can ever fit into the pattern that is being made by
the government. Or the young students of foreign languages, the boy
who plays the violin alone to himself among the grave mounds because there is nowhere else to play and whose writing in English
shows more signs of promise than that of anyone I have ever known.
They come from the territories once occupied by the Japanese. It
may be a year before they go back, and before they reach their native
villages, bureaucrats and time-servers will be there already. The young
were not sent to occupy the places recaptured from the Japanese. The
old generals, the old time-servers were sent instead. The lists
appeared—hundreds upon hundreds of men who had taken part in
the prodigious civil wars and whose names were almost forgotten
have suddenly come into the limelight again. Youth is cold shoul-
dered and not trusted with responsibilities, yet it is only the young
who could make China habitable again.

These are the things that batter on the brain while you look at
the young girl reading her books beside the small bamboo cradle in
the sun.

April 6th., Chungking. For a year, for two years I have told myself
that Chungking is pleasant in spring. Why not go? It is two hours
by air.

I remembered the white cliffs, the flooding river, the caves in the
rocks, the hardness of the place, the mud, the filth, the inevitability
of corruption in such a soil, I remembered the long winter nights
when a yellow mist comes and the loveliness of the Chialing River at
dawn—surely there is no other river so beautiful, and it was all I had
expected it to be, though sterner and more miserable than ever. I had
forgotten the scream of the automobiles, the grayness of the shop
fronts, the white cohorts of the dead.

There can rarely have been a more bumpy passage. We flew low
over flooded Kweichow and dropped a parachute with millions of
dollars of national currency to some flooded farmers, and as we sank

slowly down to sea level from the 6,000-foot heights of Kunming, we were conscious of another atmosphere. Kunming is heady wine. You feel all the time you are living on top of a mountain. Under the mat sheds in the small sand strip at Chungking you feel you are at the bottom of the sea.

Then the long climb up the steep cliffs, the grayness of the air—all greens and blues washed away, Chungking the color of granite, the roads muddy, the people wearing black, the automobiles with their trailing plumes of purple wood-oil exhaust, the sense of treachery in the air, the life slowly crumbling away. This is not the true picture, but this is how it seems tonight. Kunming has color, the patterns and shapes vibrate with their own integral life, but in Chungking the sun never shines. It shone once. Grandfathers remember the sun, but no one else remembers. And all of it is below the sea.

April 8th. The frail gray sky opened this morning to receive the sun, and you would have sworn that the day would be gray again, but the clouds cleared, the moist burning sun smothered us all, and it is summer already. We sweat in the cheap hotel bedroom. We drink iced lemonade all day, knowing we shall have dysentery; but it is better to die of dysentery than to die of thirst.

Marshal Feng Yu-hsiang is better. He looked ill when I last saw him two years ago; now there is ripeness in his cheeks, and he carries himself with greater assurance. He has been dismissed from the Executive Committee of the Kuomintang. Laughing, very pleased with himself, he lifted his cup and said: "I have two more jobs under the government. Today I have drunk a toast to express my delight that one job has been taken from me."

"And when the others are taken from you?"

"Then I shall drink more toasts."

He said: "The murder of the students shocked me profoundly. This cannot go on. We cannot afford any longer to allow fascism to go unchecked."

He has mellowed with time, and his assurance is bewilderingly evident. One has the impression that he grows stronger with the years, more robust, even more understanding. They say he still wants power. I doubt it. He is sixty-five and power can mean almost nothing to him, and his sympathies are with the powerless. He talked for half an hour of the ship he has asked the government to give him; it must be a big ship, sufficiently large anyway to allow him to take under his protection the writers and artists of Chungking who want so desperately to go to the coast. "If they stay here," he said "they will be at the mercy of every little government-paid cutthroat. We must take them down the Yangtse safely. It must be done." Very gently he dropped his huge fist on the table, not banging the table but bringing it down with so much force that it was as though a giant was demonstrating strength.

He told me a long story of his native village. The favorite concubine of the Emperor Ch'ien Lung was dying. All over China imperial emissaries were sent to demand that those with the power of healing should come to the capital. Orders were given to the country magistrates to send the men who seemed most promising. One day a young meat-ball seller called Liu-yeh-yeh was picking his teeth outside the walls of Peking, absent-mindedly looking at the imperial rescript on the walls. He seemed to be reading the rescript, and he was nodding his head from side to side. Militiamen saw him and asked him whether he could cure the concubine. Liu-yeh-yeh was suddenly struck with nervousness. He could not read, he did not know what was happening, he began to stammer, and the militiamen began to think of the reward that would be theirs if they could find the man who would cure the imperial concubine. He was taken to the palace and given into the hands of the Emperor's doctors, and at last he was presented to the Emperor, and then he was too nervous to speak, he merely shook his head from side to side. On the afternoon of the same day he was taken into the room where the imperial concubine was lying.

Liu-yeh-yeh only knew that she was ill, and that unless he cured her, his life would be forfeit.

He said, "I must think about this. Give me a room where I can think."

They gave him a room, and they gave him young attendants, and new clothes. He meditated. He strode up and down the room, and he knew that his head was in danger, and he thought: "I must think of something." He thought of his feet, and the little balls of dirt between his toes. He ordered the attendants to go away. He collected the dirt from his toes, rolled it all into a large ball, placed it in a cup of hot tea and summoned the attendants. "The medicine is ready," he said, giving them the tea. The tea was taken to the imperial concubine, who drank it. Next morning she was better.

No one was so surprised as Liu-yeh-yeh. More medicine was

required. Unfortunately he had no more medicine. He walked into
the garden, trying to make his feet dirty. The Emperor sent him a
scroll. He could not understand what was happening. He was promised a bride from the imperial family if he could cure the concubine.
Guards followed him. Panic-stricken, at a moment when the guards
were not watching, he leapt over the wall.

Then all over China there was a hue and cry for Liu-yeh-yeh.
The Emperor sent new imperial rescripts in all directions. Large
rewards were offered for the mysterious doctor who had so successfully cured the imperial concubine; but the concubine was sinking
again. All matters of state were held up. He was rumored to be going
in the direction of Paotingfu. Soldiers were sent after him. They were
waving immense embroidered flags and calling on him to stop. He
was coming to the river near a village, he saw them creeping up to
him and in utter desperation he threw himself into the river and was
drowned. The concubine was dying. A report was sent back to the
Emperor, who ordered that the body of the magician should receive a
state burial and that a large temple should be raised in the Buddhist
faith on the bank overlooking the place where the man was drowned.
The temple was to be named the Temple of the Magician, but today
it is called more properly: "The temple of the balls of dirt which
appear between your toes when you have been walking for a long
time."

And saying this, Feng Yu-hsiang roared with laughter, the immense face dark with wrinkles and the great plump hands making
staggering blows on his knees; and never had he seemed more
likeable.

April 9th, The Control Yuan. We saw him this morning in a house
close to Marshal Feng Yu-hsiang's house. Yu Yu-jen is nearly seventy.
He wore an emerald gown, and his white beard was very long. He
stood very silently in the middle of the room, bowing and smiling,
the face deeply lined. He is the greatest calligraphist in China, writing with tremendous short sweeps which half-destroy the original
character of the letter, yet the strength is overwhelming.

We talked about the murder of the students and the decay of
law in this country. The smile froze on his face. He shook his head
from side to side, and once he opened wide his hands and said: "I am
ashamed—every day more ashamed. I am the Minister of the Control
Yuan, but I have no power."

I said: "Who can we go to so that justice will be done?"

He answered: "You can go to the Generalissimo."

"Will he listen to us?"

There was no reply.

We spoke of calligraphy, and he offered to write some characters for us. He has written on calligraphy and gave us some of his writings and his recent poems.

He said: "I do what I can that justice should survive, but the Control Yuan has no powers. Dr. Sun Yat-sen desired that it should have powers—yes, the widest possible powers." He suggested that we see Dr. Sun Fo. In theory the Legislative Yuan also has wide powers.

"Then who has power?"

He refused to answer, but when I said: "One man?" he nodded his head.

A little later he said: "The president of the university has sent in his report. It will go through the usual channels."

He said he was overweighed with grief and terror for the future of the country. As a young man he had fought side by side with Dr. Sun Yat-sen; he was almost the oldest surviving member of the original Kuomintang. He had entered many ministries, taken part in many wars, made many visits to many parts of China, conferred for many days with Dr. Sun Yat-sen, and now in old age there was little to show for it except the tremendous dignity of the man. He said: "I am old—in a few days I shall spend my seventieth birthday. I have seen many things." He shook his head sadly again, for so few of those things, except calligraphy and the beauty of the Chinese land, had been pleasant.

He said: "I am old, and Feng Yu-hsiang is old. We belong to the same generation, and we are happy together. We are brothers," and I think it was then that for the first time I realized that deep, fervent, and unchanging desire of the Chinese to form small bands of brothers among themselves. In China everything is so insecure, and the brothers who are dedicated to each other survive longer. So the Generalissimo had formed his small band of brothers, which wielded great power; no power except death can dissolve that brotherhood.

Yu Yu-jen came out of the house and stood for a moment at the top of the steps, bowing gracefully, the white beard against the blue sky of his gown, an old man whose memory was failing, who knew that power had been taken from him, yet he remained upright and would remain so to death.

April 10th. Nothing surprises me any more in Chungking. I saw a man walking stark naked through the Street of the Seven Stars this morning, and hardly anyone turned to watch him; I saw a mad girl reeling and singing drunken songs, and no one paid any attention to her except a few children who followed her, whispering among themselves; I saw starved dogs fighting over a bone till the blood sprang. But worse than the things one sees are the rumors one hears—of civil war.

This afternoon, in the rain, I went to see Dr. Sun Fo in his strange circular house overlooking the Chialing River; and on the way I was responsible for the death of a man. I am appalled by what I have done, but I cannot see what I should have done, yet merely by my presence at a certain place and a certain moment of time, the man died, and another has been wounded.

Near Dr. Sun Fo's house a huge army truck was backing into the hillside. Here the road winds steeply above the Chialing River; maize grows on the slopes, and in the rain the road was slippery. I had passed the truck. The driver waved and shouted, *Ting-hao,* and I remember I turned back and grinned at him and caught his eye. He was young, with a full round face, a forage cap and his coat was open at the neck. He slipped the gears with one hand, and with the other waved again, and the army truck began to back against the hillside, and then there was a sound like a subdued sob, the wheels began to race and the truck began to bounce, very slowly, down the hillside, with all kinds of things being thrown from it—clothes, boxes, great strips of tent cloth. It happened in slow motion, and one moment you would see the wheels and the soft underbelly of the truck, gleaming black and silky, and the next moment you saw the torn hood; and then a soldier was thrown clear, to crumple in the red mud of the sloping fields, but there was no sign of the boy who had waved to me. I ran down. It took at least ten minutes to make my way down the slope, and one boy was dead, his back broken, and the boy who had been thrown clear was moaning, his face covered with blood. I tried to stop the blood flowing. Five minutes later some officers came down. Ten minutes later I was in Dr. Sun Fo's drawing room. He had said to friends of mine that he had been puzzled the last time I had seen him, because I wore muddy shorts; now the shorts were more muddy than ever, and bloodstained.

We talked of the death of the students. He said: "What can I do? We have no power. We pass laws, but the government pays no attention to the laws we pass. They invent new laws. They have invented a law relating to the duties to be paid on incoming merchandise. This is a law which the Legislative Yuan has never passed. The government has increased the duty. On what grounds?"

I said: "If there is no law, then there is no nation and there is no revolution. If this kind of anarchy prevails, then everything your father fought for will be lost."

He nodded and said: "We have done our best. We are up against forces over which we have no control. Have you seen the minister of the Control Yuan?"

"Yes, he suggested I should come to see you. Can anything be done to safeguard the lives of the students?"

He answered: "There are laws on the statute book against murderers. If we could have protection for the law——"

He did not go on. The rain poured outside. Fifty yards away they were taking the body of the soldier up the slope. He talked of a book I had written and very kindly lent me a copy of his own book. I have been reading it all evening and do not know which to admire more—the logic of the man or the passion behind the words. He has grown immeasurably since the war; his hates have grown too, and his loves. He shook his fist this afternoon and said: "Must we be saddled with T. V. Soong? He knows nothing—nothing whatsoever—about banking, and he knows nothing of economics. The whole country depends upon him, he orders our whole economy—and look where we have come to! "

April 11th. Eating cherries, I went to Feng Yu-hsiang's house in the country. For miles you go along the road north of Chungking. Here there are no mountains, only great rice lakes, a sense of desolation, crumbling ruins of mat-shed houses. And then quite suddenly the car stops, guards appear from somewhere, and you find yourself walking in the evening mist along the raised mounds between the fields, the sun sinking, the sky like a wound; there is something ill and cheerless about Chungking evenings.

I can never associate Feng Yu-hsiang with any ordinary background. Twice as large as most men, he seems to demand vast mountains and immense rivers to be his accompanists through life; and so it was this evening when the rice lakes seemed to go on forever, and huge shadows of clouds leaped across our paths. Steaming bullocks wound their way slowly through the fields; there was no sound this evening, and no sign of a house.

One should have expected it. The house was in a great gulley hollowed out from the fields, and you reached it by steps carved out of the livid rock. We could see guides coming, with lanterns; and then more guides, and then the lights of the house went on—a giant's palace, not large, but giving in this evening light an impression of immensity. On the rocks beside the path he had ordered his poems to be carved in characters six inches high—he had left his mark on Szechuan, which would remain for generations.

I have forgotten how we spent the time; he talked of Chinese characters, and he refused to talk about the condition of the country—he was *en pantoufles*, happy with his brush, with the sense of security that came from the immense overhanging rocks, this hollow dug out of the earth, the sound of a river somewhere, and the rustling of bamboos.

"Do you like it?" he asked.

"Yes, but it's not real—I've always seen you either on top of mountains, or somewhere in the bowels of the earth."

I went back by car after supper, but nothing was so good as the long journey across the dark mist-laden fields, and the journey back across the same fields turned black and silver in the moon.

April 12th. Still in search of murderers, we went to see Dr. Chiang Mon-lin, secretary of the Executive Council. Years ago I had met him in Chungking and liked him for his courtesy and his gentle devotion to a China that no longer existed. For a while, while I was in Kunming, he was president of Peking University, which was one of the three associated universities comprising Lienta; and I would see him at annual meetings, and sometimes he would pass in his car. For many years he has been head of the Chinese Red Cross. I expected to find him unchanged, helpful, hating murder, but he said nothing that would put our minds at rest.

"I have nothing to do with the universities now," he said, the voice clipped and dry, the life gone from it. "I'm getting old—I can't do more than one thing at a time."

"Is there any way in which we can safeguard the lives of the students?"

"I can't do anything——"

"But people tell me you can. Can't something be done to get the secret police away from universities, away from everything—altogether away?"

He said, the voice like a whiplash: "We must have the secret police, otherwise there is no safety for government officials. I might be shot on my way home."

I spoke of the danger in which the democratic professors found themselves. They were good men, but the military clique of the Kuomintang had threatened them.

He said: "There are men in Kunming whom I dislike intensely—it is no affair of mine what they do. The Democratic League is the tail of the Communist Party." He smiled: "A large dog wagging a little tail——"

I could hardly believe that in his position he could believe such nonsense.

"They are good men, and they are democrats, and they are in danger——"

He said: "They are not good men, they are not democrats."

It was useless to go on. The telephone bell rang. Someone was telephoning to ask whether dollars could be exchanged at a better rate than seemed appropriate according to government rules. He answered: "I will see what can be done."

April 13th. We know him as the Honorable K. P. S. Menon, which sounds intimidating, but not so intimidating as his title: The Indian Agent-General. Of all the foreign representatives to China, he is the most beloved. Men loved and admired Eggleston, the Australian ambassador, in the same way that they love and admire Menon.

We had lunch with him today. His wife wore a scarlet sari and on her forehead there was the red circle; his children were there, in saris also, and there was Wen Yuan-ning the present editor of *Tien Hsia*. The sunlight kept bursting into the large room on the shores of the Chialing River.

Wen Yuan-ning told a story of Madame Kung Hsiang-hsi, the wife of the prime minister. He had a great admiration for Madame Kung, who is the richest woman in China. He admired her for her dignity, her strength of mind, her immense interest in the financial dealings of the country; and this was strange, because Madame Kung's fortune has been amassed at the time when the people of China have starved on an unprecedented scale. Most of all he admired her strength of character, and related a story of her visit to Mussolini. "In the Palazzo Vecchio Mussolini lived and worked in an enormous room. his desk two hundred yards away from the bronze doors. The *carbonieri* led you to the doors, opened them, and you were left alone to walk across the marble floor with Mussolini glowering at you from his desk, his face becoming larger and larger as you approached. But Madame Kung was made of sterner stuff. She refused to walk across the marble floors. She stood there and held her ground, and Signor Mussolini was compelled to walk the full two hundred yards toward her. What a triumph for Madame Kung!"

The triumph, however, was short-lived; someone asked who were the people who had observed the scene.

When Yuan-ning answered: "Signor Mussolini and Madame Kung."

"It is impossible," a young Chinese answered. "Mussolini is dead, and therefore we can have no verification of the story, and are we expected to believe a story she told about herself?"

I shall remember this afternoon for the gracefulness of the saris, Menon's boyish laughter, the sunlight streaming through the window and falling on the gold rings and armbands of the colorful daughters.

April 15th, The Democratic League. Ever since I came to China, I have heard rumors of the League, which was founded in 1941. In all the weary days of civil war and murder, the ideals of the League, caught between the cross fires of the Communists and the Kuomintang, seemed greatest and most likely to succeed, given time and some well-being and great luck. They stood in the center, isolated, often attacked by both sides, always at the mercy of their poverty; for they possessed no army, and unlike the Kuomintang, which could raise money wherever it wished, and under whatsoever conditions it wished, it was poverty-stricken. The League received money in the form of private donations—no other sources were available.

I have known Lo Lung-chi, the spokesman of the Democratic League, for years. Shortly before I went to Kunming, he was dismissed from his post in the university on the Generalissimo's express orders. They said he had spoken bitterly about the Generalissimo's policies, as if that were a crime. It is true that Lo Lung-chi is often bitter, but when there is so much bitterness in the country, it seems strange that he should be marked out for a failing that is almost universal in China.

Occasionally I would call and see him in his small rooms in the former Japanese consulate in Kunming. He worked hard, spoke brilliantly, and though he lacks the power of invoking the admiration and adoration which Wen Yi-tuo invokes, his mind works along straight lines, and his honesty is self-evident. Today, when I called to see him at the headquarters of the Democratic League, he was almost unrecognizable: he had matured, and there was more precision than ever in the clear, cold voice.

"We're trying to work out the plan of mediation, and God knows it's difficult enough. We're getting somewhere, I hope. As I see it, the role of the Democratic League is to represent the moderate groups always, and to convince the extremists on both sides that moderation is necessary at this time—especially at this time. We were working all last night on plans. The Kuomintang threatens to occupy a town in Manchuria by force. The Communists refuse to surrender it. I have begged them both to settle the issue in peace— and let there be no occupation in the ordinary sense, let the city be occupied by a committee which will include one American, one Communist, and one member of the Kuomintang. This is reasonable, surely. We have almost convinced them. Later we shall know whether we have succeeded."

We spoke about the student murders. He said: "If only we could form a coalition government, then we would have guarantees that the law would be just. This above all. We must have a sense of law, or perish."

Of General Marshall he said: "There is nothing so exciting as working with him. He has a mind like a clasp knife. He knows nothing whatsoever about the problems that concern us all—the problems of personalities—but on the subject of peace I have never met a more persuasive advocate. What is certain is that if he fails, no one else will ever succeed. And perhaps he is right—the personalities are not permanent, and the Chinese pay too much attention to them and see even this terrible war in terms of the prestige of generals. General Marshall should at least be able to teach the Chinese militarists that their personalities have no weight against the suffering the civil war produces. He should know—he is the greatest general of them all."

Later I met Carson Chang, who is the head of the National Socialist Party—a party that has nothing whatsoever to do with fascism. He lives in a house near the Generalissimo's, surrounded by woods, the furniture unbelievably Victorian, and English, so that it is almost impossible to believe that you are in China. There are ebony elephants on the mantelpiece, antimacassars, ormolu clocks; and out-

side the bay windows children were playing tennis. Even Carson
Chang himself, in his brown business suit, looks like an Englishman
of Victorian times, pudgy, smiling, with a great forehead and an old-
fashioned, not hesitant, manner. As leader of the Socialists, he has
probably more power than any other leader within the Democratic
League.

He said: "What we are witnessing is the birth not of a new
China, but a very old China indeed. We are struggling slowly, and
not always successfully, to make people realize that they have responsibilities. Our members are students, university professors, school-
teachers, technicians. We simply do not know how many members
there are in the Democratic League, but of one thing we are
sure—we represent a large body of moderate opinion. We have
worked closely on the boards which have been brought into being in
an effort toward mediation. We stand for certain very simple principles, and the most simple of all—*habeas corpus.*

He went on: "We have our representatives in various towns, and
as you know they are constantly being attacked and threatened. We
know the names of the people who threaten them, but we can do
nothing—they are in positions of power. But at least we are struggling, we know that in the end the difficulties may be insuperable,
but someone will have to take the moderate path—we cannot simply
watch China being torn between two extremes. Outside China, they
know very little about us. We are supposed to be an infinitesimal
party, without power or influence. Partly true. But we do represent
great untapped forces, for the Chinese are naturally moderate and
this new passion for extremism will pass. Meanwhile we need all the
help we can get, and we hope to have constitutional government
—then, and then only can the moderates exert their power."

April 18th, General Marshall. He came back to China two days ago,
and word came yesterday that he would see me. We live in the
baking heat of full summer, the roads glaring white, dust everywhere,
the subdued roar of the city breaking on exposed nerves; but in T. V.
Soong's house near Liang Lou K'ou everything was quiet, and General
Marshall in stern khaki uniform looked as though he had lived all his
life in cool weather.

He was taller than I expected, the chin firmer, the eyes clearer;
and when he walked across the room there was an amazing elegance
in his movement. The fans whirled above his head, and the immense

painting of tigers behind him accumulated in the dusky shadows a menacing power of revolt and terror; and this was as it should be. After the blinding heat and sunlight outside there was something dreamlike in this room, which seemed immense, full of whirling shadows and tigers.

I cannot remember everything he said, but I remember a few phrases thrown out at random, the odd strength in the voice, the absence of all gestures. This is not strictly true, for during the course of the conversation he made one gesture so overwhelming that I was amazed. Suddenly, and it seemed for no reason at all, looking above my head, he flung out his arm horizontally, the fingers following the line of the arm. The strength of the gesture, for no apparent reason, directed at no visible enemy, the way the head shot up and the eyes gleamed—all these were confusing; and then I heard the scurry of feet and saw a small Chinese general scuttling away from the door, where presumably he had been listening. The general was Yu Ta-wei, the minister of munitions. With a gesture so perfect that it assumed immediate obedience, General Marshall had thrown him out of the room.

We talked of the secret police, the murder of the students, the intolerable abuses of power by the militarists; and though he said little, he nodded, and sometimes the sharp edge of the words, crisp as steel wedges, surprised and delighted me. It is impossible to convey the menace and cautious hate that appeared to exist behind his use of the words "the circle round the Generalissimo." He said: "We are doing our best under the most trying circumstances. I have not given up hope." I asked him whether there was any possibility of introducing into China a legislature independent of the judiciary. He smiled wanly and seemed to be wondering whether American justice was the appropriate model for China and passed on to the affairs of students, saying: "I think all the time of the young. What I am trying to do concerns less the political leaders of this country than the young people of China." He said again: "I think of the young all the time—all the time. I work for them."

I cannot explain the nervousness that overcame me. I was tongue-tied, baffled by the extraordinary pattern of this room—the tigers on the wall seeming at every moment to bear down on the general, the symbolism too perfect to be credible. I know a man who has been through many battles, but he never heard his knees shaking together until he was decorated by Marshall. I asked him why. "I don't know," he answered. "One gets the most damnable impression that he knows everything. It's like that. It's not hero-worship. The man isn't a hero—I don't think he's done any actual fighting, but one gets so appalled by the thought of the responsibilities he has accepted. They were so great, and he was so successful."

Now, when I think of Marshall, I shall always remember the painted and terrible tigers on the wall, the exploding eyeballs and bared fangs, and his own gentleness, and how the tigers and the general met on a hot day in Szechuan, and the Chinese general who disappeared as though he was a bullet shot from an invisible rifle, and somehow the pattern becomes one and what is certain is that if Marshall cannot succeed in bringing the contestants together, everyone else will fail.

Later. I cannot think of any greater contrast than that between General Marshall and Dr. Wellington Koo, the Chinese ambassador to the Court of St. James, whom I saw immediately after leaving T. V. Soong's house. Marshall is simple, direct, without political convictions, stern with the justice of those who have commanded wars. Dr. Wellington Koo is complex, his thoughts weave into entangled and intangible shapes; his political convictions are deep-centered, and because he is a diplomat he must think of advantages rather than abstract justice, and toy with conundrums all his life. Inevitably, thinking of him, one thinks of a spider's web glistening with dew and waving in the wind. He speaks English excellently and precisely, and it was possible to admire him and at the same time to realize that he was the diplomat of diplomats, and the wiliest of all Chinese, who have some experience of wiles.

His hair was white, the face very thin, the lips pursed into a small button, and I have never seen anyone who so much resembled the early portraits of Henry VIII. The half-shuttered lids expressed continual weary surprise at the malice of the world. He had been a diplomat all his life. He believed rightly that diplomacy still has its place in human intercourse, and he said he regretted that foreign ministers now thumped the table and spoke outright for home consumption rather than followed the old pattern, which was to speak quietly, decorating all subjects with politeness.

"Something has gone," he said, "and may not return. In the old days we could make some kind of compromise. It is not difficult to thump tables." He brought his fist down on his open palm. "You see, I can do it as well as the next man, but why do it? It will get headlines, but I am not sure that the acquisition of headlines is worthwhile. If you want peaceful settlements, then the old mediaeval policy was still the best—we spoke quietly, hardly above whispers, and tried to get a compromise, which inevitably made you lose face—but you didn't lose so much face as you do now, when you thump tables."

April 20th. The ponies struggled up the slopes bringing blocks of salt to the high hills where, as evening falls, a multitude of telegraph poles gives the impression of gallows. Evening is the worst in Chungking. Then vapors come from the earth, mist swirls, and though the poverty-stricken bamboo huts huddle in the shadow, and the sores and diseases on people's faces no longer show, the solemnity breeds a kind of remorse: in the evening your conscience strikes—why should these things be allowed? There is the same poverty as when I came here first. A few new streets have been built, you no longer need to climb 321 steps to reach the ferryboat, for they have introduced a funicular railway; and you no longer fear Japanese bombs. At night, too, you are conscious of the secret police, and even today, though I have only spent half an hour in the streets, I have seen gangs of conscripts roped together, walking silently through the dusk.

Tonight the sun set like an eye closing, so softly that we were hardly aware of the coming of darkness, passing from one darkness to another. I have been wandering round the streets, where so much of my life has passed. One walks through these streets in a state of blessedness. Candles gleam inside houses. Red lacquer ancestral altars gleam under hanging red pepper pods. The young girl takes the door from its hinges, lays it gently on the earth outside the hut and sleeps, the light from the ancestral candles burning on her cheeks.

April 29th, Kunming. The sun was strong, the rice fields gleamed in their moon shapes, the whole earth flowered in the sun. Chungking's heat has gone; we enter a more temperate land, where flowers grow all the year round and the earth is soft, and there is less suffering.

Southwest Associated University is coming to the last days of its life. We shall soon leave the mud huts. The students talk of going by truck, knowing perfectly well that there are dangerous roads and perhaps five per cent will die on the way. The roads of China are littered with dead and broken trucks. The skies are equally unsafe, particularly in Yunnan, where the wind currents are dangerous. Some speak of going by rail, but all the bridges into French Indochina are broken. The journey will be hazardous, but all hazards are worthwhile as long as they can reach Peking.

April 30th. Wen Yi-tuo is in good shape, his face very red with sunburn, no longer pale with typhus. Because he led the students down from Peking, he is looking eagerly to leading them back again. "But they want me to attend the People's Political Conference in August in Nanking, so I shall go, and then if there are any students left here——" Some student interrupted at that moment. He said only: "You must do what your conscience dictates," and then the student left. Soldiers were bathing in the pool, and the red-winged dragonflies were already spinning across the universities' small lakes.

He said: "The students have done wonders here. They have gone the hard road, and they have accepted hardship. Do you know, people offer me the most extraordinary temptations to leave China. The University of California wants me to give lectures there next summer. Why? I didn't think anyone knew of my existence. But I shall have to stay."

He spoke about his hopes for the Democratic League.

"We must use whatever pressure we can employ continually on both sides to avert this disaster of all disasters—the civil war. I am proud that the students of this university were the first to realize the danger. And no danger could be greater, for no one can win, and the Chinese people will lose."

I told him of the strange conversation with Chiang Mon-lin, secretary of the Executive Council and former president of Peking University.

"Well, if they want to believe we are the tail of the Communist Party, that is their affair. They make up their beliefs as they go along. Myself, I believe we are the tail of the Chinese people, and we'll keep on waggling."

We went across the Wen Lin-kai. I said I was going to fly to Peking immediately.

"Then your dreams will come true?"

"Yes—part of the dream."

"What's the other part?"

"Oh, peace in China—a hundred things, but peace most of all."

He held my hand.

"We must pray for peace, there *must* be peace. The rest doesn't matter." Then he grinned and said: "I am writing a poem again. I shall dedicate it to you—a very satirical poem about China, and the way so many people squabble over her." Some peasants were passing. "Do you think they want war? There is only one fair generalization about China—we are pacific people—continually at war."

May 5th, Flying to Peking. Never have I seen a landscape so wild, so rock-hewn—the livid green cliffs of lava spreading north of the Yangtse. We climbed straight into the sky, and when we looked down there was nothing but the desert of high blue hills, sharp-edged, covered with forests, uninhabited; and all this happened almost at the moment when we left Chungking—the unimaginable barrenness of the place. Li Po talks somewhere of the "desperate height of these Szechuan hills." It was true enough of Chungking itself, but here the wildness goes to extremes, you fly over mountains where no one seems ever to have lived, mottled and roughened like an elephant's skin, an immensity of peaks, with sometimes a river gleaming like fish scales below. Bucket seats. The airplane slipping and sliding down invisible sudden roads. The sensation of *falling toward* Peking.

Gradually the earth turned yellow. You were conscious of a moment when the green hills became yellow sand, and yet it is not really yellow, there are green shadows and mysterious mists, and there is green still in the crescent-shaped rice fields, and gradually the rice fields disappear, the land becomes less fertile, rock and clay, without trees. No villages—a tenantless land. Professor Chen Ta would say sometimes: "It is nonsense to believe that the population of China is four hundred million—so little of this country is under cultivation, you can travel for hundreds of miles by air and see no villages at all."

We dream of Peking, the gold palaces, the blood-red walls, the bringers of tribute who came once along these hills; but there are no signs of wealth here, a few square-cut fields and then the desolation begins again. A great white gash appears. Perhaps it is the old bed of the Yellow River, which now flows south instead of north. We have been flying for four hours. The airplane plows through dust and throws on dust its amazing shadow. And what is surprising is that through the clouds of dust you see other clouds, low-lying, and they are the only soft things traveling over the vast plain; and then, too, above the dust there shines the blue sky, deeper by far than the molten gold-blue of Szechuan, an intense dark silvery blue.

And then, five hours after leaving the airport, the sand-haze darkens, there are villages everywhere; the airplane swings low—and you have come to a place of golden roofs, everything in squares, an immense city ringed by another immense city, the square city in the center all gold and the larger city which frames it dark blue; and the maize ripening beyond the walls, and blue lakes everywhere. The intoxication of Peking! The delight in order, the marble bridges, the depth and blueness of the lakes, the wide streets with their freight of swift-moving traffic—gold tiles everywhere.

The airplane swung low over the Altar of Heaven: white marble, blue roofs, the perfect circle south of the city where offerings were made at the winter solstice, and all other things are square—the golden imperial city is square, the roads run squarely and the parks and the walls are square. Seen through this summer haze, Peking was absolutely unreal.

May 7th. Gradually over the years one makes one's peace with a city, but here there is peace at once: not friable, but perfect. It is better than all our dreaming, all proportions perfect, all colors brilliant. Over the gate leading into the imperial palace someone in an excess of hero-worship has placed a canvas picture of the Generalissimo, the face blue, the expression sullen, almost snarling. You pass the great wall with its winged cloud-pillars of victory, the marble bridges and the moats, and it is confusing to see this immense portrait overriding all things. Not even the emperor would have dared to place his portrait there; and though this is bad enough, the same face with the same expression looks down from all the other gates.

We wander all day; there are parks, pavilions, smooth asphalt-covered streets, sentries with white Japanese nose bags, the plump and fertile northern Chinese, the grace of the girls who fill the avenues with their bicycles, the utter sparkle of the sky. I have stood at the center of the world and seen all the kingdoms to north and south, standing in the midmost marble circle of the Altar of Heaven, and this was perhaps best of all; coming toward it in heavy noon through a forest of stunted trees. The city seething with life; fairs everywhere, and outside the Legation Quarter so many kimonos, so many Japanese hunting trophies that they are past counting. For the first time in seven years I have come upon second-hand bookshops. Morrison

Street, in the glaring sunlight; the immense marble halls of the Peking Union Medical College; the gaudy painted drum-tower to the north of the city; the rocks, the flowers, the weight and singular proportions of the imperial palace, and all these are perfect. There is no city that can compare with this. Life, with its urgent Chinese flow, passes before the quietness of splendid palaces; and it is all and more than we expected, and we are immeasurably grateful.

For years I have lived in small rat-infested bedrooms; now I live in a palace with two hundred rooms, great courtyards, marble lions guarding the doors; and though the palace is falling into ruins, and the ornamental gates caught fire a few weeks ago, it has a perfection of its own. Sand spills everywhere, but the yellow of the sand seems perfectly appropriate where all that is best is colored yellow. And then, too, there is a child who is half French and half Chinese who lives with me, who has stayed here in a convent throughout the war and whose presence is like a blessing, so perfectly is she endowed with all that is best in East and West. So one lives here, quietly, living behind high walls, as secretly as one could desire, and you have only to cross the courtyards to come out into the golden city.

May 12th. At night the North Lake in Peking glitters in the moonlight, and the old imperial barges float across the smooth surface, and the lovers hide among the cypresses, the dagoba shines ghostly white, and everywhere you look there are black flaring roofs which will turn gold tomorrow. The whole of this lake, all the marble bridges, all the hundreds of buildings around it, and all the temples once belonged to the Empress Dowager; now they belong to the people who crowd everywhere, quietly, with good manners, enjoying the spectacle which was reserved less than forty years ago only for princes and dignitaries.

The wind blows over the lake, the lotuses turn up their smooth undersides, and there are moats a hundred feet wide brimming with water lilies which will ripen in a day or two; already the pink tongues are bursting through. The elaborate gold carving of the decorated pillars still enchants us, and never becomes wearisome. You climb the Coal Hill and see the whole landscape before you, not rigid but spaciously ordered; an empire in a blood-red frame of walls, the wealth overflowing. In this city you move and have your being in a haze of gold splendors; and this is as it should be. Painters are regilding the roofs, men wear the softest silks and fan themselves continually. Prices are rising. Every day a new concrete block-house is set up against the possibility of a Communist incursion; but we cannot take these things seriously, we cannot believe that Peking will ever change.

I have known something of this splendor in Bali, a sense of continual rejoicing, an accepted way of living, a tradition so secure that none could break through it. There are secret police, garrison troops march through the dust, sometimes you will come upon men marching with ropes bound to their trussed arms. All this is true. The war reaches here; there are more and more block houses at street corners—for some mysterious reason there is a block house with a machine gun pointed directly at the Peking Union Medical College, where the Americans, the Kuomintang, and the Communists are trying to make a peace—yet the residual glory remains. There is hardly any poverty, for one can grow fat on maize, and maize is still cheap. There are no beggars, few prostitutes, a sense of security remains, and cigarettes are cheap and food is not yet exorbitantly dear. The havoc may come later, but in these early days of summer, wandering alone or with Jacqueline through the city, all tensions seem to be relaxed, and hopes rise like the roofs of these buildings, which twist into the sun.

May 28th. At the winter solstice the Son of Heaven sacrificed to the Honored Ones. The great yellow palanquin came through a shuttered snow-bound city, the imperial guards raced forward, the emperor threw himself down in penitence before the unawakened sun and the awakened earth. A furnace of green porcelain received the offerings; a white calf, rolls of silk, and hymns from the time of Confucius were sung.

I confess that there is no ceremony I would so much like to see performed as this. In those days there was some balance between men and heaven, and communication flowed down from one to the other. We shall never recapture those days, but at least we have no reason to believe that we have made ourselves better, in our unritualed lives; there may come a time when Peking will be meaningless, and no one will know that there was an ordered way of life which sprang naturally from the soil. The city has been built according to a priestly code, mapped out in the shape of a god—they will tell you that this part of the city represents a man's head, and that part a man's legs opened wide, and that part the utter extremities of his fingers. Rivers flow underground, and this too may be explained, but nothing explains its beauty so well as that in the days when Peking was being built, men believed in their own strength. Strength flows from these palace walls, and certainly it is not the strength of feudalism but of human worship and endeavor. Wealth flowed here from all the provinces of China, but these emperors cannot have been wholly bad who placed their wealth so tenderly and spaciously around them. The springs of religious feeling are beginning to be sealed in China, but as long as the scholars remain to study the ancient poems, we shall know something of the motives that brought this majesty about.

June 3rd. I shall fly soon to Yenan, the Communist capital, where they say it is even hotter. It may be, though I cannot imagine a heat greater than this. Yet it becomes cool in the evening, almost ice cold. The rain comes again, drowning whole courtyards, but in the morning there is only the freshness of raindew and the clearness of the sky. I have been wondering what place in the world most reminded me of Peking, and at last I have found it—an apple orchard in the south of France, ripening in the sun.

A JOURNEY TO RED CHINA

While I was in China, there were three great centers of resistance—
Chungking, Kunming, and Yenan. Chungking was the Kuomintang
capital, Yenan the Communist capital, Kunming the center with the
largest number of students, the greatest universities, and the greatest
concentrations of American power. Inevitably Kunming was compelled
to take the middle course, and the general impression seemed to be: "A
plague on both your houses—let us have peace, and let the best men take
control."

We heard little of Yenan. Very occasionally reports came through.
Yenan was a mysterious valley somewhere in the north, unapproachable
in time of war, still more unapproachable during the time of undeclared
civil war which followed Hiroshima. The Communists knew it as the
administrative center of the Shen-Kan-Ning area—Shen-Kan-Ning standing for the liberated regions of the provinces of Shensi, Kansu, and
Ninghsia. Other areas with equally strange names existed—there was
Chin-Cha-Chi, Chin-Chi-Lu-Yu, Huang Chung, and perhaps twenty
others. Within these areas the Communists claimed to govern a population nearly as great as the population of America. On the borders of these
areas fighting between the Communists and the Japanese or the Kuomintang had been continuous for nearly eight years.

By the kindness of the American air authorities in Peking I was able
to make two flights into Communist territory, one to Yenan and the
other to Kalgan. These notes were written late at night or early in the
morning after long interviews with the Communists. My main interest
was to see what could be done to prevent the civil war, which had already

begun, from spreading. I have attempted no statistical inquiry and no
evaluation of the forces at work. I was interested in people, landscapes,
the hopes men had, their poetry and universities and dances and songs.
I was impressed by the Communists and believed them to be honest
men, cautious, not domineering, scholarly, and careful in their policies.
They had firm hand shakes, clear eyes, and quiet strength.

June 8th, Journey to Yenan. You go down the long road which leads
from Peking to the Western Hills early in the morning. All the way
down the road there are stiff, gold wheat fields in the sun, and here
and there are marble memorials—stone lions, dragons, turtles. You
tell yourself that this is one of the oldest places in the world. The
walls of Peking are crumbling and all over the imperial city grass is
growing through the roof-beams and the thrones of the emperors are
falling into powder, the brocades are torn, and soon there will be
nothing left except the ancient courtyards filled with ruins. It is true
enough, but in this fresh morning air, with the blue haze on the hills,
it does not seem important. The whole place is alive with birds and
immense square fields and farmcarts and workmen—the air has never
been brighter, the colors have never been fresher, and you wonder
why you are leaving Peking to go to an old, abandoned city in northern Shensi.

The macadamized road goes straight to the West Field, where
there were at least fifty airplanes on the ground. They were camouflaged with green and ochre paint to remind you that the war was
hardly over, and they were attended by young Americans in shorts
who looked amazingly tall and fair.

In the airplane there was a doctor, a general, a girl in a red print
frock, some soldiers. The brown paper bags crackled, the pilot came
plunging down the cabin in search of the lavatory and the parachute
harnesses began swinging from side to side. We saw the gold-red
roofs of the summer palace disappearing, and soon we were over blue-
tented mountains, wrinkled like an elephant's skin, with deep green
shadows and here and there a space where a peasant had carved out
on the steep slopes a place to live and farm in. The mountains were
poor pasture. You felt the poverty of the place, and you were shocked
by the white sores on the mountains where rivers had once flowed
and would flow again in autumn, though no water fell down them
now. It was a bleak, hard, desolate unavailing landscape after the rich
yellow plain of Peking, yet it was brilliantly colored, with every variation of blue and green. Then at last the blue tents gave place to the

plains again, the earth changed color, ochre and brown, and much sooner than you had expected you were among the yellow hump-backed mountains of Shensi. Here was loess, most fertile of earths when watered, but the land looked dry, the villages in the valley looked unbelievably small. I do not know why they make China yellow on the map, for China is all colors. From the air it is lead-green over Chungking, and all the colors of the rainbow over Kun-ming. Here it was the color of faded yellow tiles. But where did people live when there was no sign of houses?

After nearly four hours, the airplane came streaking low over a plain between yellow hills, driving straight for a tall pagoda. There followed inevitably that most delightful sensation which comes when one wing shoots straight into the sky, and all the yellow hills were above, and the blue sky lay beneath. Above you were houses, not many, perhaps five or six, a river, caves in the mountains, dusty roads, and you saw the long yellow valley with its loess walls. The pagoda streaked past again. The airfield was a green field, and the first thing you noticed when the cabin door was opened was the sweet smell of dust and grass. This was Yenan.

I never discovered where the sweet smell came from. There was mint in it, and parsley, and scented flowers, and clean mountain air. There was no sign of any flowers, only the long low plain between the hills. The air was cleaner even than the air just outside the walls of Peking, which is cleaner than anything I have known in the south, a soft sweet glowing air which belongs to North China alone. Yet everywhere there was dust.

The valley was the color of yellow dust; the small huts in the fields, the stone bridges, the shops, the hills which were sometimes covered with scrub, all were yellow when seen from a distance. There were three valleys, radiating from the broken walls of Yenan, which was bombed savagely at intervals between 1939 and 1943, so that almost nothing remained. There were almost no trees, though I found peach trees later in a courtyard, and there were pear trees from which they made an excellent wine. There was date wine, too, but there was only one grove of date trees in the whole valley. For the rest it was a hard barren land, the river too low at this season to irrigate the fields, but when autumn came the river would flood its banks. It was the last place in the world where you would expect to find the administrative center of a Communist empire.

There is a river, but no sampans come down it. Women washed clothes by the river, small children paddled in it, and old men clung desperately to the slippery steppingstones. It was so small a river that we hardly noticed it when we flew over it. There were the steep loess cliffs, which glowed at all hours of the day but best of all at sunset: they hemmed you in on all sides, and there were moments when they seemed hard and menacing, and other moments when their soft contours were charming. Their colors were always changing. There were depths upon depths of yellow in those hills. It was easy to imagine that men were content to stay there. You would look out for the sunset and the afterglow, and at dawn again they glowed with an entirely different light. At midday, in the dust and the heat haze, they seemed not to be there at all—they were crumbling, or had already crumbled. Soft earth, so soft that you could dig into it with your fingernails, but sometimes at the foot of the hills you would come upon massed layers of hard white rock.

The dull blue clothes of the people fitted in perfectly with the land, and the people themselves seemed to belong there, as the men of Provence belong to southern France. The land looked old and overworked: occasionally you came upon peasants who looked older even than the land. It was bare enough in summer; in winter, at the time of frost and floods, it must look unendurably barren. But even so, after wandering around it for a few days, you felt that it was a place to stay in, where you could dig your roots deep and attend quietly to the changing of the seasons.

Later. I have come to the end of the world—we are imprisoned by these loess hills, and with the very greatest difficulty can we believe there is any world other than this. It is the oddest impression. You feel that you have come to a place so ancient, more ancient than anything else in China. It is very much like the surrealist paintings you used to see before the war. And everything is in slow motion—the horsemen ride across the valley and over the river in slow motion, and people walk slowly. They walk slowly in Peking because it is a habit there; but here they walk slowly because of the heat. The sky is a deep, ever so deep blue. The starlings chatter in the willows, and there is no breath of air to shake the leaves. Dogs and pigs lie in the shade of stones. There are perhaps sixty thousand people here, but you don't see them—they are hidden in the caves.

Of course it *is* the most ancient place in China. It was among these strange flat-topped yellow hills that the Chinese began their journeys. I am amazed by the curious resemblance of these hills to the temples in Peking. The temples are supposed to be modeled on tents, but there is no record that the Chinese ever lived in tents. These hills, when the winter wheat is ripe, resemble the flaring roofs of the imperial palaces.

June 9th, Red Virtue in the date garden. Chu Teh came along the path through the date trees, limping a little, wearing a dark blue cotton coat, blue cotton trousers, and a blue cap. It was dusk. In this light his face had the color of old bronze, very dark, and he was smaller than I had expected. He grinned and shook hands, and then you noticed with a shock that he was unlike the early portraits, he had grown much older and you could only recognize him by the boyish smile and the broken nose.

We had come a long way from the clustered huts and caves which is all that can be seen of Yenan. In the dusk the starlings went wild, the caves disappeared, there was only the dark outline of the yellow loess cliffs. The sky was dark, and sometimes you saw a wolf prowling in the distance or a solitary white-turbaned horseman coming along the river bank. They said Chu Teh lived in a date garden. There was no sign of a date garden for miles. And then suddenly, very blue against the sand-colored hills, you saw the date trees and a long low earthen wall. It was the headquarters of the commander-in-chief of all the Communist armies in China.

He looked nearly all his sixty-five years, and he resembled none of the photographs taken by Agnes Smedley and Edgar Snow. He was unshaven; there was no beard, but there were a few faint bristles on his chin. You thought at first he was an old farmer, who had seen many wars and had come at last into this date garden in northern Shensi for a long rest before he died. He gave no impression of power, but he did give an impression of dignity and composure, and a kind of quietness. You see telegraph wires among the date palms, and you wonder what the devil they are doing there. He had small bright eyes—Edgar Snow says they are large, but they are small nevertheless—and there was something birdlike even in that slow limping walk which led up to a terrace near the caves from where you could look down on the darkening valley. When he took off his cap, you saw that his hair was thinning, but it was still jet-black, and when he smiled he had the teeth of a young boy in the face of an old peasant. He was a good man, a *hao jen,* and you wondered why he kept a few soldiers around the place.

He spoke very quietly and confidently, in a husky voice, and sometimes there was in it I do not know what note of disturbing somberness, as of a man who knows that date palms live forever and all men die young. He was so obviously the good farmer that you were amazed by the legends that had grown up around him. Was it true that he had led the Long March? Was it true that he assisted Ts'ai Ao in dethroning Yuan Shih-k'ai? Was it true that once in Yunnan he had lived in great state, with concubines and opium pipes and immense wealth? Was it true that he had directed the Hundred Regiment attack against the Japanese, and countless other attacks? They were all true enough, but it was hard at first to reconcile the old farmer with the legends.

It was growing dark, the moon was rising, and there was only a single soldier standing like a shadow against the low wall. The battle of Shihpingchieh had come to an end a week before. It was a bloody engagement which lasted a month. The Communists retreated. The Kuomintang official newspapers announced that there had been 100,000 casualties on both sides. It was positional war with a vengeance. In *Red Star Over China* Edgar Snow quoted General P'eng Teh-huai: "Static warfare must be avoided. In a lengthy positional war the enemy has every advantage, and in general the chances of partisan success diminish in proportion to the duration of the battle." The Kuomintang were credited with having thirty tanks and ten bombing planes. Up to that time the Communists had never fought positional wars on any large scale. Why did they fight them now?

Chu Teh answered: "Why not? We had to hold up their advance—they were getting swell-headed. They forgot we are a strong army and capable of positional warfare. There were very good strategical reasons why we should hold them up. Shihpingchieh is an important nerve center. The enemy did not know we would defend it, did not know our strength, and fell blindly into a trap. It lasted a month and stopped quite a lot of their energy. The casualties were less than the Kuomintang have recorded. We lost ten thousand. They lost more."

Of the fate of the prisoners he said: "They killed the prisoners they captured. We did not need to kill the prisoners we captured. There is never any need to kill the prisoners we capture. They are fascists." He said "fascists" with a faint note of bitterness, hiding the real bitterness. The voice became louder and tougher. "They kill and arrest everywhere. They have prisons and secret police everywhere. We must have an end to the secret police and we must have a democratic government. If the Kuomintang had carried out the People's Consultative Council's agreements in February, there would never have been the civil war. There are three agreements—the reform of the government along democratic lines, the reorganization of the armies and the cease-fire agreements. The Kuomintang violated these agreements, rejected democratic reforms, and insisted on maintaining its dictatorship on a nationwide scale. This dictatorship claimed to rule our liberated areas. At a meeting called to congratulate the success of the People's Consultative Council, they sent in their hired thugs to attack the great poet Kuo Mo-jo and half a dozen others, including Li Kung-po.* Do you like it? Our Chinese Kuo Mo-jo is like your Bernard Shaw. Do you like it?"

He spoke with energy but very quietly. It was growing dark. An oil lamp with a brown paper shade was placed on the table among the cups of tea. A soldier came and threw a thin coat over Chu Teh's shoulders. You could see only the dark face in the glow of the lamp. He went on: "We don't want to fight a civil war, but their troops attack us, they close down all our newspapers in Peking and Shanghai, and they keep on arresting and murdering us and breaking agreements. What else can we do but resist? I say deliberately they are fascists. Under a fascist dictatorship how can we realize peace?"

I said: "Both sides are stiffening, and as far as I can see we are in danger of a civil war that may last ten years."

"If there is no democratic government, it may well last ten years. The Kuomintang must keep their political agreements. If they would set up a democratic government according to the Foreign Ministers' Conference, the civil war would end at once. We cannot—we must not have a fascist government ruled by one man and a small party clique. We want democracy and nothing else. As for the help the Americans have given the Kuomintang, let bygones be bygones—we will not quarrel about the past. The Kuomintang couldn't fight us if they didn't get gasoline for their airplanes and ships for their troops. I cannot understand why America should want to support a dictatorial government. All over the world it is a question of the realization of democracy—and democracy means a coalition government. Democracy doesn't mean secret police, dictatorship, tortures, murders, and the disappearance of people everywhere."

He was still speaking quietly, but when he mentioned the secret

* Li Kung-po was murdered by Kuomintang officers in July 1946. He had previously been attacked at the conclusion of the People's Consultative Council in February.

police his voice rose. He would mention them again and again, so that they were like an accompaniment throughout the long four-hour conversation at night.

I said: "There is an impasse somewhere, and it must be solved."

"How would you solve it?"

"I don't know enough, but I would guess three things are necessary. Reduce the whole Chinese army immediately to a token army. The Chinese army cannot fight against the great powers—America, Britain, or Russia. Put it on the frontiers of China, and it cannot fight. Put it inside China—it can only fight Chinese. Would you be prepared to dissolve the Communist army altogether, or make it a small token army?"

He thought for a while, grinned, and said: "Yes, if the Kuomintang do the same. I agree that we cannot fight foreign powers, and the army is only good for fighting between ourselves. Why not dissolve the air force and navy—we cannot fight foreign powers with them?"

"There are two other things that seem to me necessary," I went on. "The leaders on both sides should go. A democracy is best run by ordinary people. The leaders have far too much prestige. The prestige of Aristides in ancient Greece was too great—so the people got rid of him. I think it was the same thing with Churchill. It was necessary to get rid of him. The country is too small to bear the weight of its great men. Would you be prepared to go, if the Kuomintang leaders also went?"

He answered quickly: "It is not just a question of deposing some of the leaders. The Communist Party has 1,200,000 members in China. The Kuomintang has a large membership. The leaders are not important, the parties are important."

"There is a very real danger which comes from the tremendous prestige of the leaders on both sides. Would you and Chairman Mao Tse-tung be prepared to go if the leaders on the other side also went?"

"Yes, if there was a real danger, we would be prepared to go."

"Thirdly, there must be free elections, as there are in America and England."

His face lit up.

"I agree entirely, but the government should not be a government which carried out 'false democracy,' and the democratic practices of the Kuomintang are all false."

We had not got very far, because as things were in China none

of the three propositions seemed workable. They were probably necessary: it is possible that there was no other solution, but it was
improbable that any of these things would be carried out in the near
future. China was at the mercy of forces over which the people had
no control. But it was good to see Chu Teh agreeing with the propo-
sition that the leaders should go if there was "a real danger." He
rubbed his chin, grinned, and drank some tea. It was very strong tea.
I could still see only the dark reddish-brown face behind the oil
lamp.

More than anything else now he resembled the old farmer. He
was an old man, he had seen many wars and he preferred to live
among his date palms; he was looking out into the distance, the
moon had risen over the black cliffs, and the soldier was still standing
by the low parapet.

"Let us go back to what we have been saying," he said. "I agree
we must dissolve the army, or at least make it much smaller. But how
can we dissolve their secret police? We have no secret police, no
torture chambers. We can only get rid of these things with a democratic government. How can we get a democratic government? There
are elements in America which are supporting Chiang Kai-shek
against the people. I have met General Marshall. He came to Yenan.
We trust him, but we do not understand why America is supporting
the Kuomintang against us. If for one month America refused to
support the Kuomintang armies, there would be an end to the civil
war."

I mentioned the violations that had been committed, according
to executive headquarters, on both sides. He said: "I emphatically
deny that there have been violations of the truce on our side."

I was surprised by this and asked whether there were not sometimes moments when communications between the widespread and
decentralized Communist areas become difficult. Orders from headquarters were perhaps not always carried out.

"There may be delays of two or three days," he answered, "but
there is no difficulty of communication. We have radios."

"What are the possibilities of peace?"

"If we can extend the truce now or later, there may be peace. At
some time or other it may be possible to get together and work out a
peaceful solution."

It was growing darker and colder, and we went into the cave.
There was no furniture, no maps, only a small table and three battered sofas with springs pushing out through the cloth. The oil lamp

was placed on the table. You could see him more clearly now, for the walls were whitewashed and reflected the oil lamp. He looked older than ever, but he looked stronger. He said:

"We are not an independent government. We are a temporary government, without consuls or any official intercourse with foreign powers. Yet there are 130,000,000 people in the liberated areas. We want international intercourse and we want trade, but we have only three ports, Wei-Hai-wei, Chefoo, and Lungho. We would like foreigners to come here, and we guarantee their freedom of movement, and we guarantee freedom to all missionaries. We want trade—international trade. We will not confiscate and we will not break our agreements. . . . In our border areas production is steadily increasing."

I asked him to define Chinese Communism, for it was evident that Communism in China differed from Communism elsewhere.

He said: "Chinese Communism is democracy plus capital."

I very nearly jumped out of my chair.

"It is quite easy to explain," he went on. "The Chinese Communists employ the Marxist theory in their analysis of social, political, and economic conditions in China. The conclusions they draw are those that answer the needs of the people. There is not yet any Marxist Communist theory in actual practice—it is still in fact largely a capitalist system. In China today we support the capitalist system, because today the Communist system of Marx is no more than an ideal. The only prospect of Communism lies in the distant future. To be Communist now would not be realistic. China today cannot realize such a system. Today, the system that can be carried out and is needed by the people is democracy with the free development of capital. We must develop our capital resources and increase the wealth of the people and raise their livelihood, and we can only do this by industrialization and foreign investment. Our program has always been to find out what people want and to satisfy their needs—it was only by doing this that we could be successful against the Japanese. We will not confiscate the wealth of the capitalists, but we will not allow big trusts to be formed. We want democracy, free elections, and an end to the feudal rule which the Kuomintang has inherited from the Manchus."

Saying this, he had put on a pair of horn-rimmed spectacles and resembled the old farmer no longer. He was an elderly professor, who spoke quietly and distinctly and a little wearily, as though he knew beforehand that there was so much distrust against Red China abroad that it was impossible to make people realize that Communism was no longer the immediate objective.

He went on: "How can we exist without capital? Our standard of living is so low. We must have the means of production to raise the standard of living of the peasants, and we cannot have it without capital. We are not against private capital, and we cannot follow the Russian model." And then, later: "This is not Communism—this is the new democracy."

It was growing late, the lamp flickered on the rickety table and he looked more than ever the elderly professor who had returned after an exhausting lecture. A soldier came in and handed him a slip of paper. He glanced at it, and in silence handed it back again, and we were still somewhere at the end of a long low whitewashed tunnel. He talked about the Long March.

"They keep on thinking of us at that time as small guerrilla units," he complained. "We were not small guerrilla units—we were a comparatively large army, and so our activities were different from those of the Russian guerrillas during the war. We were an army continually increasing in numbers, because more and more villagers came to join us. Through the whole journey we relied for our intelligence on the villagers, and they gave us food, transport, and supplies. We had little time for training. The training came largely on the field. We had some well-trained officers. Both P'eng Teh-huai and I were old Kuomintang officers who went over to the Communists when we realized that the Kuomintang was simply a machine of oppression. During the revolution of 1911 I was a company commander. When the Yunnanese revolted against Yuan Shih-kai, I was already in command of a regiment. I was a member of Dr. Sun Yat-sen's Tung Meng Hui, a forerunner of the Kuomintang. Afterwards we were always fighting against the war lords. We were regular soldiers first and partisan leaders afterwards.

"Our tactics developed gradually. Partly they came from our experiences in the regular army, and they came too from books. One book which impressed us immensely was a book on the American war of independence. But it was not books or technical knowledge which were most useful—more useful than anything was the creative ability of the masses. We fought for political aims, our tactics depended on political aims. During the Long March we wanted to get to the northeast as quickly as possible, because it was from there that the greatest danger from the Japanese arose, and this was what the people wanted. We had artillery, mountain guns, and mortars. We were not really guerrillas—we fought positional wars in Hunan, Kweichow, Szechuan, and Kansu. We were a real army then, and we are a real army now."

For years I have been obsessed with the beauty and revelation of character which comes from Chinese calligraphy, and I was glad when he showed me some of his handwriting. It was very much what might be expected: heavy and dark, the characters crowded together, the down strokes thick and determined, each character over an inch high. There was the beauty of ruggedness and heavy deliberation, and more than anything else of determination. It was his commonplace book. He turned over the pages slowly, the thick local-made paper crackling under thumb and forefinger. On each page there appeared a character so perfectly in keeping with the man that the revelation was complete. Then very slowly he put down the book, which contained heaven knows what secrets of diplomacy and military affairs, and we went out into the garden, past the solitary guard on the parapet, the date trees, and the small gate. There were no signs of the guards. The stars shone, and some low clouds were moving up the valley in the west.

Chu Teh, which means "Red Virtue," definitely does not look like the great military leader; he has no tics, no gestures, no dramatic flair. Somehow the photographs had never suggested the heavy reddish-brown color of the deeply tanned face; they showed neither the smile nor the firmness nor the slow voice. The greatness of the man was not apparent, and he remained the old farmer until very slowly the accumulation of so much patience and quietness and instinctive strength revealed the man in his direct simplicity. This was not Feng Yu-hsiang's simplicity, which is infinitely complex. He was a farmer who had planted his trees, and whatever storms came, he was determined they would grow.

This was not greatness as we are accustomed to measure greatness. He was incapable, I think, of turning on suddenly and capriciously any personal power. He had no mannerisms—he had killed the marionette, or perhaps he was too old, and the marionette no longer possessed any validity. When you are sixty-five and have spent all your life fighting and see no end to the fighting, it would be strange if you continued to think in terms of drama. There was no drama—only a great impatience and sadness. Once he escaped arrest by throwing a white towel around his waist and shouting: "I am the cook. Why kill me, when I can prepare such good food for you?" Today, he could no longer disguise himself as a cook. He seemed to have no love for power, and the only concession he ever made to his title of commander-in-chief was to wear occasionally a drab purple cloak with a ragged fur collar. You do not grin like a boy unless you have a good conscience. Among the date palms and in the great silence of the cave tunnel he gave the impression of an old peasant who was simply saying the things that were on his mind.

A wolf was prowling on the walls of the garden when we went out; it stood there, shaggy and thin and black against the moonlight, then suddenly jumped away and disappeared in some undergrowth. As the jeep rolled through dust clouds toward the river, some more wolves appeared, but they too scattered. A cold wind came down the valley, the date garden disappeared, there was only the moonlight, the hills, and the darkness of the plains between the black cliffs. Once a candle gleamed in a cave high up the mountainside. When the candle went out, the valley looked lonelier than ever.

June 10th. The soldier came walking up the hill with a gray pack over his shoulders, his blue cotton uniform stained bright yellow with dust. He had a round red face, the color of a red pippin, and he wore the uniform of the Communist army, which is exactly the same as the uniform of all the other soldiers in China—the same blue and white enamel badge on his cap, which signifies the white sun in the blue sky, the same cut of the coat, the same puttees—but on one arm there was a small white square with the legend: 18 G A. The old Eighth Route Army has been transformed into the Eighteenth Group Army. He was about eighteen, and he walked up the hill looking in no way different from the soldiers in the south except that he looked better fed.

We watched him as he left the road, where the dogs were sleeping and the horses were plunging against the rock to avoid the only automobile that had passed that day. He went down to the river, took off his wheat-straw sandals, and bathed his feet. Then he waded through the river and climbed up the bank toward one of the caves in the hills, and for a long while we heard him singing. And for days afterward you remembered the clear smile and the sound of the voice coming across the darkening valley.

June 11th, The dance in the peace orchard. The yangko dance has an old history. It may be as old as historical China. There are songs in the *Book of Odes* that may have been danced to these simple steps and simple drum beats. Usually the dance was performed at the time of transplanting, and again at harvest, and at wedding festivals, wherever there were great feasts and ceremonies.

It cannot have changed very much through the centuries, but it was changing now. The dance remained, but the Communists were inventing a new kind of dance—the *yangko* was played at the beginning and the end, but in between there were short plays. These plays were occasionally acted separately and had grown up with the tremendous new interest in drama. Now the Communists were using the *yangko* dance and the play in a deliberate effort to change the old village customs. There were plays against witchcraft, illiteracy, and bad habits; there were plays designed to show the necessity of increasing production, co-operatives, medical work in villages, and sanitation. In the old *yangko* the leader held an open umbrella and was followed by long dancing lanes of boys and girls, heavily painted, in gaudy dresses. They raced from one courtyard to another, sang songs, danced to the sounds of a pigskin drum. The love dances were the best. In these the two lanes of boys and girls danced facing each other, swaying their bodies provocatively, clapping their palms on their knees, bending forward or leaping backward, while the clown buffooned and the audience beat time to the drums. Sometimes fireworks were let off. The dance differed slightly from village to village, but in essentials it was simply a slow dance—three steps forward and one back—which became more and more furious as the dance progressed. Sometimes there were competitions between the villages. Also, the musical accompaniment could be changed at leisure, and from time to time new songs were invented. Essentially, it was a robust dance for the young, which may have had its origin in a fertility cult, a complex interweaving of two lanes of youngsters.

When the Communists first came to northern Shensi, they watched the dances but did nothing to change them. They might never have changed them if there had been no war against Japan. In 1939 they began to realize that the dance could serve as the introduction and the finale of a new kind of propaganda, which would reach all the villages in the areas over which they ruled; for the villagers were known to have an extraordinary fondness for these dances, which they cultivated on every possible occasion. They began tentatively by replacing the leader with an umbrella (who may have represented the emperor) by a farmer carrying farming implements. They allowed the love dances to continue, but they insisted that there were other things as important, and they replaced the clown with a Japanese or a traitor. The first of the new *yangko* dances were deliberately designed to increase production, and the first of all was called "Brother and Sister Cultivating the Virgin Land." It was a clever title, for "brother and sister" in Chinese folk song have the significance of "lover and beloved."

The new play introduced between the old dances was purely experimental. It was to be performed in the open air by a small group selected from the dancers, and it had to be written with extreme simplicity so that it could be followed easily by all the villagers. There was no tradition. They improvised on the basis of the symbolic traditions of the Chinese stage. A farmer could suggest the presence of mountains by standing on his toes and shading his eyes; the crackle of machine-gun fire could be expressed by cymbals; animals were simply men wearing masks; but since the actors in the play wore their ordinary blue cotton costumes, how could you distinguish between them? You could, of course, make them announce to the audience that they were tax collectors, government officials, farmers, labor heroes, or people fleeing from the Japanese. It was not difficult, but it was a waste of time, and traditional Chinese stage, by using deliberate artifices of gesture and symbolic costumes, had long ago got over this difficulty.

In the peach orchard near the small house where Mao Tse-tung lives, the *yangko* dance was being played. The setting was perfect, and because it had rained recently, the peach leaves gave off a heavy scent. The audience formed a circle around the dancers. On one side there were Western violins playing together with Chinese violins, on the other sides there were cymbals and flutes. The dancers came rushing in, tall Shensi boys with white knee breeches, brightly colored waistbands and green shirts, with their heads in colored kerchiefs. They danced amazingly well, beating both sides of the drums and singing a song of welcome, which changed later into a song in praise of democracy and peace. The drum beats became louder, the beat more insistent, and they were followed by boys and girls with heavily rouged faces who began to weave within the magic circle of the garden incredibly complex patterns to the tune of the violins, the cymbals, and the drums. You could recognize the ancient pattern of the love dance, though the words had changed, for they formed two lines and came together and parted, and raced and clapped hands and in general followed the pattern of the ancient steps of the dance; and though the songs had been changed, the imitation of the emotions of love remained. And then very suddenly, in a final roar of drum beats, they departed and their places were taken by the protagonists of the interlude.

There were two interludes. The first was a comic movement in the drive against illiteracy, showing how a small farmer sends a letter from the town to his old father, saying that the price of beans had gone up. The old man could not read. He asked help from another farmer and was told that the price of peas had gone up. He knows that if he leaves his fields near harvest time he is in danger of losing his crops, but the price has gone up so much and he is so avaricious that he decides to set out with his peas. He goes to the town. He cannot find his son, and he discovers that the price of peas has not gone up at all. Cursing, he returns to the farm and discovers that his son has forestalled him, his crops are ruined, his daughter-in-law, who can read, is insulting him and life is no longer worth living. Some of this is spoken, but most of it is song. The audience is roaring with laughter—the old man is near tears and even toward the end argues bitterly against book-learning. "You can't make children by book-learning, you can't raise crops by book-learning, it's all a waste of time." He dances round the ring in an agony of remorse, shaking his head, nervously lighting his long silver pipe, forever bewildered by the magic power of the words he has misunderstood, until in the end, with the blissful smile of the initiated, he promises faithfully to learn to read.

It was a morality, and absurdly simple, but it was evidently effective. It was not a theoretical incident; it was an incident that had happened very often, and it was played dramatically and effectively by actors who knew how to imitate the finest gestures of the peasants. They spoke in the local dialect, there were purely local jokes, and though doors were opened according to the same gestures that take place on the Chinese stage, and a twelve-hour journey on foot from the village to the town was accomplished in two minutes, it was clear that the audience could identify itself with the actors.

And then the dancers came in again, the interlude was over and the pure dance took the place of insistent propaganda. Once again there was the beat of the drums, the heavily painted faces, the swirl of skirts and waistbands, and the clear voices of the singers. The thumping of their feet on the earth, the small clouds of dust, the tremendous force of the drums—they were things that you remembered for long afterward, because they seemed so appropriate to these thickset, sturdy people. There was nothing professional in their dancing; they danced with a kind of natural abandon, and because they liked dancing, and because they were young. So had they danced in the time of Confucius, and so too would they dance when all our present quarrels are over.

June 12th, The Communist general. He was vice-commander-in-chief of the border armies, not tall, though he gave the impression of height, but dark and swarthy, and like nearly everyone else in Yenan he grinned like a boy. He had been ill of a stomach complaint for a long time, but looked healthy and even vigorous, and he wore the usual wheat-straw sandals and faded blue cotton coat without insignia. He walked heavily and determinedly; his hands were fine and covered with innumerable dark wrinkles, and sometimes when he spoke the eyes seemed to fill with pain. He was General P'eng Teh-huai. He had been fighting since he was eighteen.

The military leaders in the border areas belong to no special type, but among them you notice very soon two dominant trends—those who resemble peasants, though sometimes they were never peasants, like Chu Teh, and those who resemble scholars, like Mao Tse-tung and Chou En-lai, though they are scholars who have never taught or studied for any length of time. P'eng Teh-huai resembled a thickset peasant even to the heavy curve of the shoulders and the dark sunburned hands. He did not seem, like Chu Teh, to be completely at ease in the world; nor was he nervous. He was a man who had hated and fought passionately, but with a clear brain, with little education but immense driving force. He had led one of the four armies which composed the Long March, and now, as he spoke of those days which were already disappearing into legend, there was an odd sadness in his voice. The old voice came from the youngish face. So perhaps had Napoleon's generals spoken in the years before Waterloo, remembering the victories in Italy and the Nile.

He spoke about the past for more than three hours, delighting in his reminiscences.

"If you go back a long way, you can see how it all began. You have to go back to the time when Sun Yat-sen was still alive, and the Whampao Academy was being born, and from Canton there was being planned the long march to the north against the warlords. It was 1923. Under Sun Yat-sen there was peace between the Communists and the Kuomintang, and in Whampoa Academy itself there were important Communist leaders like Chou En-lai, Lin Po-chu, and Li Fu-chun.

"Sun Yat-sen had proclaimed that only a people's army could fight the war lords in the north, and in fact it was a people's army which began the march from Canton. During the first stages of the march, until the army reached Wuhan, there was complete co-ordination between the Communists and the Kuomintang. The march had three main purposes: to resist foreign imperialism, particularly the Japanese, to wipe out the war lords, and to create a democratic government. But when we reached Wuhan, it became clear that the right wing of the Kuomintang was not prepared to resist foreign imperialism, was indeed prepared to make overtures to them. On April 12th, 1927, there was the Kuomintang *coup d'état.*

"The Great Revolution failed. There was a reign of terror, and hundreds of men were arrested and later killed. The Kuomintang, instead of collaborating with the revolutionary forces, co-operated with the feudal forces in order to overthrow the revolutionary movement.

"There followed the Nanchang uprising, organized by General Yeh Ting and supported by Madame Sun Yat-sen and many other liberal elements. General Chu Teh, at that time, was only a regimental commander in Yeh Ting's armies. No one had ever heard of him until then. The uprising failed. Chu Teh led a thousand survivors through Kiangsi into Hunan.

"As I say it now, it is not very exciting—names of battles, places, marches. But they *were* exciting, though the old revolutionaries have gradually forgotten them. The battles all become one. But at this stage there occurred battles that are remembered by us, for suddenly Mao Tse-tung comes on the scene.

"In 1927 Mao Tse-tung was organizing peasant self-defense corps in Hunan. At first they had no weapons—only sharp sticks, spears, bayonets. Later they were to capture rifles from the Hunan provincial troops. Mao Tse-tung was moving around the area of Tingchiang in eastern Hunan, and then he came south to Chingkansan, an extraordinary range of mountains, not very accessible, which produces two or three good crops a year and where you can live in some kind of isolation. Mao mobilized the peasants and redistributed the land. Chu Teh came up from the south and joined him. He had begun with hardly a thousand soldiers, and by now he had hardly more than 2,000. Out of these 2,000 and the peasants on Chingkansan two regiments were formed—the 28th under Chu Teh, and the 31st under Mao. I have forgotten why these regiments were given these numbers. Perhaps there was no reason, or they wanted the enemy to think they had many regiments. It was the first time Mao

Tse-tung had met Chu Teh, and it was the beginning of the formidable combination which was to be known later as Chu-Mao.

"So there were two regiments defending the mountain, and several guerrilla units armed with old spears and swords and whatever
else they could lay their hands on. It was the winter of 1927. The
Hunan provincial troops and the Kiangsi troops were sent against
them, and there were even Yunnanese forces under Chu Peh-teh. It
was the first of the annihilation campaigns. I wasn't there, but Lin
Piao was there. Lin Piao, who comes from Hupeh, was a battalion
commander of the 28th regiment under Chu Teh. He was unknown
then. They were to hear about him later.

"We did not stay on the mountain. When we had broken their
attacks, we attacked. We destroyed five regiments under Chu Peh-
teh at a place called Yunghsin on the eastern borders of Kiangsi and
captured 7,000 rifles. This was the beginning of our military strength.
Afterward, in the spring of 1928, Chu Teh led his troops to southern
Hunan, taking the main forces away from the mountain stronghold.
Chingkansan was left now weaker than ever—there were only guerrillas
and untrained troops to defend the mountain. The Kiangsi and
Hunanese troops heard that the mountain was undefended. They
brought between 20,000 and 30,000 troops against the mountain,
against Mao Tse-tung, and perhaps 400 well-trained guerrillas. This
was all he had, but he was well entrenched, the peasants on the
plains would work for him, and they managed to break up the
enemy's supply lines.

"Remember that in those days there were no airplanes, no railways, no tanks, no trucks. The defenders knew the terrain and concealed the grain, and it was not impossible for them to put to flight
armies vastly superior to theirs by sudden, devastating attacks. We
had an excellent intelligence system, and besides Mao Tse-tung,
whose military training came from the field, there were regular
officers like Chang Tse-ching, who was later killed in action. At the
battle of Wangyangchieh, Mao Tse-tung and his guerrillas routed an
army of 20,000 men. The victory partly belonged to Chang Tse-ching,
who was regimental commander at the time, but it was Mao who
organized the peasants and constructed a vast intelligence system
and directed the campaign. The mountain was still in our hands. We
waited for another annihilation campaign, for we had no strength at
this time to attack.

"I say 'we' did this, but I was not there. I knew very little about
what was happening until the third of the annihilation campaigns, in

the winter of 1928. At this time Mao Tse-tung and Chu Teh left the mountain and went to Fukien and southern Kiangsi to organize the peasants. I was left in charge of the defenses of Chingkansan.

"In July 1928 I had organized an uprising in Pingchiang in northeastern Hunan. I heard about the defense of Chingkansan, and after the uprising failed, I led about a thousand men to join the mountain soldiers. By this time our forces had grown. I had a thousand men, and the peasants were flocking to the mountain, so that we had between 4,000 and 5,000 men altogether, with a considerable number of bayonets and rifles. But we were still weak in numbers compared with the enemy. They said publicly they had 60,000 well-trained and well-equipped troops. They may have had about 45,000. At that time Chu and Mao were somewhere in western Fukien. The enemy had good leaders. Their officers were all regular Kuomintang officers. They had three armies, with Chu Peh-teh in command of the Third Army. But we defeated them, first in hundreds of skirmishes and later in battle. It was the first time the Kuomintang used radios: we did not even have telephones. Nevertheless we drove them away. Actually we never had radios at all until after the battle of Changsha in 1930. Even if we had had radios, we would not have known how to use them.

"We occupied Changsha for ten days in 1930. It started with the anniversary meeting at Pingchiang the year after the uprising. Ho Chien's troops arrived, but we routed them about six *li* away and then decided to follow them. We had nothing to lose, and they were very frightened. Changsha was defended by five regiments—a total strength of about 30,000. To attack Changsha with our 10,000 was technically impossible—the city was difficult to attack and favors the defender—but our morale was high, and we were bitterly determined to show the war lords that peasants can muster enough force to get through. We got through. We fought a nasty engagement on the Nanling river fifteen *li* from Changsha and attacked with bayonet charges, since our main weapons were bayonets. It was costly. We had between 2,000 and 3,000 casualties. There was fighting along the approaches to Changsha the whole day and part of the night, and even when we had entered the city, there was still fighting going on outside. It was a hard war, and in ten days Ho Chien was bringing so large a force against us that we evacuated.

"We had started from small beginnings. We were still small. In the Nanchang uprising we were still smaller. After the defeat in Kwangtung, there were left only Chu Teh's troops numbering about a thousand and Mao Tse-tung's peasant guerrillas armed with spears and homemade bayonets—and there was the uprising I directed at Pingchiang. Now we had large resources in equipment, and we were beginning to think we were a real army. We withdrew from Changsha to southern Kiangsi. The enemy began to launch another annihilation campaign under the direct orders of Chiang Kai-shek. We defeated them, we captured their signal officers and began to learn how to use radio. We were 10,000 when we captured Changsha. Now we were at least 17,000, for our losses were more than made up by farmers and workers who joined the army.

"The uprising at Pingchiang was an entirely independent peasant uprising. I did not join the Communist party until March 1928. I had no real military training, though I studied for a while in the Hunan Military College. Military schools are useful for giving you technical knowledge, but you learn more on the field, and battles are largely fought with morale—it was hatred of imperialism and warlordism that drove us on. The oppressing powers are always more powerful in military equipment, but they lack the morale of the oppressed. The American War of Independence lasted eight years. We modeled ourselves on the Americans, and were prepared to consider ourselves lucky if we could win in twenty years.

"We have never had any time to collect a history of our wars. I am giving you what I remember, and I cannot recollect all the details. In the Long March I was commander of the Third Group Army. We started from Kiangsi with 70,000 men, and when we reached northern Shensi there were no more than 10,000. Mostly they died from natural causes. In western Szechuan the air was so thin that we could hardly breathe, and in the grasslands there were almost no villages and no people, and it was all a kind of desert and we often starved. Best of all the battles was the crossing of the Wu River in Kweichow. We were surrounded. We had already crossed the river, but the enemy lay on both sides of us. We drove back again across the river, and put half the enemy to flight, and then drove against those who were on the south bank. The Kuomintang forces were led by a good general, Wu Chi-wei—he had won many victories in the past, but we destroyed his army.

"The river was about 400 meters wide. There were five regiments of Kuomintang troops entrenched on the bank, and all the ferryboats had been taken over to the opposite side. We silenced their guns with our own mortars and machine guns, then one man swam across the river and brought a single boat back to our shore. We sent the boat back under heavy fire with twenty men in it—backward and forward until we had established a bridgehead of 300 soldiers. They knew we had landed, but in the dark they could not tell how many we were. Then we captured their ferryboats, and put all the men we could spare into them, and routed them."

He could not remember all the events that had taken place in the famous crossing of the Tatu bridge.

"It's a long time ago, and I cannot remember it all. There were so many rivers—the Gold Sand River, the Hsiang River, the Wu, and the Yangtse. I remember the bridge was about 140 meters wide, with six or seven iron chains placed about thirty centimeters apart. It was a shaky bridge at all times, and the current was too strong for us to cross by rafts or pontoons. So the soldiers crossed one by one, hanging down from the bridge, hand over hand, their only weapons hand grenades and pistols, for a rifle would be useless. The current was terribly fast. The bridge was a hundred meters above the level of the water. I cannot remember very much, but I remember the people falling into the water, and there was nothing we could do to help them."

We had lunch then. He ate little except milk and porridge; he still suffered from stomach ulcers—part of the legacy of the Long March. He talked about the recent changes of tactics in the Communist army.

"We have been fighting guerrilla wars for twenty years, but we have also been fighting positional wars. The Kuomintang still regards us as partisans and guerrillas, but the battle of Shihpingchieh should have taught them better. We have American equipment now—captured from the Kuomintang.

"We cannot be defeated, but it is probably true that we cannot win. We cannot be defeated because we have the support of the people, who are the source of our soldiers, our supplies, and our intelligence. They can harass the enemy and keep all intelligence away from the enemy. Then we have another thing they have not got—the close co-ordination between the officers and the soldiers, and their determination for self-sacrifice. Lastly, we allow our commanding officers tremendous flexibility in command.

"There were times in the past when we had heavy equipment, or captured it from the Japanese, and then we had to destroy it, because we could not use it. Sometimes the same thing happens now. What is the use of having a tank when you have no gasoline, no spare parts, no repair shops? We burn it, because the enemy would use it against us if they recaptured it. We have done the same with heavy guns. So, in general, we avoid positional war because our troops are not so well equipped as theirs and often we find ourselves numerically inferior. We have no constant source of supplies, as they have. At the very beginning of the battle of Shihpingchieh we had only one regiment in the town, reinforcements did not arrive until twenty days later. The Kuomintang had American equipment, but their morale was low; and so we fought them without any great difficulty and held up their advance for a month. We can do this whenever we like. We are an army now, and because we are fighting for democracy, we have never been tougher or more determined."

June 13th, Mao Tse-tung's head. I was beginning to think that it would never be possible to see Mao Tse-tung. They said he was busy, the threat of civil war hung more menacingly than ever in China, and he was working through the night on papers and dispatches. You reminded yourself that Yenan was the administrative center for a population of over a hundred million. On those clear summer mornings, when the air was bright and deathly still, it did not look like it, but it was nevertheless true. The destiny of China was being decided in Nanking and Yenan, the small yellow backwater which had been forgotten by the world.

Mao had flashed past in an overladen jeep on the day I arrived. He looked strong and well in his blue cotton clothes, the face tanned by the sun, and I noticed that he had large hands that clutched the side of the jeep as it went through potholes of yellow dust. They shrugged their shoulders and said: "You probably won't see him again."

Meanwhile there were other people one could see, and in the intervals there was Mao's book, *The Coalition Government*, to read. It was a curiously impressive book, written in a dryly humorous style, without bitterness. It was very long, and they said the whole book had been delivered as a speech in a single day—nearly 200 pages of it. There were moments when you came face to face with the man, movements of quietly passionate fervor, without rhetoric. He did not grow larger as you read the book, but he grew more human. You began to see how his mind worked.

"Our starting point," he wrote, "is to serve the Chinese people earnestly and wholeheartedly, and never to be severed from the people; to set out always from the point of view of serving the people's interests, not serving the interests of a small group or oneself: and to give equal responsibility to the people and the guiding organization. Experience during the last twenty years has taught us that all tasks, policies, and methods that were correct corresponded to the demands of the people at that definite time and place, and all that were incorrect were separate from the people's will."

Or again:

"Our comrades must not think that what is unintelligible to us is also unintelligible to the masses. Very often the masses stride ahead of us and want urgently to advance forward, while our comrades do not act as leaders of the broad masses, but on the contrary reflect the opinion of some backward interests. Every comrade should be taught to comprehend that the highest criterion of all our statements and activities is whether they correspond to the highest interest of the broadest masses, and whether they are supported by the broadest masses. Every comrade should be taught to comprehend that as long as we rely on the people, firmly believing in the infinite creative power of the people, then we may be able to overcome all difficulties, no matter how serious they are, and no enemy will be able to overwhelm us, but will be overwhelmed by us."

And then finally, in the only note of passionate protest in the book, which is also a note of passionate faith:

"They must understand that no matter how tortuous the path may be, the independence and liberation of the Chinese people will be realized and the time for it is already at hand. The great aspirations of countless martyrs during the last hundred years must be fulfilled *by our generation*. Whoever desires to prevent these aspirations from being translated into fact, that man will fail."

Meanwhile the undeclared war was going on. Chungking and Yenan radios were bitterly assailing one another. We sat over the radios and wondered which particular incident would later be taken by historians as the beginning of the war. It was neither peace nor war—only a ragged nervous interval, while we held our breaths and prayed that the final incident would never take place.

Three days after my arrival I went to a play based on an incident from *All Men are Brothers*. In front of me in the audience was Mao Tse-tung. It was not difficult to recognize him; he had long blue-black hair, fine cheek bones, and an immense sweeping forehead. He was enjoying himself completely. No one came in to bring telegrams concerning the civil war. At one moment when the feudal landlord was abusing the captain-general of the peasants, he became lost in a

horrible fit of giggles, turned to his companion, and seemed to be in
danger of sliding under his seat.

The play was splendid and exceedingly simple. You knew that
the captain-general of the peasant armies would inevitably capture
the fortress of the white-faced feudal chief, and that the feudal lord
and all his sons would be scattered to the winds. You knew, or you
thought you knew, that virtue would be rewarded; and it was only a
question of waiting four and a half hours before the good received
their rewards. But four and a half hours, looking at the stage whose
setting was a gigantic square of bright blue cloth seen under arc
lamps, is a long time. It became increasingly necessary not to be
blinded and to seek some kind of rest by looking at Mao Tse-tung's
head.

It was a good head, and unusually expressive. The shoulders
looked powerful, and perhaps because he is a Hunanese he made no
effort to hide his emotions. I have seen photographs of a man's back
that are more revealing than his face. It might be possible—the clang-
ing of the instruments and the high-pitched voices and the fantastic
richness of the colors of the stage were becoming intolerable at
times—it might be possible, I told myself, to learn something about
him just by considering the head.

Other reflections occurred to me. The play was a morality, as
primitive in its calculated simplicity as *Everyman*. It was also very
relevant to the times, for there was no doubt in the minds of anyone
in the audience that the captain-general of the peasant forces represented Mao Tse-tung and the white-faced old man with the long gray
beard represented the Generalissimo. But chiefly it was a morality,
and like all good moralities there was represented for you the whole
world: not only peasants and soldiers and chariot-driving generals,
but cooks and servants and gatemen and officials. It was a play describing the passions of the people and virtue triumphant. The heroes
wore the finest silk, the finest dragon-painted gowns; the evil wore
ugly red and black masks which gave them the appearance of tigers.
It was Shakespearean and impenitently romantic; and seeing Mao
giggling almost to sickness it was possible to come to one conclusion
about him—he remained the romantic, in spite of the hardheaded
deliberate speeches which are so organized and biting that they read
like the works of Mr. Sidney Webb.

The captains come in with their nodding plumes, their crowns of
emeralds, their robes of flowing jade and red-gold, with their wives
and ministers. The handsome youth whom you last saw in a gown of

ruby enters now in a white gown embroidered with yellow dragons. With every scene there is a change in costume for the leading actors, and you fail to notice that the background is simply a sky-blue sheet which burns the eyes.—The music is like an incantation; it keeps you awake, but it sends you half-asleep, an exceedingly repetitious music without harmony or melody or any melodic theme. By this time you have forgotten that you have been gazing entranced at the stage for over three hours. There are no pauses, no intermissions. You are assailed by rich colors, by the blare of trumpets, by the roar of the audience which has by now completely identified itself with the actors. You begin to look again at the back of Mao Tse-tung's head, or some of the other heads in the front row.

There was Chu Teh; there was Lin Po-chu, the chairman of the government of the border region that extends round Yenan, who looked like the manager of a bank; there was Tung Pi-wu, Communist delegate to Chungking, who resembled a professor; there was vice-chairman Li Ting-ming, an old landlord who sucked continually at a silver-stemmed pipe and wore a blue cotton cap rakishly in spite of his sixty-seven years; there was General P'eng Teh-huai, who had led one of the four armies that comprised the Long March, the only man there who resembled in the least the popular idea of a Communist guerrilla, with his rough, laughing, brutal peasant face, and his fine hands. There was Madame Mao Tse-tung who was (though no one will believe it) more beautiful than Madame Chiang Kai-shek. There was Mao Tse-tung, in a well-cut brown Sun Yat-sen uniform, looking up at the actors as he leaned forward, planting his elbows on his knees, grinning continually. And behind them, in vast crowds, were soldiers and girls and peasants and farmers and government leaders and students.

But he made no speeches. When the citadel was attacked at last, when the actors with wooden swords had capered around the stage, when all the feudal landlords lay dead or were supplicating mercy on their knees, when the walls disappeared in the smoke of blinding saltpeter flames and the dead bodies had risen and run off to the wings, when the last procession of virtuous peasants and smiling heroes had circled the stage, everyone got up and walked out into the night. I saw only one soldier with a bayonet—the leaders of what is known as Red China were not being guarded very efficiently; or perhaps there was no need to guard them. Mao bowed to several people he knew. A moment later he passed me again outside, looking gray and huddled in the darkness as he tried to find his place on the

waiting truck. He bowed, then disappeared. The headlights went on
from the two jeeps, and then once again the night was blinding with
light.

June 14th, Faces. All were sunburned, for there is little shade in these
valleys except in the caves and most men spent their lives in the
fields. Mostly they were northern faces, deeply lined, with square
foreheads and handsome features, but sometimes and more often than
you expected you saw the aquiline features of descendants of the
Turkic tribes that came down from the north; they were darker, and
often the men were taller.

For years the valley of Yenan lay on the frontier. Tribesmen
came down from the north and intermarried with the original stock,
and from Sian in the south people fled northward. As in Vienna and
Okinawa and in all those places where there have been mixtures of
widely differing stocks, those who survive seem often the handsomest,
and these people of Yenan were handsome and sturdy above the
average. I never saw a girl who was not delightful to look at. On old
Chinese tapestries and paintings of the T'ang dynasty you will come
across girls and women with pear-shaped faces. I have thought this
kind of beauty had vanished until I came here and saw a girl walking
along a road, who resembled one of the pear-faced goddesses on the
tapestries. They say there are hundreds of them in this region, but
they seem to be growing rarer. They are called *gua-nien-tzu,* and may
be descended from the court beauties who once decorated Sian, when
it was known as Ch'ang-an, the capital of the empire. I never saw a
man with one of these faces, but I saw at least four girls.

Once I saw a man riding furiously on horseback and the horse
was one of those heavy-cruppered horses which appear in T'ang dynasty paintings. As he rode through the dust, he resembled a prince,
the face very red and heavily bearded, the saddlecloth bright blue and
embroidered with Persian roses, and he wore bright yellow sleeves
and a red cape fell from his shoulders. He seemed to come straight out
of the past.

Landscape. The heat was terrible. It was the kind of landscape that
Van Gogh would have liked to paint—the dust rose like flames. And
yet life went on, a small peasant cart with immense wheels went
down to the river, the few mat-shed shops were still open, and people

walked slowly down the street, kicking up bright yellow fans of dust.

That morning a Kuomintang airplane had flown high over Yenan. We went out to watch it, puzzled by its presence. What would it find? Only a baking hot valley with dust clouds rolling. If they dropped bombs, it would only make a few more dust clouds. There was nothing at all in Yenan except the river, which was growing shallower each day, a few ponies which shrank into the walls of the cliffs and a few peasants. Yet they kept on sending these airplanes, and it was always puzzling.

And sometimes the earth seemed dead, without life, with nothing growing, a lost country which no explorer would ever find. Chu Yuan wrote a story of the peach-blossom fountain. He described a country he reached through a cleft in the mountain near a spring where peach trees were growing; beyond the mountain he came upon a race of people with flaxen hair who had escaped from the empire in the Tsin dynasty and knew nothing of the coming of the Hans. They tended their fields and wore their hair in loops and they were content to live as they were. There were peach trees in Yenan, and it was not impossible to believe that you had come into this undiscovered country. The people looked contented. There was millet and wheat enough for everyone, and a little rice. Men dug out of the friable soil a hard living. They plowed the slopes, and every flat-topped mountain was crowned with its plain of ripening wheat.

There was so little shade. All that remained after the bombing of the old city were the walls and the gates. At noonday men clustered under the wall's shade or sat in the dark shadows of the gates, motionless, saying nothing, too hot even to move their legs when jeeps and lorries passed through. It was too hot even to fan yourself. The dust rose—when a car passed quickly it would lift a column of dust fifty feet high and half a mile long. There was nothing anyone could do about it except to bathe in the muddy river.

I have forgotten why we went down to the river that day, but I remember the three boys sleeping on the shore. They had bathed and there were still bubbles of water on their skins. There was no shade, but they had spread out their clothes under them and put up sticks near their heads from which hung their immense farmer's straw hats. The hats protected their faces, but their bodies remained in the sun, and what was extraordinary was that their chests were burnt dark brown, but their thighs were white, and then again below the knees the brownness emerged. They were all about sixteen, but they slept soundlessly, in the heavy stupor of heat, not noticing our approach.

They were farm boys, and their arms and hands stretched out on the dust were burnt darker even than their chests. When I think of those heavy summer days, I think of the farm boys in their heavy slumber, and how difficult it was sometimes to move when the sun was vertically above us. But in the early afternoon life flowed back again into these rich, desolate valleys.

The school in the caves. High up on the cliff walls there was all that remained of the Lu Hsun Academy. We went there on a baking day, and near the academy the jeep rolled over the cliff bank and fell twenty feet into a pigpen. The driver was thrown clear. He was dazed and frightened and confronted with twenty large black pigs, which ran screaming in all directions. The sun was startlingly bright and you saw the boy with oil smeared all over him, waving his hands, while the pigs tried to leap at him. One pig was crushed under the wheel. A peasant came with a three-foot knife, searched for the vein in the neck, and dug the knife in up to the hilt.

It was not the perfect beginning to a visit to the university. We were all shaken and a little dazed. Most of Lu Hsun Academy, known as Lu-I, had left Yenan to settle in Kalgan, but part of Yenan University, known as Yenta, remained. The classrooms and dormitories were in caves, the professors lived in caves, and the libraries were in the best caves of all.

Previously the college possessed an extraordinary importance as the only large center of learning in the Communist areas. Like all the other Chinese universities, it had suffered atrociously during the war years. Everything was inadequate—books, scientific instruments, even paper. They made crude glass test tubes in a factory, they hammered out scientific equipment in the local arsenal. But there was a time when Lu-I had been the advance guard of most of the educational work in the north. The innovations in the *yangko* dance were developed there. Drama had been given special importance, and it was among these caves that the best of the new dramas were written. Best of all was *The White-Haired Lady* which was about the daughter of a tenant farmer who failed to pay his rent. The landlord took the daughter as his concubine, and finally drove her away. She hid in the mountains, going out only at night to find food in the temples, and gradually, because she never lived in the sunlight, her hair turned white. For twenty years she remained there, until the red army came into the neighborhood, and they found her and gave her a normal life.

The students of Yenta were well fed, they wore the same blue cotton clothes as the peasants, and their work in the university was deliberately aimed at keeping the students in the closest possible contact with the peasants. The courses were short-term courses—accounting lasted one year, law one and a half years, education two years. The professors were often professors who had escaped from Kuomintang areas.

The fortunes of the war had brought a strange collection of English books to the library. There was John Buchan's *The Three Hostages* and *Mr. Standfast*, R. W. Seton-Watson's *Munich and the Dictators*, a collected edition of Walt Whitman, four Bibles, H. G. Wells's *The Shape of Things to Come*, the poems of Virgil, Liddell Hart's *The War in Outline*, Madame Chiang's *Messages on War and Peace*, twenty Penguin Shakespeares, and William Faulkner's *Absalom, Absalom!* On political science I could see only two books by Lenin, Gide's *Political Economy*, and Bernard Shaw's *Intelligent Woman's Guide to Socialism*. There were about seventy books in English altogether, and you wondered where the devil they had come from.

The professors received no salary, but were given everything in kind—even to the carton of cigarettes that arrived on their tables on the first of each month. I went into some of the caves where the professors lived: they were as comfortable as all the others in Yenan, the caves whitewashed and gleaming, the furniture solid and well varnished. There was an orchestra, a small clinic, a clothing store where the clothes of the students and the professors were supplied. I asked them whether they preferred to live without salaries. One of the professors answered: "It saves a lot of time if you get all the services free—almost no shopping is needed." I did not see one person who did not look vigorously healthy.

"The best days are over," the president of the university told me. "Once we had all the best professors and the best students. What is left is only a quarter of what there was. If you had come here a year ago, you would have seen the yellow cliffs blue with students, but look at it now." But when you looked up the cliffs, they were still blue with students, and I suppose they will remain there until Yenan once more becomes a forgotten village in northern Shensi.

June 17th, *The dead.* You do not see any signs of the dead in Yenan. In all other Chinese towns you see the grave mounds rising north and east of the city, and sometimes on all sides, and there the dogs play and scamper among the grasses, and the rooks come. The burial places are also the execution grounds, and since you must sometimes wander on the outskirts of the city to see your friends, or to go to neighboring villages, you are always in danger of seeing a man with his arms tied behind his back, kneeling, and by his side a rough, pinewood-plank coffin. But in Yenan there are no grave mounds, and no dead.

The reason is that all the earth must be plowed. There is no room for the dead. And if the dead are invisible, so are the people invisible: there are days when you can walk in the outskirts of Yenan and see almost no one at all—in the heat they are all hidden in the caves. All round Yenan, on those clear hot summer days, there was a curious emptiness. Nothing stirred. No one came out of the military headquarters, and you forgot that inside the mountains men were sitting in shirt sleeves over telephones, taking down radio statements from all the stations in the world, giving orders, making plans for the future of China. The future was hidden in the dark caves.

June 19th, The cave of the ten thousand Buddhas. The waves of honey-colored suffocating sand came rolling along the road, but inside the printing shops everything was cool. The printing presses were high up on the cliff face and you reached them through an ornamented green-tiled gateway. Cut out of the cliffs were inscriptions in praise of Buddha, and near the gateway there was a small wooden board on which was written: *Liberation Daily.* An old temple had become the headquarters of the most important Communist daily in China.

In Peking, Shanghai, and Nanking all Communist newspapers were banned. No newspaper was allowed to print news from Communist sources; in the whole country there were only seven Communist newspapers, and these were produced in the border areas. These were the newspapers for general circulation, but every army possessed its own printing press and hundreds of magazines were in circulation. Of all these newspapers the *Liberation Daily* was probably the most influential.

I had not expected to find modern machinery high up in these caves, but least of all had I expected to find caves like these. They were not cut from loess: they were cut from rock, and from every wall there were Buddhas gazing down at you. Here were small black printing presses, some powered by treadle, others by steam, roaring and hammering, and beside them were the great guardian gods, life-size, with the paint still on them. And in another cave, twenty times vaster, made in the shape of a great square and stacked with ream upon ream of brown paper, were ten thousand Buddhas.

It was curious and enchanting, and among them were some of the best Buddhas I have ever seen. There were row upon row of small Buddhas reaching from the floor to the ceiling, and here and there you saw a much larger Buddha of the T'ang dynasty, almost feminine in its elegance of expression and gesture, reclining or blessing, untouched and unharmed by the centuries. On some of the Buddhas faint colors remained—malachite green, and red, and blue. It was annoying to remember that at the greatest period of T'ang dynasty art the Buddhas were all painted, but how well they had survived! The paint had flaked off, but the unchanging stone remained. Mostly, there were the rows of small Buddhas, but there were at least eight larger carvings, and there may have been more among the stacks of paper, hidden in corners. The printing presses were the new prayer wheels, and the new priests were these boys in fading blue cloth who ministered to them.

Among them was at least one which would have melted the mouths of the curators of the world's museums. One Buddha lay in a half reclining posture, fingering his stone necklace with one hand and blessing the world with the other. The nose had broken off, but you could still see the chaplet of flowers in the headdress and the Grecian folds of the gown. There were no lights in this storeroom except oil lamps, and when it grew dark, the stone glowed. And perhaps nothing had changed through the centuries, for the first people in the world to use paper were Buddhist priests, as Aurel Stein discovered in the Gobi, and more than a thousand years before the Communists came here, there may have been stacks of paper and printing presses in caves nearby.

It was oddly disturbing to find the Buddhas there. The square temple, with its huge stone altar and smoke-blackened ceiling, the tens of thousands of Buddhas lining the walls, enforcing by their sheer repetition a sense of disturbing calm, all these were unexpected in Yenan, and more than ever unexpected in the printing press.

Mao Tse-tung. Photographs are unfaithful and give no impression of the man with the long streaming blue-black hair, the round silver rimmed spectacles, the fine cheek bones, the pursed, almost feminine lips, and the air of a college professor. Usually, you see him in photographs wearing a cloth cap, and you notice the round peasant face and the small nose and the heavy eyes—but the moment the cap is taken off the peasant disappears. It is true that he hardly ever remains the same for more than a few minutes on end, so that one moment he giggles like a boy, and the next moment the soft voice takes on depth and authority and a quite extraordinary resonance. He is fifty-three and looks thirty.

Partly, of course, it is the fault of the legend. If you remember the Long March, if you remember Edgar Snow's famous story of Mao Tse-tung undoing his trousers and scrabbling for fleas, or taking off his trousers altogether when he entered Lin Piao's cave one sweltering hot day and gazing at a map on the wall, then you will be perfectly satisfied to regard him as part military genius, part peasant leader, and part barbarian. Agnes Smedley describes how she was shocked by his femininity. It is perfectly true that there is a streak of femininity in him, as there is in all Chinese scholars to the extent that their gestures are graceful, they speak in carefully modulated, soft voices and sing their poems falsetto. There is something of the same femininity in Chu Teh, whose voice has a tenderness that would resemble weakness in any Western general, though no general has been tougher than Chu Teh. Ultimately, a man is what he is without his cap. Remove the cap, and Mao Tse-tung gives all the appearance of a scholar, with all the odd chameleon strengths and weaknesses that come from an intense absorption in scholarship. The course of study he has set himself is the revolution of China.

I watched him carefully for more than three hours in a bare room that was the Yenan equivalent to the foreign office drawing room. He was not at first sight impressive. No flashes of electric energy radiated from him, and for a little while I was not even conscious of his presence. He wore black cotton slippers and a brown woolen Sun Yat-sen uniform. When he shook hands, he lifted his elbow to the height of his shoulder, an odd gesture, which suggested that his hands had been mauled before by foreigners. Yet he did not in the least give the impression of weakness. He had burly shoulders and his hands were large, like peasant hands. He smiled delightfully, and when he spoke the voice was very low and almost inaudible. He had a high forehead and his face was bronzed.

It was a party given for three professors who had come down from Peking; among them there was an old man who had been his teacher many years before. There was Mao Tse-tung, Chu Teh, an American major, the three professors, an interpreter, and myself. Mao was very much the host, and though the professors wanted to talk about him, he insisted on talking about Chu Teh. "It was extraordinary. Chu Teh had the courage to go through the grasslands *twice*. It was dangerous to go through it once, but twice——" The legend of the Long March returned; he had no desire to sidetrack it, and answered the professors' questions gravely. They wanted the whole history of the Long March. The Communists were old men now. The Long March was still the legend around which their lives revolved; they were absorbed by their recollections of the march as others are absorbed by memories of their youth. He spoke of the grasslands again. "We killed our oxen and horses for meat, and carried them on our few remaining baggage animals, and then in the end we ate the baggage animals and carried the meat ourselves. The best fighters we ever had to face were the aboriginal tribes—the Miaos, the Fans, the Mis, and the Huans. We learned from them more than we learned from anyone else." And then again, a little later: "We have to thank the Generalissimo for driving us into all those strange places—we would never have seen them if it had not been for the Generalissimo." Someone asked him how they had managed to come through unharmed. He answered: "The vast territories of China and the backwardness of everything." He said later: "There are territories near Sikong where there are so few fishermen that the fish just aren't afraid of people." It was a rambling and desultory dinner table conversation. The electric light came from the power plant belonging to the American Observer Group on the other side of the river. It was late tonight. When it came on, it was already deep dusk; and when the light burst over our heads, he giggled again. He looked self-conscious only when the American major began to photograph him with a flashbulb. He ate slowly and carefully, and he would look up for no reason and smile at someone. You expected there would be coffee and liqueurs, and perhaps the college servant would come in in a moment with brandy on a silver salver. Then the party came to an end, he accompanied his guests to the door, bowed, and shortly afterward disappeared to accompany them a little farther down the road.

He had said he would return and talk to me, and I waited alone in the bare room with its portraits of Sun Yat-sen, Chiang Kai-shek, Truman, Stalin, and Attlee on the wall. It was so odd to find the portrait of Chiang Kai-shek, and odder still to notice in the corner portraits of Mao Tse-tung and Chu Teh. The interpreter said they had great difficulty finding a portrait of Attlee—no one knew what he looked like, and hardly anyone had heard much about him—but at last they had found one in *Life* and enlarged it. Mao Tse-tung came back. He sat on a stool and put another stool between us; the dinner things were being cleared away, he was no longer the genial host but a man prepared to talk about the civil war, socialism, China, the heavy things that lay on his mind. He looked grim now. The line of the mouth became hard and determined, the voice deeper, the gestures far more restrained. But I hadn't come to talk about politics—I wanted to learn more about his poems. He grinned again. "They're really very bad—terribly bad. I just write poetry to waste time."

It was useless. Whatever you said about his poetry, he had one final, absolute answer—it was shockingly bad, and he would be ashamed to have it seen. It was nonsense, but the kind of nonsense that gave him pleasure, for he giggled again, knowing only too well that the poetry was good. He had written a poem called *"The Snow,"* which had become famous all over China. "I gave it to my friend, urging him not to let anyone see it, but he published it without my permission."

Then the hardness returned, the romantic disappeared, and in its place was the cool brain that wrote *New Democracy* and *The Coalition Government*. They are hard-hammering books written in ice-cold composure and with a formidable logic. Calmly, logically, he spoke about the civil war, and there was nothing at all original in what he said, but in the manner of it there was a hidden strength and a quiet purpose. I had said something or other about the failure of the Spanish Republicans during the civil war against the massed artillery of the Germans. He said: "In the first place, Spain is not China. There were only 8,000,000 people fighting against Franco, but the Chinese liberated area numbers a population of 130,000,000. The Spanish Republic fought for three years. We have fought for twenty-one years. But from the very beginning up to now, we have desired peace and we do not want this war to be prolonged."

He went on: "There are some people abroad who are giving aid to the Kuomintang. These supplies should be stopped, and the democratic peoples of other countries should oppose the sending of ammunition to the Kuomintang. There are people abroad who do not want or approve of democracy in this country: these people are acting in consonance with the reactionaries in China. Let them know that whatever happens, if we are faced with mechanized war, we shall fight on, if necessary with our hands and feet."

I asked him what were the conditions for peace in the civil war. He said: "When there is democracy, the civil war will end. The people who are fighting us really do not want to realize democracy at all."

He was dubious—or had not read enough—about socialism in England. He thought the socialist government's policy of taking over the heavy industries was partly dictated by the necessity of the export trade. He was glad there were no British soldiers in China, but said that British intervention in Indonesia was "not correct." He liked the phrase "not correct" and used it often. He said: "There are some people abroad who hope to extend the civil war in China—they are doing everything they can to extend the war. But on our side we do not want war, and we look forward to the time when all democratic elements in all countries are united toward the common aim of peace. It is as simple as that." And then again: "We are not afraid of being defeated for we shall not be defeated," and then he made a gesture with his hands and feet to explain that they would fight with their hands and feet to the last man. It was the second time he had done this. He talked for a little while about the aims of his small government, saying as Chu Teh had said before that in the civil war neither side could win, it was better to have a coalition government, and that China could not afford a civil war either now or at any other time. The voice grew deeper, the scholarly graces vanished, and you noticed for the first time the inflexible temper that lay behind the air of refined scholarship. Like Chu Teh, he was unimpressive at first sight and possessed no tricks of expression at all. But gradually he showed his quiet power. It was then, and only then, that the peasant, the scholar, the politician, and the military commander seemed to be fused together. A few moments later he left and walked up to his house. All you saw in the darkness were the stooped shoulders colored with the blood-red light from a lamp which a soldier held as he walked behind him.

June 21st, The poet. He wore his blue cotton coat like a cape, and though he must have been fifty, he walked with a swagger, his black beard coiling in the wind. He was K'e Chung-ping, the poet, a man who sang for the people and thought it was not worthwhile to write poetry unless the people sang it. He came from Yunnan, and may have had tribal blood in him, and when he sang his own poems or the poems he had learned from the peasants in the mountains, his red, bearded face took on an aspect of extraordinary gravity and repose.

There were many in Yenan who regarded him as the greatest of the popular poets. Years ago, in Shanghai, he wrote a long epic describing the Red armies. It was before the Long March, yet the description of the hardships endured by the armies until they reached the Wind Fire Mountains was like the hardships Mao Tse-tung and Chu Teh had endured. No copies of the epic, which had 20,000 lines, have survived; all were confiscated, and the poet himself was imprisoned three times, once by the war lord Sun Chuan-fang and twice by the Kuomintang. "The worst of it is that your teeth fall out, and your hair falls out, and it is years before you can forget the bite of the manacles on your legs. It was worse than Dante's *Inferno*. The food was bad, and mixed with gravel and chaff; the only vegetables I ate were dried cabbages."

He could not remember much about the poem—prison had put an almost blank wall between himself and the past. He could remember odd verses, which he was good enough to write down, and the verses he liked best he asked permission to sing. He sang them superbly, stopping half-way to ask if he was boring his audience; but the audience had long ago agreed that they had never known a poet who sang his own poetry so well. He had a great fund of folk songs, and insisted that the real poetry of the country lay in the fields and villages. He liked particularly poems of love or utter grief, for grief digs deep roots in China; and these he would sing as though the grief had only that moment struck him, in a piercing voice, the eyes closed, the expression agonized. There was a Yunnanese song he had heard in his native village of Kuang-nang, nine days' journey from Kunming. He would begin slowly in a deep voice:

> *The sunset and the flowers fade,*
> *The bees come to taste the flowers,*
> *The bees come, and the flowers are faded.*
> *The elder brother looks at the sister's open grave.*

Nothing could be simpler, and nothing could be more complex, for the elder brother and the sister were evidently lovers according to a Chinese poetic tradition; grief and love were inextricably joined together.

The long poem *Feng Huo San* (Wind Fire Mountain) seems to have contained innumerable short poems interspersed with declamations and descriptions, battle scenes and songs sung around camp fires while the soldiers toiled toward the mysterious mountain where all their hopes would become real. It was significant that the title itself should come from an old Chinese ballad. There was, for example, the song of a drunken goatherd:

> *Drink down the fine sweet wine!*
> *Seal your hundred-flower hearts.*
> *I am a wandering saint.*
> *May you laugh at the third watch of the night,*
> *On the fifth watch you may have tears.*

> *I ride on my black-headed horse*
> *Through forty li of roads,*
> *Past fifty li of mountain caves.*
> *O pluck the poppy flower,*
> *And be drunk with sleep!*

> *I am the saint of the south mountain.*
> *There are witches on the mountain of the north.*
> *There are dark caves.*
> *O brother, go to the north mountain.*
> *O sister, go to the south mountain.*
> *I am the saint from the south!*

Grief, the lover's grief, entered into the songs sung by the soldiers after battle:

> *Some day there will be judgment for the dead!*
> *We shall know who killed the headless corpse.*
> *Have the mountain spirits killed him?*
> *On the second moon they come to this boy's grave.*
> *Brothers and sisters come to look at the dead.*
> *O mountains filled with lamentation!*

> *No one must weep for the beloved,*
> *The tea flowers are beginning to blossom.*
> *Why weep and destroy your eyes?*
> *The reeds flower on these white-haired nights.**
> *The boy you dream of is still young. . . .*

---

* At weddings in China the couples drink "white-haired wine" as a sign that they will grow old together.

It was no wonder that he was regarded as a great poet when he could turn the simple ballad rhythms and the ballad imagery into songs that could be still sung by the people. Ai Ching was a poet's poet, who knew his craft perfectly, but he did not *sing*. K'e Chungping sang because it was the only voice he possessed—he had been too long in prison to believe that there was anything else worth doing. He sings of his imaginary Red army coming toward the end of its journey, seeing the Wind Fire Mountain in front of them:

> *Now in April, with a thousand toils, ten thousand hardships,*
> *We have come at last into our worldly inheritance.*
> *O the great sons and great daughters!*
> *The road shines with blood, yet we sing the war song.*
> *As long as the two ends of a wheat stalk are pointed,*
> *There will be pure springs on the high mountains.*
> *O, our stomachs are full of noodles dipped in sauce.*
> *The mountain roars, the wave surges.*
> *Only when you work hard do you realize the taste of wine*
> *   and meat!*

There was a perfection in his work which was sometimes startling, and you wondered why, of all the books which have become lost, the long revolutionary epic with the glorious title *Wind Fire Mountain* should be among them.

June 27th, Kalgan. I came back to Peking from Yenan a week ago. I remember there was sun every day in Yenan except on the last day. Mao Tse-tung and Chu Teh came down to the airfield in the rain, in their sandals and blue cotton clothes, while the sky looked utterly gray and the valley was lost in the rain mist. For the first time in eleven days there was no sun on the valley; and somehow it seemed wrong. There is sun nearly all the year round in northern Shensi, a hard glittering baking sunlight, which hardly changes in its intensity, though the seasons change.

The valley of Kalgan is twenty times wider than the valley of Yenan, a great curving sweep of valley rising toward dark mountains. The mountains do not oppress you, and they are magnificently formed, with peaks and promontories and huge black buttresses. There were two cities, the old dark walled city, tortuous and decaying, and the new city of reinforced concrete built largely by the Japanese. They had had eight years to build the place, but they had not finished when the three Communist columns came from north, east, and south on August 27th, 1945, and threw the Japanese in confusion. The Japanese have departed, but Kalgan was full of their traces—there were *tatamis* everywhere, and there were gaunt gray buildings and factories. What was surprising was the newness of the Japanese town, and how incomplete it was; here there would be a building, and there a vegetable patch, and farther on another building. So it must have been in the American West in the early days. Kalgan was always a frontier town; it lay on the Great Wall; it had existed at least as long ago as the Han Dynasty, for a famous Han governor inscribed on the city gateway in his own hand: "O good and great country," and the inscription remained. The Empress Dowager had passed through here on her return from exile in Sian. Feng Yu-hsiang had once made the city his headquarters. On the Nankao Pass, between Kalgan and Peking, innumerable battles had been fought, and it was there that the last defenders of Peking in 1937 were mown down by the Japanese. But Kalgan had changed completely. Among these pepper-colored plains and sharp-toothed hills, the impact of modern industrialism was being felt. At this time only one other industrial city was occupied by the Communists—Harbin.

Kalgan, at the center of the Chin-Cha-Chi area, is conscious of its industrial potential. The factories are everywhere, and smoke pours from the chimneys. This was modern industrialism: railroads, mining and reinforced concrete. It was a city of peasants and workmen, the shepherd boys tending their sheep on the sand hills in the shadow of a factory, and at midday, in the shade of the poplars, the workmen in blue cotton were resting. The old Chinese walls were crumbling. From now on it would be concrete, not stone. It was heady wine for the Chinese who came here for the first time after living in villages and fighting as guerrillas. An industrial city, white, clear, and shining in the sun.

June 28th, The palace of Prince Teh. The palace lay under the shadow of Great Divine Son Mountain, a bleak range of blue mountains east of Kalgan, and was menacing enough in the rain. Even when the sun shone these savage cliffs looked menacing, and the small pagodas perched on the summits of the sheer foothills did not look like pleasure houses: they were pagodas of iron, starkly etched against the lowering sky, almost terrifying. But the palace, with its marble dragons and painted eves and innumerable courtyards folding into one another, was completely delightful. Until he fled, it was occupied by Prince Teh, whose other titles were Prince Demchukdongrob, Lord of West Sunid, of the Silingol Banner in the north of Chahar. He had occupied the palace on the invitation of the Japanese, with his concubines and retainers, a tall man, with a close-cropped skull, already ageing; and they said he had the keenest eyes of anyone in Mongolia and the greatest ambition to imitate Genghis Khan and carve out of Asia a new kingdom for his people. Before the surrender of the Japanese, he had fled to Peking and then to Chungking, where he was received with due ceremony as the leader of the Mongol Horde. The Communists said: "He lived here under the Japanese, therefore he was a traitor, and we would have killed him if he had not fled."

The palace was now occupied by the Communist governor of the province, a thickset man with fine mobile features and a reputation for good calligraphy, hardheaded and earnest. It was this man who had most of the responsibility for seeing that Chin-Cha-Chi suffered as few growing pains as possible. He was obviously overworked, but what was amazingly attractive was that he did not resemble in any way any preconceived idea of a governor. The mayor of Peking, Hsiung Ping, looks like a governor—fat, and of course immensely wealthy. Governor Sung of Chin-Cha-Chi could have been a precision worker in a factory, a professor, or a civil servant, or anything you please. He had a heavy forehead; you could feel the power behind it; you were conscious that he would stand no nonsense; like Mao Tse-tung he had developed a curiously flamboyant calligraphy, but he spoke in a quiet slow voice. He was amused with the idea of living in Prince Demchukdongrob's palace and sleeping in Prince Demchukdongrob's bed. He was amused, and he was a little sad, and he always looked slightly lost in the reception room with the gilded pillars and the yellow satin embroidery on the chairs and sofas.

And then others came in, General Nieh, the military governor of the Border Area, and General Tsai—both had been on the Long March. Nieh had studied in Paris and Belgium. For a while he studied chemical engineering at Charleroi University. He had a keen pale intelligent face, a good forehead, the manners of the eighteenth century. He had directed with two others the operation over the Tatu Bridge. He laughed easily and splendidly, and he liked telling stories and possessed a quiet, mordant humor. General Tsai looked like a factory worker. He had lost an arm in the Long March. The mouth was bitter and indrawn, but the eyes were large and transparently clear. He said very little, but what he said was always to the point. He was vice-chairman of the military-political bureau.

There were many others, but what was surprising was that they could easily be divided into two types—those who had returned from France or Belgium, and those who had remained in China. You could distinguish the types at once. Neither looked like the current conception of what a Communist leader should look like. You would see these people in any American or English town, you would be friendly with them and get to like them. They felt that the government of the Kuomintang was a travesty of government, but they knew that they were unprepared to take over the power. They were conscious—no one could be more conscious—of their limitations. They did not look sly, and not one of them resembled the pot-bellied compradore type which spills over Nanking. They would not beg for help, and they did not care very much if they were misunderstood. They liked good food, but they didn't care very much if there wasn't any. They liked good wine—there is excellent grape wine produced in Huahsien on the road between Peking and Kalgan—and they drank innumerable toasts for no particular reason except that there were a considerable number of bottles available. And then, when we went out into the courtyard, where it was still raining and the marble lions looked more arrogant than ever, you half expected to see Prince Demchukdongrob surrounded by his concubines and walking in the rain, for nothing can be more pleasurable to a Mongolian than to walk in the rain, and nothing fills him with a greater love for the vast plains. But instead there were Communist delegates in blue cotton suits, looking rather shabby except for General Nieh who wore a uniform captured from the stores left by the Japanese.

June 29th, More about Mao Tse-tung. It was said all over Yenan that Mao hated to talk about himself. For four nights he had discussed his own biography with Edgar Snow. It was necessary at that time: the Long March of the Communist armies was unknown, its leaders were unknown, and even the objects of the Long March were unknown. But at that time Mao had said he would never write about himself again, he was not important, the movement among the peasants, the farmers, and the factory-workers was far more important than any single man. Probably he meant all this. It was infinitely difficult to get any information about him.

But in Kalgan there lived a man who had known Mao Tse-tung

since he was twelve years old. His name was Hsiao San, he was editor of a newspaper and looked like a professor at the Sorbonne. He was born like Mao Tse-tung in Hsiangtan in Hunan, and though he had left China for two long periods of study in France and Russia, he had kept up a correspondence with his childhood friend. He lived in a small Japanese house, with the usual patterned and uncomfortable sofas, the usual *tatamis* and sliding panels and rooms that were so small that they resembled wooden prisons. I got him to talk about Mao Tse-tung.

"Mao is the most complex person we have," Hsiao San said, when I spoke about the incredible difference that existed between Mao bare-headed and Mao wearing a peasant cap—the scholar could so easily turn into a peasant, a schoolboy, the vicar at a harvest festival, the poet, the soldier, and the political leader. "None of us have really understood him. I have known him longer than anyone else, but I have never got to the root of him.

"When he was sixteen and I was twelve, I met him for the first time. He was hurrying down a road with a parcel of books under his arm. I had seen him before—he always had books. A few days later I lent him a book with articles about Peter the Great, Wellington, Washington, Lincoln, Rousseau, Montesquieu, Napoleon, and perhaps twenty others. He read the whole book in one night, and gave it back to me, saying: 'We need great people like these in China.'

"There was a free library in Changsha. He would stay there all day, reading, reading, reading. He didn't read with any deliberate plan—he read everything, everything without exception, politics, economics, history, *The Dream of the Red Chamber*, which he admired immensely, the histories of famous generals. He noticed that in all the epics and legends of the past there were always victorious emperors and generals, but no victorious peasants. He was himself the son of a peasant. His father had been in the army. When he returned from the wars, he bought twelve *mou* of land and made young Mao work with him in the fields. The father was often brutal and cursed him, quoting Confucius and saying that the son should obey the father implicitly. In answer, Mao quoted another chapter from the *Analects* where the father is enjoined to treat the son mercifully. It was from that time, I think, that there dates Mao's implacable opposition to Confucianism.

"In 1911 he was eighteen, and had been for a short while conscripted in the army. He was still reading furiously, but now he was reading chiefly the works of Adam Smith, Darwin, and Spencer, which had been all translated into classical Chinese by the celebrated translator Yen Fu. At this time he read a book by Chiang Kan-fu on socialism. If you read it now, you would think the book was ridiculous—it was a terribly muddle-headed book, but it contained some good quotations and it belonged to the school of thought that owed much to the Reform Party in China under K'ang Yu-wei and Liang Ch'i-ch'iao. It was half-baked, like so much that was being written by Chinese at that time, but it was the first time Mao had heard of socialism. All his sympathies, all his scholarship, all his memories of life in the field and in the army seemed to lead to one conclusion—he would become a socialist. Later he read three books: the *Communist Manifesto*, Kautsky's *The Class War*, and a history of socialism by someone whose name I've forgotten. He was completely thunderstruck by these books.

"At that time he wanted to be a teacher—or rather, he did not know what he wanted to be, but he thought that if he was a teacher, he would have time for reading, and writing. He wanted passionately to be a writer. He still went to the library early in the morning, slipped out of the library for lunch and read again until the library closed. He had little money, and his parents were complaining. He entered the normal school. He passed through the entrance examination with flying colors—the principal of the school publicly posted his essay on the wall and commended him. At first the principal could hardly believe it could be written by one so young. At this time he was absorbed in Chinese history.

"It was the time of the European war. I still saw him nearly every day, and now I noticed that he was passionately reading every newspaper he could lay his hands on. The war fascinated him. He knew all kinds of details, and he could explain during our evening walks what it was all about, what important factors there were, and where it was leading. In 1920 I went to France. Mao himself had organized some of the groups that went to France—you could study and work for your living at the same time. Many of the people who went were his friends, and he begged them to go. For himself he preferred to remain in China where he could work out his own destiny. He was already conscious of his leadership.

"He has won battles, but his knowledge of war came from his wide reading, from his association wih the peasants, with the legends of the past, and with an incident that occurred at the normal school. Soldiers came and wanted to take it over. This is the kind of thing that happens all over China—soldiers try to take over schools because they are the largest available buildings. It is happening now in Peking. Mao organized the defense of the school. He drilled the students and the professors, and however unlikely it sounds, he gave orders to the senior professors which were instantly obeyed. We even bought arms in Changsha to defend the school, and medical supplies. We kept the soldiers out and Mao Tse-tung remarked: 'Well, this is the first time I have taken military command.' He seemed to know that it wouldn't be the last.

"He is fifty-three now, and he has been many things in his time. He has led armies, he has been secretary to the old reactionary Hu Han-min, he has been editor of an official Kuomintang newspaper—the *Political Daily* which was issued in Canton before the Northern Expedition, he has been director-general of propaganda under the central committee of the Kuomintang; but it was only this year that he assumed for the first time the acknowledged leadership of the Communist party. There have been many changes within the party, many quarrels. But what he likes to remember most is the days when he wandered around the districts of Hunan in great poverty, wearing a sun helmet, a white shirt, white trousers, and sandals, and organized the peasants.

"Three or four times he nearly died of weakness during the Long March, which he directed with Chu Teh. They went through nine provinces, Kwangtung, Hunan, Kwangsi, Kweichow, Yunnan, Sikong, Szechuan, Kansu, and Shensi. Many stronger men died on the journey. He was strong—he put tremendous significance on physical health in his youth and liked wandering through the countryside in all weathers—but he looked ill when it was over. He still looks after his health carefully. He eats less pepper and smokes fewer cigarettes, and doesn't read late into the night any more, unless he has to. His speaking voice is not good, but when he makes speeches he has all the air of an old peasant. He is not an actor. He has no dramatic appeal. He talks simply. He delights in being as scientifically accurate as possible, but at the same time he is a dreamer and a poet. His poetry is a kind of secret vice. He won't show it to anyone except his closest intimates like Chu Teh or Lin Po-chu. I spent nearly ten years in Russia, coming back in May 1939, through Urmchi, Lanchow, and Sian, and the odd thing was that he seemed hardly to have changed at all."

July 1st, The poet Ai Ching. They said in the south that he was a man of about forty, very rugged and bearded, who took no care of his clothes and wandered over the country singing his poems and never so happy as when talking with some other wandering peasant. It was all wrong; he was nothing like this, and yet it was easy to understand from his poetry how the legend arose. The poetry is robust, hard, filled with a kind of sunlit energy and defiance, and sometimes the hardness would disappear and in its place there was pure lyric feeling, a quietness like that which descends on ancient Chinese poetry. He was famous for the long poems on soldiers fighting against the Japanese—there were *The Trumpeter* and *The Man Who Died a Second Time*, and there was a host of others, which reflected the roughness and energy of the times. It was easy to imagine him tall and bearded, stalking over the northern plains, a Chinese Whitman who cared only for the sufferings of the people.

In a sense the legend was true—he *was* the Chinese Whitman, and he had sung of the sufferings and deaths of the soldiers more than any other poet in China, and far better. He did not look like Whitman. He looked like a young scholar, perhaps twenty-five, with a brown, sensitive, mobile face, a fine forehead, and immense eyes. Like almost everyone else in Kalgan he wore a thin blue cotton suit and a blue cotton cap. The hair was long and blue-black; in immobility the lips seemed carved from red sandstone; he had almost no gestures and carried himself with a natural grave dignity, though he often grinned like a schoolboy. You would say at first glance that he was a scholar, at second glance you were certain he was unlike any scholar you had ever seen.

I saw him nearly every day I was at Kalgan, and tried sometimes to discover the springs of his poetry, since he alone of all Chinese poets has sung perfectly about the war. I asked him whether he had seen war at close quarters, and he said he had seen it very rarely and then only accidentally when he was on some propaganda work near the front line. But he had seen drought and famine and the insides of prisons, and he had seen the new China growing up in the north; he had lived for years with the villagers and soldiers and watched their sudden fury against the Japanese. "The best thing was the people. That was why I wanted to live among them, encouraging them to write and editing their magazines and writing for them—above all *for them*. We were cut off from the world. There was the blockade in the south, there was the Japanese blockade in the east, hardly anything came to us from Russia. And in a way it was good, for the writers had no other source except the people." Like others, he would say the word for people—*lao pai hsing*—with a special tenderness.

One morning, when he seemed less occupied than usual, I asked

him for details of his life. He was not very interested in his biography
and seemed to think it was almost of no importance at all. "Not very
much—just prison and painting a little, and working."

"Why did they send you to prison?"

"I was arrested in the French Concession, and they kept me in
prison for nearly three years—dangerous thoughts, I suppose." And
then a little later: "I was born in 1910 in Chinghua *hsien* in Chekiang. My father was a small landlord, who had graduated from a
middle school and had a little modern education. I was born on the
farm. I learned by heart all the classical things that were taught in the
schools near the farm; then when I was fifteen I went to a middle
school at Chinghua. After that, I thought I wanted to be a doctor
and studied medicine for half a year. It was no good—I was not made
to be a doctor, and by this time I had decided I wanted to be a
painter. My parents did not want me to go abroad—they knew nothing of other countries, and besides it was a time when the Chinese
still had little love for foreigners. It seemed monstrous to go and
study painting in Paris. But still I went, and they sent me a little
money, and I earned some more by drawing designs for Chinese
porcelain in France. Yet I depended on my father's money, and in
the end, when he sent an ultimatum—no more money if you stay
abroad—I returned, very reluctantly. There were other reasons for
returning. In 1931 the Mukden incident occurred and Japan invaded China. The French seemed to be in sympathy with the Japanese, and you felt as you walked around the streets of Paris that the
Chinese were despised. But I had learned something—I knew how to
paint a little, I had been to Arles, I had seen the paintings of Van
Gogh, I had read a great deal, chiefly in French. I was beginning to
think I might be a poet and began to write seriously for the first time
on the boat coming back to China—they were immature poems, and
all of them are lost now.

"I left Marseilles on January 28th, 1932. I remember the date,
because it was also the date of the Shanghai incident—the Japanese
attacked Shanghai. The fighting had ended by the time I returned
home. I went straight to my native home in Chekiang and found that
my parents still wanted me to become a high official; gradually, when
they discovered that I had no intention of becoming an official, they
began to hate me. In May I left them and went to Shanghai—it was
useless to go on in the small village. In Shanghai I met Lu Hsun. I
had studied the social revolution in France and was becoming more
and more a socialist, so I studied and taught in a small study group

called—for all these study groups had that kind of name—the *Chun Ti* study group. *Chun* means spring and *Ti* means earth, and it meant 'the awakening of the earth in spring.' It was a rather mild group, but our thoughts were evidently 'dangerous thoughts.' It was banned on July 12th, and I was arrested.

"I had written very little poetry in Paris, and more on the boat, but now in the prison in the French Concession in Shanghai I began to write in earnest. The French, mercifully, were not so strict as the Chinese. There was just enough food, and I could smuggle the poems out of the prison, and through friends we could get good food sometimes and magazines from outside. I was released in October 1935.

"I had met Lu Hsun once before going to prison, and now I decided if it was humanly possible to be a professional writer. I gave up painting altogether and plunged into poetry and literary magazines. It was a time of peace, though the peace was soon to be broken, and literary magazines were growing up like mushrooms. Now and then they would be suspended, or they would change their names. It was a time of awakening. I stayed most of the time in Shanghai and developed a close friendship with Ho Feng, the critic, and Tien Ch'ien, the poet; and then at the beginning of the war, in July 1937, I went to Hankow and later I became a teacher in the National Revolutionary University in Shansi—this was an eminently respectable university, in spite of its name, being sponsored by Marshal Yen Hsi-shan, the war lord of Shansi.

"Meanwhile the war went on, and Marshal Yen Hsi-shan was not entirely the 'model governor' he pretends to be. Two months later I went to Sian and organized resistance groups against the Japanese. It was a time when the writers became organizers. They were propagandists—they had to be. They had to tell the people what they were fighting for, and never to stop fighting until the Japanese were out of China. Afterward I returned to Hankow and then to Kweilin, where for a while I edited the literary page of a newspaper.

"We were terribly unsettled in those days—always moving about. I stayed in Kweilin for a year, then I went to Hunan and taught Chinese in a middle school for another year. The school was very liberal; I was happy there. But gradually it became known that the school had liberal tendencies, and the government became alarmed and closed up the school. The times were dangerous. We thought of what we should do and decided to go to Chungking—the safest places are the large cities, for you can hide more easily.

"In January 1941, there occurred the New Fourth Army inci-

dent, when this Communist army south of the Yangtse was ordered
to move north of the Yangtse. It obeyed the order but was surrounded by Kuomintang troops and 4,000 were killed. It was in this
civil war fought in the midst of the war against Japan that General
Yeh was captured—he was imprisoned for five years and died, as you
know, this year in an airplane crash not far from Yenan. Like hundreds of thousands of others, I began to wonder whether the Kuomintang was prepared to fight to the utmost against the Japanese.
Partly with the help of General Chou En-lai, and partly with the
help of one of my students who had become an officer in Marshal
Yen Hsi-shan's army, I went to Yenan. The journey was dangerous. I
was disguised as a staff officer in Yen Hsi-shan's army. There were six
or seven of us, and one famous writer was disguised as our aide-de-
camp. We had the right papers, but we didn't look very much like
soldiers. We passed altogether forty-seven sentries. In March we arrived in Yenan. Since then I seem to have lived continually in an
atmosphere of annihilation campaigns."

He had shown no bitterness at all during this long account until
he came to the end; he said "annihilation campaigns" like a rat-trap
closing. He said nothing more for a long while.

"It was not so bad—we got down to the people at last. This was
the important thing. You know, for years we had lived in cities. We
wrote about the people, but we did not know the people. In Shensi
we had time to learn the folk songs of the people, I began to realize
we were all too much influenced by Western literature. We read
Mayakovsky and the French poets, but they were not Chinese, and
they were badly translated. They told us a great deal, but they did not
tell us the thing we wanted to know most. Once I read Mayakovsky's
Cloud in Trousers in a French translation. It was a tremendous
shock. It opened up immense possibilities, but most of us copied the
method too literally, and we did not realize that he was speaking
about a particular Russian situation. Our own situation in China had
little enough to correspond with the situation in Russia in 1916.
When I was younger, I read Byron, Heine, Pushkin, Goethe, Whitman, Verhaeren—I translated *La Cité, La Plaine, Les Douze Mois*
—Mayakovsky, Essenin, a hundred others. Some of the influences
remain, particularly Verhaeren, but what I wanted in my poetry is
that the greatest influence of all should be the Chinese people.

"I believe that art and the revolution must go together; they can
never be separated. We are political animals, and sometimes we must
write as political animals. If the revolution fails, the art will fail, but

insofar as is possible the artist must be a revolutionary. A revolutionary and artist must represent his times. Therefore he must write propaganda. One writes propaganda for the same reason that the Christian painters painted Madonnas—I write about the people and a particular social system because I have faith in them. It is possible for us to have the same faith in democracy as the people in the mediaeval Church had for their God.

"Now more than ever I realize that we were wrong in our beginnings. We thought we must write something entirely new, not knowing that the tradition remains, and we can never escape entirely from the tradition. We forgot that there must be *harmonie*." When he said "*harmonie*" his face lit up; one derived the impression that all problems were resolved in this mysterious word, a word that possesses an almost Chinese significance and force. "It seems to me that in the future our poetry will change, and all our culture will change with our poetry. It will change in three directions. We shall take the best, the most revolutionary poems of the past, and we shall continue to take influences from the West. We need simpler tunes—tunes the people can sing. We do not need the delicate fragile emotions of the intellectuals.

"So far we have not always succeeded in our new poetry—the best things we have produced in northern China during the blockade were not poems, but *reportages* and woodcuts. These sprung from necessity. There had to be *reportages*, because the soldiers and the people wanted them. We did produce some illustrated books with photographs, but they were rarely good. We had expert cameramen, but rarely had good materials. And so it was with everything—the men were good, but we were being besieged and the materials were bad, unless we captured them from the Japanese.

"We had at least one good poet—Tien Ch'ien. He has a more vigorous style then Mayakovsky's, a succession of rousing hammer beats, and he has a tremendous gift for stating things simply. He is still very young, and unfortunately became famous too early, before he had matured. Occasionally he wrote love poems, but most of his poems were concerned with the war and problems of production —they were two very real things when we were fighting. Most of us at first tried to write as we had written before: it took a long time to realize what were the most important things. But Tien Ch'ien saw them at once, and it is only recently that he has taken a real interest in folk song. They say he is a propaganda poet. It is true. And why not? We had to win the war, and there were exactly two fundamental things—production, which meant our own survival, and our continual attacks against the Japanese. But sometimes Tien Ch'ien, using this new hammer-beat language he had invented, made terrible mistakes—he distorted Chinese phrases, and where the tone of a character should be soft, he made it hard, and where there might have been easily remembered rhythms, he deliberately distorted the sounds into hammer beats; and you cannot remember his poems easily.

"Thinking about it now, it seems that we did what we could, and on the whole we were successful. We subordinated everything —our lives, our customs, our traditions—to winning the war. It had to be. We had everything to gain by organization. No one starved, and no one was without weapons. We relied on ourselves, and we knew that China would have to rely on herself for victory. And gradually, over all those long years, we built up in the north a system of democracy that can never fail, because it represents so intimately the demands of the peasants, for after all we are a nation of peasants and will always be a nation of peasants, and this is what is important."

He had spoken very quietly, rarely using gestures, and sometimes his eyes would wander to the glass cases placed against the wall where there were Buddhas and wooden goddesses which had come from abandoned temples. He had cut himself away from the past; now he was busy attempting to find the past again. For him most of the old Chinese poets I admired were worse than useless: they had no social message, no sense of political responsibility. There remained a few poets—Tu Fu and Po Chu-I were among them—who spoke of the sufferings and aspirations of the people. This was what was important. China was going through her revolution now, and until the revolution was accomplished, there was neither time nor energy left for beauty. I said that at first I was shocked in the Communist areas by the drabness of the people, who all wore cotton clothing and seemed so like each other. Gradually I noticed that the cotton uniform possessed vast advantages: you no longer looked at clothes—you looked at faces, and each face was different.

"And besides," he went on, "what else can we wear? We have our uniforms, as you call them, though they are not uniforms; but if we wear the clothes you see in Peking, how can we go among the peasants, how can we expect the peasants to tolerate us? It is important that we should be as like the peasants as possible. This is not a disguise. We take to it naturally. The body is not important, but the face tells everything—— We must learn once again to look directly at people's faces."

He spoke of many other things, of writers and the difficulties of printing, of his extraordinarily beautiful wife and children, of the horrors of living in a house that had been built by the Japanese and was cluttered with *tatamis* and sliding panels and labor-saving devices and little wooden platforms where you placed a solitary bowl of flowers if you were Japanese; but he preferred to have flowers all round him. He lived quietly and methodically. He was still editing magazines, still teaching, still writing, and sometimes he would wander off among the peasants and live with them, for fear that literature would claim him too ardently. His whole wealth consisted of his bed, some furniture, a chest littered with manuscripts, and a Japanese sword. He had killed the demon that desires money and had only one belief: that at this period in China's history it was necessary to serve the people.

July 2nd, Ting Ling and the blind storytellers. I had been wanting to see Ting Ling ever since I came to China, for of all the novelists since Lu Hsun she had seemed the best. She could describe lovers, the morning mists, the trials and strains of the young Chinese before the Japanese war with an immediacy that gave her writing a curious similarity wtth D. H. Lawrence. It was all there. She saw cleanly; and her lovers were as real as her landscapes. Yet during the whole course of the war we heard almost nothing about her, and some wondered whether she was dead. It was rumored that she had published three or four books in Chungking under assumed names, that she had died in battle, that she had become the Red commissar for something or other and lived in a state of free love. I sent a note around to say that I would like to see her. We had mutual friends. She came. I did not interview her; she interviewed me on all the writers I knew in the south.

She is hardly more than four and a half feet tall. She is Hunanese, and there is a special sweetness about the smiles of those who are born in Hunan. She spoke in a low voice, very feminine, without gestures, wearing the usual blue cotton coat and blue baggy trousers; but once again you noticed, in this country where clothes are emblems of rank, that the blue cotton sets off the face perfectly; and you are conscious only of face, hands, the curve of the shoulders. She looked thirty, but she is over forty. She had fine teeth, and her black hair was drawn straight back from the brow; you realized that she must have been an extraordinarily attractive girl, and that she is herself the heroine of most of her novels.

She spoke of the odd fate that her work has received abroad. A few of her short stories were published in translation by Edgar Snow, a play was translated into English and performed in India. *The Mother* was translated into Japanese during the occupation, she had read the book again recently, it did not please her, she wanted to revise it, making it the first of a trilogy dealing with the women of northern China. She had published one book in Chungking during the war under an assumed name. She had never been a Red commissar, and she was happily married and had two children. She had spent all her time during the war editing magazines, organizing drama groups, and writing *reportages*.

"We had to write for the people, because we were living in a time of revolution, and nothing else was important. Most of my early writings are valueless. Those stories of the emotional crises of young women in Shanghai—they have little enough meaning for me now. What is important is to get the people on paper, to find out how they really behave, how they think and act and love one another, and above all how they fight, and to do this authentically, not relying on the imagination—to do it with real feeling and understanding. You cannot write about the peasants unless you have lived with them for years, and because China consists so largely of peasants, you cannot write about China at all unless you have lived with the peasants.

"When a writer sits down to write, he does not say: 'I shall write for the people or not for the people.' His characters, the people he describes, depend on his daily life, on his observation, on his love for them. He can write, if he pleases, about young women suffering emotional and spiritual crises in Shanghai, or about the habits of cultivated scholars, but the peasants will not read them or listen to them. We had to develop an understanding of them, to go down among them, to suffer with them; and their crises are not like the crises in Shanghai. They are made of simpler stuff, but how difficult to render them on paper!

"My early works were a kind of continual *Sorrows of Werther*. Sometimes, too, I wrote of the peasants, but reading these things now I realize how often I misunderstood them. Lu Hsun spoke about their faults, their lack of education, their pitiful obedience to feudal laws. It was true at the time. It is not true now. They are maturing incredibly quickly, and they know now that they have rights and duties, and that they will never again suffer under the old feudal forces. They are making a world good enough to live in. They are learning to read—every village has its reading classes—and they are learning to write. I spent as much time as I could trying to find young writers among the peasants. They were not many, but they were good.

"What I wrote about the peasants in the past lacks life. I had to begin to think how to write all over again. In 1942 Mao Tse-tung made a speech calling upon the writers to study the peasants, to move among them, and to be as much at their service as the government administrators. I was doing this long before his speech, but I still did not understand them. I discovered that style was not important, that it was dangerous to invent a style, that one should write in such a way that the writing is a mirror of the people. I tried to break my old style and create a new style, but even that was no good—style, too, must come from the people, from the rhythms and sounds of the voices you hear around you.

We learned that nearly all past Chinese literature was divorced from the people. *The Book of Odes* contains songs sung by the people, but we are no longer the same people we were two thousand five hundred years ago; our feelings have changed; conditions have changed; and only the scholars can read and understand the old terminology. When we write the new *Book of Odes*, it will be utterly different from anything that has gone before. We must go back to the songs of the people."

Wandering among the mountains of Shensi, disappearing for months on end in remote villages, or organizing dramatic groups, she had listened to the songs of the people and studied them until she could almost identify herself with the old singers. They had a naked, original strength, often satirical, occasionally brutal, but there at least she had heard the real voice of China. Her face lit up when she spoke of the blind singers in the villages—this was real, this at last was the music she had been listening for.

"In every small district there were professional storytellers supported by the villages. Their stories are sung to music. They have a *pipa*, a kind of guitar with four strings, and they have other instruments which they perform all at the same time. There is a kind of flat board laced to the leg beneath the knees—they can tap on it with their fingers to give an accompaniment to the *pipa*, or they can beat on it with a bronze clapper, or they have a sounding board above the knee to beat on. They sing without gestures, wholly absorbed in their song; and the song is very long, usually an interminable story of heroes in the past, of kings and the downfall of dynasties, of amazing battles and great deaths.

"The people knew the stories by heart, and sometimes, but very occasionally, these blind musicians used to invent new stories. There were hundreds of stories, and the people knew them all and never tired of listening to them. The storytellers would move from one family or one village to another—new ones were constantly coming in. We invited these storytellers to Yenan. We took down their stories and studied them, and we started to ask them to tell stories about the resistance of the peasants to the Japanese. It was propaganda, if you like, but the resistance had already led to innumerable good stories. We have sent writers to live with them and learn from them. We have sent other writers to get them to sing the new stories. They were men with fantastic memories and fantastic imaginations. We found after a while that they could invent stories prodigiously —as much as ten stories in half a year. Then they went back to their villages.

"Now, all over Shensi, there are these storytellers. In the evening, when the farmers have returned from the fields, they listen to the blind old men with the bronze clappers and the *pipas*, telling stories of the old heroes like Chu-ko Liang or of the young soldiers who fought in tunnels and blew up the Japanese with land mines. The stories are told in dialect; they belong to the people; they are continually growing and budding and forming new stories. We feel now that the art of the storyteller has never been richer than in the places we have liberated from the Japanese, and the writers from the coastal ports are humble before the achievements of the blind men who wander from village to village. There, at last, is the intimacy between author and audience which we lack, the direct communication, the splendor of the legends that belong to the present time.

"We still need to study the West, but in the end we found the best storytellers among our own people."

I saw her many times again in Kalgan, striding down the road or coming to the stuffy hotel to discuss the importance of India or the places where the most beautiful women were born or what had happened to the friends she had not seen for nearly ten years, but the impression that remains is of a woman who wanted to spend the rest of her life among the peasants, and perhaps even wishing that she was a blind musician wandering among the tented hills of Shensi. She hated to discuss politics, which was a pity; she had a fine clear-cut mind. She spoke of the peasants as Ai Ching spoke of them, conscious of their enduring greatness and of all men's ignorance about them until the war made it possible for people to see and write about them clearly for the first time. They were there. She was one of them, born beside a small river in northwestern Hunan.

"There are four hundred and fifty million of them," she said. "It is time we learned about them."

July 6th, The desert and the sown. The airplane left Kalgan one burning summer day and headed for Mongolia. Once again there were the bronze mountains in the sun, no clouds, the white scars of the unflowing rivers and here and there on the mountain slopes were small temples among green trees. No day could have been brighter and nothing could have been smoother than the flight of the airplane. The pilot said we were going to Suiyuan, the most northerly of the provinces of China proper, in the direction of the Ordos plains; but when we looked for the plains we saw only the sweep of the mountains going on forever, until at last we came to a region of yellow-blue earth that seemed even at that height to be barren and uninhabited. We were already in Suiyuan. From the air you saw the railway line, the green fields, and nothing else.

Chi-ning is a small walled town on the railway to Pailingmiao. It stands in the middle of a vast plain, dominated by the immense power station and water tower of white concrete—you can see only the walls, the station, the tower, and the railway station, and for the first time it occurs to you that all over Asia there are towns like this along all the railway lines. There had been no need to make an airstrip; the plain was enough, a plain where there are few roads, no animals, and the only sign that people once passed by here were the hillocks of stone erected for the dead. I hoped to see camels, but none came. The air was pure, and the sky was touched with the green grass, which went on forever. In the distance were the faint blue mountains low on the horizon. The town was in the hands of the Communists; the first field team had come here.

It was comfortable there, lying under the shadow of the plane with a great wolfhound that had appeared from nowhere, or talking to a girl student who had walked from Yenan two weeks before, a bad journey, without compass or maps, always a little afraid of straying into enemy territory. She had come with three or four others. It had rained often. Kweihua, the capital of the province, was in Kuomintang hands. There was still the possibility that Kuomintang troops might attack Chi-ning. Even while we were there two P-38s came high over the city and circled around.

It was poor country, growing only sheep grass and *yu mei*, and it was deathly still during that long morning of full sunlight. The girl said: "In winter it is desperately cold. There is snow on the ground, but the skies will clear." And you wondered whether the field team would still be there, and what fortunes of war there were for this small brown city on the plains.*

Later. The plains came to an end, and the russet-red mountains with their green shadows returned again. There were no rivers, almost no farmsteads, there were a few trees near the monasteries, but the whole earth seemed broken up with the white cracked fissures of rivers that have long ago been forgotten. It is one of the dominant impressions that remain of northern China—the rivers have gone, and they have left in their places only the salt-white tracks where they once flowed. It was midsummer. They would flow again in autumn, but they would not flow as they did once before desiccation had affected those great buttressed plains.

It was wild, and it was sad. The checkered fields, with their millet, their winter wheat and corn and vegetables—there was no sign of them. Perhaps there were farmsteads huddled at the foot of the mountains in the shadows, but you could not see them, though we were flying low, perhaps not more than 5,000 feet. China is a hard-bitten land. She never looked so hard-bitten as when we flew southeast from the beginning of the Ordos plain.

And then suddenly—it was the last thing you expected, for your eyes were so accustomed to the yellow mountains and the cracked earth that you forgot there were other mountains—you come to the foothills and see before you, covered in cloud, the great blue hills that guard Peking.

It was all over. Yenan, Kalgan, Chi-ning, the vast experiments, Mao Tse-tung leaning forward heavily, Chu Teh's red face in the light of the oil lamp, the soldiers riding up the valley in clouds of dust with the Persian patterns on their saddle bows, the loess caves, the pagodas, and the ten thousand Buddhas, and the intensity and

* Chi-ning was captured by Kuomintang forces in September 1946. Kalgan fell, after a brief and fierce battle, early in October 1946. The field teams were dissolved in February 1947 under Secretary Marshall's orders.

seriousness of these people—these you could remember, as you remember legends, but like all legends they belonged to the past. Once there was the legend of the Long March. Later there was the legend of the border areas, when farmers and soldiers fought off the Japanese for eight barren years. New legends would come—there was no end to them.

July 16th. Every night I must tell Jacqueline a fairy story about the princesses of Persia. I do not know why it must be Persia, though she insists upon it, though she knows perfectly well that the Persia is really Peking. She comes in her pajamas and snuggles into my arms, fantastically certain of her place, even though I am working or reading; and then we must argue about the names of the princesses, and she will insist on the most ridiculous names of all, and then go to sleep—or so I think, until she wakes up when I am gazing down at her, quite silent before her beauty, the faintly Chinese eyes, the faintly yellow skin, the mouth and cheekbones which are wholly European. She has the gaiety of the French and the intolerable wisdom of the Chinese.

In this old ruined palace there are so many courtyards that I am continually losing myself. To enter the house you must step through mountains of debris, for the great gates and porticos burned down in January; over the high walls you can see the brick pillars still supporting the charred *nanmu* wood, and I have such a horror of this stupid destruction that I cannot enter the palace without a sense of revolt. They say that the ornamental gates went up in flames because the electrical connections were out of order, and there was a most brilliant scarlet flame and even better than the flame was the scent of the wood, which was first placed here when the palace was built to the glory of one of the eight iron-capped princes, who were the sons of the Emperor Ch'ien Lung. I confess I envy him. I should have liked to see the moment when these things happened, but it seems absurdly unfair that after all this waiting in exile in the south of China, this amazingly beautiful entrance should be denied to us. And now the whole palace is crumbling to ruins, and the Japanese have littered some of the smaller courtyards with their *tatamis* and the plaster ceilings are falling down on us, and there is so much corruption among the estate officers that we dream only of having a small house somewhere in the west city, for fear that we shall live, like the author of *The Dream of the Red Chamber,* in a place where "all order is perishing and only vice survives." The strangest people live here. Old women peer out of gnarled courtyards, among the wistaria trees. This palace could tell many things if it spoke, and I suspect that it would speak most often of the terror it feels at its own decay. Once through all these courtyards officers of state came to lay their petitions before the prime minister of China, who worked in a room which is now haunted by an untuned piano. Once, too, there was vast wealth here, but that has been stolen by the same estate officers who now hide their stores of flour in the darkest alleyways. There seems to be no hope for the palace of the iron-capped princes. It will go on decaying, the tiles will continue to fall from the roof, the servants will continue to steal and the old relatives of the prime minister will continue to make their living by cheating at mahjong parties and by taking service with corrupt officials. So it is perhaps with everything in Peking. There are only a few places where the glory remains, but how prodigious a glory it must have been before the speculators and the usurers and the officials took pride in defeating one of the loveliest works of men.

July 19th, The Hunting Park. There is nothing in Peking as old as the Tower of London, but the past is more visible here than in any city I have ever known. For six hundred years there has been a settled condition of living, an unchanging ritual of life. On the way to the Western Hills we passed an immense fortress with moat, drawbridge and gates, and grass growing all over it. We passed a mausoleum built by the Japanese in honor of one of their Chinese collaborators. It was all bright red and gold, with flaring roofs and marble steps. At the gates of the Hunting Park bronze dragons stand in attitudes of majesty. Nothing had been lost. Stillness, proportion, the sense of fitness —they were all there though no huntsmen ride through the park and the old pleasure palaces are covered with weeds.

When Hsiung Hsi-ling was prime minister, he asked for the grant of the western quarters of the Hunting Park to build an orphanage. There were famines in Honan, and great floods. He was a poor man, but he collected three hundred thousand taels from his friends and built an orphanage here, and made it one of the best in the Far East. The children were well cared for. The most modern equipment was installed. There were workshops, porcelain kilns, a printing shop, temples. The Empress Dowager sent him on a mission to the West, with the humble aim of learning what would be of most use to

China, and though his days as prime minister have been forgotten, and the wild scheming of his friends, the Reformers, is old history, he made this orphanage, which remains. He was evidently proud of his work, for here and there you will come upon the scrolls he wrote, or his own calligraphy outlined in stone above the lintels, and sometimes there is his photograph, an old man with a small white beard and heavy eyelids, not frail, not determined, a man who gives an impression of abiding honesty and simplicity, himself the last of the rulers of China to have believed faithfully in the past. He was a Buddhist scholar with a deep reverence for the imperial tradition. He hid the Reformers of 1898 in his own house and accepted no bribes and died poor, having given everything he possessed to the orphanage except a part of his palace in Peking. In his will he wrote that he bought his palace out of his hard-earned savings and only once received a gift from Yuan Shih-k'ai; and it is clear that he loved nothing except that the orphanage should survive.

It had survived well enough, through wars and civil wars, but when we reached it this morning, we wondered whether he would have approved of the changes. At the entrance to the Hunting Park there were Kuomintang soldiers, trigger-happy. It was not difficult to believe that somewhere in the Hunting Park there were also Communist soldiers, for the Western Hills mark the frontiers of Kuomintang control and fierce battles have been waged here at night against the Japanese. But the Hunting Park was unchanged. There were the forests of white pines, the acacias and the pears, the small lakes, the stone plinths from which palaces once arose, a confusion of brambles and arching trees, all sweet-scented. The orphanage looks new, though the children have scabies and are not well cared for. Hsiung Hsi-ling built houses on the sloping shores of the forest at a time when houses cost hardly more than a laborer's monthly hire; he could get away from the fret of his palace in Peking and gaze at the goldfish in the pool or dig for buried treasure—there was one superb green vase that had come from the grave of a princess in the park. He set it beside a pool full of reeds and fishes, and shaded by acacia trees, near a small one-storied hunting lodge where he often stayed. I shall never forget this place for the quiet and the gleam of gold in the pool and the serenity of the forest, and most of all I shall remember it for his exquisite good taste. One can see him so perfectly in this setting, an old man in a maroon gown, coming here as often as possible to drink the spring water which bubbles from a black cave. The orphanage is corrupt now; there seems to be no one with power to put it on its feet again; there are far too many teachers for far too few orphans; too much of the food brought from America is going to the supervisors.

Among these lakes and mountain streams, the enchantment remains, an enchantment that is not overpowering like the gold tiles and the proportions of Peking, but shadowy and insubstantial as a dream. The tall green pillars engraved with Buddhist sutras gleamed in the sun. The ice-cold spring was bubbling. A shadow darkened the sun, and as we wandered down the steps to the car and saw the great plain stretching yellow to the walls of Peking, we knew we were determined to come again and live here and try to make the orphanage once again the perfect thing it was in the past.

July 20th, Nightmares. Dreaming of Chen Kung-p'o, who was executed last month. We have all been dreaming about it, because the details in the Chinese newspapers were so completely authentic. The strange intolerable disease of the Chinese for the facts of death, which they know only too well. Everything about the last hours of the traitor was recorded—how he stayed awake on his last night and wrote one more letter to the Generalissimo, and then when they came in the morning, he asked that the letter should be sent, even though it was unfinished, and arranged to pay the executioner for a speedy death, and went in his stockinged feet to see some others who were awaiting trial, saying nothing, but holding their hands and looking into their faces, while the tears fell endlessly from his eyes. He desired that his body should not be allowed to putrefy, and he requested that after his death his body should be enclosed in ice. The way he walked slowly across the prison yard, and how he was shot by a single bullet from a Mauser that killed him before he reached the wall. We know these things only too well, for too many people knew Chen Kung-p'o and there is still some doubt whether he was any worse than many members of the government who made fortunes during the war. They say that Chen Kung-p'o died poor. It may be true, because he belonged to the old order and did his best according to shifting lights. But what is intolerable is that his death has suddenly brought us face to face with one of the insoluble problems of the Chinese scene: treachery.

Five days ago, in a street in Kunming, the cold and abstract violence of the Kuomintang military clique led to the death of Wen Yi-tuo, who was my friend. I dare not dream of him; if I do, all dreams forever will be shadowed by him. I have not written about his death before, because I could not. He was the greatest man I ever met in China, the most scrupulous, the most happy in his work, the most popular of all the professors at Lienta, the man with the sweetest smile and the most mature brain. His name means "the one and the many of learning," and hence by implication all that can be understood by learning. He started life with an intense desire to paint, went to America, returned with his mind full of colors, helped to build up the architectonics of modern Chinese verse and having written two slim books of poems, decided to dedicate the rest of his life to an examination of the ancient Chinese classics in the light of modern criticism. We were so often together that I cannot remember when we first met. At the time when I knew him first he wore a reddish beard, and he would explain, as though excusing the color of his hair, that he thought he was descended from tribesmen. His body was frail. He had starved during the war, and taken, while Dean of the College of Chinese Literature, so many various odd jobs in middle schools that he had no time for himself. When the students were murdered in December, he did his best to make sure that justice would be done, and in doing this incurred so much enmity that we knew even then that his life was at stake. He had a fine speaking voice which would sometimes become dark with passionate remonstrance. He cared nothing for his own life, and on March 17th this year he marched at the head of the funeral procession of the students through the streets of Kunming and gave the saddest of all the farewells at the grave.

I would wander around the lake with him, and sometimes in the early afternoon or late at night I would come upon him at his table, his head bent over the seals he was carving against time, so that he could feed his children—he hated this waste of time, even though the seals sometimes brought good money, and he would say he preferred to be teaching for eighteen hours a week in the middle schools, where at least he could inculcate a love for Chinese traditions.

He was ill last year of typhus, after a journey to the petrified rocks in the south of Yunnan; and then I would see him in his ragged blue gown walking slowly with a stick through the campus. Students would run up to him asking for interpretations of the classics; always he spoke to them with especial sweetness. His classrooms were filled to overflowing, and there would be perhaps forty students listening through the windows. He had a quiet contempt for the professors who thought it unnecessary to speak with students about political problems. He believed the present government of China to be corrupt, and said so openly, with no shadow of fear on the fine high-boned face. I took him once to see the American consul, and what was most delightful was Wen Yi-tuo's unspoken delight in being in an American home. He had a hard-bitten mind and was obsessed by the poverty and degradation all around him; once he nearly broke under the strain; he recovered easily and never showed the least sign of strain afterward. He led the long march of the students from Peking to the southwest at the beginning of the war, and we had thought of him always as the man who would lead them back again. It was no more than we expected of him. But we did not expect him to die in the way he did, returning after a meeting, shot down in cold blood by four gangsters with American silent revolvers. He received six bullet wounds and was dead almost immediately. His son, who was standing a little away from him, saw the father fall and threw himself over his father's body, crying "Let me die for you, father," and then fell unconscious, for the gangsters put four more bullets into him. They say the father's body will be cremated, and he will be buried near the students who died last December. The son has recovered, though he is still not out of danger. From his hospital bed he has told a strange story of how the assassins stood over him and said before shooting him: "We must shoot you to save our lives, but we will not kill you. Later, when you have recovered, you may take revenge on us."

July 23rd. In three days I shall leave China and then fly home. I thought, after five years, I had roots here, but the roots are drying up. Death and corruption and unimaginable beauty, and the lion awake at last, and yet not sufficiently awake, and the worst is the evil all around us, and the best lies with the young. I am glad I lived with them, and yet not sorry now to leave, for there must be other countries as good. I saw the landscape and very nearly exorcised a childhood dream, and lived for a while in the valley of Yenan, and knew Wen Yi-tuo, and helped a few, and was helped by many; and what was left, except the pain, can never be put on paper, or even dreamed on. The beauty lay everywhere, and most of all in the faces of the children. And it was kind of whatever fates control us to leave the best to the end—Kunming, Yenan, gold roofs of Peking.

July 28th, On the plane to Shanghai. This morning, the ultimate day, Peking was the same, a mist rising, dust whirling along the ground, an awful feeling of heaviness, as though one wanted to stay here forever.

Writing this in the airplane, drowsy in the overheated cabin, not caring, knowing that the best is over and Shanghai is a nightmare, not caring, and yet angry a little, because this time we did not fly directly over Peking but skirted round the walls and flew directly south. The last we saw of Peking was the gold glow in the sky, as of a burning, above the city.

Nanking. A red gash in a purple hill, where Sun Yat-sen lies at the top of far too many steps, the city black as ants, floods all around; no yellow tiles, only dark roads, bleak and miserable, crisscrossing interminably. And then to Shanghai again, seven hours after leaving Peking, an eternity of mist and rain, the rain discoloring everything—even, at last, the sea.

July 30th, Shanghai. So overwhelmingly tired that I locked the door of the hotel bedroom and went to sleep after wandering round the city all day in a relentless pursuit of tickets, visas, passports. Someone must have opened it with an outside key. A shaft of orange light; a girl and a hotel coolie come in noisily.

"Want girl?"

"No."

"Want boy?"

"No."

"You American?"

"No."

He pushed the girl toward the bed; she wore a flowered dress, and pulled her skirt above her knee.

He said: "$75,000 dollars. You pay me now."

I tried to push him away.

"Okay—$50,000 dollars. You ask for girl, eh?"

"No."

"Okay—$40,000 dollars. You see."

Somehow they were pushed out, but someone was playing on a Chinese violin in the next room, and somewhere across the landing someone was screaming; and in the morning it was worse still, the hotel unswept, the prostitutes still wandering around the evil-smelling building. I took a ricksha out into the country, as far away as possible from the Bund and the sweating gray skyscrapers; and there were small villages, and the sunflowers were growing on the grave mounds, and the people looked thin and worn, and the smoke belched from Shanghai in the distance. Escaped at last to stay with the Indian agent, far from the center of the city, grateful for his calm, his dark eager humorous face, and the quietness which, like all Indians, he carries with him as we carry clothes.

August 1st, Nanking. I flew this morning to Nanking to say farewell to Feng Yu-hsiang. Nanking was quiet, dust-laden, bathed in heat and silence, the streets wide and clean; impossible to understand why it had looked so black and menacing when I saw it from the airplane on my way to Shanghai. It is his birthday. He said sadly that he had today been removed from the active list on account of age—he would have preferred to be a soldier to the end. In the heat and the dust we went out onto the Lotus Lake, Feng Yu-hsiang sitting in the prow, his servant fanning him, and then one by one the red lanterns came out, bobbing over the rushes and lotuses. He said quietly, looking up at the first stars: "There is an old proverb. A clean sky and lotuses are like scholars," and then he went on to talk of Wen Yi-tuo's death. He looked older now, limping a little, the eyes half-closed, the great head red in the light of the lanterns. "A clean sky and lotuses—those are the most beautiful physical things, but more beautiful still are the great scholars, and this man who was killed."

August 3rd, Madame Sun Yat-sen. Wondering what would happen if I stayed longer in Shanghai, for there are some things in this huge, grimy, domineering, relentless, noisy and bloodshot city that should not even be contemplated, we came at dusk to the gates of Madame Sun Yat-sen's house. Guards with fixed bayonets stood at their posts. There were chains on the great iron gates, and three bars; but once you are allowed inside the gates, everything is peaceful again, there are flowers everywhere and the house stands among trees.

She wore a white gown, her face very pale and unbelievably beautiful. There were lilies in a Chinese jar on the table, and a painting of Dr. Sun Yat-sen looked down from the wall. She looked twenty, and there were moments when she gestured or pursed her lips and looked eighteen. She talked of her peace hospitals and of her recent statement, calling upon both sides to cease their conflict, and of the Chinese general who had accused her of Communism in a deliberate and unavailing effort to incriminate her. She complained against the censorship, the terrors to which so many Chinese, and so many foreigners, bowed; and she spoke most softly when she mentioned the secret police. "It was not like this before. Dr. Sun would not have approved of them." And then again: "I had looked forward so much to the end of the war—now I am ashamed." Nobility was there, and grace, and goodness. The pale face, the sleek shining hair, the long white gown, and the girl's smile over the polished table. The rain thundered and roared beyond the quiet room, but in the center of the room, pouring tea, smiling faintly and not in the least mysteriously, she spoke of the time when peace would come, or frowned because there was still war. "In my mind for a very long time the hospitals have been first. This is how it must be—but why, when we think of the health of children, do those others think of guns?"

August 4th. No man is lonelier than on an airfield in the morning mist; the airplanes half hidden, the clouds low, the sun breaking, and everything is fresh, but the airplanes look like prehistoric monsters unmoving on the sandy field. I am haunted still by Madame Sun Yatsen, and shall be forever. I have seen a photograph taken twenty-five years ago; nothing has changed, the lines of the face as unchanging as the eyes, the sleekness of the hair as unchanging as the expression of the pursed lips. She spoke, I remember, not with bitterness, but with a kind of terrible Chinese despair, seeing no hope unless there was a coalition government, knowing that her husband was being forgotten by those in power.

Shivering here on the airfield, seeing the mist rising, the sun flooding across sand, deadened almost by the weight of these last five tragic years, it seems unthinkable that this evening I shall be in India, where life may be no better but at least there are no civil wars. All human wars are victories for the sun and the rain; famine and floods come, and the raveled earth grows weeds where there was once corn; and sooner or later if these wars endure, China will become a desert. For twenty years after the Taiping Rebellion there were deserts in the Yangtse valley, the land which was most tamed became the most barren.

We had hoped for so much. We did not know or guess that this would happen. We lived among simplicities, the Japanese the only enemy; and then at last we found the enemies among ourselves. The naked game of the world is being played in China. On this ravaged country we can see better than elsewhere the forces at work—the decay of the old religious systems, the terrible dangers that accompany the introduction of industrialization in an agricultural community, and the final birth of a new social consciousness, slow and groping, but clean and vigorous, healthy with the health of the young. We have seen these things through eyes shadowed by tragedy, and no place on earth can be so tragic as China.

Clean-cut, silvered with clouds, the river ran below, and the floods came like a sea, and the red hills, and the river widening, flowing over the land, more beautiful than ever among the rich rice fields of Hunan, until the gaunt blue mountains rose again in Szechuan, and at the end of the journey Burma was dark with immense green shadowy forests, and India grew out of the dusk, like an evening cloud. For five years of war I had been in China, and now as we come down on the airstrip above Calcutta it seems like a moment of time, no longer than it takes for lightning to score a dark land, where men are seized in terrible gestures of war and the lakes are shining and somewhere among the suddenly illuminated temples beside the shore there are lovers and scholars; and this too remains. The best were the scholars, the farmers, and the soldiers; the worst were worse than anything one can imagine. The best remains.

Index